Comrades

By Brian Moynahan

Comrades

1917 — Russia in Revolution

BRIAN MOYNAHAN

Little, Brown and Company
BOSTON   TORONTO   LONDON

First Edition

The author is grateful for permission to reprint the following copyrighted material:

Excerpts from *Memoirs of a British Agent,* by Sir Robert Bruce Lockhart. Copyright ©
1932 by Robert Bruce Lockhart. Reprinted with permission of Macmillan London and Robin
Bruce Lockhart.

Excerpt from "Spring Rain," by Boris Pasternak, translated by Robert Kemball. Reprinted
with permission of Ardis Publishers.

Excerpts from *Writer's Notebook,* by Somerset Maugham. Reprinted with permission
of A. P. Watt Limited on behalf of the Royal Literary Fund.

Excerpts from *Black Night, White Snow,* by Harrison Salisbury. Reprinted with permission
of Doubleday, a division of Bantam, Doubleday, Dell Publishing Group, Inc.

Excerpts from *The Russian Revolution,* by N. Sukhanov, translated by Joel Carmichael.
Copyright © 1955 by Joel Carmichael. Reprinted with permission.

Excerpts from *The Demesne of the Swans,* by Marina Tsvetaeva, translated by
Robert Kemball. Reprinted with permission of Ardis Publishers.

Excerpts from *Lost Splendor,* by Felix Yusupov. Copyright © Librairie Plon. Reprinted
with permission.

All the photographs are reprinted with
permission of the David King Collection.

Library of Congress Cataloging-in-Publication Data

Moynahan, Brian, 1941–
    Comrades: 1917—Russia in revolution / Brian Moynahan.—1st ed.
        p.   cm.
    Inclues index.
    ISBN 0-316-58698-6
    1. Soviet Union—History—Revolution, 1917–1921. I. Title.
DK265.M853   1991
947.084′1—dc20   91-28727

10 9 8 7 6 5 4 3 2 1

MV NY

*Published simultaneously in Canada by
Little, Brown & Company (Canada) Limited*

PRINTED IN THE UNITED STATES OF AMERICA

For
Michael and Julie Joseph

Contents

viii / Contents

Map of Petrograd on pages 18–19
Map of European Russia on page 87

Author's Note

All dates are given according to the Julian (or Old Style) calendar in use in Russia before February of 1918. In the twentieth century, this was thirteen days behind the Western calendar. Thus the date used here of March 1, 1917, for example, corresponds to March 14, 1917, in the Western calendar.

No emphases have been added. Where italics are used, they appear in the original document.

Russian names are given in their accustomed Western spelling rather than in systematic transliteration.

Principal Personalities and Parties with Some Contemporary Descriptions

Alexandra. Granddaughter of Queen Victoria, "unbalanced and hysterical" but had about her "something strong, earthy, passionate and proud." Empress.

Alexeev, Mikhail. "Dogged, calm and reasonable," sometime commander in chief, and grieving witness to the disintegration of the world's largest army.

Blok, Alexander. Symbolist poet, seducer, and weathervane to the emotions of the revolution.

Buchanan, Sir George. Monocled and silver-haired, he "can look the stage diplomat but inspires loyalty." British ambassador.

Chagall, Marc. The great painter who thought Lenin had turned Russia "upside down the way I turn my pictures."

Chaliapin, Fedor. Operatic basso, born in a Kazan slum.

Chernov, Viktor. Exile and ideologue who showed "not the slightest stability, striking power, or fighting ability." Social Revolutionary leader.

Chkheidze, Nikolai. Chairman of the Petrograd Soviet, a man with "every talent for being led in a halter, jibbing slightly now and then." Menshevik.

Dan, Fedor. Siberian exile, a "mild-faced, baldish figure in a shapeless military surgeon's uniform," Editor of *Izvestiya*. Social Revolutionary leader.

Dzerzhinsky, Felix. Convict and Siberian exile with eyes that "blaze with a steady fire of fanaticism" under "eyelids that seem paralysed." Head of the Cheka, forerunner of the KGB.

Francis, David. A "kindly old gent" whose "knowledge of anything beyond banking and poker is severely limited." U.S. ambassador.

Gippius, Zinaïda. Poetess, beauty, and anti-Bolshevik diarist.

Gorky, Maxim. Vagrant and dockhand turned journalist and bestselling dramatist of slum life. A man with "no power to inflict harm or suffering," who first sympathized with and then turned on the Bolsheviks. Publisher of *Novaya Zhizn*.

Guchkov, Alexander. Son of a Moscow tycoon, duelist, and adventurer. First war minister of the revolution. Octobrist.

Kamenev, Lev. Former exile, a "quick-moving little man with a wide vivacious face," a conciliator who "lacked sharp edges." Bolshevik moderate.

Kerensky, Alexander. Radical young lawyer and "hot hurricane and bridegroom" of the revolution. Justice, war, and prime minister. Affiliated to Social Revolutionaries.

Kornilov, Lavr. Wiry Cossack combat general with the "heart of a lion and the brain of a sheep." His tenure as commander in chief unwittingly saved the Bolsheviks.

Krupskaya, Nadezhda. Known as "the Fish" for her bulging eyes. Lenin's wife.

Krylenko, Nikolai. An "epileptic degenerate of the most repulsive type" who, during 1917, progressed from humble ensign to commander in chief. Bolshevik.

Kshesinskaya, Mathilde. Prima ballerina, "none more lithe," former mistress of the tsar, and owner of an art deco palace taken over by the Bolsheviks.

Lenin, Vladimir. "Crazy with vanity," with the air "more of a provincial grocer than a superman," irreplaceable to his party. "Lenin the Thunderer sat in the clouds and then — there was absolutely nothing down to the ground." Bolshevik leader.

Lvov, Prince Georgy. "More like a country doctor than an aristocrat," the "tired and wan" first prime minister of the revolution.

Martov, Julius. A "spare, hobbling figure" who broke with Lenin in the Social Democrat split. Suffered from "Hamletism — he is *too* intelligent to be a first-class revolutionary." Leader of the Menshevik left.

Miliukov, Pavel. "Muscular and active with no surplus flesh," renowned historian who had lectured at the University of Chicago. Foreign minister in first revolutionary government. Cadet leader.

Nicholas II. Melancholic and wistful, suited "to be a country gentleman growing turnips." Last of the Romanovs. Tsar.

Paleologue, Maurice. An "incorrigible snob" but an acute diarist. French ambassador.

Parvus. Obese German agent, with a stomach that "vibrated like a sack of grain," who persuaded Berlin to back Lenin on the grounds that he was "much more raving mad" than other revolutionaries.

Protopopov, Alexander. The last interior minister of the tsar, who "resembles an excitable seal," sleek and allegedly syphilitic.

Rasputin, Gregory. Monk, lecher, and hypnotist, with "eyes of strange lightness, inconceivable in a peasant face, the eyes of a maniac." The Friend of the empress.

Rodzianko, Mikhail. Burly and bald, a "mettlesome fellow seeking always to impress." Chairman of the Duma, Octobrist.

Savinkov, Boris. Terrorist, escapee from condemned cell, morphine addict, and "loner with a fixed gaze and sealed lips." Kerensky's assistant at the war ministry. Social Revolutionary.

Shulgin, Vasily. "Proudly whiskered and patrician," conservative nationalist and Duma deputy.

Sukhanov, Nikolai. "Cantankerous and honest" journalist and former exile with "yellow-gray browless face." Member of Soviet Executive Committee. The great diarist of the revolution. Independent, veering toward Menshevik left.

Tereshchenko, Mikhail. Sugar millionaire, finance and foreign minister, "extremely lively and charming" but inexperienced. Cadet.

Trotsky, Leon. Siberian escapee, writer, orator, New York exile, "a four kind son of a bitch but the greatest Jew since Jesus." Progressed from anti-Lenin freelance to committed Bolshevik.

Tsereteli, Irakli. Siberian exile, a "tall, lean, ox-eyed Georgian." Interior minister under Kerensky. Menshevik.

Vyrubova, Anna. As "commonplace as a bubble in biscuit dough," confidante of the empress and with her "the real ruler" of prerevolution Russia.

Yusupov, Felix. Transvestite aristocrat who regarded his murder of Rasputin as a "scenario worthy of his favorite author Oscar Wilde."

Zinoviev, Gregory. Early editor of *Pravda,* with "pallid skin and high-pitched voice." Close aide of Lenin but opposed to violent takeover. Bolshevik moderate.

PARTIES

Octobrists. Most right-wing of the major parties, representing the richer land and factory owners. In favor of vigorous war effort. Led by Alexander Guchkov.

Cadets (Constitutional Democrats). Mainstream liberals favoring a parliamentary monarchy and aggressive continuation of the war. Led by Pavel Miliukov.

Social Revolutionaries. Peasant-based and thus the largest party in Russia throughout 1917. Terrorist tradition. Favor a republic, all land to the peasants. "Defensists" who supported defense but not offensives at the front. Led by Viktor Chernov.

Mensheviks. Moderate splinter from original Social Democrat leftists. Believe in broadly based and democratic socialism. Defensists. Led by Julius Martov.

Bolsheviks. Extremist offshoot from Social Democrats. Support a narrow party dictatorship and prepared to use violence to achieve it. Defeatists in favour of immediate peace with Germany. Later known as Communists. Led by Vladimir Lenin.

Left Social Revolutionaries and Menshevik Internationalists drift toward Bolshevik position.

INSTITUTIONS

Soviets. "Councils" broadly representing the interests of soldiers, workers and peasants, and the intellectual left. Dedicated to preserving and extending the radical elements of revolution. Established in many places but dominated by the Petrograd Soviet and its Executive Committee.

Duma. A weak form of parliament, without real legislative or executive powers, introduced by the tsar to buy off the abortive revolution of 1905.

Comrades

I

Scene-Set

THE AUTUMN OF 1916 in Petrograd was gray and drizzling, with a quick fall of yellowing leaves and a bitter wind that whipped off the river along the quays. Half-frozen ice drifted down the Neva in thin gray flakes. The capital smelled of damp, coal smoke, sea salt, and carbolic. It was the most northerly city of any consequence in Russia, on the sixtieth parallel at a level with southern Alaska. It was dark from midafternoon to midmorning.

Poets passed the nights in a cellar bar called the Stray Dog. With prohibition in force, they slipped bootleg vodka into pineapple juice and drank it from teacups, listening to Anna Akmatova in a black silk dress read her famous call to decadence:

> We are all winners, we are all whores
> How sad we are together.

The city was thick with senseless ennui.

The war had entered its third year, and was going badly. The Romanov family had ruled Russia as a personal fief for 303 years. The city, eccentrically sited by Peter the Great in marshland on an isolated and vulnerable periphery two centuries before, was the symbol of their personal power. Nicholas II, the current tsar, controlled an empire that traversed most of the meridians of the eastern hemisphere and on the Bering Strait scraped over the edge of the western.

For all the immensity of its possessions, a sixth of the land surface of the planet, the autocracy was approaching a crisis. "More and more every day the signs of trouble multiplied," the daughter of the British ambassador noted, "and yet nothing was done to avoid the inevitable crisis."

More than five million Russian troops had been killed, wounded, captured or were missing. "In a year of war the regular army vanished," said General Alexei Brusilov, a senior commander. "It is replaced by an army of ignoramuses." The Germans had overrun Russian Poland. Fourteen armies held a front that stretched from Riga on the Baltic to the Black Sea and across it to Erzerum and Persia. "Colorless, expressionless, endless regiments marching through dead cold," a trooper wrote. "They were not individual Russians any more; they were not men who were going to die for their country, they were just men who were going to die." The high morale of 1914 had gone. "Under the mask of servile submissiveness lies terrible anger. . . . Just strike a tiny little match and everything will go up in flames."

Trains of wounded from the front slid daily into the Warsaw Station. In the Hospital of Saint George, they lay in the quiet white-and-blue wards with tired suffering eyes. Thousands of refugees from the lost territories were crammed into wooden sheds and cellars near the station, often shoeless, the children still in the thin cotton frocks of their summer flight.

Queues outside the bread shops stretched down the length of the streets. It was said that each line had women in it who were paid by the Germans to incite the people against the war and the autocracy. Bakeries had their windows broken at night. The economy was in crisis, but fashionable Petrograd was as yet little affected. Smart hotels, the Astoria and the Europe, were booked up.

Speculators flourished. "The sharks are working their gigantic jaws," reported the financial paper *Birzhevya Vedomosti*. A third of grain stocks were held by banks anticipating price increases. The Moscow branch of the Russian Asiatic Bank dealt in thousands of tons of sugar and had warehouses filled with cotton. Profiteers dealt in drugs as well as food. A kilo of aspirin, one and a half rubles in 1914, now cost two hundred. Quinine was up from four to four hundred rubles a kilo.

Cabarets, the ballet, and opera thrived. "We danced the Last Tango on the rim of trenches filled with forgotten corpses," said Vasily Shulgin, a right-wing politician. Fedor Chaliapin, born in a Kazan slum, the finest operatic bass of his time, was singing Don Quixote, and Mathilde Kshesinskaya, the tsar's lithe ex-mistress, danced Giselle. In the intervals in theaters and the opera house, the bright eyes of women sparkled with forced merriment, an air of unreality on every face. A guest at an official reception for a Japanese prince complained of "too much glare, silver and plate, food and music, too many flowers and servants."

Saint Petersburg had been famously vigorous in the arts and sciences before the war: it was given the more Russian name of Petrograd in the first months of the war. It was preeminent in soil science, petroleum chemistry, and hydrodynamics. Dmitri Mendeleev formulated the periodic law of the chemical elements at the university and Alexander Popov first used the aerial in radio experiments. Ivan Pavlov's talents had won an early Nobel Prize and the physiologist was continuing his study of conditioned responses in dogs. Igor Sikorsky had produced the world's first four-engined aircraft at the Russo-Balt plant. On the eve of the war, the four-hundred-horsepower *Grand* cruised above the city for six hours, with sixteen people and a dog aboard in a passenger compartment with a sofa and washroom. Russia had the fourth largest economy in the world, after the United States, Britain, and Germany.

The achievement in music, with Igor Stravinsky, Serge Rachmaninov, and Serge Prokofiev, was as great. Serge Diaghilev had stormed the West with his Ballet Russe. Marc Chagall and the expressionist Vasily Kandinsky painted with a brilliance matched only in Paris. Maxim Gorky, one-time scullery boy and dockhand and vivid chronicler of slum life, and the poet Alexander Blok maintained the city's literary tradition. The futurist poet Vladimir Mayakovsky wore an earring and painted red-and-black algebraic signs on his powdered face.

Literacy was growing rapidly — the liberal newspaper *Russkoe Selo* had a circulation of 2.5 million copies, among the highest in the world. An English traveler on a prewar trans-Siberian found the soldiers on the train reading Gogol and Pushkin — "they begin anywhere in the book and stop anywhere, and always find it interesting." Every station bookstall from Moscow to Harbin had a copy of Jerome K. Jerome's *Three Men in a Boat*, and "every peasant seemed to have read Milton's *Paradise Lost*."

War dissipated the energy. Russians felt cut off by the West, which treated them "like some kind of astral body." Paintings appeared to "lose their vivid color, their freshness, brilliance, spirit, and soul." Alexander Blok feared the state of *odichaniye* — "going savage." "Black, impenetrable slush on the streets," he wrote. "The streetlamps — only every third one is lit. A drunken soldier is being bundled into a cab (will they hang him?)" No one was in any doubt that there would be a revolution. "No one is even talking about it," said Zinaïda Gippius, a poetess and baroque beauty and a sharp-tongued observer in the literary salons. "We have gone numb."

The suicide rate tripled, becoming an epidemic among the young and underlining the silent forces of disintegration at work in society. Two-thirds of the victims were under twenty-eight.

Among the rich, divorce was the new and universal fashion. Madame Zimin, a millionairess, played bridge every Sunday with her "three husbands — two ex, and one real." There was a "tolerance beyond the range of Western civilization" and the wives of English bankers and diplomats held up their hands in pious horror.

Prince Serge Obolensky, an earnest young noble back on leave from the front, noted that a "smart set had grown up, a lot of society ladies, young divorcées, very different from what had existed before." They partied wildly to fashionable gypsy orchestras. Alexander Blok womanized almost frantically, and his wife Lyuba repaid him with her own infidelities. "I have had 100 women — 200 — 300 (or more?)," Blok wrote. "But really only two: one is Lyuba; the other — all the rest." A young poet, Boris Pasternak, found life in the cities to be "gay with the brilliance of a florist's window in winter."

Forty thousand prostitutes, many barely past puberty, catered to the needs of foreign businessmen and officers from the swollen garrison or on leave from the front. Army morale was deteriorating. Officers overstayed their leave, packing the smart restaurants and gambling halls. Hotels "thronged with officers who should be at the front. There is no disgrace in being a 'shirker' or in finding a sinecure in the rear."

Blok had got himself an easy billet with an engineering unit stationed near Minsk in the country house of Princess Drutskoy-Lyubetsky. The princess was an amusing hostess — she had trained boa constrictors for the circus before the war — and she fed Blok's unit suppers enough to kill them. Even so, the poet found that the "stench of the soldier's greatcoat is not to be endured," and he contrived to spend most of his time in the capital.

A general, attending a performance of the ballet *Nuits Egyptiennes* at the Maryinsky Theater, was overheard to say that there were too many troops in Petrograd and that they were turning dangerous. Four thousand men of the Preobrazhensky Regiment were crammed into barracks built for twelve hundred. In the dark, fetid air the men made speeches from supper until morning. The garrison was badly officered, idle, and corrupt, "in fact good for nothing but to supply recruits for the army of anarchy." If God did not spare Russia a revolution, the general went on, "it will be started not by the people, but by the army!"

Tsar Nicholas, on the advice of the Empress Alexandra, began taking a Tibetan potion in the autumn to ward off exhaustion, insomnia, and depression. Judging by its effects, foreign diplomats reckoned the elixir to be a mixture of hashish and the yellow flowers of the nauseous-smelling henbane plant. The empress took opium to relieve a nervous stomach. Morphine addiction was becoming commonplace, fed by supplies from military hospitals. The habit started with doctors and chemists and spread to officers, officials, engineers, and students. Everyone knew the cabarets where the trade was carried on.

The newspapers were full of "caviar," the black blotches of the censors' marks.

The lower depths of the city bore the brunt of the shortages and speculation. Prewar governments had been niggardly book-balancers. The war plunged the regime into freewheeling debt. Expenditure, 3.5 billion rubles a year prewar, was up to 15.3 billion in 1916. A third of prewar income had come from the banned vodka trade. The war was costing Russia 40 million rubles a day, more than Britain or France. New income and excess-profits taxes raised only enough in a year to pay for four and a half days' fighting. The solution lay in borrowing, from allies and through domestic war loans, and in recourse to the printing press. Money in circulation rose from 2.4 billion rubles in 1914 to 8 billion in 1916. The ruble slid from 94 to 155 to ten British pounds.

With that came inflation. Eggs and soap were up fourfold in price since the beginning of the war, meat had tripled, and flour more than doubled. "Raise up the red banner of revolt against our executioners, murderers, and robbers," ran a pamphlet circulating in the factory districts. "Revolution is the only reply to the war and the high cost of living."

The city was losing social cohesion. Almost three-quarters of the population — which had doubled since the turn of the century to more than two and a half million — had been born elsewhere. Wartime factories sucked in workers, who now numbered four hundred thousand. Labor in the metalworking plants was up by 135 percent; in chemicals, it had doubled. The bulk of the new arrivals were single young men and women. Many Petrograd children were sent to be brought up by grandparents in the countryside and the old returned to their villages. Two generations, children under ten and adults over fifty, were largely missing.

One in six of the new arrivals were foreign, the bulk Polish and Baltic refugees, but including exotics — Chinese, Koreans, and Persians. The Russians rarely came from nearby provinces. The big recruiting grounds for labor were the central provinces and the northwest; Pskov, Novgorod, Smolensk, Yaroslav. The newcomers fell into the lowest reaches of industrial life, the men working in the hot shops, foundries, rolling mills, and forges, the women in textiles and ammunition plants. They brought their peasant clothes and habits with them, chewing sunflower seeds so that the pavements outside their lodging houses were covered with black husks like carpets of flies.

The municipality was spending a third more on public health and sanitation than it had in 1913, but that money bought less than half the services. A five-hundred-million-ruble development plan, to include more parks, tramlines, waterworks, sewers, and hospitals, had been shelved. The Neva was heavily polluted by industrial and human waste. The infant mortality rate in the working-class Vyborg district, on the right bank of the river, reached 25 percent. The water supply spread typhoid and intestinal disease. In a city with a young population, almost half of the deaths were caused by epidemic and infectious diseases.

Rents tripled through shortage of housing and were among the highest in Europe. More than three people shared a room on average, double the figure for Paris or Berlin. The chairman of the Vyborg sanitation committee claimed that workers were more cramped than those buried in the cemetery. Fewer than half the dwellings had running water or sewage. Tenements had an "impossible atmosphere — exhalation of people, wet clothing, and dirty linen; everywhere dampness and dirt." Holes in the wall were stopped with rags, and in the autumn rains legions of cockroaches and bugs climbed above water lying two inches deep on the floors.

Though the 1916 harvest was good, the army drained supplies, transport was lacking, and peasant farmers were reluctant to sell grain for devalued cash that bought little. The military had commandeered about a third of railroad rolling stock. Overuse and sloppy maintenance were wearing out the remainder. Thousands of freight cars were caught in distant snowdrifts. Seaborne cargoes of Welsh coal ceased at the outbreak of war and the Germans had overrun the Polish coalfields. Demand was thrown on the Donbass mines, which already supplied Moscow and the southern industrial belts. Petrograd received 18 million pounds of grain in December in place of the 133 million it required.

During the year, the last traces of sensible government seemed to have been swept away. Spiritualism and the occult, the "Dark Forces," came out of the fashionable salons where society ladies had long dabbled with them and appeared to control the appointment of ministers. The name of Rasputin, the empress's doppelgänger and the personification of dark force, was seldom pronounced aloud, as people feared it would bring them bad luck. He was called "the Unmentionable" or "the Nameless One."

At Rasputin's insistence and that of his helpmate Alexandra, the country had gone through five interior ministers and three war ministers in the space of ten months. Wags suggested that a sign should be hung outside the cabinet room saying: "Piccadilly — Every Saturday a New Program."

The honeyed and servile body of Boris Stürmer, a Rasputin protégé, now combined the offices of premier and foreign minister, a man whom a predecessor said had "left a bad memory wherever he occupied an administrative post." Foreign ambassadors despised him. The American ambassador was David Francis, an octogenarian from Saint Louis, an expert banker and poker player, but so at sea with politics that the British diplomat Bruce Lockhart said that he "doesn't know a revolutionary from a potato." Francis was maddened by Stürmer's habit of stopping in front of a long mirror during interviews and "surveying himself in evident satisfaction, while he turned up the ends of his mustache in the style of the German Kaiser." Maurice Paleologue, the French ambassador, an incorrigible snob but an acute diarist, found that Stürmer "emits an intolerable odor of falseness," and Britain's Sir George Buchanan wrote to London that he was "a man on whose word no reliance can be placed."

Stürmer had the advantage, crucial in 1916, of the assiduous cultivation of Gregory Rasputin. His flattery was rewarded in a long letter campaign the empress carried out with Nicholas for his promotion. "Lovy, I don't know that I should, but I should still think of Stürmer," she wrote to the tsar. "He very much values Gregory which is a great thing. . . . Our Friend said about Stürmer to take him for a time at least, as he is such a decided loyal man."

His predecessor as premier, Ivan Goremykin, had been a bizarre enough choice to run a great empire at war. On his appointment at seventy-five, Goremykin said: "I am like an old fur coat. For many months I have been packed away in camphor. I am being taken out now merely for the occasion." He spent much of his time reading French novels and going to sentimental "Piccadilly weepers" at the theater. Stürmer brought a new standard of corruption to high office when he replaced Goremykin in February 1916. In November, his secretary was arrested for blackmailing a bank. The tsar continued to think Stürmer to be an "excellent, honest man."

The empress attacked General Alexei Polivanov, the hard-working war minister rated by the British military attaché as "undoubtedly the ablest military organizer in Russia." Polivanov's contempt for Rasputin set Alexandra against him: "Is he not Our Friend's enemy?" Polivanov complained in early March when Stürmer outfitted Rasputin with War Office cars too speedy to be followed by the police agents assigned to report on his nightly whoring and drinking. "Get rid of Polivanov," the empress wrote to Nicholas. "Lovy, don't dawdle, make up your mind, it's far too serious." Polivanov was dismissed on March 25.

Rasputin and the empress whittled away at Serge Sazonov, the able foreign minister who had held the post since 1910, through the summer. Alexandra described Sazonov as "long-nosed" and a "pancake" with dangerously liberal views. In July, Sazonov took a vacation in Finland. Stürmer and the empress scurried to put pressure on Nicholas, absent at army headquarters, the Stavka. Sazonov was sacked, and the street balladeers pilloried Stürmer as a German agent as he acquired his second great office of state:

Fresh comes Stürmer from the palace
In his diplomatic role.
Deutschland, Deutschland über Alles!
Russland, Russland, lebe wohl!

The interior minister was a key to the survival of the autocracy. He controlled the Okhrana, the secret police who were headquartered in a low building with yellowing walls and barred windows in the center of the city. From this place of "secret and shameful aspect," Okhrana agents had by 1916 virtually eliminated the influence of revolutionary parties. The leaderships were in exile, in the West or Siberia, or dormant. Undercover men had infiltrated the few underground groups that were still operating, picking up emissaries sent by the exiled Bolshevik leader, Vladimir Lenin, within days of their arrival.

In September, the empress told the tsar that Rasputin was begging him to name Alexander Protopopov to oversee this instrument of repression and intelligence-gathering. "He likes Our Friend for at least 4 years," she explained, "and that says much for a man." In October, Nicholas appointed Protopopov, small and neurotic with "bright, wild eyes that shifted all the time," a sleek-haired amateur of the occult who "resembled an excitable seal" and who was widely held to be syphilitic. The Petrograd rumor mills soon had the new interior minister proposing a separate peace to the Germans. As to syphilis, though some more charitable observers credited his obvious ill health to a progressive spinal disease, his behavior hovered between eccentricity and madness. Diplomats thought him "certainly not quite sane." Protopopov designed his own uniform of field dress, sword-belt of undressed leather, high boots, and spurs. He kept an icon close to his desk and carried on conversations with it, explaining that everything he did was by "His advice."

Rasputin urged that Protopopov be given authority in another essential area, the organization of food supplies. The empress transferred supply from the agriculture to the interior ministry without bothering to first inform the tsar. "I had to take this step upon myself as Gregory says Protopopov will first have all in his hands," she wrote to Nicholas. "Forgive me, but I had to take this responsibility for your sweet sake." Protopopov was soon accused of creating food shortages in order to provoke riots as an excuse for repression.

A Union of Towns, a voluntary body of mayors and experts, had been established shortly after the outbreak of war to deal with organizational weaknesses. It mounted the only systematic campaign against infectious disease and for the resettlement of refugees, ran its own trains with alarm bells to warn of cholera, smallpox, and typhus, and, together with the rurally based Union of Zemstvos, maintained 92 percent of the country's hospital beds. The union, not the government, had organized the manufacture of gas masks after the first German gas attack in May of 1915.

The union gave the government a blunt warning in October 1916. "Power should not remain in the hands of those who are unable to resist secret influence," it said, "and who cannot organize the resources of the country." Alexander Protopopov, recognizing himself in the description, banned the union's meetings and set the Okhrana to pursue the eight doctors, six engineers, twelve scientists, and sixteen experienced mayors who made up its central committee.

The same month, workers broke into the French-owned Renault works in Petrograd and murdered four foremen, shouting "No more war!" A crowd from the Vyborg working district protested against inflation by marching to the Finland Station, singing the "Marseillaise" and carrying red flags. Troops from the 181st Infantry Division, called to put them down, fired on the police instead. Cossacks were needed to drive the infantrymen back into their barracks at lancepoint. The ringleaders were court-martialed and faced execution.

By October 28, seventy-seven factories had stopped work in sympathy with the soldiers in the biggest strike of the war. "The hangman's hand is raised above your heads," the accused men were reassured by the strikers, "but it will shake when faced with the powerful protest of the people rising up from slavery." Despite lockouts and threats to draft strikers to the front, the shortage of supplies for the front forced the government to back down to strikers for the first time in the war. None of the infantrymen was executed.

The premiership, foreign policy, internal security, and food supply were concentrated in the hands of what Paleologue called "two renowned scoundrels," appointed on the recommendation of Rasputin and an empress who believed in his "wonderful, God-sent wisdom." Okhrana agents in the capital reported that the "mood of opposition has gone very far — far beyond anything seen in the broad masses" before the abortive revolution of 1905. They felt that a "devastating chaos of catastrophic and elemental anarchy" was threatening. "Many things caused this," the Okhrana noted. "A scarcity and rise in the price of basic commodities, war weariness, rumors that excited the population, etc." As the catchall "etc." indicated, no single reason for the crisis could be isolated. The Romanovs, the writer Dmitri

Merekhovsky thought, had reduced Russia to the "fifth act of a tragedy played in a brothel."

The autocracy rested on these foundations as winter arrived. In December, Meriel Buchanan watched as the spell of "that endless gray autumn" was broken. The waters of the Neva froze into a dazzling surface, the slush and dirt of the streets were covered by heavy snowfalls, the heavy weight of the clouds lifted, and "the golden spires and snow-covered roofs shone beneath a cold, clear sky." There were still holes in the ice, where the water accelerated as it was confined between the piers of bridges.

One such hole provided the dumping place for Rasputin. He was consigned to it, not by Marxist revolutionaries, but by a transvestite fop, a grand duke and a politician so right-wing and anti-Semitic that he was later held up as a fine example of a proto-Fascist.

II

Yankee Doodle Dandy

LIKE LENIN, Felix Yusupov had a much-loved elder brother who died violently. The nature of these deaths, however, showed the gulf between the circumstances of the two men, and between the casually gory prelude to revolution conducted by the one and the calculated terrorism of the other. Alexander Ulyanov was hanged in 1887 on a gibbet in the Schlüsselburg Fortress, at the point where the river Neva starts its descent to the sea, for plotting to assassinate the then-tsar, Alexander III, with a bomb concealed in a medical dictionary. He was buried in a common grave within the prison walls. His brother Vladimir Ilyich Ulyanov, later to adopt the name Lenin, was then a seventeen-year-old schoolboy.

Twenty-one years later, in 1908, Prince Nicholas Yusupov was killed in a duel fought on an island in the Neva with a young Lieutenant in the Horse Guards over the honor of the latter's fiancée. Felix Yusupov was twenty, a dabbler in transvestism and the occult, waiting to go up to Oxford.

A fellow aristocrat claimed that Yusupov had undergone a "profound religious conversion" as a result of his brother's death. This conversion, however, amounted to little more than the application of his overripe mind to politics. Felix was a near-caricature of a spoiled young man, scion of the richest family in Russia: his mother's annual income was estimated at 1.3 million rubles, equivalent to a ton of gold, and his great-great-grandfather, Prince Nicholas Yusupov, had been a confidant of Catherine the Great and an acquaintance of Voltaire and Pushkin. Felix liked to boast that his ancestor was a debauchee who kept three hundred portraits of his mistresses and never traveled without a menagerie of monkeys, dogs, and parrots.

It would have taken a month to visit the thirty-eight Yusupov houses and estates, had Felix wished to do so. He did not. The main Moscow palace, one of three, had been built by Ivan the Terrible. It frightened Felix, who "imagined the ghosts of the wretches who died in chains" in the underground passages that connected it to the Kremlin. Yusupov holdings in the Crimea included a 125-mile stretch of coastline, so rich in oil that the peasants used surface deposits to grease their wagon axles, and the treeless mountain of Aï-Petri, highest on the coast, which his father had given to his mother as a birthday present. The most important southern estate was at Korëiz on the Black Sea. "We also had a house on the bay of Balaklava," Felix recalled, "but we never lived in it."

He was happiest in the ocher-washed palace on the Moika canal at Saint Petersburg, a city full of people he could outrage with impunity. The palace was decorated with spoils from an earlier revolution, the French. The furniture in the *petit salon* had belonged to Marie-Antoinette, the rock-crystal chandelier on the main staircase to Madame de Pompadour. Paintings by Fragonard, Watteau, and Rembrandt were later to prove valuable portable assets. It was on the Moika that, as a child, he started dressing up in the miniature Louis XV theater. He would play at being his ancestor, Prince Nicholas. "Wealth, splendor, power," he said, "I could not do without them."

The family flaunted its eccentricities. Felix's grandmother devoted herself to collecting stamps and snails. The latter she crushed underfoot, convinced that the resulting goo made the finest fertilizer for the rose bushes. Her gardeners wisely ignored her. His father found a dirty, evil-smelling dwarf on a fishing trip in the Caucasus and brought him home to become Felix's tutor. On Sundays, the tutor wore a dinner jacket and yellow shoes. Arabs, Tartars, and Kalmucks were retained to add color to the Moika palace. A manservant was employed solely as a lamplighter. When electricity was installed, Felix noted with glee, the man was so bored that he drank himself to death.

Felix first experimented with transvestism when he was twelve. He took one of his mother's dresses, borrowed a wig from her hairdresser, and went to the section of the Nevsky Prospekt where prostitutes gathered. The Nevsky was the main thoroughfare of the city, with smart shops, hotels, and banks running along it. In French, Felix told the men who accosted him that he was already engaged. He reversed languages with his mother's friends, who normally spoke French and whose Russian was foreign-accented. "My brother and I found this irritating," wrote Felix. "We always answered old ladies in Russian when they addressed us in French." He progressed from the pavements of the Nevsky to the Bear, a fashionable restaurant. "By day I was a schoolboy, and by night a fashionable woman," he said. Dining with some officers, he amused himself by using a string of his mother's pearls as a lasso and aiming it at their heads. The string broke, some pearls went missing, and his father discovered his secret.

Ten days spent confined in his room had no effect. Visiting Paris with his brother, he wore drag at a performance at the Capucines theater. He was flattered when the lecherous King Edward VII asked his brother for the name of the girl he was escorting. Back in Petrograd, he appeared as a chanteuse at the Aquarium, a nightclub with tanks on the walls from which the fish stared impassively at Felix's admirers.

His brother's death induced some change. Felix spent more time in Moscow, which he thought more Russian than westernized Saint Petersburg — a "mix of piety and dissipation, of religion and self-indulgence," a description that applied as prettily to himself. A visit to see Maxim Gorky's new hit play, *The Underworld*, sparked off an interest in the lower orders. He went to the Viasemskaya-Lavra section of Saint Petersburg, a slum quarter, disguised this time as a beggar. He was not impressed. "All around us the dregs of humanity, both men and women, lay half-naked, drunk, and filthy," he wrote. "The unfortunate wretches quarreled, copulated, used the filthiest language, and vomited all over each other."

Yusupov did not doubt the system of autocracy or his own privileged position within it. His contemporary Serge Obolensky, who did, read natural history, physics, and agriculture at Saint Petersburg's university, using his vacations to increase the butterfat content in the model dairy on his estate through selective breeding. Yusupov was looked after by a valet, a chauffeur, and a housekeeper when he went up to Oxford. He installed a macaw in his rooms and smuggled in a bulldog, disguised as a baby to evade the British quarantine laws. In February 1914 he married Princess Irina, a niece of the tsar and a noted beauty. His relations with the imperial couple were not good; the empress, aware of his transvestite escapades, thought him corrupt.

The hostility was returned as the war went on, encouraged by Yusupov's parents. His father was forced to resign as governor-general of Moscow in 1915. The Yusupovs blamed this on the influence of a "pro-German camarilla" led by Rasputin and the empress. Felix said that his father was dismissed because of the "draconian measures" he had taken to free Moscow from "occult domination by the enemy."

These measures were anti-German riots, which Prince Yusupov was slow to bring under control since he felt that a "healthy demonstration" would be a warning to Alexandra and her friends. Looted Bechstein and Blüthner pianos were piled into bonfires that spread to the wooden houses and threatened a serious conflagration. The tsar was willing to overlook the governor-general's lack of control, but his officials warned him that Prince Yusupov was a "megalomaniac of the most dangerous kind," so full of his own importance that Moscow was in danger of becoming an independent satrapy. Family humiliation deepened when Yusupov's mother, Princess Zinaïda, criticised the empress during an audience in 1916. Alexandra heard her out in silence and dismissed her from court: "I hope never to see you again."

Through the summer of 1916, Zinaïda bombarded Felix with letters from the Crimean estates. In rough code, in which Rasputin became "the book" and the empress was "Validé," a mocking use of the Crimean Tartar word for "great mother," she wrote her son that "Nothing can be done unless the book be destroyed and Validé tamed." Yusupov, though "rather prone to perverse imaginings and literary representations of vice and death," found violence against an empress unthinkable. Rasputin — an outsider and a peasant — was another matter. Yusupov needed small prompting to slip into a fresh disguise, as the savior of the motherland.

The two men had met shortly before Yusupov went up to Oxford in 1909. "A low, common face framed by a shaggy beard," Felix wrote of Rasputin. "Coarse features and a long nose, with small shifty eyes sunken under heavy eyebrows. . . . There was something base in his unctuous appearance, something wicked, crafty, and sensual." Rasputin was then thirty-eight, the son of a drunken and probably thieving *muzhik* peasant from a wretched hamlet on the borders of western Siberia. Born without a family name, like many peasants, he was known simply as Gregory in childhood. His adopted name Rasputin, from the Russian for "womanizer," reflected one of his main preoccupations. This predilection did not prevent him from being presented, in the guise of a "man of God," to the sexually correct imperial couple at the end of 1905.

The intensity of Russian religious feeling and its mysticism fed many sects. The *raskolniks* were the most numerous, persecuted "Old Believers" who held to forms of orthodoxy outlawed for two and a half centuries. Less than twenty years before, the people of a *raskolnik* village on the Dniester had refused to take part in the official census, which they believed to be the work of the Antichrist. They dug four tunnels and held their own burial service before they jumped singing into the pits, walling them up from the inside to die of suffocation.

Khlysty sectarians sought erotic ecstasy in mass orgies and then atoned by whipping themselves with birch rods. The number of *khlysty* was put at 120,000, although there was a prurient tendency to overemphasize both their numbers and the way in which they strove to attain "celestial communion" through "monstrous scenes of sensuality, lust, and incest." Pacifist *dukhobors* stripped themselves naked in protest when the Cossack recruiting sergeants came calling. The *dusheteli* were stranglers who cut short the pain of the dying by choking them, from "motives of human pity and retrospective pity for Christ and His Calvary." *Skoptzy* castrated themselves to escape the pressures of the flesh. *Stranniki*, in birchbark shoes and ragged coats tied at the waist with string, wandered the Siberian wilds in the hope of escaping from the kingdom of the Antichrist, dependent on charity.

The influence of these sects — "and how many more!" Paleologue exclaimed — was mirrored in Petrograd society by those who dabbled in the occult and the divine. Séances were fashionable. Alexander Blok attended one and complained of having to sit "with my little finger crooked round the little finger of a fat, hoarse old lady tall as a grenadier." The empress and the tsar, though the Lord's annointed and supreme guardians of the Orthodox Church, were not immune. Like many of their subjects, they were "more sincere, or at any rate more Christian" than their official church.

The first mystic at court was a French charlatan, "Dr." Philippe Nizier-Vachot, who fell from favor after he confirmed a phantom pregnancy of the empress as real and was back in France when Rasputin first appeared in Saint Petersburg in 1903. Rasputin's simple fervor impressed the empress's confessor, the archimandrite Theophanes, who was unaware that Rasputin had been expelled from Kazan for drunkenness and that, in Tobolsk, he had seduced the wife of an engineer and begun to enjoy society women. Rasputin had the appetites of the *khlysty* wanderers, although there was no proof that he was a member of the sect. Piety mingled with his indulgence. He had made the pilgrimage to Jerusalem, he knew his Bible, and he was believed to have hypnotic powers.

Descriptions of the color of his eyes varied from "steely gray" and "pale blue" to "dark and deep"; even his enemies agreed that they had exceptional focus and brilliance. Tamara Karsavina, the most beautiful ballerina of her generation, once passed Rasputin in the street and recognized him at once through his "eyes of strange lightness, set close, inconceivable in a peasant face, the eyes of a maniac."

Rasputin was skilled at exciting credulous aristocrats, particularly women, with his foul language and manners. His hair was long and matted. He used his beard as a napkin for the fish and potatoes he wolfed with his fingers. His teeth were blackened stumps from neglect and from the sugar in the port and madeira be consumed with smacking lips. When admirers arranged his first audience at court, the Siberian treated Nicholas and Alexandra with "gross familiarity" from the outset, calling them "Papa" and "Mama" and embracing them with the Russian triple kiss. They were en-

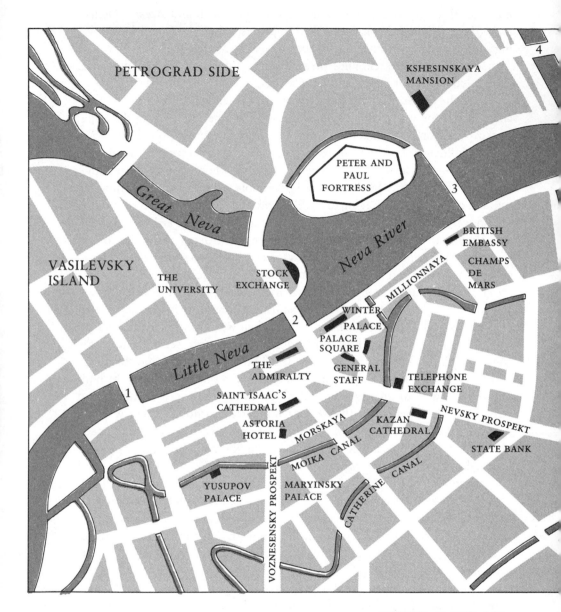

PETROGRAD

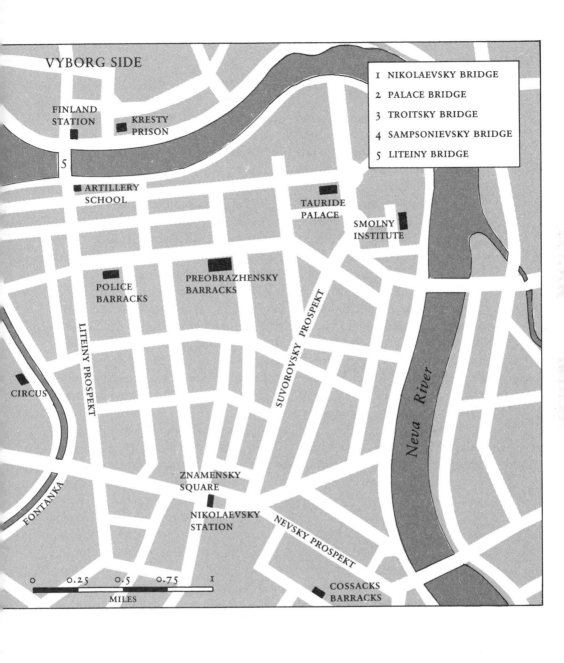

VYBORG SIDE

1 NIKOLAEVSKY BRIDGE
2 PALACE BRIDGE
3 TROITSKY BRIDGE
4 SAMPSONIEVSKY BRIDGE
5 LITEINY BRIDGE

FINLAND
STATION

KRESTY
PRISON

5

ARTILLERY
SCHOOL

TAURIDE
PALACE

SMOLNY
INSTITUTE

POLICE
BARRACKS

PREOBRAZHENSKY
BARRACKS

SUVOROVSKY PROSPEKT

LITEINY PROSPEKT

CIRCUS

Neva River

ZNAMENSKY
SQUARE

NIKOLAEVSKY
STATION

FONTANKA

NEVSKY PROSPEKT

0   0.25   0.5   0.75   1

MILES

COSSACKS
BARRACKS

chanted by his simplicity, a contrast to courtier sycophancy, and found in it the "voice of the Russian soul."

Rasputin was aided by the hemophilia of the son and heir, the Tsarevich Alexis. The defective gene that caused this condition had been passed down to her male descendants by Queen Victoria, Alexandra's grandmother. Alexis suffered from hemorrhaging so painful that it distorted his body. Rasputin was able to bring the boy relief. It is not known, although it was much rumored, whether he used his powers of hypnosis; it may be that he simply calmed the tsarevich, reducing his capillary blood flow, and thus allowed the bleeding to slow when the boy's fatigued body drifted into deep sleep. But those who knew the boy agreed that Rasputin was able to ease the condition. "Rasputin's presence in the palace was intimately connected with the prince's illness," stated the family's Swiss tutor, Pierre Gilliard. "Alexandra believed that she had no choice. Rasputin was the intermediary between her and God. Her own prayers went unanswered but his seemed to be."

Rasputin extended his influence into politics, gathering around him a shifting collection of charlatans, financial adventurers, and ambitious politicians. Aron Simanovich, an able and subtle jeweler, acted as his secretary and adviser. An early backer was the so-called "therapist" Zhamsaryn Badmaiev, a purveyor of narcotics, stupefactives, anaesthetics, and aphrodisiacs with names like Elixir du Tibet and Lotus Noir, and a practised swindler who had extracted two million gold rubles from the imperial government to finance a phantom uprising in Mongolia.

The link between the empress and Rasputin was maintained by her dumpy confidante, Anna Vyrubova. A woman so dull that a conversation with her was compared with "talking to a phonograph," Vyrubova protected Rasputin when a major scandal broke at the end of 1911. Sated by his conquests of society ladies, Rasputin transferred his interest to a nun. When seduction failed, he tried to rape her. He was summoned to explain himself to the heavyset Bishop Hermogenes of Saratov and a young monk-mystic, Iliodor, whose following among the poor matched Rasputin's hold on the rich. The bishop beat Rasputin over the head with a cross, leaving him bleeding and swearing that he would never again go near the imperial family. Theophanes, the imperial confessor, turned on his former protégé.

Vyrubova took Rasputin's messages of contrition to Tsarskoe Selo, the "tsar's village" fifteen miles south of Petrograd, from his lodgings on Gorokhovaya Street, respectable rooms with oak furniture and "an air of middle-class solidity." Rasputin weathered the storm despite the erotic rumors that linked him carnally with the empress. If Rasputin kissed women, Alexandra said, it was because it was a form of apostolic greeting. Besides, "saints are always exposed to calumnies." Hermogenes was deprived of his see and exiled to a monastery in Lithuania, Theophanes sent by immediate decree to the Crimea, and Iliodor imprisoned in a penitentiary monastery near Vladimir.

Iliodor escaped to Finland, selling a manuscript about Rasputin to an American publisher. The young monk had first, however, sought with some success to inspire women seduced and abandoned by Rasputin to gain their vengeance. An ex-lover stabbed Rasputin in 1914. A doctor who examined him found his genitals to be shriveled, as in old age, and thought that syphilis and alcohol had rendered him impotent.

The first open attack on Rasputin was published in the summer of 1915 in the *Moscow Stock Exchange Gazette*, which described him as an "abject adventurer." The interior minister who permitted publication, Prince Stcherbatov, was replaced without any reason being given or necessary. When a senior gendarme officer, General Vladimir Dzhunkovsky, had Rasputin arrested after a row — "women screaming, broken glass, Rasputin drunk and lecherous" the British consul and secret service agent Bruce Lockhart reported — at a fashionable Moscow nightclub, the Yar, Dzhunkovsky was dismissed and sent to the front.

By the autumn of 1916, with the cabinet dominated by Rasputin nominees, criticism was a constant drumroll. On November 1, Pavel Miliukov, a liberal leader and a renowned historian who had lectured at the University of Chicago, rounded on the government in a speech to the Duma, the quasi-parliament in Petrograd. He accused the premier, Boris Stürmer, of living up to his German name. "Judas is the traitor among us," he thundered. "Was it not madness to appoint as a prime minister a man with a name and a face apart from our sympathies and methods, a man of a race with whom we are at war! Are the trenches the steps toward riches for the premier and his clique?" Miliukov was aiming higher than mere politicians. He read out, in German, the verdict of a Viennese newspaper on Stürmer's appointment: "That is the victory of the court party assembled round the young tsarina."

The attack emboldened Yusupov, living alone in the Moika palace, to act on his mother's urgings. A few days later he met Mikhail Rodzianko, the Duma chairman, a burly, balding man with a powerful contempt for the government. "What can one do when all the ministers and most of the people in close contact with His Majesty are tools of Rasputin?" Rodzianko asked Yusupov. "The only solution is to kill the scoundrel, but there's not a man in Russia who has the guts to do it." Yusupov haunted the Duma sessions in the chamber of the Tauride.

Stürmer was replaced on November 18 by Alexander Trepov. The new premier was more competent and sympathetic but, having tasted Stürmer's blood, the opposition wanted more. Yusupov was in the Duma gallery on November 19 to hear Trepov screamed down for forty minutes while his pleas to "postpone our feuds" went unanswered. After Trepov sat down, an extreme right-wing deputy, Vladimir Purishkevich, directly challenged Rasputin. Purishkevich urged ministers to fall at the feet of the tsar and assure him that the "crisis at home cannot continue, the multitude is muttering in its wrath, revolution threatens, and an obscure *muzhik* shall govern Russia no more!"

Two days later Yusupov visited Purishkevich at his apartment, where they discussed the mounting public revulsion and the danger to the autocracy for two hours. Purishkevich asked what his visitor proposed. Yusupov's eyes, if not as penetrating as those of Rasputin, were remarkable enough for the ballerina Anna Pavlova to say that he had "God in one and the devil in the other." He fixed them on the older man and said, "Remove Rasputin." The two shook hands on it, and Princess Zinaïda's "book" was prepared for destruction.

The co-conspirators were an odd couple. Yusupov regarded the assassination of Rasputin as a "scenario worthy of his favorite author Oscar Wilde." Vladimir Purishkevich was a conscious counterrevolutionary who had no argument with autocracy and saw the plot as a necessary step to preserve it. A vehement man, energetic in his fifties, bearded and bald, and known for provocative behavior — he liked to appear in the Duma with a red carnation jutting from his fly buttons — Purishkevich was also a Jew-baiter. He had been a moving force in the notorious Union of the Russian People, a government-funded group that inspired anti-Semitic pogroms by the Black Hundreds gangs during the abortive 1905 revolution. He had become a one-man patriotic center during the war, organizing hospital trains, canteens, and delousing stations. He named his good works for himself, advertising one as the "Tea Room of State Councilor Purishkevich."

Two further plotters were recruited by Yusupov. Both were personal friends. Grand Duke Dmitri, a favorite of the empress and first cousin to the tsar, was three years younger than Felix at twenty-six, "flighty and impulsive," and a heavy drinker. Captain Sukhotin of the crack Preobrazhensky Regiment was a patriotic and devout monarchist worried by the damage Rasputin was inflicting on a tsar who, in orthodox hagiography, represented the image of Christ on earth to the masses. The first action against the excesses of the monarchy was being taken, not by the dormant revolutionary left, but by monarchists.

A plan was sketched out. Yusupov was to lure Rasputin to the Moika palace, on the pretext of inviting him to meet his wife. Since shots might be heard in a nearby police station, Rasputin was to be poisoned in a cellar room before his naked and weighted body was sunk in a branch of the Neva. Purishkevich brought in an army doctor with access to potassium cyanide, Stanislas Lazavert, who worked on one of his hospital trains.

The coming revolution was to be distinguished by lack of secrecy, its coups and countercoups tattled over days before they happened in a nation suffering from a "compulsion to open its mouth." These first plotters anticipated the trend. Purishkevich discussed the plot with fellow members of the Duma and revealed the date set for the murder, December 16, to the monarchist Vasily Shulgin. On that day, Purishkevich said with pride, "We will kill him." Whom? "Grisha," he said, using Rasputin's diminutive. Shulgin tried vainly to convince him that the rot in Russia went deeper than Rasputin. Purishkevich also revealed details of the plan to at least one newspaper reporter. Yusupov had discussed the murder with a Duma deputy, Vasily Maklakov, assuring him that Alexandra would disintegrate as soon as Rasputin had gone. With the empress in a mental institution, Yusupov predicted, the tsar would soon turn into a "good constitutional monarch." Rasputin's mentor, Aron Simanovich, got wind of a plot from punters at a gambling house he ran. Okhrana agents reported to Alexander Protopopov at the interior ministry that a move against his patron was underway.

Rasputin had an unwitting opportunity to evade the plotters. Alexander Trepov thought that it would be impossible for him to remain as premier unless Rasputin was removed from influence. Rasputin was known to be bribable — Protopopov was paying him a thousand rubles a month from police funds — so Trepov offered Rasputin 200,000 rubles in cash and a monthly stipend if he would go back to Siberia and leave politics alone. Rasputin refused.

Although he was particularly on his guard in December, Rasputin had no reason to suspect Yusupov. The young aristocrat had been cultivating Rasputin for months. Felix had submitted to hypnosis, during which he felt that heat was pouring into his body "like a warm current" as his body went numb. "All I could see was Rasputin's glittering eyes," he recalled. "Two phosphorescent beams of light melting into a great luminous ring." Though Felix felt "polluted each time I met him," he had little difficulty in persuading Rasputin to accept his invitation to meet his wife. Princess Irina was one of the beauties of the day.

Yusupov fretted over the décor of the cellar. He wished to give it a lived-in look, and a Yusupov lived well. He decked it out with Persian carpets and a bearskin rug, oak chairs, curtains, a cabinet of inlaid ebony, and a crystal and silver crucifix. The room was ready by 11:00 P.M. on

December 16, a Friday. A samovar bubbled on the table and there were rose cakes and glasses of Madeira wine on the sideboard — Rasputin was not a vodka drinker. Wearing rubber gloves, Dr. Lazavert carefully ground up crystals of potassium cyanide into powder and placed the poison inside the cakes. Each of the three glasses of wine beside the cakes had three decigrams of cyanide dissolved in a few drops of water. Four centigrams was a lethal dose. Lazavert tossed his gloves on the fire, a blunder since the room filled with the odor of burning rubber.

Yusupov collected Rasputin from his apartment. Felix felt shame for the "despicable deceit" of inviting a guest to his own murder, and fear of his victim. "What had become of his second sight?" Yusupov wondered. "What use was his faculty for reading the thoughts of others, if he was blind to the dreadful trap that was laid for him?" Rasputin was wearing a silk blouse with a cornflower pattern and smelt of cheap soap. He was looking forward to meeting Yusupov's lady. The two men drove to the palace. Music was playing on the first floor. The conspirators had bought a record of "Yankee Doodle Dandy" to play on the gramophone to suggest that Princess Irina, in fact in the Crimea, was entertaining girlfriends upstairs.

In the cellar, Rasputin was delighted by the ebony cabinet, opening and closing its many drawers. He ate a rose cake, the bitter almond scent of the cyanide passing unnoticed. He was not yet in the mood for wine and asked for tea. The cake had no effect and Yusupov lost his nerve, going upstairs to the room where his fellow conspirators were cranking the gramophone. They persuaded him to return. He tempted Rasputin into drinking two glasses of wine and eating some more cake. Rasputin merely complained of "a tickling in my throat." He asked Felix to pick up his guitar. "Play something cheerful," he said. "I like listening to your singing." The murder had dragged on for two hours without a corpse. At 2:30 A.M., after Rasputin complained at the incessant jangling of "Yankee Doodle Dandy," Yusupov said he would see if his wife's guests were leaving.

The upstairs team was as nervous as Yusupov. Dr. Lazavert went out to get some fresh air and fainted. Either the doctor had made a mistake with the dosage of cyanide or the flustered Felix had given the victim unlaced cakes and wine. Another possibility was that speculators had sold the army adulterated supplies. Purishkevich said that it was pointless to wait for the poison to take effect and that Rasputin should be shot with Grand Duke Dmitri's Browning revolver. Yusupov asked for the honor of firing it. He took the weapon and went back into the cellar. Rasputin was sitting with a drooped head and labored breathing. "My head is heavy and I've a burning in my stomach," he said. "Give me another glass of wine. It'll do me good." He swallowed another Madeira "at a gulp" and revived. Despite his cargo of poison, he suggested that Felix go to the gypsies with him. "All our thoughts belong to God," he leered. "But our bodies belong to ourselves."

Rasputin was still playing with the cabinet. "Gregory Efimovich," Felix said, "you'd far better look at the crucifix and say a prayer." Felix raised the revolver. "My arm grew rigid, I aimed at his heart and pulled the trigger," he recalled. "Rasputin gave a wild scream and crumpled on the bearskin." The others rushed down. Rasputin seemed dead and they prepared their alibis. Captain Sukotin put on Rasputin's fur hat and coat and drove off with Dmitri and Dr. Lazavert in Purishkevich's open car, to convince any watching policeman that Rasputin had left the Moika alive.

In the palace, Purishkevich relaxed over a cigar at a job well done. Yusupov went back into the cellar to look at the result of his handiwork. The corpse stirred and opened "green viper eyes." With a violent effort, Rasputin got to his feet and rushed at Yusupov's throat with a roar. "He sank his fingers into my shoulders like steel claws," Felix said. "His eyes were bursting from their sockets, blood oozed from his lips." Yusupov tore himself free, losing an epaulette from his military cadet uniform, and ran to warn Purishkevich. Rasputin had climbed the cellar stairs and was crawling away through the snow in the courtyard when the older assassin caught up with him.

The Siberian could still speak coherently: "Felix, Felix. I'll tell it all to the tsarina." Purishkevich fired twice as Rasputin dragged himself along an iron fence that led to a gate into the street. Taking more careful aim, he hit Rasputin in the back and then fired a shot at his head. Rasputin collapsed in the snow as Purishkevich closed in to kick him in the head.

The shots attracted two soldiers. Purishkevich told them that Rasputin, "enemy of Russia and the tsar," had been killed. The men embraced and kissed him, thanking God the deed had been done, and helped him drag the body back into the palace. Dmitri and Captain Sukhonin returned from their alibi excursion, this time in the grand duke's closed car, to collect the corpse. It was wrapped in a heavy linen sheet, driven to Petrovsky Island, and dumped from a bridge through a hole in the ice. The conspirators failed to weight it and they left a boot on the ice by the bridge.

The cover-up was as messy as the murder. An on-duty policeman arrived at the mansion to make inquiries about the shots. Purishkevich took him aside and identified himself. He asked the policeman if he had heard of Rasputin, a wonderfully superfluous question in 1916 Petrograd. When the policeman agreed that he had, Purishkevich said, "Well, he's dead and if you love the tsar and the country you must be silent about this and tell no one." The policeman told his superiors within twenty minutes. Yusupov, "full of courage and confidence at the thought that the first steps to save Russia had been taken," went to the palace of his father-in-law, Grand Duke Alexander. There he told what had happened.

Felix constructed a cover story to explain the shots the next morning. News of the murder was already circulating — the ballerina Tamara Karsavina had been woken early in her apartment a block away by her maid, who said that the milkman was claiming that Rasputin had been "done in" at the Moika Palace. Yusupov told General Grigoriev, the local police superintendent, that there had been a little horseplay in which a friend had tried to shoot one of the watchdogs in the courtyard. He refused to allow the chief police commissioner to search the palace — dark stains were still visible on the cellar staircase — and denied that Rasputin had been a guest.

The justice minister, Makarov, interrogated Yusupov and asked why Purishkevich had told the policeman of the murder. Yusupov, sticking to his story of a party that had got out of hand, said that Purishkevich was drunk. Makarov knew Purishkevich well. "He never drinks," Makarov said. "What's more, if I'm not mistaken, he belongs to a temperance society." In a classic of criminal understatement, Yusupov said that he had "a strong feeling that neither General Grigoriev, nor the chief commissioner, nor the minister of justice was taken in by what I told them."

This was a miniature of the incompetence that was to stamp the coming revolution. The conspirators' plans for the future were as typical. They had none, even if, as many suspected, they had fired the first shots of a revolution. The act itself was sufficient. "From now on we will do nothing more and will leave to others the task of carrying on our work," Yusupov told Mikhail Rodzianko, the Duma president. "Pray God that concerted action will be taken, and that the emperor's eyes will be opened before it is too late." He agreed that he had no plans to prevent his disaffection from reaching the *narod*, the "dark people," beneath him.

III

The German Woman

RASPUTIN'S CORPSE LAY UNDISTURBED in the ice throughout Sunday, December 18. Tchaikovsky's *Sleeping Beauty* was playing at the Maryinsky Theater with Smirnova as premiere danseuse. Her leaps, pirouettes, and arabesques were said to be no more fantastic than the stories going from lip to lip in the stalls. Those with telephones were aware of the Friend's disappearance, and in passing on, the news was embellished with tales of the occult. During the interval Count Nani Mocenigo, the counselor at the Italian embassy, said to Maurice Paleologue, "We are back in the days of the Borgias!"

The French ambassador was worried at the extent of the galloping hatred for the empress. "Countess R — ," an acquaintance, had just returned from a clothes-buying sortie to the fashionable dressmaker Lomanova in Moscow. "If the emperor appeared on Red Square today, he would be booed," she reported. "The empress would be torn to pieces." All classes were involved in open attacks on the "German woman," the *Nemka*.

Police found the body on Monday, when the telltale boot was seen on the ice under the bridge. It was taken three miles to the Tschema veterans' home, on the Tsarskoe Selo road, a mournful and melancholy place on the plains south of the capital. An examination by Professor Kossorotov established three bullet wounds as the cause of death. There was no evidence of poisoning. The conspirators seemed to have given Rasputin the wrong wine and cakes. The body was laid out on the written instructions of the empress by a hospital orderly and a nun, Sister Akulina. Nobody else was permitted to see the body, though there were supplicants in plenty.

Sister Akulina was devoted to Rasputin, holding that he had exorcised the fits and convulsions to which she was subject. She spent much of the night washing the body and wounds and dressing it in fresh clothes before it was consigned to a casket. A crucifix was placed on the breast, and in the thick peasant hands Sister Akulina placed a letter. "My dear martyr, give me thy blessing that it may follow me always on the sad and dreary path I have yet to traverse here below," it read. "And remember us from on high in your holy prayers! Alexandra."

The evening papers carried brief, two-paragraph stories on the murder. They caused a sensation. Many went to burn candles in thanksgiving in the cathedral of Our Lady of Kazan. As news of Yusupov's involvement spread, people knelt in the street outside the Moika Palace. Along with the euphoria went a feeling of "resignation to evil happenings." One such happening, Felix Yusupov claimed, involved the Martha and Mary Convent, whose abbess was the Grand Duchess Elizabeth, the empress's sister. During the night offices at the hour of the murder, "priests had suddenly gone mad, blaspheming and shrieking; nuns ran about the corridors howling like souls possessed and lifting their skirts with obscene gestures." It must, the cynics said, have been a pretty sight; the nuns' habits had been designed by the Moscow religious painter, Mikhail Nesterov.

The empress and her companion Anna Vyrubova prayed over the corpse at the Tschema veterans' home on Tuesday. They smothered it with flowers and icons, a gesture that struck Paleologue as more pathetic than touching. For him, this "baneful tsarina and her pernicious companion" were weeping over the swollen corpse of the "lustful *muzhik* whom they loved so madly and whom Russia will curse for centuries." Reports reaching the diplomatic corps said that Alexandra was "outwardly calm but silent and absorbed."

Nicholas heard the news at the Stavka, the army field headquarters in Mogilev, a dreary place on the banks of the Dnieper with four horse-drawn tramlines and a park with hilly views to the river. The army had commandeered the Bristol, a four-ruble-a-night hotel on the Dvoryanska, a muddy avenue of leafless chestnuts. The café-chansant served as a map room. The hotel and the municipal bandstand and railway station had been repainted in the tsar's honor, their fresh blues and creams exaggerating the peeling gloom of the remainder.

Mogilev was 490 miles south of Petrograd, a rail journey that had taken nineteen hours by the prewar Kiev express and now lasted two days. Nicholas set off at once to comfort the empress.

On Thursday night, December 22, Rasputin was buried in a plot of ground on the edge of the imperial park at Tsarskoe Selo. The hasty ceremony was conducted by Father Vassiliev, archpriest to the Court. Nicholas and Alexandra attended with their daughters and Anna Vyrubova. Seeking to minimize the involvement of the imperial family, the Okhrana started rumors the next morning that the body was buried in an obscure monastery in the Urals.

At the weekend, over cards and liqueurs in the Imperial Yacht Club, the grand dukes aired plans to remove Alexandra to a nunnery. Sometimes Nicholas was to go too, to be replaced by one of themselves. Mikhail, his kindly and weak-willed brother, was one candidate. He had left Russia before the war after a clandestine marriage to the ex-wife of a captain in his regiment. He had come back with the war, but his command of a Cossack brigade had been disastrous and he had been shuffled off to an obscure inspectorship. Nikolai Mikhailovich, the tsar's cousin, had a more realistic claim, for his relative liberalism had won him the nickname "Nicholas Egalité." Cynical, disparaging, and jealous by temperament, he was a historian who "worked only with words," and was "too fond of scandal" to act decisively.

No secrecy was observed in these intrigues. On Sunday, Petrograd rang with details of a coming coup. One theory was that a famous fighter pilot, Captain Kostenko, intended to crash his aircraft onto the imperial limousine. Another had several grand dukes plotting to use four regiments for a night march on the palace at Tsarskoe Selo to force the emperor to abdicate in favor of his son and a regent. Prince Gabriel Constantinovich gave a supper party for his mistress, a former actress, on Monday, December 26. The guests included Grand Duke Boris, the industrialist Alexei Putilov, a dozen officers, and a squad of elegant courtesans. They talked nonstop about the conspiracy and the details of which regiments were to be seduced. All this was done with "the servants moving about, harlots looking on and listening, gypsies singing."

Tongues loosened by streams of Brut Imperial were heard by Okhrana agents. Nicholas and Alexandra were informed. They sent the grand dukes no Christmas presents that year and soon moved them and Rasputin's murderers out of Petrograd. Grand Duke Dmitri was ordered to join the army staff in Persia, Yusupov exiled to his family estates in the south. Vladimir Purishkevich had already gone to the front, where the military police were keeping an eye on him. The other grand dukes were sent to their estates or away on urgent naval business. The press was forbidden to mention Rasputin's name.

It was as difficult to conceive of the overthrow of a three-hundred-year-old absolutism in the middle of an unlost war as it was to imagine its unreformed survival in peace. No revolutionary seriously discussed the possibility, hoping at best to regroup after the war, when the more advanced proletariat of the Western countries might have given a lead. This view overlooked the actuality of an emperor and empress who had so undermined themselves that other Romanovs were turning on them in panic.

Every major group with an interest in stability had been alienated. Industrialists despaired. Alexei Putilov, who employed twenty-seven thousand at the steel and engineering works bearing his name in Petrograd, had been saying for more than a year that tsarism "is lost, beyond hope." Putilov was an indifferent businessman — his factories relied on government subsidies to stay solvent — but politically shrewd. He reckoned that the bourgeoisie would initiate the revolution, "thinking they are saving Russia," but would prove too thin a class to sustain it. Amid "interminable anarchy," the middle class would give way to workers and peasants.

The Union of Towns, with its heavy makeup of professionals, was under Okhrana surveillance. Civil servants were contemptuous of their ministers. Moscow had added distaste for the rulers to its old dislike of "effete" Petrograd. General Alexander Krymov, one of the army's better commanders, told Mikhail Rodzianko that the army would welcome a coup with joy and that the High Command thought that revolution was "imminent." The grand duke Alexander Mikhailovich warned Nicholas that, strange as it seemed, it was the establishment that was preparing the revolution. "We are participating in an unheard-of spectacle," he wrote to his cousin. "The revolution comes from above and not from below."

Nicholas was an autocrat who had no natural authority; Rasputin had said that he "lacked insides." His wistful eyes and the worried set to his mouth and shoulders showed through the stiff bearing and naval beard in his official photograph. Power "hung over him like a shroud." At five foot seven, he was overshadowed by his gargantuan uncles. Other Romanovs fitted the part, physically at least; his father, Alexander III, was a bearlike man over six feet tall. Nicholas was handsome, neat, and conventional.

"The tsar is not treacherous, but he is weak," the German Kaiser Wilhelm said. "Weakness is not treachery, but it fulfills all its functions." Nicholas's bad luck was a legend — dangerously so, for he behaved as though he believed it himself. His Christianity was deep but submissive. He had preceded his marriage with some signs of vigor — a world tour, taking the dancer Mathilde Kshesinskaya as a mistress — but these signs were not in much evidence after. The wedding celebration itself turned to tragedy, with at least two thousand of his subjects crushed to death at a coronation fete outside Moscow. His heir Alexis, eagerly awaited after four daughters, was a hemophiliac.

At the outbreak of war, an informer had told the French ambassador that people had "long been convinced that the Emperor is manifestly doomed to

misfortune." Besides, the superstitious said, "the lines of his hand are terrifying." Palmistry conspired against him.

Nicholas had qualities. His natural dignity and charm made it difficult
for his critics to despise him. He was a caring father, his children loved and
secure, and a devoted husband — Rasputin thought him "made for family
life and to admire nature." He was conscious of the feelings of others and
endeavored to contain rather than give rein to his own. He kept himself in
trim, eating and drinking little, with a kennel of eleven English collies to
accompany him on his daily walks. He treated subordinates with a gracious
and somewhat shy kindness. He had no vanity, refusing to watch newsreel
footage of himself at the front.

An autocrat's virtues — sensitivity to danger and ruthlessness in eradi-
cating it, the instinct to exploit others — were absent in Nicholas, however.
Conscious of his own shortcomings, he was awkward in the presence of
talented men, a position he avoided wherever possible by appointing me-
diocrities. Half-baked schemes — the takeover of Tibet, the building of a
bridge across the Bering Strait — masqueraded in his mind as grandeur, and
the shabby adventurers who proposed them as imperial architects.

Yet Nicholas believed deeply in his role as autocrat. When the British
ambassador Sir George Buchanan suggested shortly after the Rasputin murder that he should regain public support, Nicholas replied, "Do you mean
that I am to regain the confidence of my people or that they are to regain *my*
confidence?"

He manifestly did not fill the part. As Supreme Commander, his intelligence was held to be that of an average Guards colonel, not a flattering
comparison. He had no experience of command beyond a brief period as a
subaltern with a squadron of cavalry a quarter of a century before. He laid
no claim to strategic or tactical insight and played little part in the conduct
of the war. He spent his afternoons in Mogilev going for brisk walks along
the Dnieper bluffs, and his evenings watching movies. His favorite was a
twenty-reel Pathé serial called *The Streets of New York*. Eight of his more
responsible ministers had formally warned him of the dangers of going to
the Stavka headquarters in Mogilev and leaving his capital in the hands of
depot battalions and reservists. His mother, the Dowager Empress Maria,
was so horrified she "nearly had a stroke. . . . Everyone would regard it as
being at Rasputin's orders."

The affection of his people, which served him in place of their respect,
was evaporating. They started to feel, early in January of 1917, that the
tsarina-empress could "not alone be guilty."

*   *   *

Nicholas's greatest misfortune was held to be his empress. This was partly a matter of convenience. The tsar-emperor was nominally Russian, though generations of dynastic marriages by the Romanovs had reduced his native blood to less than one part in a hundred. Alexandra was nominally German, a Hessian princess, and undeniably foreign. Her mother, Princess Alice, was a daughter of Queen Victoria. Alice died of diphtheria when she was six and Alexandra — previously warm and happy enough to have earned the nickname "Sunny" — became quiet and withdrawn. Victoria took a close interest in the upbringing of her favorite grandchild, and Alexandra was often at Windsor Castle. Bernard Pares, an Englishman attached to the Russian army, observed that "she was in the deepest sense a Victorian Englishwoman." Nicholas had first courted her on the banks of the Thames at Walton. She spoke Russian with a strong British accent.

Alexandra's appearance and deportment — tall and slender with a delicate complexion, supple figure, and reddish gold hair — were held to be "English looks." So were her dark blue eyes, and the strain of inflexibility and Puritanism shown in the spartan beds and open windows she decreed for her children. Attacks on her benefited from the camouflage of patriotism.

Women in Russia had an influence and strength beyond their apparent servility. Several were serving in the army, openly after petitioning the tsar, or masquerading as men. The novelist Ivan Turgenev had found women to be stronger in character, decision, and temper than their menfolk, an observation all applied to Nicholas and Alexandra. "In the matter of lovemaking it is almost always the woman who takes and retains the offensive," Maurice Paleologue noted. "It is the woman whose orders are accepted and whose will prevails." This was often the case in politics, revolutionary and autocratic, for the "share of women in terrorist plots is very important and often decisive."

Somerset Maugham, the British writer who was on a secret service mission to Russia in 1917, was struck by the "aggressive way in which women treat men. They seem to take a sensual pleasure in humiliating them in front of others." Maugham found Russian men to be "femininely passive, they cry easily."

Women were active in all the prewar revolutionary movements. Vera Zasulich opened the assassination season in the late 1870s by shooting the Saint Petersburg police prefect at point-blank range. The "frighteningly single-minded" Sophie Perovskaya, daughter of a former governor-general of Petrograd and a noted beauty, and mistress of the assassin A. I. Zhelyabov, aided in the murder of Alexander II in 1881. A tiny blonde with pale blue eyes and pink-and-white cheeks like a china doll, she urged the reformist "People's Will" movement to convert to terrorism and gave the signal to the bomb throwers waiting for the tsar. She was hanged in the last public execution in Russia, in front of a crowd of eighty thousand. The executioner was drunk and there was no drop to the scaffold, simply a wooden stool to be kicked away; she took several minutes to die.

Vera Figner, a medical student from a well-to-do gentry family, was implicated in the same assassination. Her 1884 death sentence was commuted to life imprisonment, and after twenty years Figner was released from the Schlüsselburg Fortress. In 1917, she was writing caustic articles in the feminist press. It was she who found Paleologue to be a snob.

Another Sophie, Sophie Gunsburg, organized an attempt on Alexander III. The political prisoner Maria Vietrov martyred herself in 1897, pouring lamp oil over herself and burning herself to death after she had been raped by a gendarmerie officer. Dora Brillant kept watch at the Kremlin during the murder of the empress's brother-in-law, Grand Duke Sergius, in 1905. Maria Spiridonova, a tiny girl with big gray eyes and a nervous habit of playing with her pince-nez, was nineteen and a member of a Social Revolutionary assassination squad when she lay in wait for the top police official of Tambov province on a station platform in 1906, and shot him dead; in 1917 she was serving life imprisonment in Siberia. The "pretty girl with bright, hard eyes under her astrakhan cap" was a standard ingredient in revolutionary groups.

The empress was a mirror image on the right. Frail and withdrawn in public, Alexandra detested formal events, her veins standing out on her cheeks at a state dinner, "obviously struggling with hysteria" as her labored breathing made the diamonds sparkle on her bosom. Her hatreds were fierce and many. They included her own and her husband's relations, as well as liberal politicians whom she thought should be hanged or meet with "strong railway accidents." She campaigned for the tsar to replace Grand Duke Nicholas as Supreme Commander — "you must show you have a will and way of your own and are not led by him and his staff" — in part because the uncle was too painful a contrast to her Nicholas. The grand duke was six foot six, his boots coming up to the belly of his horse, and "the most admired man in the army." He had also threatened to have Rasputin hanged if he came to the Stavka. "Can't you realise," Alexandra complained to her husband, "that a man who has turned traitor to a man of God cannot be blest, nor his actions good."

She seldom spoke to her sister, the Grand Duchess Elizabeth, who had founded a religious community for women after her husband had been dismembered by the bomb thrown by Dora Brillant's friends in Moscow. Her sister disapproved of Rasputin. Her mother-in-law, the dowager empress, so loathed Alexandra for ruining her son that she had taken herself off to Kiev to avoid the pain of watching it.

Alexandra's only close friend was Anna Vyrubova, the coarsely built daughter of a minor court official, commonplace as a "bubble in the biscuit dough." Her "thick gleaming hair, narrow skull, red neck, clammy back, and huge thighs" aroused revulsion in outsiders. This "mound of warm and ample flesh" seemed not to have a mind, beyond her servility and devotion to the empress and their shared obsession with piety and Rasputin.

No one else penetrated into the family circle. Vyrubova sat with the family each night as they played draughts and patience, did puzzles, and read aloud "thoroughly proper English novels." It was, a princess complained, as if "they lived in rooms that are never aired." Vyrubova had no office and no salary — only occasionally could Alexandra get her to accept a cheap jewel or dress. Yet, a diplomat observed, since Nicholas rarely made a decision without his wife's approval, the "net result is that it is the empress and Madame Vyrubova who really govern Russia."

Alexandra's unflagging dynastic aim was to preserve the autocracy for "Baby," the ailing tsarevich: "We must give a strong country to Baby, and dare not be weak for his sake." She poured out her simple philosophy to the tsar in letters and telegrams to Mogilev, three or more a day. The notion that Russians were fit only to be coerced was an old one. "It is scarcely possible for a people to be as fitted for slavery as the Muscovites," a writer noted in 1706. "They are so corrupt by nature that they will do nothing of their own free will but must be driven by hard and cruel blows."

Alexandra agreed. She described the people as errant children who loved "to feel the whip — it's their nature — tender love & then the iron hand to punish and guide." Constitutionalism, she warned Nicholas with a "kind of cold fury," was a chimera that would destroy the state and amounted to treason. She urged him to be firm, to "be Peter the Great, Ivan the Terrible, be Tsar Paul — crush them all under your feet." She wanted to "pour my will into your veins," for "I am your wall behind you and wont give way."

Though she always wrote to Nicholas in English and was never comfortable in Russian, those who met her were astonished at the intensity with which she had converted to the religion and the psyche of her adopted country. Paleologue thought that she had the Russian's "moral unrest, chronic melancholy, vague sorrows, the see-saw between elation and despondency, the haunting obsession of the invisible and the life beyond and the superstitious credulity." Her moral sense, though it had her tending wounded soldiers as a volunteer nurse, did not extend to her responsibilities as tsarina; she indulged both her own and her husband's shyness, and the imperial family was rarely seen at the Winter Palace in Petrograd.

Instead, Alexandra withdrew into isolation at Tsarskoe Selo. The imperial park, secluded behind a high iron fence patrolled by Cossacks, had a lake with a marble bridge and a fleet of pygmy ships and a model Chinese village sited among clumps of lilac. Its blue-and-white Catherine Palace, with three hundred rooms, had been designed by Rastrelli in 1752. Alexandra preferred to live simply in a wing of the smaller Alexander Palace, five hundred yards away. Here, the empress spent much of her time in her mauve boudoir — the English furniture, carpets, and curtains all this color — refusing to attend social functions or to be exposed to her people. The boudoir had, visitors noted, a portrait of Marie Antoinette as well as a photograph of Queen Victoria.

Strong sexuality combined with Alexandra's religious hysteria. She shared the same bed as her husband and her letters show that the physical attraction between them was still urgent. She jealously cocooned her "Nicky" or "darling mannykins" — to him she was "Alix" or "Sunny." The few at court who stood up against the Rasputin cabal, like Prince Vladimir Orlov, director of the military chancellery — "Fat Orlov," because he was so obese he could not see his knees when he sat down — were dismissed. Placemen flourished, like Prince Meshchersky, known as the Prince of Sodom.

Alexandra knew she was hated. She rationalized it without difficulty. She said, "almost choking with rage," that it was only the "corrupt and godless society" of Petrograd, which "thinks of nothing but dancing and dining," that disliked her. She held that socialites were jealous of her "because they know I have a strong will and when am convinced of a thing being right (when besides blessed by Gregory) do not change my mind & that they can't bear."

Her mailbag comforted her. Scores of letters and telegrams arrived in Tsarskoe Selo daily, the writers whose scrawled signatures they bore blaming the country's ills on the grand dukes, treacherous politicians, and intellectuals. She kept a pile of this correspondence on her desk after the murder. It warded off her increasing bouts of depression, the melancholy evenings spent listening to a Romanian chamber orchestra and peering silently into the flames of the drawing room fire.

When visitors came, she invited them to leaf through the letters. Did they not beseech her, "our beloved sovereign, mother and guardian," to "save us from our enemies. . . . Save Russia"? Had she not the daily consolation, she wrote, of knowing from her mail that the "whole of Russia — the real Russia, poor humble, peasant Russia — is with me?"

Alexandra dismissed Petrograd as an aberration. It was small, ranking fifth among European cities, and smaller still in terms of the country it governed.

It accounted for rather more than one percent of the population of the empire, and its troublesome workers for barely one-fifth of one percent. Eighty percent of the English lived in towns, almost two-thirds of Germans, and half of Americans. Peasants made up more than four-fifths of the Romanovs' subjects and their armies. The "dark people," as they called themselves in a phrase both obsequious and menacing, were the bedrock of the autocracy.

Rare Western travelers found an "awful sadness" about the countryside whose supposed loyalty so comforted Alexandra. The grasslands were "like the sea, except at sea, there were always companions close at hand." On the steppe, there was only the driver of the trap, hunched more or less into a circular shape, chewing sunflower seeds one by one, the wheels throwing up dust clouds that hung in the air after their passing like the wake of a ship. "You saw some landmark, a grove of poplars perhaps in a hollow," an Englishman wrote, "which looked a mile off, and found it took over an hour to reach it." The song of grasshoppers formed "a continuous pedal accompaniment." Kites flew in languid circles and there were curlews in the wilder parts. Apart from crows, hooded or black, there was little other animal life.

In high summer, the temperature on the steppe could reach ninety-eight degrees Fahrenheit and the air quivered in sheets of blue and green to an intimidating horizon. Severe cold swept in waves from November to late March, windless days with bands of pale pink at dawn and the brilliance of the day sliding into sudden dusk that flared the nostrils with its freezing. Landlords who could afford it abandoned their estates for apartments in the nearest large town, the richest in Moscow and Petrograd.

The single street in the villages often straggled on for over a mile, lined with single-story cabins made of dun-colored mud bricks or logs caulked with oakum. Poor *muzhiks* lived in a single room. An icon held the place of honor in the corner, a candle beneath it. Families slept on wooden shelves, or on the dung-fired stove in winter. The mattress was a pile of sheepskins, which a visitor found to "harbor more animal life than was pleasant." A central square of bare earth held the church and its pale green domes.

Slabs of earth for building blocks and slices of dung and straw for fuel covered acres of land in summer as they lay out to dry. Behind them, the open steppe started abruptly beyond the tilled plots. In winter the steppe appeared to reach into the village, the land being without hedges or fences and so immense and flat that the curvature of the earth was seen at its extremity.

The men were "sallow in complexion, lank in figure, with straight yellow hair and a heavy expression of face." Often bearded, they wore peaked caps, blouses, and cotton shirts with woolen trousers. It was a sign of wealth if these were stuffed into a pair of boots. The poorest wore *lapti*, crude sandals made, like the roofs of the huts, from the plaited bark of birch or lime trees. Women wore kerchiefs and bright blouses. The peasants matched the melancholy of the steppe with a deep pessimism. "How strange is the fact that in their language," an Englishman wrote, "the word for 'harvest' should be *strada*, 'Suffering!' "

Army service apart, few peasants ventured farther than the nearest town, which might be two or three days away by cart. The gray houses in provincial towns seemed like "heaps of refuse" to Maxim Gorky, their roofs overgrown with weeds and dusty grass. Churches stood out against the soiled background, their white walls looking like clean patches on dirty rags.

Alexandra's correspondence told the truth, in that the *muzhiks* had no interest in radical politics. They called revolution *ravnenie*, leveling, and they were traditionally more interested in manor-burning and land seizure than in socialism. A shepherd told Gorky how they dealt with a schoolmaster-agitator. "He studied himself into such a state that he began teaching the youngsters that all sorrow came from the tsar," the shepherd said. "I don't know how the tsar had offended him. So Fedka Savin, the village elder, did the right thing — he sent word to the police. Fedka got a gold seven-and-a-half-ruble piece for it, and the teacher was dragged off to the jail by the policeman that night. That was the end of him and his learning."

The letters Alexandra received, however, were fakes. The police regularly staged patriotic demonstrations in the capital by paying men to carry banners praising the autocracy. The British correspondent Arthur Ransome saw a band of "scallywags" come out of a police station with flags rolled up around sticks. The men unfurled them, marched around the city for an hour, and returned to the police station to hand in their banners and collect their pay. The letters from the provinces, like the banners, were forged by police agents on the orders of Alexander Protopopov at the interior ministry. He wished to induce a feeling of well-being in his imperial mistress.

The Petrograd Okhrana methodically opened genuine correspondence from the provinces in the special "black room" provided for such spying. These letters showed none of the contented patriotism fed to Alexandra. The demands of war, conscription, requisitioning, and inflation were making villages withdraw into themselves, hostile to all outsiders. "The countryside is becoming impoverished and ruined," a writer from Irkutsk complained. "Horses and livestock have been taken, there's no one to plow and nothing to plow with. . . . Perhaps the landowners are getting rich, merchants and various rogues are getting rich, but the people, the common people, are undoubtedly growing poor. They are making all the sacrifices and enduring the entire burden of this war."

The Russian draft system was eccentric. Only sons, only grandsons where the father was dead, and, for a long period, breadwinners were exempted. So were some minorities — Central Asians, Finns. Poland had fallen to the Germans. The recruiting sergeants, with their squads of Cossacks, harvested only half as many men in the frontier provinces as elsewhere. As a result, conscription fell heavily on individual Russian and Ukrainian villages. Simbirsk had three-hundred-acre farms without a male worker. Grand Duke Nikolai Mikhailovich said that no Russians remained on his Black Sea estates. In one village 829 men had been mobilized out of a total of 3,307 souls, and of those 115 men were casualties. Like other big landowners, however, the grand dukes benefited from the 130,000 prisoners of war who were working on the land.

The governor of Kherson warned at year's end, "Here, hardly a third of the land can be sown, and people will die of hunger for want of labor." The proportion of unsown land had doubled since the beginning of the war, from 6.4 to 13.5 percent. In London the *Economist* warned that the demands of war were turning "one of the richest producing countries in the world into one which can only with difficulty feed its own people."

The mood round Ekaterinoslav was troubled: "They keep on taking people. . . . Police officers and the powers that be are on guard, trying to find sedition, but there's so much of it everywhere, they cannot stamp it out." Assaults on *obtrubniki* — peasants who had taken advantage of the prewar agricultural reforms to buy land — and on land surveyors multiplied. Boundary markers were destroyed, a direct threat to landowners. Some villages had mass disturbances. Shops were looted, mainly by the wives of absent soldiers who wrote from the front urging their families to hide everything the authorities wanted to requisition, livestock, grain, hay, carts. "Watch out for the landowners," the soldiers warned.

Although crop prices had roughly doubled, they had not kept pace with the supplies peasants needed from the towns. Kerosene was up by 210 percent, textiles by 262 percent. Matches were so expensive that tinderboxes reappeared. A kilo of horseshoe nails that had cost 3.4 rubles in 1914 was up to 40 rubles in 1916, while a pair of boots that had cost 7 rubles in prewar Simbirsk now sold for 40. Often goods were not available at all. A report in 1916 found that manufactured articles were in short supply or nonexistent in forty-six provinces. Even scythes had been imported before the war. In the province of Tambov, almost nine-tenths of the peasants had no metal tools.

The *muzhiks* retaliated by hoarding grain or feeding it to their animals.

Cattle, pigs, and horses were being fed a third more grain than the towns and army combined. In Khabarovsk, Chita, and the Ural region there was no flour, meat, sugar, or kerosene — "in a word, there is only hunger, cold and despair." The Moscow Okhrana warned that the antagonism between the city and the village was clearly seen for the first time in Russian history. A Moscow journalist, Konstantin Paustovsky, went to the provincial town of Yefremov to discover "what Turgenev's Russia is thinking." He found streets smelling of sour horse manure, gravestones overturned, and the woods full of bandits. Idiot beggars sat on the church steps and "white ticket men," exempted from military service, roamed the streets. There were only two other guests in Paustovsky's hotel, a fortune-teller and "Princess Greza," a man who wrote an agony column for cheap magazines.

The writer Ivan Bunin, wintering on his estate, was surrounded by *muzhiks* who "grow more furious every day." He sat on his bed and waited for them to come and burn down his house; they had already run off his horses. The editor of the religious journal *Kolokol*, returning from the villages, said that everyone was "hawking round the prophecy which Gregory had often uttered to Their Majesties: 'If I die or you desert me, you will lose your son and your crown within six months.'"

As Alexander Protopopov stepped up the supply of false letters to the empress, the governor of Tula warned Protopopov's own ministry that "such terrible times have set in that I don't know how to cope. . . . I am sitting on a powder keg."

The country was not writing to Alexandra, but mocking her. A café joke had the young tsarevich weeping in the palace. "What's the matter, Alexis?" asked a visiting general. "Well, you see, when the Russians are beaten my father cries," said the boy. "When the Germans lose, my mother cries. When am I to cry?" The *nemetskoe vasilye*, the "German plague," was replacing Jews as a universal butt and had attached itself to the Darmstadt-born empress.

It was, perhaps, a wonder Alexandra was not murdered in a country with a rich tradition of political assassination. She was well protected at Tsarskoe Selo. A Cossack escort regiment of 650 men cantered round the park and avenues at intervals of fifty yards, day and night. Men of His Majesty's Regiment were stationed in the corridors, on the staircases, in the kitchens and cellars, and in sentry boxes of the palace. The entrances and exits were screened by the police of the imperial court, who frisked visitors, tradesmen, and gardeners. They kept photo files on terrorists and dissidents. The emperor's personal police, three hundred strong, were responsible for her safety on the rare occasions when she left the palace.

A surer short-term defense was the mood of inertia. People felt themselves spectators, waiting, Zinaïda Gippius said, for a "drama that is certain to occur, but of whose plot and cast they have only the dimmest idea."

On Sunday, January 1, the tsar received the New Year's congratulations of the diplomatic corps at Tsarskoe Selo. The year 1917 started in a burst of sudden cold with a temperature of thirty-six degrees below zero Fahrenheit. The windows of the court carriages taking the ambassadors to the palace were too thickly frosted to look out of, and the horses were smothered in ice. Maurice Paleologue was taken aside by the director of ceremonies as he entered the gilt-and-parquet ballroom to be presented. "Well, Ambassador, haven't I been right all these months in telling you that our great and holy Russia is being led to disaster!" the courtier whispered. "Don't you feel that we are now on the very brink?"

The tsar seemed sick and preoccupied. Alexander Trepov, worn down by the empress's hostility to his premiership, had resigned five days before. With this blunt and faithful monarchist, the ambassador thought, had gone the last pillar and safeguard of tsarism. Trepov's replacement, Prince Nicholas Golitsyn, was sensible enough not to want the job. Golitsyn had warned Nicholas that the regiments in Moscow were talking openly of proclaiming another tsar. Nicholas had ordered him to accept, telling him "The empress and I know that we are in God's hands. His will be done!"

A former premier, Count Vladimir Kokovtsov, saw Nicholas on January 6 and scarcely recognized him, so much had he aged, his cheeks sunken and his eyes without color. He had a "strange and sickly smile, almost an unconscious one without expression." Kokovtsov thought him on the verge of a nervous breakdown. Closeted with his family and Vyrubova, the tsar spent his mornings on such niceties as abolishing German court titles, his afternoons walking, and his evenings watching movies and playing puzzles. One film was *Madame du Barry*, with bloody scenes of guillotining in the French revolution, another the spiritualist thriller *Mysterious Hands*.

Without Rasputin's glue, visitors sensed that the imperial couple were falling apart. "They couldn't get on without him," one reported. "He was their mainspring, their toy, their fetish. He oughtn't to have been taken away from them. Since his departure, they haven't known which way to turn. I expect the wildest follies from them now!"

They prayed to Rasputin's spirit. "He is," Alexandra wrote, "still close to us." Some ministers — or so a rumor breaking surface on January 13 had it — went further and communicated with the dead. Prince Kurakin, a bald and hook-nosed necromancer, was said to have raised the ghost of Rasputin. Eager for influence over the empress, Kurakin had at once sent for Protopopov and Dobrovolsky, the justice minister. The trio were said to be locked in "secret conclave for hours every evening, listening to the dead man's solemn words" and passing them on to Alexandra.

A suggestion from the imperial dentist, Serge Kostritsky, that a responsible ministry was imperative was met with indifference. "That would be useful," Nicholas murmured, but he added that it would be impossible until after the war. Madame Rodzianko, wife of the Duma president, sensed that the couple had passed beyond any persuasion. "They are confident that force is behind them and the whole country must be squeezed in their fist." As she wrote, "Police and troops are everywhere in force, patrols tramp the streets in expectation of revolution."

IV
Iced Nights

THE TWELFTH ANNIVERSARY of Bloody Sunday, the massacre in front of the Winter Palace that opened the 1905 revolution, fell on a Monday in 1917, January 9. Three hundred thousand Petrograd workers marked it by coming out on strike. In Moscow, a red banner was raised in Theater Square for the first time in the war. The capital was getting 21 freight cars of grain a day in place of the 120 required. Signs were posted on bakery doors: "There is no bread today, nor will there be."

The arrival of Allied missions led to a sudden burst of gaiety at midmonth. Cars ferried visitors from the Hotel de l'Europe to dinners and dances in embassies, at the Grand Duchess Maria Pavlova's palace, and at the Yacht Club. The big royal box at the ballet glittered with French, English, and Italian uniforms. The tsar gave a state banquet. The menu was modest — cream of barley soup, glacéed fruits, veal Marengo, cucumber salad, ices — but it roused anger in the breadlines.

By the end of the month the delegates had gone and the city slipped back into routine. It was bitterly cold. The streets filled with ice and snowdrifts piled up on the sidewalks. "With every day the food question becomes more acute," Okhrana agents reported. "Never before has there been so much swearing, argument, and scandal. That the population has not yet begun food riots does not mean they will not in the nearest future." Seven hundred new Okhrana agents and mounted police were recruited.

The danger of spontaneous fury concerned the Okhrana more than organized revolution. Mainstream opposition came from the liberal Cadets — or Constitutional Democrats — the bourgeois party led by Pavel Miliukov, caustic but muscular and active with no surplus flesh at fifty-eight. The Cadet model was English-style parliamentary monarchy. Frustrated by government hostility, they nevertheless held the country's quasi-parliament, the Duma, to be a real if fragile gain from 1905. Nicholas had consented to the Duma only to buy off that year's revolts. He crossed himself before, and wept after, signing the decree establishing it, feeling that "in this act I have lost the crown. Now all is lost." The Duma had, however, no executive powers; it exercised no choice or control over the cabinet; and its legislative functions and the franchise on which it was elected were severely limited. The tsar had suspended its sittings several times. Personal disillusion with Nicholas was deep, as Miliukov's attack in November had shown, but the Cadets supported the monarchy, with the proviso that the Duma be given real authority.

To the right of the Cadets were the Octobrists, richer land- and factory-owning monarchists. They accepted the limited constitution squeezed from the tsar that month in 1905, but wished him to fulfill its promises. These included a government acceptable to — though not, as the Cadets insisted, responsible to — the Duma. The most prominent Octobrist was the Duma chairman, Mikhail Rodzianko. A fellow Duma member thought him a "mettlesome spirit" always seeking to impress — "Look what a splendid fellow I am! . . . How I foiled Rasputin, how I did this or that, what I said to the tsar, and so on . . ." Rodzianko was a big man, well over six feet and three hundred pounds, with a voice to match — "on a still day he can be heard for a kilometer." His English was good and David Francis, the U.S. ambassador, not a Russian speaker himself, was relieved to find an "affable and approachable" politician he could understand.

Alexander Guchkov was the Octobrist party leader, fifty-five, with alert gray eyes and close-cropped iron-gray whiskers, an intriguer and the wealthy son of a Moscow tycoon. Guchkov was ambitious, with a streak of adventurism that had taken him to fight for the Boers against the British in South Africa when he was in his mid-thirties as well as to duel a colonel, S. N. Mayaseyedov, whom he accused of spying, before the war. When the colonel fired first and missed, Guchkov threw down his own pistol, saying, "I don't want to save him from his natural fate — hanging." Mayaseyedov was in fact hanged as an Austrian spy in 1915.

The Okhrana was aware that Guchkov, intemperate and angry, was talking of a palace coup with fellow industrialists who were members of the war industries' committee. The police did not dare arrest prominent men, but the workers' group on the committee was rounded up on the evening of January 26. Arresting radicals was an instinctive reaction when the city was in a volatile state, although the British journalist Arthur Ransome thought that picking up men who were helping with the arms effort was lunatic.

Opposition to the autocracy by the left had been split for years and remained so, as its major figures were dispersed and feuding in Siberia or in the West. The Social Revolutionaries — populists, in the sense that their movement was broadly based and less obsessed with doctrinal niceties than their Marxist rivals — were the most numerous, and their past was evidence of the batterings suffered by Russian radicalism. In the summer of 1874, several thousand university students — many from the law faculty at Petrograd University, where student poverty was said to "combine with active brains to produce a state of permanent irritation" — went out into the provinces to teach the peasants the joys of liberation and communal living. These *narodniks*, "men of the people," found the *muzhiks* more interested in denouncing them to the police than in listening to city-bred idealists, and they made little headway. Terrorists took over the movement, calling themselves the "People's Will" and spawning a long record of assassinations, including Sophie Perovskaya's assassination of Alexander II. Survivors returning from Siberian exile in the 1890s formed the Social Revolutionary party.

In 1901 Viktor Chernov, a former Moscow law student who had served time in the Peter and Paul Fortress, set up a small unit in Berlin to review the terrorist campaign. By nature a theoretician, indecisive, and "merely a lit-térateur," Chernov abandoned the assassinations to take up the original students' approach again of converting the peasantry. Chernov dismissed the Marxist view that the peasants' instinct to own the land they worked was reactionary. The Social Revolutionaries, known as SRs, promised the *muzhiks* a land share-out without compensation for landlords. Land seizure appealed powerfully in the countryside, where the main Social Revolutionary strength lay. By 1917, however, Chernov had been abroad for ten years, currently in Switzerland, and other SR leaders — Irakli Tsereteli, a fiery and elegant Georgian, and the precise military surgeon Fedor Dan — were in Siberia.

Karl Marx had been wary of socialist prospects in Russia. "I do not trust any Russian," he wrote to Friedrich Engels. "As soon as a Russian worms his way in all hell breaks loose." His suspicion seemed justified. The censor had allowed a translation of Marx's *Das Kapital* into Russia in an edition of three thousand copies in 1872, on the grounds that the book was too dull to be harmful. Marxist ideas were introduced to Russia with more effect by Georgy Plekhanov — if, typically with Russian revolutionaries, from afar. Plekhanov was in exile in Switzerland. Plekhanov came from a bourgeois family, but held that Russia was an exception to the theory that a bourgeois revolution was a necessary forerunner of eventual rule by the proletariat. "In Russia," Plekhanov wrote, "political freedom will be gained by the working class or it will not exist at all."

Plekhanov's Social Democrats held their first meeting in secret in Minsk in 1898. The infant party mounted its second congress five years later in a rat-infested warehouse in Brussels and, having been moved on by the Belgian police, in a London church. The congress resulted in a split. Vladimir Lenin, a scornful emigré who Bruce Lockhart thought "at first glance looked more like a provincial grocer than a leader of men," called for an elitist organization with membership restricted to professional revolutionaries. Julius Martov, popular and attractive enough for other emigrés to nudge each other in respect when they saw him, thought this a "siege mentality." He argued for a broader and more democratic party than that allowed for by Lenin's dictatorial elite.

Martov and Lenin had been unlikely comrades. Martov ate with his followers at the bustling La Rotonde bistro in Paris, a city he loved. Lenin loathed Paris — "What the devil made us come here!" — and took his disciples to a miserable café on the avenue d'Orleans, where they drank sickly grenadine and soda. The second congress, in 1903, ended the friendship. Lenin, due to the small attendance in London, narrowly won the vote. The Social Democrats divided into two factions, Lenin's Bolsheviks, for "majority," and Martov's Mensheviks, for "minority."

In practice, the Mensheviks well outnumbered the Bolsheviks, but such ironies seemed of no importance in early 1917. Lenin had returned briefly to Russia too late to influence events in 1905. The running had been made by a young Menshevik, Leon Trotsky, chairman of an interesting but short-lived revolutionary institution, a "Soviet," which had attempted to coordinate the rising. Now, all three were in exile and impotent to affect events in Russia: Martov and Lenin in Switzerland, Trotsky in New York. Lenin's professionals had proved so inept that the few Bolshevik cells remaining in Petrograd were all penetrated by the Okhrana. Lenin himself was telling the few Swiss who would listen to him that he did not expect to live to see the revolution.

The word "Soviet" meant simply "council" in Russian. The 1905 Soviet in Saint Petersburg began as a strike committee. Its members came from factories and from intellectuals — the word *intelligentsiya* was also coined in Russia — of the revolutionary left. In the few weeks of its existence, it grew into a rough-and-ready popular parliament, organizing demonstrations, handing out weapons for use against strikebreakers and developing an executive committee dominated by radical socialists. The Bolsheviks, far from being closely linked with the Soviet, initially boycotted it. When it was dispersed, the leaders of the Soviet were imprisoned or forced into Siberian or foreign exile.

A table was used a few months later by the American journalist Louise

Bryant to enlighten the readers of the *Philadelphia Public Ledger* on the three main political blocs that had emerged, on the parties, the classes supporting them, their attitude to socialism and the war, and the form of government they preferred. Her list was the political shorthand of the day, accurate enough and simple. In it, the Cadets were described as the party of "liberal landowners, industrialists and professional men," hostile to socialism, wishing to continue the war, and favoring a constitutional monarchy at best and a bourgeois parliamentary republic at worst.

Menshevik and Social Revolutionary moderates, backed by the "*intelligentsiya*, white collar workers, and the better-off peasants," did not think the time ripe for full-blooded socialism, though they hoped it would eventually come, and in the meantime supported a parliamentary republic run by a coalition of the bourgeoisie, *burzhui* in Russian, and socialists. They wanted peace, though not at the expense of a break with the Allies.

Bolsheviks, and the extreme wings of the Mensheviks and Social Revolutionaries, aimed their appeals at "industrial workers and the poorest peasants." They wanted immediate socialism with a proletarian dictatorship; a republic based on the Soviet. Hostile to the Allies, they demanded immediate peace. Louise Bryant, who was a Bolshevik sympathizer, described a Soviet as an "organ of direct proportional representation."

Petrograd was an awesome target for a revolutionary. Peter the Great had built it and populated it in the style of the dynasty, by compulsion. Work gangs were requisitioned at the rate of forty thousand men a year, marched in under military escort, often in chains to prevent desertion. Tens of thousands had died of disease and exposure as they raised the city above its marshes on piles. Peter's successors had continued the work and the city now floated on an immense body of water "like a bark overladen with precious goods," its autocratic purpose instantly recognizable.

From the dome of Saint Isaac's Cathedral, the eye wandered over a mass of barracks, ministries, and palaces. To the north, across the Neva bridges, loomed the low silhouette of the fortress island of Peter and Paul and the soaring, slender spire of its cathedral. All but one of the Romanov tsars were buried in the cathedral, and the dungeons of the fortress, entirely surrounded by water, had entombed a glittering clientele of dissidents from Peter's own son Alexis to the novelist Fedor Dostoevsky. Alexis, murdered by his father, lay in a vault beneath the cathedral. The punishment cells had iron sheets over their windows, with a small corner that opened as a flap. A noon gun was fired from the fortress, a daily reminder to the tsar's subjects across the water of the ease with which the autocrat could suspend their freedom.

The symbols of power ran in an unbroken stretch for three miles along the southern, left bank of the river and its pink Finnish granite embankment. Well to the east of Saint Isaac's were the foreign embassies, the district court, the artillery school, and the barracks of the crack Pavlovsky and Preobrazhensky regiments. Closer, the dull brownish red of the Winter Palace and the Hermitage faced out over the Neva for five hundred yards. The Romanovs had their winter quarters in this complex and it housed a collection of antiquities and paintings that took up thirty-six pages in the Baedeker guide. The tsar's study looked out over the palace square to the General Staff building, which also lodged the finance and foreign ministries in a crescent a third of a mile long.

To the west of the palace square was the equally vast block of the Admiralty, 450 yards long with a gilded spire that tapered 230 feet above the gateway. The War Office and the police prefecture were in the shadow of the cathedral to the northeast, the riding school of the Horse Guards and the main military academy to the west. Three in ten adult males wore a uniform of some sort.

The city also dominated the civilian life of the empire. The left bank was divided into three semicircles by the Moika, Catherine, and Fontanka canals. These were intersected by three streets radiating from the Admiralty, the Nevsky, Gorokhovaya, and Vosnesensky. Private palaces intermingled with the great buildings of state along the river and canals. Their severe and faultless lines, softened by the pastel colors of the stucco and the constant sheen of ice and water, added to the angular and limpid beauty of the city.

Vasilevsky Island, to the northwest of Saint Isaac's Cathedral, and holding the long red facade and birch trees of Petrograd's university, was the intellectual heartland. Petrograd students were a distinct breed, a university proletariat shabby and pinched in blue caps and tattered greatcoats with "fanatical and prematurely aged looks." A quarter of those tried for political crimes after the 1905 revolution were students or members of the liberal professions. The colonnaded stock exchange at the tip of the island handled four in five of all share transactions. The gardens outside had an animal market, where rare birds and dogs from the remote parts of the empire were held in cages. Steamers tied up at the quay from the big Baltic Fleet base at Kronstadt, an island at the entrance to the Gulf of Finland an hour and a half away.

Three-quarters of the assets of Russian commercial banks were held by banks headquartered in Petrograd. The steel and coal industries of the Donbass, the oilfields of Baku, and the copper and gold mines of Siberia were controlled from the bankers' parlors south of Saint Isaac's on the long avenues of the Nevsky and Morskaya. German businessmen had gone with the war, but the British still had their cricket and yacht clubs and shared their church with the Americans. The city's industrial plants — the most advanced in the country, capable by 1917 of producing aircraft, engines, wireless sets, and sophisticated chemicals — released plumes of smoke into the air around the compass.

Workers lived throughout the city. They were not tidied away in ghettos, as they were in Western cities. Somerset Maugham thought that this gave the Nevsky more character than New York's Fifth Avenue or London's Bond Street. He noted that the crowd on the Nevsky "does not consist chiefly of one class of population, but of all; and the loiterer may observe a great variety of his fellow creatures, soldiers, sailors, and students, workmen and bourgeoisie, peasant, talking incessantly."

In the wealthy central districts of Admiralty and Kazan, men in ragged work blouses roomed in cellars and garrets with the bourgeoisie sandwiched between them. On Vasilevsky Island, the slums of the harbor district round the commercial docks ran up to the Bolshoi Prospekt and the apartments of officials and professors. The biggest concentrations of workers were on the Vyborg side on the right bank of the river. The Vyborg proletariat had simply to cross a bridge to get to the heart of the city, though they passed the redbrick pile of the Kresty Prison to do so.

Petrograd lent itself to peaceful demonstrations, provided the bridges were not raised. The streets were wide, the Prospekts almost forty yards across, and straight so that the approach of a crowd had a sort of slow-motion menace. A banner carried over the Alexander Bridge was visible from the Nevsky over a mile away. Size made it awkward to control crowds, for cohesion and mass were easy to maintain on the spacious avenues and squares.

Against this, the width of the streets and the lack of cover left a crowd exposed to counterforce. For two hundred years, the Romanovs had controlled the behavior as well as the physical shape of their creation. The riverine city had more barracks than bridges, fifteen in all. Every major point was within a half hour's march, most within ten minutes. The barracks of the Cossacks, the key security force trained in the use of horse, knout, and saber to disperse crowds, were on the western side of the city between the Nikolaevsky Station and the Alexander Nevsky monastery. They could reach the center at a trot in twenty minutes.

The number of troops in Petrograd at the beginning of 1917 was the highest recorded in the city's history, 170,000 compared with a peacetime garrison of half that. A further 152,000 were stationed nearby. They added to the stability of the city only on paper; Okhrana agents, who would have to call on them if conditions deteriorated, thought them to contain "much raw, untrained material, unfit to put down disorders." Some companies were made up of shell-shock cases from the front. Troublemakers drafted for inciting strikes in Petrograd and the Donets coal mines undermined morale. The fourteen Guards battalions were reserve units. Many of the Cossacks came from the most impoverished regions of the Kuban and the Don. Cossacks were traditionally volunteers, but these had been drafted. They resented leaving villages stripped of male hands, where the writer Mikhail Sholokhov said, amid "abandoned huts, roofs falling in and overgrown with thistle, wandering cattle strayed through the open gates, seeking shelter from the rain in weedy, grass-grown yards." The police trusted only the training detachments of the Guards battalions.

General Alexander Balk, the city governor, had a standing plan for disorders that dated back to 1905. Police and mounted gendarmes were the first to be used, with Cossacks and other cavalry reinforcing them if needed. In the last resort, infantry would be called out of the barracks and command would pass from the police to the military. Cooperation between troops and police was poor, however, and the police themselves were split in three groups: municipal police, Okhrana secret police, and gendarmes.

Alexander Protopopov, though he told Nicholas that only twelve thousand troops were fully reliable, considered that he had enough to deal with any disorders, believing that the rest of the garrison would not mutiny. Balk was not so confident. Marines stationed at Tsarskoe Selo to defend the imperial family were forbidden to read newspapers or visit Petrograd for fear of revolutionary infection. The police were issued with machine guns and trained to use them in street fighting.

On February 10, General Serge Khabalov, commander of the Petrograd Military District, prohibited public meetings and reminded workers that martial law was in force and all resistance to authority would be put down by force of arms. Mikhail Rodzianko saw the tsar for tea at the same time. The Duma chairman warned the monarch that unless there was an immediate responsible government, uncontrollable anarchy would break out. Nicholas did not reply and showed him the door. At dinner that evening, the Grand Duchess Maria Pavlova said that the empress listened to only one adviser now, Protopopov, who "consults the ghost of Rasputin every night."

On February 14, led by workers from the huge Putilov works, ninety thousand came out on strike and demonstrated on the Nevsky with banners reading "Down with the war! Down with the government!" University students and girls from the Higher Courses for Women were present in numbers and sang a lusty "Marseillaise." Police agents reported that army officers were mingling with the crowds for the first time. "You shouldn't be fighting here," a group of ensigns yelled at the police. "They ought to send all you fatsos to the front."

The Duma reconvened the same day. It called for democratic reforms and improvements in the food supply, but there was a sense of anticlimax. The Cadet deputy Vasily Shulgin, an extreme nationalist who had nevertheless defended a Kiev Jew accused of eating Gentile babies in a prewar cause célèbre and been arrested for his pains, a contrary and courageous man, felt that the nearness to revolution was so terrifying that the debaters softened their speeches at the last moment. "Behind the white columns of the hall grinned Hopelessness," Shulgin said. "And she whispered: 'Why? What for? What difference does it make?'"

As the Duma went through its ritual debate, Governor Balk was reporting that the city had received thirty thousand pounds of flour a day over the past week instead of the normal two hundred thousand. There was panic buying of dry rusks for food hoards. A small helping of potatoes, 15 kopeks before the war, was now difficult to find at 1.2 rubles. Wood had become so expensive that the temperature in fashionable apartments was barely above freezing. Sugar was scarce, a double hardship since working people sucked their tea through a sugar lump. Restaurants laid off their orchestras.

The transport crisis was deepening. "We have grain for mills that have no fuel, flour where there are no freight cars to haul it, and cars where there is no food," the chairman of the Union of Towns complained. The temperature dropped to twenty-two degrees below zero and throughout Russia more than 1,200 locomotives were out of action with burst boiler tubes. Plants making spares in Warsaw were in German hands. Heavy snowfalls blocked tracks deep into the countryside and there was a shortage of village labor to clear them. It was estimated that 57,000 wagons, many with food aboard, were snowbound. The railways were flimsy at best — the rails were light, the track bedding weak — and three-quarters of the officers in the railway battalions, who were now responsible for much of the network, had no technical training.

A last attempt was made by the military to influence the tsar. General Gurko, who had just presided over the Allied conference, visited Nicholas in Tsarskoe Selo on February 13. He pressed for immediate constitutional reform. Nicholas was uninterested, complaining that Gurko had gone on at such length that he was too late to attend Vespers.

On Saturday, February 18, workers in the Putilov gun-carriage workshop came out for a pay raise. They were only 486 strong in a workforce of 26,700, but the strike spread rapidly to the machine and assembly shops and the shrapnel works. The following Wednesday the factory director, a seconded military man, General Dublitsky, ordered a lockout.

Nicholas left Tsarskoe Selo for the Stavka headquarters at Mogilev that afternoon. As he settled in the train for the journey, he read the farewell letter Alexandra had tucked under the pillow of his berth. "Our dearest Friend in the other world also prays for you," she reassured him. "Dearest show the power of your fist — that is what Russians need." She continued, with almost sexual connotation: "They themselves ask for this — so many have said to me recently: 'We need the knout.' . . . Now they have begun to 'feel' you they have begun to quiet down."

Women, who made up over a third of the work force in the city, waited in the iced nights from three in the morning until the shops opened at nine and then labored by day. Some husbands were at the front and few of the remainder thought it their duty to help with chores. At a bakery on the Liteiny, Maurice Paleologue was struck by the sinister expression on the faces in the queue. Thursday, February 23, was International Women's Day. The textile factories on the Vyborg side employed mainly women. Vyborg was particularly angry since the authorities had ordered that the bread and flour stocks of workers' cooperatives should be added to the general city supplies. The eleven cooperatives in Vyborg, which had been feeding over a hundred thousand workers and their families, were outraged.

In midmorning, women at the Neva Thread Mills heard demonstrators outside demanding bread. "Into the street! We've had it!" the women shouted, flinging open the windows on the first floor of the mill. The women went down into the street and marched on the Nobel machinery works. They crowded into an alley next to the plant and pelted the windows with snowballs. "Down with hunger! Bread for the workers!" they yelled. The men linked arms with them amid shouts of "Hurrah!" and set off down the broad Bolshoi Sampsonievsky Prospekt.

Local Bolsheviks in the Vyborg district were planning strikes for May Day. Far from wishing to stir up trouble in February, the Bolshevik committee member V. N. Kayurov was sent to a women's meeting to "urge people to refrain from abortive deeds." The district committee thought the mood so highly charged that it appealed for the "maintenance of discipline and restraint." Its advice was ignored throughout the day. At the Erikson plant, workers scrambled onto their machines and piles of metal to listen to the women's pleas to strike. Radicals in the plant held a hasty meeting and decided to follow the lead given by the textile women. Kayurov was furious. The small Bolshevik organization in Petrograd played almost no part in any of the events of the next week.

Nikolai Sukhanov, to become the revolution's great diarist, was its only first-rate analyst present in Petrograd. Cantankerous and honest, he pilloried the regime in fluent and biting articles under this assumed name. As Nikolai Himmer, his real identity, he was working in the irrigation department on plans to water the Turkestan desert. His civil service superiors knew that Protopopov's interior ministry had an arrest warrant out for him as Sukhanov, but interdepartment rivalry gave them particular pleasure in protecting him.

Sukhanov was equally unaware of destiny. "Not one party was preparing for the great upheaval," he wrote. "Everyone was dreaming, ruminating, full of foreboding, feeling his way." He himself had heard a couple of typists talking about the food shortages and unrest in the agriculture ministry two days before. "D'you know, if you ask me, it's the beginning of the revolution!" Sukhanov did not believe them for a second. As he watched the events of Thursday unfold, he thought the disorders identical to scores he had witnessed before.

After the lunch break, workers in the Arsenal came out in a large column when marchers banged on the gates and windows. Cossacks and police chivvied them toward the Finland Station, where they jammed up against lines of trams. "The moment has come," speakers shouted from the station steps. "The time has come. We must carry through our cause." A police officer drew his pistol to stop the crowd breaking into an aircraft plant. It was knocked from his hands, he was beaten, and the crowd stormed the gates.

The afternoon was warm and snow melted on the balconies to drip gently onto the sidewalks. The workers felt themselves masters of the city. They boarded trams, forced the motormen to stop, made the passengers get out, and overturned them. The Vyborg workers headed for the Liteiny Bridge, bypassing police and troops by crossing the ice-covered surface of the river. They moved along the Liteiny to the Nevsky with shrill cries of "Khleeba!" — "bread." The big Filippov bakery on a corner of the Nevsky was sacked. The police, "pharaohs" to the crowds, did not interfere.

At 5:00 P.M. a thousand-strong demonstration left Znamenskaya Square and headed for the Nevsky. Disorders broke out there at about 7:00. The crowds were too thick for the police to disperse, and they stayed among the fashionable shops and hotels until late into the evening. At the Moscow Gate, a crowd with gray, sullen faces was listening to a speech when the cry went up, "The pharaohs are coming!" The speech stopped abruptly. Stones were thrown at the advancing mounted police and the square filled with moans as the police in a frenzy went to work with their whips and sabers. The crowd dispersed, only to form again when the horsemen cantered off to another target.

Cossacks and cavalry cut through the crowds, but there was no shooting and few arrests. Governor Balk characterized the movement as food disorders. Okhrana agents, skilled barometers of opinion, were not so sure. They noticed that the speakers haranguing the crowds did not hide their faces or pull their caps down over their eyes, as they normally did. The demonstrators were unusually persistent, a ripple that would not die down. "Strikers, who were dispersed in one place, would soon assemble in another, displaying dogged determination in all of this," the secret police reported. They also noted that *masterovye*, skilled craftsmen, had begun to join the strikers. There were signs that the military garrison did not have the same stomach for their work as the police. Okhrana men heard some soldiers of the Semenovsky Regiment saying they would only shoot in the air.

At the Duma, a young Socialist lawyer, Alexander Kerensky, gave an emotional speech about the wave of starving women "for whom hunger is becoming the only tsar." He urged someone to do "what Brutus did in classical times," an open call to murder the tsar, which was excised from the Duma record. The empress wrote to Nicholas the next day that she hoped "Kedrinsky" would be hanged. She said that "young kids are running about, shouting that they haven't got bread" — but this was just to create excitement and the result of the warm afternoon. "If the weather was cold, they probably would have stayed at home," she concluded. "All this will pass and become quiet."

Countess Olga Putyatin, a volunteer nurse in the Anglo-Russian Hospital on the Nevsky, saw nothing remarkable beyond the normal long lines outside food shops. At a dinner party in the French embassy Thursday evening the main topic of conversation was the big party Princess Leon Radziwill was throwing the following Sunday. "No one knows anything exactly," Zinaïda Gippius wrote in her diary. "Like looking into turbid waters — we look and cannot see how far away from the collapse."

The train bearing the tsar steamed on down the single track to Mogilev. In Tsarskoe Selo, the children and Anna Vyrubova were coming down with measles. Alexander Protopopov, in a mood of "morbid euphoria," was driven home down the Nevsky late at night. It was brilliantly lit by the searchlights on the Admiralty spire. There were few people about. "The day of the 23rd was not all that bad," the interior minister confided to his dairy. "Several policemen were injured; but there was no shooting."

V

"Out of the Way, Obsolete World"

THE MORNING of Friday, February 24, dawned fine, with clear skies and a warm sun. At eight o'clock a big demonstration began in the Vyborg quarter and marched to the Liteiny Bridge, moving across its whole width and forcing back a line of mounted police. At the end of the bridge, one part of the crowd surged through a cavalry unit onto the Liteiny Prospekt. Alexander Protopopov's orders not to open fire but to work with whip and lance remained in force. Sensing this weakness, the strikers became bolder. A police agent in the Shchetinin works reported that bread was no longer mentioned at a strike meeting. The slogans now were *"Doloi Voiny! . . . Doloi Tsarskoi Monarkhy!"* — "Down with the War and the Tsarist Monarchy."

By 3:00 P.M., crowds had broken through to Znamenskaya Square, a favorite rallying point. Mounted police failed to disperse them, their horses shying under a hail of stones and chunks of wood. The Cossacks did not support the police. The crowd gave them a "Hurrah!" and they bowed low in response. A youth climbed onto the huge equestrian statue of Alexander III, nicknamed the "Hippo," that dominated the square. "Comrades!" he said, raising his right hand above his hatless head. "Russia's blood continues to flow from beneath this brainless cast-iron blob."

The Cossacks, their hair worn long on one side and combed back and up to offset their canted *papaha* hats, were the most mobile riot squads. They carried trusses of hay on the saddles of their wiry horses so they could patrol for twelve hours at a stretch, riding with short stirrups and a characteristic upright stance. They had *nagayka* whips and sabers as well as carbines. Women softened their aggressive instincts. On Bolshoi Sampsonievsky Prospekt, a crowd of more than two thousand from the Erikson mills was cornered by the Cossacks. The women surrounded the horsemen in a solid wall. "We have husbands, fathers, and brothers at the front!" they cried. "You too have mothers, wives, sisters, children. . . . We are demanding bread and an end to the war!" The nervous officers ordered a charge. The Cossacks skirted the crowd and rode back to their former position amid cries of "Hurrah!" A Duma deputy asked himself what sort of demonstration it was when people were cheering Cossacks.

By late afternoon, the police estimated that two hundred thousand were on strike. The blue caps of students were studding the crowds. On the Nevsky, demonstrators realized, the promenading crowd was sympathetically disposed toward them. Smartly dressed shoppers smiled at them as they flooded from one part of the city to another, a reminder of the start of the 1905 revolution, when stockbrokers and doctors had come out in sympathy with strikers. "Everywhere animated faces and enormous lines but the majority of the people seemed to be joking," Countess Olga Putyatin observed. "I saw nothing threatening."

Soldiers in some of the military hospitals waved bedsheets and uniforms out of the windows in sympathy. Vladimir Zensinov, a journalist and Social Revolutionary, spent the day roaming the central streets. He found the crowds of *seryi liud* — common people — to be "excited but not irritated." Most of all, he sensed the curiosity that lay behind their excursions into the smart shopping streets. When they came across a line of troops, they made up obviously fabricated excuses to be let through. The soldiers, looking around to make sure their officers were not looking, let them pass. The good humor did not extend to the police; twenty-eight were beaten up as young demonstrators hurled stones and chunks of ice at them.

The Council of Ministers, the cabinet, was preoccupied with the food situation. The disorders were thought to be under control, though when the premier, Prince Nicholas Golitsyn, left the meeting his chauffeur had to take a roundabout route to avoid the crowds on the Nevsky. The Belgian ambassador visited the empress at Tsarskoe Selo. She was calm, saying that the army was loyal and could be relied on. Protopopov, or so the foreign minister Nikolai Pokrovsky maintained, was spending the evening "conjuring up the ghost of Rasputin."

Nicholas had arrived in Mogilev and spent a quiet day. He went for a drive and a stroll, stopping in at a local monastery to kiss an icon of the Virgin. After tea, he read a book on Caesar's conquest of Gaul. He played dominoes in the evening. Three of his children now had measles. He did not think the situation in Petrograd warranted his return.

He was not alone. The Bolsheviks believed the troops would crush the strikers. The army had always done so before. "None of us thought that the movement then underway would be the last and decisive battle," Alexander

Shlyapnikov, an expert in the political underground and the ranking Bolshevik in the city, said. "We held no such belief." Nikolai Sukhanov, however, had no doubt by now that a revolution had begun. Arthur Ransome thought so as well. The British correspondent had been caught by Cossacks in two demonstrations, but all he had to show for it when he undressed were a couple of bruises where he had been accidentally squeezed between two horses. Ransome had found the Cossacks benevolent and cheerful and thought the autocracy was making a great mistake in relying on them.

It froze hard during the night, ships out in the Neva trapped firmly in the ice.

The strike became near-total on Saturday, February 25, a startling event in wartime. Workers at the biggest plant on Vasilevsky Island, the Pipe Plant, which made mortar tubes and big guns, came out. A reserve battalion of the Finland Regiment was called in, and a young striker was shot by an officer during a scuffle. At 9:00 A.M., fourteen thousand workers at the Obukhov factory joined the strike and headed for the city center. Workers in the New Parvianinen works, sitting on the ceiling trusses, chanted the revolutionary verse:

> Out of the way, obsolete world
> rotten from top to bottom.
> Young Russia is on the march!

"The atmosphere was tense," one of the workers, Kondratev, said. "We would live or die together in the struggle." They poured out onto Bolshoi Sampsonievsky Prospekt.

Only essential services — gas, electricity, and water — continued to function. The movement spread to the suburbs. Officers coming out after a night in the gypsy houses on Novaya Derevnya Island were met by demonstrators. Few trams were running and newspapers stopped publishing. Mounted police again ringed the Liteiny Bridge. A senior official, Police Chief Shalfeev, gave the traditional order: "Disperse! Fall back!" He was pulled from his horse and beaten with sticks and an iron hook used to switch tramway points. Police opened fire and claimed that shots were returned from the crowd. The crowd broke through over the bridge.

Whooping youths stripped a grocery store of its chocolate bars. A patrol of Cossacks ignored them. On the Liteiny, an urchin sold mother-of-pearl buttons liberated from a haberdashers at a ruble for six dozen. Some soldiers joined in looting Jewish-owned shops. It seemed possible that the movement would degenerate into a pogrom. During the night, General

Serge Khabalov, the Petrograd military commander, had posted notices warning that those on deferment from military service would be called up if they had not returned to work by Tuesday. The three days' grace was read as weakness, and the posters ripped down.

By midmorning on February 25, the Nevsky and the adjacent streets were again full of demonstrators, singing the revolutionary ditty "Comrades, Boldly in Step." Stores, restaurants, and cafés pulled down their blinds. Cab drivers disappeared, along with their rich clientele in beaver hats and fur coats. The streets were a mass of working men's caps with stiff visors, double-breasted work coats, women's headscarves, and rough cloth great-coats. Countess Putyatin watched from the Anglo-Russian Hospital as the Cossacks touched their caps to acknowledge the hurrahs and rode carefully through the crowds. Nikolai Sukhanov realized that the "wall between the two camps — the people and the authorities — was not so impenetrable; a certain diffusion could be felt between them."

Office workers, shopwalkers, and a few professional men began to join the marchers. The police noted that students were showing complete sym-pathy and that high school students were taking part in the disorders. The university came out on strike and students from the Psychoneurological Institute, where Pavlov taught, set off for Znamenskaya Square. The Social Revolutionary Vladimir Zensinov, his journalist's interests aroused, marched with them.

At 3:00 P.M., the clatter of horseshoes was heard from the direction of the Nikolaevsky Station. A detachment of mounted police appeared in the square. Inspector Krylov, the officer commanding the unit, rode in front in a gray greatcoat tightly laced with straps. A bugle was sounded twice to warn the crowd to disperse. Before the third and final blast, there was the crack of a single shot followed by a volley. "I started running with the crowd, losing one of my galoshes," said Zensinov. "When I looked back, I saw canes, hats, galoshes on the snow — but there were no people on the square." It was only later that Zensinov learned that the first shot had been fired by a Cossack at Inspector Krylov, the officer in the greatcoat. Krylov was, as far as anyone could judge, the first victim of the revolution on the government side — and he had been killed by a Cossack.

Not all the troops were as sympathetic. A squadron of the Ninth Reserve Cavalry Regiment opened fire on a crowd on the Nevsky, killing nine. But they had been brought in from Tsarskoe Selo and were immune to the mood of the city. As the sparkling afternoon wore on, Countess Putyatin noted from her window over the Nevsky, the "people began to command." They halted carriages with officers in them and forced them to turn off the Nevsky onto the avenues running on both sides of the Fontanka Canal. An officer who refused was pulled out and his sword was bent in two and thrown into the canal.

Police snatch squads were still able to make arrests, but the crowds were now bold enough to mount rescues. A mob stormed into a holding point at 46 Nevsky Prospekt, releasing the sixty prisoners it found in the courtyard. Another twenty-five detainees were freed from a house in Kazan Street. Police were being beaten up so frequently that they were afraid to operate alone or in small groups. Some changed into civilian clothes or wore gray army greatcoats for disguise. An undercover agent with the pseudonym of "Kochegar" — "the Fireman" — complained that some Cossack units had a protective attitude toward the crowds and "encouraged them with promises: 'Put the heat on higher.'" Sukhanov noticed that demoralized policemen were beginning to disappear from their posts.

The crowds were not fueled by any deep theories. Sukhanov heard a grim-faced onlooker ask, "What do they want?" "They want bread, peace with the Germans, and freedom for the Yids," his companion replied. "Right in the bull's eye," Sukhanov thought, delighted with this "brilliant formulation of the great revolution."

A group of intellectuals and politicians, whom Sukhanov met up with later in the afternoon in the flat of the radical lawyer Nikolai Sokolov, had no such concise view. Arcane argument raged. Sokolov's friend Alexander Kerensky, a fellow defense barrister for revolutionaries in prewar trials, was theatrical and emotional, flaying the bourgeois deputies in the Duma for "panic and confusion." Kerensky had no plans of his own, however, and soon began to lose his temper. Sukhanov found himself supporting the "defensists," who opposed offensives against the Germans but, unlike the "defeatists," thought that the front should be held as the necessary price for getting the bourgeoisie aboard the revolution. "This was against my own principles," he fumed.

Moving on to Maxim Gorky's apartment, Sukhanov found the writer engaged in a shouting match with two of his editors. Sidelined by the street, the *intelligentsiya* — a body particularly respected and well defined in Russia — was reduced to ill-temper and frustration.

Liberals were also stormbound by events. The Cadets were mournfully celebrating the anniversary of their newspaper, *Rech*. "Champagne could not dissipate the sullen mood or loosen tongues," a guest reported. "It was awkward to look at each other and ask the meaning of the shots we heard in the streets which were trying to scatter the people." The guests kept whispering: "'What insanity! We need the army.' . . . But no one was listening."

A plainsclothesman with the code name "Limonin" sat in on the afternoon meeting of the Petrograd Bolshevik committee. His meticulous report showed it to be floundering badly. The only practical steps the committee discussed were the issuing of a leaflet and a plan to start erecting barricades the following Monday. The leaflet — the undercover man neatly attached a draft of it to his report — urged the workers to "take to the streets to struggle for their interests." Perhaps three hundred thousand were already doing that as the draft was prepared. On the vital issue of controlling the strikers, the committee proposed to reconvene itself in an apartment on Bolshoi Sampsonievsky Prospekt the next morning.

The Okhrana man noted the address in his report.

The other revolutionary parties were no better placed. The Social Revolutionaries, who had been penetrated by the Okhrana agent Kochegar, lacked even a nominal central organ. "The Social Revolutionary party organization was in a shambles," Vladimir Zensinov, a member of the Social Revolutionary central committee, admitted. "Here and there isolated party members carried on work on the outskirts and distributed homemade proclamations without any coordination." The Mensheviks could not compete even with that. "The leadership of the movement and of the actions of the masses was not visible," said O. A. Ermansky, a member of the Menshevik Initiative Group. The group did not live up to its name. It held no meetings and "existed only as a sum of its parts, not as a whole."

The Duma, the writer Zinaïda Gippius thought, was in the same "revolutionary position" as a streetcar thrust across the street. The disorders simply washed across it. The Duma continued to discuss the food crisis, though this was easing as stocks were released to the bakeries.

Serge Khabalov was soothing in the situation report he sent as military commander to Mogilev at 5:00 P.M. "Attempts by workers to enter the Nevsky have been successfully stopped," he claimed. "Cossacks are dispersing those who have broken through." But the scale of the disorders was clear from his chilling postscript. Khabalov admitted that he was drawing on ten cavalry squadrons from outside the city. The huge garrison, which all but outnumbered the strikers, could not cope.

The tsar spent the day quietly in Mogilev; unaware of the behavior of their brethren in the capital, he chose to wear a uniform of the Caucasian Cossacks. The empress sent him two telegrams. In the afternoon she said that the city was quiet, but by the evening she was reporting that "things are still not well." Nicholas sent an icy reply to Khabalov before sitting down for dinner: "I command the disorders in the capital end tomorrow. They are impermissible in the difficult time of war with Germany and Austria. Nicholas."

Khabalov was not amused when he received this missive at 9:00 P.M. "How could [the disorders] be stopped by the next day?" he asked. "When people said 'Give us bread,' we gave them bread and that was the end of it. But when inscriptions on banners read 'Down with the autocracy,' what kind of bread will calm them?" There was only one solution. An hour later Khabalov addressed the evening conference of the chiefs of the city defense sectors. "We have a last resort, and we must use it," he told them. "If the crowd is aggressive and carrying banners, act according to regulations. I mean, warn them three times, and after the third warning, open fire."

The city was nearly deserted as the temperature plunged after nightfall. On the Vyborg side, barricades were being built with overturned trams and telegraph poles. The premiere of Lermontov's *Masquerade*, with its mournful requiem to the poisoned heroine in the last act, was playing to a small audience at the Aleksandrevsky Theater. There were only fifty people in the Maryinsky Theater, and gaps in the orchestra, when Maurice Paleologue went to hear a new symphony by a young composer, Saminsky. The ambassador did not appreciate its "startling dissonances and complicated harmonic formulae."

Paleologue was more impressed by the desolation on his way home. His was the only car on the Moika Bridge. Troops were massed in front of the Litovsky prison and a picket of gendarmes tried to keep warm around a fire on the bridge. "Are we witnessing the last night of the regime?" his companion asked him.

It was a question that occurred to several ministers when the cabinet met at midnight. They thought a new cabinet with individuals acceptable to the Duma would have to be formed. Feelers were put out to moderate deputies, who replied that only a ministry legally responsible to the Duma would be tolerated. This was rejected.

Prince Golitsyn met with Mikhail Rodzianko. The Duma chairman tried to persuade Golitsyn that tsarism had a final chance, if Golitsyn resigned as premier, if the empress went permanently to the Crimea, "if . . ." The prince was seventy years old, a "good-natured Russian squire and an old weakling." When he had taken the thankless post, he explained that he did so "in order to have one more pleasant recollection." He was not willing to go yet. "You want me to retire," he shrugged. "But do you know what I have in my folder?"

To Rodzianko's astonishment, Golitsyn produced a decree already signed by the tsar dismissing the Duma. Only the date for the dissolution of the parliament needed to be filled in. "I am keeping this for emergencies," Golitsyn said. He proposed a meeting with leading Duma members. "Let's get together and chat," he said. "It's no good living at daggers drawn the whole time." Rodzianko said he would arrange one. It never materialized.

The ministers moved on to discuss the dissolution of the Duma. All but three ministers, Alexander Protopopov among them, disapproved. Golitsyn prevaricated. He would have talks with the Duma men later. The meeting broke up at 4:00 A.M. The authorities, Sukhanov realized, had to go "beyond the dead point, and with one stunning blow simultaneously destroy the morale of the masses and check the disintegration within the army. A risky, desperate, and perhaps final attempt had to be made without delay."

As the exhausted ministers were driven home in their cars and sleighs, the last throw was being made. Two paddy wagons, filled with known militants picked up in night raids by the Okhrana, were being driven across the city. General Khabalov's proclamation was being posted on walls and shopfronts. "I forbid all street gatherings," it read. "I announce to the population of Petrograd in advance that I endorse the use of arms by the troops and that they are to stop at nothing to bring order to the capital."

Sunday, February 26, started with deceptive calm. There was a holiday atmosphere in the center of the city. A light fall of snow overnight gave way to a bright sun with a pleasant light frost and blue sky. Fashionable churches filled with well-dressed ladies in furs, and officers on leave promenaded from the Hotel de l'Europe after their breakfast coffee, picking their way between patrols of cavalry. Police with binoculars looked down from the firewatch towers, high circular buildings with iron masts above them for displaying warning signals.

During the morning, the Petrograd Bolshevik committee kept their rendezvous. Alerted by the Okhrana agent Limonin, fifty infantry and mounted police surrounded the apartment and seized them without fuss. General Khabalov was able to cable Mogilev that the city was quiet. A few working-class families in their Sunday best strolled with their children down the Nevsky, which was cordoned off every hundred yards or so by troops.

Shortly after the noon gun boomed from the Peter and Paul Fortress, large crowds from the Petrograd side and the Vyborg began heading for the Nevsky to heighten the effect of their demonstration by appearing in the city center. Scuffles broke out at the bridges and again they crossed the ice. Khabalov ignored a suggestion to use artillery to break up the ice. The marchers did not grasp the significance of the large infantry units which met them in the center. They were also unaware of the police machine guns set up in the firewatch towers, above the Alexander Nevsky monastery and on the roof of the Nikolaevsky railway station, all strategically placed to overlook the Nevsky. Znamenskaya Square lay directly in front of the Nikolaevsky Station at the end of the Nevsky.

A mass of people moving down the Nevsky ran into a training detachment of the Pavlovsky Regiment near the Moika Canal at 1:00 P.M. The troops knelt and raised their weapons. Although the front ranks of the crowd tried to stop, those at the rear pressed forward. Two volleys were fired. "The majority fled, some fell, a number of them dead," the Menshevik O. A. Ermansky recalled. "People had to step in puddles of blood of the dead and wounded sprawled along the road and sidewalks." Watching from the windows of the Anglo-Russian Hospital, Countess Putyatin saw people running or flinging themselves in the gutters and behind tram poles, while the dead lay "like poor lumps." A dozen wounded were brought into the hospital. A young Guards officer carried in his dead cousin, thinking that he had simply fainted.

There was general firing in the Nevsky area. Ambulances raced along the boulevard. People hugged the pavement, while youths taunted the police from around corners. Secondary school students in Red Cross armbands and white aprons gave first aid to the wounded.

Crowds tried to fraternize with troops on Znamenskaya Square, but the riflemen responded to the appeals with curses and threats. The Cossacks had been replaced by the training unit of the Volynsky Guards Regiment. Its commander, Captain Lashkevich, issued a warning and blank shots were fired. The crowd remained solid, confident that live rounds would not be used. Only after the first volleys were fired did it flee, leaving forty dead and many wounded on the cobblestones. A group of students, singing and carrying red flags, met a similar fate on a bridge over the Catherine Canal. "Suddenly there was a deafening rattle, tra-ta-ta-ta! Machine gun fire!" said a survivor. "An officer yelled: 'Anyone who wants to live had better lie down!' Two corpses and many wounded lay on the bridge."

Blanks seemed to have no effect on the excited marchers. "When troops fired warning volleys into the air, the crowds refused to disperse and greeted them with laughter," the Okhrana logbook for February 26 noted. "Only live ammunition fired into the thick of the crowd could scatter the mobs." Simple intimidation had failed. The troops would have to shoot to kill, and go on doing so. Many demonstrators hid in the big courtyards that lie at the center of Petrograd buildings, and went back on the streets after the firing stopped.

The schoolgirls at the Empress Catherine Institute for Young Ladies of Nobility enjoyed the day. Zinaïda Shakovsky, a ten-year-old, was saying good-bye to her mother and brother after their weekly visit when she heard the "strange, soon to be familiar sound" of gunfire. It was like "the dry and regular fall of hail" and was followed by shouting and screams and the tramping of horseshoes on the pavement. Maids stuck mattresses into the windows overlooking the Fontanka quays and the girls were shepherded to the safety of a classroom overlooking the inner gardens. The sudden intrusion of the twentieth century into this old-fashioned world was welcomed. The girls were thrilled to hear a mistress use an unfamiliar word, "Revolt," and to be able to behave in an unladylike manner. They slept that evening on the classroom floor. A maid was wounded shutting the windows. People in the crowd were shooting with captured weapons at what they thought was a police machine gun on the roof.

Alexandra visited Rasputin's grave during the afternoon. Writing to Nicholas at 3:30 P.M., she said, "It seems to me that it will all be all right. The sun shines so clearly and I felt such peace and quiet at His dear grave. He died in order to save us."

Less convinced at a happy outcome, Mikhail Rodzianko asked General Khabalov to use firehoses instead of bullets. Khabalov said that regulations forbade the use of firemen and added that "some say drenching with water produces the opposite effect — it stimulates." Rodzianko then cabled Mogilev. "Situation serious," he said. "Anarchy in the capital. Government paralyzed. . . . Disorderly firing in the streets. . . . Essential immediately to order persons having the confidence of the country to form a new government. Any delay deadly." The telegram arrived at 5:00 P.M., the tsar complaining, "Once again that fat Rodzianko has written me some kind of rubbish which I am not even going to answer."

On his walks round the city, Sukhanov noticed that not all the troops were attending to repression with gusto. The crowds were slowly filling up with soldiers' gray greatcoats. Some patrols were not marching but strolling round the city. A cordon of grenadiers at the Troitsky Bridge was standing easy, despite the presence of an officer, and carrying on animated political conversations with civilians.

At 6:00 P.M., a police sergeant, Kharitonov, reported a first but isolated mutiny. He was on duty near the barracks of the Pavlovsky Guards, located in the riding school of the court stables on the Champs de Mars. The reserves were confined to barracks, with only the more reliable regimental training unit being used on the streets. The Fourth Reserve Company got wind of the massacre perpetrated by the training detachment on the Nevsky five hours earlier. Upset, the guardsmen broke into the armory and seized thirty rifles. They moved toward the Nevsky under an NCO with the intention of persuading their comrades in the training unit to stop shooting.

The men met a mounted patrol of ten policemen on their way along the Catherine Canal. "The soldiers abused the police, calling them 'pharaohs,'" Sergeant Kharitonov reported. "They [the soldiers] fired several volleys at them, killing one policeman and one horse." The novelist Leonid Andreyev, watching from his apartment on the Champs de Mars, rang his neighbor Fedor Chaliapin to find out what was happening. Neither the writer nor the great basso could make sense of it. The Pavlovsky's commander, Colonel Eksten, and the regimental chaplain went off in pursuit of the mutineers. There was a melee. When Eksten drew his revolver, his hand and then his head were slashed off by his men with sabers. "Later a detachment of the Preobrazhensky Guards was summoned," Kharitonov's report concluded. "It disarmed and surrounded the mutineers."

Nineteen of the mutineers were packed off to the Peter and Paul Fortress. The incident seemed closed, and the tsar was not informed. At 9:20 P.M., Nicholas cabled the empress from Mogilev that he would leave for Tsarskoe Selo on Tuesday. He played some dominoes before going to bed.

The regime thought it had won. Alexander Balk, the city governor, declared that the troops had produced "brilliant results," with the streets almost normal by twilight. At the evening cabinet meeting, Prince Golitsyn decided to ask the tsar to appoint the war minister General Mikhail Belayev as overall commander in place of Serge Khabalov, whom he found "slow-witted and totally confused" and whose hands were beginning to shake under the strain. The cabinet agreed to suspend the Duma. The decree suspending it was sent to Rodzianko, its chairman, at his apartment. General Belayev was looking forward to having the Pavlovsky mutineers tried and hanged as soon as possible.

At an evening gathering of socialists in Kerensky's apartment, the most left-wing of them was gloomy about prospects. I. Yurenev, close to the Bolsheviks, said there would be no revolution. "The reaction is gaining strength," he said. "The unrest in the barracks is subsiding. It is clear that the working classes and the soldiery must go different ways." Alexander Shlyapnikov rejected the idea of forming armed squads of workers, thinking it would irritate already hostile troops.

At 11:00 P.M., Paleologue noticed one house that was a blaze of lights, with a long line of carriages outside it and lackeys in powdered wigs at the door. Princess Leon Radziwill's famous party was in full swing. The ambassador got a glimpse of the limousine of Grand Duke Boris as he passed. The regime was still enjoying itself. Whether it continued to do so, the Okhrana agent Limonin reported, "depends entirely on the behavior of the military units. . . . If the troops turn against the government, then nothing can save the country."

VI

His Majesty the Russian People

THE REST OF THE COUNTRY had little idea of what was happening in Petrograd. Count Alexei Bobrinskoy, a young officer from a family with estates of 150,000 acres, had been spending a short leave hunting in the Novgorod forests. The game was plentiful. He shot a lynx, and raced across thirty miles of smooth and snow-covered road in a horse-drawn sledge to catch the fast night train to the capital. He arrived at the Nikolaevsky Station at 7:00 A.M. on Monday, February 27. He hailed a porter and gave him his Purdey shotgun and valise, and collected the lynx from the luggage van. The only intimation of trouble was the ten rubles a sledge-driver demanded for the one-ruble trip to his home. "The people have gone mad," the driver said. "They are shooting in the streets." Nothing happened on the journey, though Bobrinskoy paid the exorbitant sum.

Troops in the training unit of the Volynsky Guards had held a meeting the previous evening on their return from Znamenskaya Square, where they had shot demonstrators on the orders of Captain Lashkevich. The men decided not to act as "executioners" any further. They declared that they would harm no one but would attempt to win over the rest of the battalion and "join the people." The unit formed up on parade in full battle order. At 7:00 A.M. Captain Lashkevich arrived to take the salute. Instead of the normal greeting of "At your service," Lashkevich was met with a "Hurrah!"

Lashkevich asked an NCO, Sergeant Kirpichnikov, what this meant. The sergeant did not answer. Lashkevich ordered the parade at ease, took a paper from his pocket and said it was an order from the tsar. He had no chance to read it. Another hurrah was followed by shouts: "We won't kill any more. Enough blood!" Sergeant Kirpichnikov politely asked the "gentlemen officers" to leave. The parade banged their rifle butts on the ground and the officers made off. As Captain Lashkevich crossed the parade ground, shots were fired through the small winter ventilation windows in the barracks. The troops watched Lashkevich "suddenly fling his arms wide and crash to the ground face down into a snowdrift." He was killed, Kirpichnikov claimed, by "a well-aimed stray bullet."

Having murdered their unit commander, the Volynsky Guards had to spread the mutiny as far and as fast as possible to avoid the firing squad. Rifles were seized from the battalion stores. The officers were confused. No overnight orders had been issued to cover the risk of mutiny, despite the Pavlovsky incident. The officers' judgment of their men was sketchy, since the average stay of a soldier in the garrison was only six to eight weeks. Some of the recruits were young boys who had not yet taken their oath of loyalty to the tsar.

As the officers hesitated, the men moved. A police officer named Vassiliev, in charge of a mounted police detachment stationed in the cavernous Preobrazhensky barracks, was alerted by a telephone call. He was told that the Volynsky men had mutinied and were making for the adjacent Preobrazhensky parade ground, where the battalions were drilling. Vassiliev grabbed his combat equipment and rushed off. "Right in front of the barracks was deployed a gray, disorderly crowd of soldiers who were slowly proceeding toward the Liteiny Prospekt," he said. "Above their heads two or three dark banners made out of rags were visible."

An NCO ran out of the crowd and stopped Vassiliev. "Your honor! Don't go, they'll kill you!" the man yelled. "The commander of the battalion is killed, First Lieutenant Ustrogov is killed, and some officers are lying by the gate. The rest have run away." Thoroughly frightened, Vassiliev went into a nearby school for engineer ensigns. He tried to reach his own detachment on the telephone. There was no reply. When a police sergeant, Liubitsky, got through to Okhrana headquarters to report the Volynsky mutiny, the stenographer was so amazed that she logged the call in the wrong century, as 9:00 A.M. on February 27, 1817.

The wedge-shaped section of the city between the Liteiny and Suvorovsky Prospekts to the west and east, and Basseinaya Street and the river to the south and north, was a military stronghold. It contained the barracks of the Horse Guards, the Household Troops and gendarmerie, the gunners' schools and artillery headquarters, the riding schools, and the officers' casino. To the east were the barracks of the Preobrazhensky Regiment, the oldest in Russia, founded by Peter the Great. Before the war, its men had been bearded and tall, as the Pavlovskys were shaven and flat-nosed, but these handpicked regulars were now dead or at the front.

The Preobrazhensky Chapel was surrounded by a railing formed of Turkish cannon captured by the regiment and was decorated within with Turkish flags taken in 1828 and 1829. The pillars were sculpted like palm trees, with every frond a plaster lance. The vast spaces of Preobrazhensky Place were overlooked by the Nicholas Military Academy and the museum and parade ground commemorating the late-eighteenth-century commander, Marshal Suvorov. On its eastern edge was the Suvorov Church, the simple country church where the great general had prayed, and which had been transported timber by timber from his native village.

This ensemble was the sacred place of the Russian army. Here was concentrated General Khabalov's might, guardsmen, mounted artillery, field engineers, gendarmes, cavalry, and infantry. On Sunday, the officers had been comforted by the close-knit, reliable backs of the soldiers shielding this fortress from the mobs a few hundred yards away on the Nevsky and Liteiny.

An officer in the military academy, Serge Mstislavsky, looked from the window. Laundry, stiff from the cold, was hanging on clotheslines. The parade ground was empty. He could make out small gray figures at the entrance to the Volynsky barracks, gathering together, waving their arms up and down. Then he saw soldiers running away, "stooping close to the ground, crouching in ditches, past heaps of garbage and behind stacks of wood, running and crawling." They had no caps and some no overcoats, only unbuttoned jackets. He could hear shooting.

Some of the fleeing NCOs and officers hid in the Suvorov Museum. Others made for the academy. An academy colonel asked, hopefully, if the men were drunk. "Not a bit of it," said the sergeant. "Completely sober." More refugees, preceded by their officers, arrived for sanctuary from the Litovsky and Preobrazhensky regiments. Gloom fell on the academy common room. The duty officer rushed in to announce, "The Preobrazhensky men have just bayoneted Bogdanovich." Bogdanovich, the regimental commander, had refused to hand out cartridges and weapons. The academy instructors walked round the common room quietly, making sure that their spurs did not jingle. Only an ancient lieutenant-general, shaking his gray sideburns stubbornly from side to side as if in a private argument, consoled himself. "Nonsense," he muttered. "They'll return and repent. Where can they go? . . . Hmmm. That's precisely it. Where can they go?" He pressed the servant's bell. "I wonder, hmmm . . . what's keeping the tea?"

On Sunday, at most four hundred troops had mutinied for not much more than an hour. By 10:00 A.M. on Monday, there were ten thousand mutineers. Proximity aided the process. Volynsky rebels had only to march two hundred yards to arrive at the gray barracks of the Sixth Engineer

Reserve Battalion. "Come out, comrades!" they yelled. The engineers took to the street with their band playing. They were on the Liteiny Prospekt, with its cheering crowds, in twenty minutes. A lad from the Volynsky marched with them, flapping his arms like wings and crying, "We're going forward into the unknown!"

At 11:30 A.M., American diplomats in the Austrian embassy on Sergievskaya Street telephoned Ambassador Francis to report that mutineers had broken into the arsenal next door and had murdered General Matusov, its commandant. The Americans, still neutral in the war, were looking after Austrian interests and the welfare of the 1.25 million Austro-Hungarian prisoners in Russian hands. Francis rang the foreign ministry to ask for a guard to be put on the embassy to protect officers who had fled inside it. A ministry official said he would ring Francis back. He did not do so, and this was the last U.S. communication with the imperial foreign ministry.

The soldiers soon lost unit cohesion in the crowds. Some handed over or sold their rifles and sabers and exchanged their caps with civilians. "That's it," an onlooker in a ragged hat cried. "Look at the soldiers! No pharaoh will stand up to them." Maurice Paleologue, walking to the Liteiny, found flames mounting from the law courts. The crowd cut the hoses of the firemen who arrived to deal with it. Revolvers from the sacked arsenal were handed out to teenagers, who swirled out of side streets, shouting and firing in the air. Arthur Ransome saw a group of them shooting at pigeons perched on overhead streetcar wires.

Caught in cross fire between loyal troops and rebels, Paleologue beat a hasty retreat. From the British embassy, General Knox, a British military observer, saw an immense mass of soldiers being led by a diminutive but immensely dignified student. They had red cloths attached to their bayonets and they seemed to move silently, as though the watchers in the embassy windows were spectators in a gigantic cinema.

Count Vladimir Kokovtsov, former premier and finance expert, was taking his dog for a walk with his wife when the animal was startled by rifle fire and bolted under a gate. Kokovtsov was trying to get it back when the gate opened and Octobrist party leader Alexander Guchkov came out with Mikhail Tereshchenko, a young sugar millionaire. Guchkov told Kokovtsov that the Duma was hoping to form a new government, in which Tereshchenko was to be finance minister, and asked if the count would keep himself available to give financial advice. Kokovtsov said he would.

Alexander Kerensky had been woken by his wife, Olga, at 8:00 A.M. He took a telephone call from Nikolai Nekrasov, a professor of statistics and a leader of the liberal wing of the Cadets. He was told that the tsar had suspended the Duma, that a mutiny was taking place, and that he was wanted in the Tauride palace at once. "It came to me as a jolt," Kerensky recalled. "But I soon perceived that the decisive hour had struck." Kerensky dressed quickly. His relations with his wife were poor — his new mistress was her first cousin. "When he walked out of the flat that day, Alexander Fyodorovich never returned to live with us," Olga recalled. "That was the final breach in our family life."

He hurried on the five-minute walk from his apartment on Tverskaya to the Tauride, an elegant eighteenth-century building a few hundred yards north of Preobrazhensky Place that housed the Duma. The Duma's lack of executive power made it a sham as a parliament, but it was, nevertheless, the only elected national body of significance. As power slid from the top, its first natural stopping place was the Duma. The Duma deputies, however, found their new significance difficult to grasp. Kerensky found them "wandering idly about. . . . No one felt capable of doing anything at all or had any plan of action." He proposed that Mikhail Rodzianko be empowered as chairman to open a regular Duma session, ignoring the tsar's *ukase*.

This was rejected. The deputies knew only that some sort of mutiny was taking place, and that if they backed it prematurely they might be charged with treason. They split. Nikolai Chkheidze, the senior Menshevik in the Duma, was a neatly bearded Georgian with "every talent for being led on a halter, jibbing every now and then." For once, he was decisive, calling for a revolutionary government. Rodzianko, on the other hand, was still hoping that Nicholas would appoint a responsible new ministry.

The prudent majority settled for the creation of a provisional committee of Duma members "for the restoration of order and for liaison with persons and institutions." They did this with as much enthusiasm, a deputy said, "as if we were electing members to a fisheries commission." The wording was vague enough to keep the members' necks out of the noose if the street mobs lost out to the tsar, and the meeting was held in a private room to avoid any obvious flouting of the order to suspend sittings. Rodzianko was to chair the new body.

Though he joined the committee, Alexander Kerensky was in a bridge-burning mood. He was sure that the mutiny could become a movement deep enough to break the autocracy provided that it found a focus, and that it was his destiny to lead it. He wanted immediate contact with the troops. He telephoned his wife to contact Social Revolutionary colleagues and ask them to urge the mutineers to rally at the Duma. He waited for the mutineers anxiously, fellow deputies ribbing him about the nonarrival of "his" troops. They came at about 1:00 P.M., the tramp of their feet preceding them like the "sound of distant surf." The nervous Duma would not go to the revolution, the caustic right-winger Vasily Shulgin said, so "one way or another the revolution had gone to *it*." The incoming tide, Shulgin added acidly — blond peasant soldiers with scraps of red rag tied to their greatcoats, students in blue caps, laborers in dirty black work jackets — should be called "His Majesty the Russian People."

Shulgin wondered who would lead them. A soldier came up to him and asked, "Do you happen to have them in the Duma?"

"Have what?" Shulgin replied.

"Officers."

"What kind of officers?"

"Oh, any kind will do."

"Why?"

"I told my fellows it won't do to be altogether without officers," the soldier said. "They are angry with the ones we do have. But how can we get along without them? It isn't right. For order's sake, there must be officers. . . . Perhaps you have some in the Duma who will do?"

Kerensky ran out through the main entrance to greet the mutineers, and dazzled them. Speaking with quick and jerky eagerness, he posted what he christened a revolutionary guard at the door. His figure in his lawyer's black jacket became that of a notability to onlookers. "He stood there *determined*," Shulgin said, sensing that the soldier's query was being answered. "He grew. He grew in the mud of the revolution." Shulgin thought that Kerensky was one of those rare people "who can dance on a marsh. . . . It had little hillocks on which he could find a footing." An onlooker whispered, "He is their *vozhd*, their leader."

Kerensky was thirty-six, a "noisy lawyer flying high" who had found his moment. He was born in Simbirsk, a town of 65,000 set on a bluff amid watermeadows and cherry orchards on the middle reaches of the Volga. Sleepy and conservative, a place where minor gentry wintered and the summer nights were "breathless with the songs of nightingales," Simbirsk was remarkable mainly for the contrasting energy of the young radicals who fled it. Lenin had studied at the Simbirsk Academy, where young Kerensky's father had been director, writing Lenin a glowing report on his graduation.

While Lenin held for his birthplace nothing but malice, Alexander Kerensky remembered it with affection. He was an important boy, in white suit and pink Eton bow, his uncle the parish priest and his father the headmaster. He thought himself a "very loyal little subject of the tsar," living in an "enormous, splendid apartment" provided to the family by the government. "The beauty of the Volga, the chimes of evening bells," he wrote. "The bishop sitting solemnly in a carriage drawn by four horses, the convicts with heavy chains, the pretty little girls with whom I went to dancing lessons." These early interests — eternal Russia, injustice, women — had remained. Kerensky left Simbirsk for Turkestan, where his father was appointed the chief inspector of schools. To his early Slavic upbringing, respectable and restrained, the diarist Nikolai Sukhanov thought that Kerensky added "the tempestuous Turkestan temperament with its inclinations to pomposity, preciosity, and theatricality," useful qualities for a lawyer.

A teacher watching Kerensky playing Khlestakov in a school performance of Nikolai Gogol's *The Government Inspector* noted acutely that the "figure of this lovable lady-killer and unwitting con-man might have been created for him." Kerensky's face was sallow and almost deathly pale, his eyes narrow and Mongolian, and his frantic intensity made him "seem to be permanently in pain." But he was energetic and his bouts of melancholy were short. He picked himself up easily. Zinaïda Gippius thought him "not very clever," but found him "specially understandable and pleasant with all his boyish-brave ardor." People liked Kerensky.

He became involved in radical politics at Saint Petersburg in his teens. Many law students were seduced by the "smoky room, the table loaded with samovar and plenty of sandwiches, the group of a dozen men and girls." Kerensky had no time, however, for fashionable terrorism or Marxist internationalism. He felt that Marxism, with its "austere completeness and orderly logic," was "borrowed entirely from abroad" — his own ideas, though "indistinct and inconsistent," were "rooted in the native soil." His group, a member said, "dreamed about a new world, but they were unquestionably humanitarian and utterly Russian in every respect."

Kerensky started a legal aid office in the city after graduating from the Saint Petersburg law faculty, advising workers on their rights and representing them without fees. He got to know the lowest strata of urban life with an intimacy unknown to Lenin. In 1904, he married Olga Baranovskaya, an intense girl with an oval face and lustrous black hair, the daughter of an army officer — his own mother was a general's daughter. Shortly after the wedding, walking home happily aglow by the Winter Palace, he saw the tsar standing deep in thought on a balcony. Kerensky claimed that he was struck by a keen presentiment, that "we would meet sometime, somehow our paths would cross."

During the 1905 revolution, Kerensky founded a socialist newspaper and served four months in the Kresty Prison after a friend's revolver was found in his apartment. A prison sentence was an obligatory qualification for any middle-class revolutionary — the bulk came from backgrounds similar to Kerensky and Lenin — with pretensions to leading the workers. Kerensky was thrilled with his luck. "The stigma of bureaucratic descent was removed under the showerbath in prison," he said. "I was now one of us in radical and socialist circles."

After his release he became a "political defender," one of an elite band of barristers who took on difficult political cases. He was poorly paid. He lived with Olga and their sons, Oleg, born in 1905, and Gleb, two years later, in a cheap flat behind the Nikolaevsky Station, its walls "shining with water," before moving to rooms above a funeral parlor. But it was high-profile work. His triumphs, all clients escaping the death penalty after a peasant rising in Estonia, more than outweighed the failures, 17 executed in Riga. In 1912, troops shot dead 170 striking miners in the Lena goldfields in Siberia. The massacre caused deep revulsion throughout Russia, and Kerensky made a national reputation when he was appointed to the inquiry commission.

He was elected to the Duma a few months later. The heavyweights in the smoking room thought him a "puppy," for his speeches were emotional and left his whole body trembling with sweat pouring down the pale cheeks, but the gallery adored him. He could adopt a "definitive Shakespearean tone," which irritated colleagues with its superiority. But his spontaneity swept away all barriers with a mass audience, and he was personally kind. Though he was too young to have known Lenin as a child in Simbirsk, he was typically generous to Lenin's family. In July of 1914, with war looming, he met one of Lenin's sisters on a Volga steamer. "Look now," he said. "You'll see Vladimir soon." "Why?" she asked. "The war will change everything in Russia," he told her eagerly, "and he'll be able to return home."

Kerensky's Okhrana file, another necessity for a radical, grew bulkier during the war. The Bolshevik deputies in the Duma had been arrested at the start of the war, despite their apostasy in renouncing Lenin's "defeatism" in court. Kerensky agitated for their release. In near isolation, he denounced anti-Semitic atrocities. He went in person to Kuzhi, a small town near the front in Kovno where Jews were being lynched for supposedly hiding Germans in their cellars so that they could surprise Russian troops at night. He examined the cellars and, for a time at least, prevented further pogroms by exposing Jewish "treachery" as a myth.

His Okhrana file described him in 1915 as the "instigator of the recreation of the local Social Revolutionary party, broken up by previous arrests." The leaderless Bolsheviks in Petrograd were impressed enough to write to ask him if he would carry out "joint revolutionary work." Bolshevik feuding and class-based ethics had no appeal. "Hatred and malice," he wrote, "hatred to the end towards political opponents is incomprehensible to us." His dislike of violence was reinforced by a visit to Tashkent during intercommunal riots, when hundreds of Russians and Central Asiatics were raped and murdered following Asian protests at conscription. Kerensky had, to a marked degree, the respectable Russian's distaste for *niepriyatnosty*, "unpleasantnesses," a word that covered anything from pogroms to arson.

He fell ill — "white, like paper," Zinaïda Gippius found, "though he doesn't calm down but bounces about." In February of 1916 he had a tubercular kidney removed. He was close to death for a month. During his convalescence, he took up with Olga's cousin, Lilya Baranovskaya. The gossip noted that Lilya was herself married to an army officer, and had her own child.

Kerensky continued to live under the same roof as Olga and their two young sons. His friends found it naive. Naive, too, was his appearance for his friend Count Orlov-Davidov in a scandalous divorce case in the autumn of 1916. The count had married a French singer who said that she was pregnant by him. The count's butler discovered that, far from being with child, she had bought a baby in preparation for the "birth," and the count became a laughingstock. Kerensky took personal loyalty too far in this case, some thought, for a serious politician.

Sukhanov had his doubts. Not about Kerensky's sincerity, for he rang with a "conviction that was all-compelling," but about his ability to fool himself. He felt that Kerensky had persuaded himself that he was a socialist, a son of the people. He believed it well enough, and so did the people. But underneath it, the diariest held Kerensky to be by taste and temperament the "most consummate middle-class radical."

For the moment, though, his "supernatural" energy had a vacuum to work in and he grasped at it. His Okhrana nickname was "Speedy."

Serge Khabalov was in a state of near-collapse, the military commander's jaw trembling as he wandered from room to room in his headquarters. The chief of the Fourth Police District of Petrograd, General Vladislav Galle, was summoned to discuss the city plan. Galle found that it did not exist. The old plan had divided the city into sectors, each under the control of a unit that was now mutinying; there was no new plan. News came in that a squadron of armored cars, supposedly disabled and parked in a military garage, was rumbling down the Nevsky with red pennants flying.

A shock detachment was organized under a much-decorated Preobrazhensky officer, Colonel A. P. Kutepov. He scraped together six companies of riflemen, fifteen machine guns, and a squadron and a half of cavalry. With this small force, Kutepov was supposed to restore discipline among several mutinous regiments in the huge area from the Liteiny Bridge to the Nikolaevsky Station. Kutepov said he needed at least a brigade. The punitive counterforce set off into the city.

By early afternoon, with four corpses lying outside the U.S. embassy at 34 Furshtatskaya near the Preobrazhensky barracks, and five wounded officers seeking sanctuary inside it, about twenty-five thousand troops had mutinied. The mutiny was an event so rapid, so unprecedented in a garrison far from the front but under wartime discipline, that those involved found it inexplicable. "Let there be no mistake," Arthur Ransome wired to the *Daily Mail* in London. "This is not an organized revolution. It will be impossible to make a statue in memory of its organizer." Serge Mstislavsky, the military academy officer and a clandestine Social Revolutionary, tried within a month to discover who had brought out the Volynskys and precipitated the mutiny. Seven members of the regiment claimed the honor; none of their accounts had anything in common. Mstislavsky concluded that the regiment had been "led out by an eighth, nameless person" who had not sent in his account of the matter.

Mstislavsky was equally certain that no political party played any part. His own Social Revolutionaries had been found "fast asleep, like the Foolish Virgins" in the Gospel. "The truth of the matter," he wrote, "was that outside of small factions stewing in their own juices . . . the socialist parties were completely bankrupt."

The mutineers were used to discipline, and touchingly grateful to officers who came over to their side. An unknown ensign on a horse joined a large group that was shuffling about to no purpose. "Brothers, I'm with you!" he cried. "Forward!" they responded. "The lieutenant is with us. Hurrah!" A Bolshevik who helped to take over the Finland Station, Mikhail Kalinin, admitted that he was embarrassed when soldiers yelled to him, "Where are our leaders? Lead us!" He did not know what to do with them. Then he realized that they were close to the redbrick walls and towers of the Kresty Prison. "If it's leaders you want, Kresty is right here," Kalinin said, "but first you have to free them." The soldiers broke through the gates and 2,400 prisoners were freed. V. V. Schmidt, who had been arrested the morning before with the Petrograde Bolshevik committee, found himself on the pavement with a rifle being pressed into his hand.

Prisoners in the Litovsky Castle and the 958 men in the house of detention on Shpalerny Street were also freed. About three dozen women convicts filed out of the Litovsky, wearing prison gowns and scuffing through the snow in their slippers. Most of the political prisoners headed straight for the Tauride, across the Neva. "The police didn't even oppose the crowd," said Lenin's sister, Anna Ilyichina, who had also been arrested in the Okhrana sweep thirty-six hours before. "They gave them the keys immediately. They just opened our cell and told us to come out."

The ex-prisoners from the Kresty arrived at the Duma at about 2:00 P.M. They included the members of the workers' section of the military industries committee who had been rounded up in January, men with experience of practical organization and firsthand memories of the 1905 Soviet. The freed prisoners joined with left-wing deputies, largely Mensheviks and Social Revolutionaries, to establish a new workers' council. Kerensky found them an office at the far end of the Tauride Palace, while the Duma committee worked in another wing.

A Provisional Executive Committee of the Soviet of Workers' Deputies was formed. Two Duma members, Kerensky and Nikolai Chkheidze, were appointed to it to serve as a link with the Duma. This organizing committee worked hastily, issuing proclamations to set up a supply base for the wandering mutineers in the Tauride and calling on citizens to feed them. It also appealed to workers' representatives, at one delegate per thousand workers, to attend the first session of the Soviet to be held at 7:00 P.M. that evening. Two provisional committees were thus in existence in separate wings of the palace by midafternoon, one dominated by moderate bourgeois members of the Duma, the other a radical and self-styled Workers' affair. In its opening hours, the revolution was giving ample proof of its ability to spawn committees.

Linguistically, there is little in Russian to distinguish "Duma," or assembly, from "Soviet," or council. The Duma had functioned as an elected assembly, intermittently, only since 1906, and the Soviet for a matter of weeks in 1905. Nevertheless, the gulf that Kerensky and Chkheidze were trying to bridge between the two was already wide. The Duma saw itself as the sober precursor of a fully fledged parliament that would represent the respectable elements in society. These included the most moderate socialists, but not "riffraff." The Soviet was devoted exclusively to radicals and workers, seeing itself as a lifeboat for their interests, and eager to maintain the momentum of revolution.

Conservative Duma men like Vasily Shulgin were overcome by the disorder, the stench of unwashed men, and the constant physical threat posed by the mob surging through the Tauride. Loyal monarchists quit the Tauride in disgust, cursing the "mentally ill Kerensky" for joining the Soviet committee.

The first prisoners of the revolution were being brought into the palace. Ivan Shcheglovitov, a former justice minister, arrested by a student in his apartment, was a prime candidate for lynching — he had described the tsar as the "image of Christ upon earth" and regarded constitutionalism to be a heresy against God. Kerensky cut through the muttering throng in the cream-and-gilt ballroom of the palace. "Your life is in safety," he told the trembling Shcheglovitov. "Know this, the Duma does not shed blood." Taking a boyish glee in his new role as policeman, Kerensky took his fellow deputies aside to show them the key to the room in which he was confining the fallen bureaucrats.

The regular police were in full disintegration. They did not expect any quarter, for if the revolution failed, they would be the hangmen of reaction. The crowds knew where they and their families lived. "Many times the crowds caught policemen and lynched them," a Petrograd schoolboy, Arvids Jurevics, recalled. "I saw on our street a man white as a sheet, being pulled away. He wore a *shinel*, the long police greatcoat, and a *papaha*, a gray fur hat. The police were dressed a little differently and you couldn't mistake them. He was taken away and was shot just around the corner."

A crowd caught another young policeman near the Fontanka Canal and dragged him bleeding to a part where there was open water. A horrified baroness watched him plead for his life: "Brothers! Don't drown me! I swear by God I did nothing wrong! I didn't hurt anyone! Brothers!" He was thrown into the canal. He made the sign of the cross and started to swim. The crowd, furious that he might escape, hurled paving stones at his thrashing body until it disappeared.

Pitirim Sorokin, the young Social Revolutionary journalist and academic, thought it was a miracle that Kerensky was preventing mass lynchings in the Tauride. Sorokin came across a mob on the Liteiny howling at the police, "Ah! Pharaohs! Your end is coming!" A man pointed at the red glow from a burning police station and went into a frenzy: "We are going to destroy all government offices, burn, smash, kill all police, all tyrants, all despots!"

Some police held out on rooftops with machine guns. Others tore off the distinctive greatcoats and put on work blouses or army tunics. A year later Meriel Buchanan saw one survivor, an old sergeant who had often guarded the British embassy "covered with orders and medals," dressed in rags sweeping the steps of a shop on the Nevsky. Station houses were attacked and burned and the policemen in them murdered. The Okhrana received no telephone reports after noon, and itself had not long to survive. The Petrograd police director, Alexei Vassilev phoned his own headquarters from his apartment and ordered the staff to leave. Within a few minutes, a crowd stormed the building, set it on fire, and threw the records and files into the courtyard. Later in the day, with his wife and a passport made out in a false name, Vassiliev abandoned his apartment and fled to a friend's place.

The prima ballerina Mathilde Kshesinskaya was warned to get out of her art deco palace near the Peter and Paul Fortress. As the ex-mistress of the tsar and current lover of a grand duke, she was too intimate with the regime to be safe. Shooting had gone on around her house all day. With her fox terrier Dzhibi under one arm and a suitcase full of jewels under the other, she abandoned it.

Alexander Protopopov fled the interior ministry, taking with him a briefcase with the memorabilia of his period in office, letters to and from the empress, letters from the now-measles-stricken Anna Vyrubova, and police pictures of the corpse of Rasputin. He headed for the relative safety of the Maryinsky Palace.

When the crowd saw an officer or nobleman riding in a car, they would jump on it, push it, and sometimes turn it over, but the occupants were generally unharmed. It was mainly teenagers who enjoyed this sport, but the schoolboy Arvids Jurevics saw one determined old lady pushing her shopping bag against a car to stop it. A dark blue limousine with the imperial gold eagles on the doors got a special cheer. It flew a red flag on the hood and was filled with mutinous sailors from the imperial yacht.

By 4:00 P.M., General Khabalov retained control only of his own headquarters, the Maryinsky Palace, the Admiralty, the Winter Palace, and the Peter and Paul Fortress. Smoke from the burning law courts, prisons, and police stations drifted across the sky. Cars and trucks raced around the darkening streets with red flags flying and machine guns in the back. "In practically all of them," Sukhanov said, "you observed women." A little group of English ladies braved the streets to attend the weekly sewing party at the embassy, "talking in hushed tones of what might be the result of all this." The American naval attaché, Captain McCully, reported at 6:00 P.M. that he had seen a cavalry regiment riding quietly away and "abandoning the city to the mutineers." Countess Nostitz, the American wife of a Russian general, complained that an officer had just died in her drawing room. He had been shot for refusing to hand over his sword.

Hooligans and professional thieves celebrated the absence of police by breaking into apartments. Countess Kleinmikhel was dining when servants burst in. "Run! Run!" they cried. Bandits had broken into the building and were making their way upstairs. The countess led her guests to refuge in a house opposite. From there they watched as a group of soldiers and sailors were served their meal on silver plate and ordered up bottles of wine from the cellar.

*   *   *

The cabinet assembled at 7:00 P.M. in the Maryinsky Palace, protected by a company of troops. Several thousand men were a few hundred yards away outside the Winter Palace, including Pavlovsky units that had arrived unexpectedly with a marching band. Their loyalty was uncertain.

Kutepov's expeditionary force was melting away. During the afternoon, the colonel came across a common phenomenon of the revolution, the mob that agreed with the last person to harangue it. He succeeded in rallying large numbers of Litovskys and Volynskys, promising them that they would not be shot for mutiny. They lifted him on their shoulders, but an agitator shouted, "Comrades, he's lying. They'll shoot you." They abandoned him. Kutepov holed up in the mansion of Count Musin-Pushkin. He was unable to contact Khabalov by telephone and several of his officers had been shot. No rations had been sent for his troops and, although he had bought bread and sausages for them from a shop that was still open, they were hungry. The mob outside the mansion was smashing the streetlights and shouting his name. "A large part of my force mixed with the crowd and I understood that we could put up no further resistance," Kutepov said. "I went home and ordered the door locked."

It was no longer clear who was in command, the trembling Khabalov, the war minister General Mikhail Belayev, or Colonel Zankevich, chief of the General Staff. A decision was made to declare a state of siege, in Khabalov's name. When the decrees were hastily printed — on the Admiralty presses since the city printing plant was in rebel hands — there was no way to post them. "I had neither glue nor brushes," said Alexander Balk, the city governor. "General Khabalov said some way must be found to hang them, but by the way he spoke I got the feeling that he didn't attach much importance to the decree." The decrees were eventually stuck on the spikes of the palace railings, where the night wind blew them away.

One other decision was made by Russia's last tsarist government. Prince Nicholas Golitsyn suggested that Protopopov might offer himself as a sacrifice and resign from the cabinet. The interior minister agreed, saying hysterically that there was "nothing left now but to shoot myself." He slipped away from the Maryinsky Palace and spent his next hours cowering in a tailor's shop. That apart, nothing was done. "We walked about in distraction," said Golitsyn. "We saw that the situation was deteriorating and anticipated we would be arrested." At 8:00 P.M., Khabalov cabled the Stavka at Mogilev to admit that he had been unable to fulfill the tsar's command to restore order. "Only a handful of men from different regiments have remained loyal," he reported. "They are concentrated at the Winter Palace. . . . They and I will continue the struggle."

Khabalov and Zankevich went out into the palace square. They hoped to be able to hold an oblong around the Winter Palace running between the Neva and the Moika Canal. The Pavlovsky Guards, tired of waiting in the freezing night and unfed, evaporated. After a misty day, it had started snowing and the temperature had fallen to fifteen degrees below zero. There were not enough troops to hold more than the palace itself. A rumor that a mob was arriving swept through the Maryinsky. The lights were put out and when they came on again a minister was found hiding under the table. After 10:00 P.M., the cabinet slipped away from the back of the building.

The ministers might have drawn some comfort if they had realized the chaos that surrounded the mutineers. Mstislavsky had come out in his revolutionary colors and was attempting to organize the rebel forces, on behalf of the Soviet rather than the Duma, from a room in the Tauride Palace. He was using a page torn from a prewar tourist guide as an operations map. He knew, which the ministers did not, that the Finland Regiment, the cadet schools, and a bicycle battalion were still loyal. The infantry in the suburbs was unaffected. The Cossacks and much of the cavalry were neutral at best. Mstislavsky was uncertain whether a body of troops on Senate Square were "theirs," but sure they were not his. In conventional terms, Mstislavsky thought his position was "quite catastrophic."

During daylight, the crowds on the streets had acted as a living barricade to Khabalov's forces. The streets had emptied with nightfall. From the Astoria Hotel, the liberal Vladimir Nabokov was looking down on the Morskaya, deserted apart from a lumbering armored car and an occasional soldier running fast and hugging the walls. Pitirim Sorokin was going home after attending a meeting of writers. He was depressed to find that his fellow writers were already working on which newspapers to censor, reminding him of Flaubert's dictum that "in every revolutionist is hidden a gendarme." Sorokin found only a few onlookers outside the burning High Court building, their "faces in the red blaze looking demoniacal as they shouted, laughed and danced." There were corpses in the snow.

None of Mstislavsky's "forces" were coherent units. He had gaggles of volunteers commanded by a sprinkling of antiregime officers, none of them local men. The soldiers, frightened of the morrow, were insisting on written orders, which Mstislavsky scribbled on sheets of Duma writing paper he found in his desk, feeling that he was scattering his orders "like rose petals into a raging storm." He had no artillery; his four machine guns could not be fired for lack of lubricants, while the still-loyal bicyclists, a bridge away in Vyborg, had fourteen in working order. Mstislavsky sent a volunteer to buy some Vaseline from the nearest chemist. The lad came back, embarrassed, twirling a silver ruble in his hands. The shops were shut, it was late, and the would-be revolutionary had not wanted to wake up the shop owner. Two of his last officers were dispatched to stop a large mob from breaking into the government alcohol warehouse by the Tauride Park, a wise precaution: when Ambassador Francis checked the streets round the U.S. embassy toward midnight, he came across fifteen soldiers, all drunk. Francis rang the U.S. consul general in Moscow, Madden Summers, but was told all was quiet there.

Mstislavsky thought that Khabalov had only to break out of Petrograd with all possible speed and wait for reinforcements on the outskirts. Having isolated the city, the tsarist general could start a concentric advance at his leisure with loyal regiments from the front. This was how the French general Gaston de Galliffet had suppressed revolutionary Paris in 1871, and it was what Mstislavsky's few fellow professionals in the Duma building expected to happen now. An infantry captain peered around the door. "A fellow could get into trouble around here," he said, shaking his head. "Just as much chance as a snowball in hell."

The politicians elsewhere in the Tauride were at loggerheads. The Soviet had met in the Catherine Hall at 7:00 P.M. with about 250 delegates. Troops, dirty and disheveled, swarmed into the hall and shocked the janitors, who thought it would take a week to clear their bootmarks from the polished wooden floors. The men announced themselves to cheers: "We're from the Pavlovsky . . . the Litovsky . . . the Sappers . . . the Chasseurs . . . the Finnish." Sukhanov found that the delegates were listening to the soldiers "as children listen to a wonderful, enthralling tale they know by heart."

Nikolai Chkheidze, as the ranking Menshevik, was the obvious nomination for chairman of the Soviet. Kerensky and the Menshevik Matvei Skobelev became vice-chairmen. Over Bolshevik objections, Kerensky and Chkheidze were mandated to represent the Soviet on the Duma's provisional committee. The meeting also elected a permanent executive committee with ex officio membership for all socialist groups. The Bolsheviks had two members out of the fourteen. The Soviet decided to publish its own daily *Izvestiya*, "The News," reviving a title suppressed in 1905.

As the Soviet organized itself, the Duma chairman Mikhail Rodzianko was making a dangerous trip across town to ask Grand Duke Mikhail to contact his brother in a final attempt to persuade the tsar to appoint a responsible government.

Nicholas had already ignored a warning from his wife. In the morning, Alexandra had ordered an icon to be paraded around the palace corridors in Tsarskoe Selo with prayers chanted for the sick children. Her valet de chambre overheard a soldier mutter, "You trample on the people and you carry idols about." If that was the first whiff of revolution at Tsarskoe Selo, the empress was well aware of the gravity of events in the capital. At 1:03 P.M., the stalwart of autocracy, her philosophy enshrined "in the three words pas de concessions," cracked. "Concessions essential," she cabled Mogilev. "Uprising continues. Many troops have gone to the side of the revolution."

Nicholas did not reply. Neither did he comment on a frantic cable from Rodzianko that arrived at Mogilev a few minutes later. "The hour of your fate and that of Russia is at hand. Tomorrow may be too late." This telegram was, as Vasily Shulgin was to mock, already "a year and a half too late." The tsar took his normal postlunch walk along the highway running north along the Dnieper toward the pretty town of Orsha.

He dined with his chief of staff, General Mikhail Alexeev, and General Nikolai Ivanov. The war minister, Mikhail Belayev, had cabled Alexeev from Petrograd at 7:00 P.M., warning him that the situation was out of control. "Fires have broken out and we have no means to combat them," the war minister reported. "Genuinely dependable units must come at once." The tsar was impressed by Ivanov's boasting over the dinner table. The general told how he had single-handedly put down a mutinous band of sailors at Kronstadt in 1906 by bellowing at them, "On your knees!"

Ivanov did not cut much of a figure with his fellow generals. One thought he had degenerated since the Kronstadt incident and was now a "flabby old man, possessing neither strength nor energy" and having a "meager grasp of the political situation."

The tsar thought otherwise. After the meal was over, Nicholas appointed Ivanov commander of the Petrograd military district, and ordered that he be given reliable units from the front and a personal bodyguard of a Saint George's Cavalry battalion. Toward 10:00 P.M., Grand Duke Mikhail telephoned Nicholas from Petrograd at Rodzianko's suggestion. The tsar refused to speak to him. Alexeev took the call, the grand duke asking him to urge his brother to dismiss the cabinet. It took half an hour for the grand duke to get a reply: Nicholas would leave for Tsarskoe Selo at 2:30 A.M. that morning, but there would be no changes in the cabinet until he arrived. In the meantime, General Ivanov was to leave for the capital.

Rodzianko returned to the Tauride with the news that the cabinet would not be changed. He was urged to announce that the Duma provisional committee would take power immediately. "Take it," Vasily Shulgin pressed him. If the Duma refused, "dogs and scoundrels" would not. By that Shulgin meant the Soviet in the adjoining wing. Rodzianko wavered: "I am not a revolutionary. . . . I won't go against the tsar's power." He asked for fifteen minutes alone in his office to think it over. "All right," Rodzianko said when he emerged. "I have decided to take power, but from now on I insist all of you obey me unquestioningly." He turned to Kerensky: "Alexander Fyodorovich, this means you especially."

The Duma committee lodged its bid for power before the Soviet. It rankled. At midnight, Rodzianko appeared in the office where Nikolai Sokolov, a Social Revolutionary lawyer and Soviet member, was working with Mstislavsky's Soviet military commission. Rodzianko brought with him Colonel Engelgardt, a Duma member and general staff officer sympathetic to the revolution. "The Duma provisional committee has assumed responsibility for restoring order in the city," Rodzianko announced. "The colonel has been appointed commander of Petrograd."

He said that the Soviet had already formed its own military commission and that there was nothing for the colonel to do. "Right now we have no need of high and mighty appointees," Sokolov said as Englegardt flushed with anger. "What we need are revolutionaries. And it is absolutely intolerable that the Petrograd Soviet, at present the only real force, should be entirely removed from the command it has created itself." Rodzianko pounded the table: "No, gentlemen, you forced us into this business and so you've got to listen!" A brawl was close to breaking out, but Mstislavsky whispered to Sokolov, "Who cares if it's Engelgardt — it's no skin off our nose. They can name anyone they want, we won't let go of the reins."

Breathing heavily, Rodzianko left with Engelgardt, an open split between Soviet and Duma narrowly averted. Later in the night, the Duma committee appointed temporary commissars to replace the vanished ministers. There were twenty-four in all. The bulk were Cadets and Octobrists. All were Duma deputies. With that, the exhausted politicians stretched out to sleep. They had, the poetess Zinaïda Gippius noted, created a revolutionary government that, Kerensky apart, contained not a single revolutionary.

A thin screen of soldiers was posted round the Tauride. No counterattack came. A little after midnight, Belayev informed Mogilev that he had telephoned the Maryinsky Palace and had been answered by a revolutionary. Only the communications and foreign minister had not fled, and they were hiding from the mutineers who now roamed the building. Grand Duke Mikhail, waiting in the General Staff building for the firing to die down so that he could drive home, demanded that the loyal troops be withdrawn from inside the Winter Palace. "I do not want them firing on the people from the house of the Romanovs," he said. The loyalists in the palace were hungry and thirsty. A general who asked for a cup of tea was told that the palace administration had standing orders not to serve it before 8:00 A.M.

The palace defenders were turned out of their makeshift beds into the early hours. Khabalov and Zankevich led the remnants of their forces across the square into the Admiralty building. The men were short of ammunition, food, and water. During the night, most of them slipped away.

The imperial train did not leave Mogilev until 5:00 A.M. on Tuesday. Russia had no government and its autocrat was on a train moving through snowy flatlands at twenty-five miles per hour. An hour later, Nikolai Sukhanov was woken in the Tauride by a pair of noisy soldiers. Exhausted politicians lay wrapped in broadcloth and fur coats on tables and the floor. Kerensky, his frock-coat spread out around him, was "bent like a pretzel," his mouth wide open, snoring gently. The soldiers were cutting Ilya Repin's famous portrait of Nicholas out of its frame above the debating chamber with their bayonets.

VII
The Ghost Train

As SUKHANOV WATCHED the portrait being prized out, he wondered what had happened inside the heads of these soldiers, "dumb slaves of the despot," only twenty-four hours earlier. The grunted, monosyllable remarks they made as they worked with their bayonets were so mundane the diarist did not bother to note them down. He disentangled himself from his *shuba* fur coat, and listened. Sporadic firing was continuing from some loyalist troops.

The Vyborg bicyclists held out until midmorning on Tuesday, February 28. Captured machine guns and some light field guns were firing on them from across the Sampsonievsky. The attack was inaccurate but the flimsy barrack huts offered no protection and were slowly disintegrating. Their CO, Colonel Balkashin, was a popular officer who had kept the respect of his men. He decided to surrender to prevent further casualties among them. He ordered a ceasefire and crossed the broad boulevard to the angry crowd, insisting that his men were not responsible for bloodshed and had acted under his direct orders. Balkashin was shot in the heart and died instantly, his action seeming to be the one clear case of outstanding personal courage recorded in Petrograd in those days.

At 11:30 A.M., General Ivanov grilled Serge Khabalov from Mogilev over the Hughes wire, a keyboard and telegraph apparatus which worked like a crude telex machine. Ivanov hoped that he would be able to move his punitive force directly into the city by rail. He asked the Petrograd commander which railway stations and city districts were secure. "None," replied Khabalov. "The entire city is in the hands of the revolutionaries." What authority existed? "I don't know," said Khabalov. Were all ministries functioning properly? "The revolutionaries have arrested all the ministers."

What police units did he have at his disposal? "None." How much food did he have? "I have no food supplies."

While Khabalov's replies were going over the wire, the garrison in the Peter and Paul Fortress surrendered. The Pavlovsky troops arrested after the brief mutiny on Sunday evening were freed from two cells in the Trubetskoy Ravelin. Instead of facing a firing squad, they were carried out on the shoulders of a cheering crowd. A few minutes later, at 12:25 P.M., Mikhail Belayev informed Mogilev that the tsar's command for all ministers to obey Ivanov could not be carried out. Only four ministries were answering the telephone.

Nicholas remained out of touch on his train. An American pastor had noted that Russian trains "plod along at a pace which an able-bodied cowboy on his bronco would outstrip." On many sections of the line, the rails weighed only forty-two pounds to the yard instead of the normal seventy-four. Sleepers were made of uncured green timber that had split, and the rails were held on them by small clamps instead of steel cradles. As the empire slipped fast away, the emperor was in slow motion.

The streets and the Alexander Gardens surrounding the Admiralty, the last redoubt, were filled with armed workers and soldiers preparing to attack. The Admiralty was defended by six hundred tired, hungry, and demoralized men. Their officers ordered them to return to their barracks. At 1:30 P.M., Belayev reported that all organized resistance by loyal troops in the capital had broken off. A policeman's head, severed by a saber, lay in the street a block from the U.S. embassy. The commercial attaché's cook saw it on her way to work and was hysterical for several hours.

It was not until about 4:00 P.M. that the rebels milling about outside the Admiralty finally plucked up the nerve to burst into the building. It was empty. Frontal assault was not the order of the day; the murder of officers, increasingly, was, and Tuesday was a dangerous day for men in epaulettes to be caught on the streets. They were often the victims of rumors that "lone machine gunners," officers and police, were firing on the crowds from roofs and church belfries. These snipers were known as "Protopopov's men," and a grim little ditty about him ran:

> *A pious man, of all such people*
> *who can say why he went mad*
> *and on the very top of steeples*
> *placed machine guns that he had.*

The stories were persistent. A week later, it was being said that the frozen body of a policeman had been found by his machine gun in the attic above the Fabergé jewelry shop on the Morskaya, dead of cold and starvation. Most obituary notices blamed the police for deaths: "Killed in the street by the tsar's police, firing from ambush — Red Cross sister, Manefa Georgiebna Thorchovskaya . . ." But the low number of casualties shows that the Protopopov men were a myth. In all, the revolution caused no more than 1,300 casualties, and many of the 170 or so dead were to be killed in naval bases.

There were many sources of gunfire. Looters were working the city. It was as well that Mathilde Kshesinskaya had fled the evening before; the ballerina's palace was sacked on Tuesday by men who fired in the air when bystanders became too curious. Paleologue and Buchanan watched four lorry loads of coal being taken away from the palace cellars, reflecting that their own embassies were near freezing for lack of fuel. Two thousand men, many of them violent criminals, freed themselves from the hard labor prison beyond the Nevsky Gate. Those who were chained and handcuffed took themselves to the smithy of a nearby Cossack regiment and unshackled each other. Opening the storeroom, they seized weapons and swept off into the city.

Trucks with rifles and bayonets sticking from them like "enormous hedgehogs" roamed the streets. Hijacked private cars roared past, soldiers and youths lying on the mudguards with rifles and letting off occasional volleys through excitement and joie de vivre. Soldiers appeared at the U.S. embassy demanding a car. David Francis told them there was only a Ford, which he used to go to the city's nine-hole golf course, and that it had broken down.

During the afternoon, Alexei Bobrinskoy, fresh from hunting lynx, watched a crowd in pursuit of human quarry rushing along the Neva quay near the Hermitage. The young officer heard someone say, "It was a jolly good thing we shot him — he was sniping at the crowd from his window." He asked who. "Ah, some general of the tsar, but we finished him off!" Shots had been fired in the air by drunken soldiers and a woman cook had pointed at the house of a long-retired general. The mob burst in and killed him. His wife escaped by the back door. The house was looted and the furniture smashed, chairs and tables thrown into the street.

Another phantom gunman provided the pretext for sacking the Astoria Hotel, a favorite watering hole for officers on leave. A regiment was marching past it, band playing, when shots were said to have come from the roof. Soldiers smashed in the big plate windows on the Morskaya with their rifle butts. All the Russian officers in the hotel were arrested and an elderly general who put up some resistance was killed in the hall. British and French officers billeted in the hotel managed to get the women and children among the guests away to safety.

NORWAY

SWEDEN

Baltic Sea

GERMANY

POLISH PROVINCES

AUSTRIA-HUNGARY

RUMANIA

White Sea

FINLAND

ARCHANGEL

OLONETS

VOLOGDA

ESTLAND
LIVLAND
PETROGRAD
NOVGOROD
KURLAND
PSKOV
KOVNO
VITEBSK
TVER
VILNA
GRODNO
MOGILEV
SMOLENSK
MINSK
KALUGA
OREL
VOLHYNIA
CHERNIGOV
KIEV
POLTAVA
PODOLIA
KHARKOV
BESSARABIA
KHERSON
EKATERINOSLAV
TAURIDA

YAROSLAV
KOSTROMA
VIATKA
PERM
MOSCOW
VLADIMIR
NIZHNI NOVGOROD
KAZAN
UFA
RIAZAN
SIMBIRSK
TULA
PENZA
ORENBURG
TAMBOV
SARATOV
SAMARA
VORONEZH
DON
ASTRAKHAN

KUBAN
STAVROPOL

Black Sea

TEREK

Caspian Sea

TRANS-CAUCASIAN PROVINCES

TURKEY

0   200
MILES

EUROPEAN RUSSIA

Many streetlamps and the overhead wires for electric trams had been broken. No cabs ran and fashionable ladies with urgent business took low peasant sledges with straw in the bottom. Officers were best advised not to go out, because the crowd "disarms them, molests them, kills them." Meriel Buchanan saw men swagger past the British embassy with officers' swords buckled to their waists as trophies.

A former Russian military attaché in Washington, General Stackelberg, was shot when mutineers forced their way into his apartment. His mutilated body was tossed into the street, where cavalrymen rode their horses over it. A cousin of schoolgirl Zinaïda Shakovsky's mother, married to a colonel, slept on a couch in her apartment with her Red Cross uniform spread over the blanket. "If they come in here, it might protect me," she said. A family friend, General Grigoriev, was wakened by a group of drunken soldiers. He put on his cook's apron and a white cap and led the search for himself.

As Arthur Ransome crossed the Champs de Mars, a cavalryman galloped over, pulling up in a flurry of snow and pointing a revolver in the correspondent's face. "For the people or against the people?" the horseman demanded. "I am English," Ransome replied. "Long live England!" said the trooper, and rode off.

Ministers, generals, and police in civilian clothes, "disguised, frightened, humbled like the small shopkeepers whom they used to bully," begged disciplined-looking units to place them under arrest. A steady stream arrived at the Tauride all day. Alexander Protopopov arrived with a "hopelessly harassed and sunken face" in the afternoon from his hideout in a tailor's shop. *Izvestiya* had come out that morning with a front-page story praising Kerensky's "magnanimous and magnificent" treatment of the former justice minister, Ivan Shcheglovitov. "Here Kerensky was revealed," the newspaper said. "An actor to the core, but a man with an honest repugnance to shedding blood." Protopopov read it and thought it safest to give himself up. An ugly crowd surrounded the ex–interior minister at the entrance but Kerensky strode through it, his "eyes afire and hand raised," to roar, "Do not touch this man!"

He led Protopopov into the palace ballroom, full of angry soldiers and resembling a "third-class provincial railway station when troops were embarking, smelling like leather, uniforms, and bread." The crowd froze with hatred when it spotted Protopopov, his "mustaches trembling," and Kerensky guided him through to the Pavilion of Ministers — the holding point for members of the old regime — motioned to a settee and said, "Have a seat, Alexander Dmitriyevich." "At first sight they looked like the top brass at a gala," a journalist wrote. "The shining shoulder straps and decorations of the generals, and quite a few bald pates. . . . A large office desk was covered with empty glasses." The room was silent, though, for the prisoners were forbidden to speak.

Vladimir Sukhomlinov, the scented and pomaded former war minister who had directed the disastrous campaigns of 1914 and 1915, was brought in later in uniform. He was suspected of treason, and his contempt for machine guns and rapid-firing artillery — he held them to be "unmanly" — helped cause the enormous casualties in the first months of the war. Soldiers threatened to lynch him. "I hastened to protect him with my own body," Kerensky recalled. "I yelled that I would not allow them to kill him and dishonor the revolution. They could only get him over my dead body." The men insisted on having Sukhomlinov's epaulettes. He handed them over himself, taking a penknife from his pocket and slowly cutting them off.

A few doors away in Room 41, Colonel Engelgardt, who knew Sukhomlinov well, was attempting to reimpose garrison discipline through the military commission. Some military normality reigned here. Engelgardt, a racehorse owner and rider — "he took some prizes," Serge Mstislavsky remarked bitchily, "but never in steeplechases" — had turned up to work in his General Staff uniform. Dandyish clerks and two or three coquettish girls, their hair in buns held neatly together with combs, were typing away.

Engelgardt issued a stream of orders to protect the installations he thought important. Guards were to be posted outside the State Bank, the Savings Bank, and the Winter Palace. To Mstislavsky's disdain — how ancien régime could he get? — the colonel also sent men to palaces of the Grand Duke Mikhail Nikolaevich and the Grand Duchess Maria Pavlova. All units were instructed to arrest drunks and people shooting in the air. A squad was given the duty of stopping cars running aimlessly about. Mikhail Rodzianko arranged for the shabby troops on watch in the Catherine Ballroom to be replaced by a guard of smart cadets.

A "clammy horror" overcame Mstislavsky as he watched the mounting evidence that the Duma men's desire for order was outflanking the Soviet's radical spirit. The revolutionaries who had run Room 41 before Engelgardt's arrival on Monday night were being replaced at their desks by "bandbox-fresh little squirts." What it boiled down to, Mstislavsky said, was that the "patent leather boots had taken over." He had no faith in these closet monarchists. He noticed Engelgardt blushing with embarrassment when he was obliged to arrest a naval officer. How would they deal with Ivanov's punitive detachment?

The tensions of *dvoevlastie*, the duality of power between the Duma provisional committee and the Soviet, were already established. Mstislavsky was overpessimistic in feeling that those on his side, who wanted to deepen the revolution and whose instinctive loyalties were to the Soviet and not the

Duma, had lost: the monarchists among the Duma men were equally depressed.

Vasily Shulgin, proudly whiskered and patrician, found Tuesday to be "even more of a nightmare" than Monday. The crowds were shouting "*Svoboda, Svoboda*" — Freedom, Freedom — until he felt sick to his stomach. Everywhere he found "bands of orators, beastly 'hurrahs,' the hateful 'Marseillaise.' " He noted that the people cramming into the Tauride were beginning to greet the Soviet, whose executive committee was working in the next room to that of the Duma committee.

"Yes, one feels there is something with a double head," Shulgin wrote. "But it is not a double-headed eagle." The Soviet was becoming a "second government," filled with emotional people whose every other word was "landowner, tsarist clique, Rasputin, serfs, police." Deputations from institutions, societies, and unions were lobbying frenziedly and the telephones never stopped ringing. There was "no beginning, no ending, no middle" to it all.

Nikolai Sukhanov was little happier in the Soviet executive committee. Its popularity was indeed increasing, but that involved Nikolai Chkheidze as its chairman in having to drag himself away to greet each new delegation that arrived. The tired and sleepy old Georgian would put on his fur coat, give a resigned shrug, and disappear from the meeting. There was no secretary to take minutes, which mattered little since there was "nothing to report beyond 'chaos' and 'emergency reports.' " Every few minutes an emergency erupted, which almost always turned out "not to be worth a barleycorn." The Soviet session itself was so overcrowded that it resembled a "mass meeting in a riding school."

The one way to get things done was to buttonhole Kerensky. Sukhanov was charged with protecting the presses where *Izvestiya* was being published. He went to the Tauride Ballroom, grabbed Kerensky, and held him until he had rounded up a posse of volunteers to go to the printing shop. Only Kerensky, in a swill of would-be leaders, was able to settle matters at a stroke.

Trucks filled with mutineers reached Tsarskoe Selo in the afternoon. Alexandra was busying herself with her sick children. "I kept seeing her beside my bed," the ailing Vyrubova wrote, "now preparing a drink, now smoothing the cushions, now talking to the doctor." In the evening, the local garrison mutinied and threw open the prison. There was a skirmish with a palace patrol in the park. The empress went out into the minus-fifteen-degrees cold to visit the palace defenders with her plucky seventeen-year-old daughter Maria, who was now sickening with measles. Alexandra brought the men into the palace by groups to get warm and have tea. The noise of songs, music, and shots drifted across the park from the town.

Paleologue was convinced that the monarchy was ending. He watched a Romanov turncoat, the ambitious Grand Duke Cyril, leading his marines in his naval captain's uniform to place them at the disposal of the rebels. A delegation arrived in Petrograd from Tsarskoe Selo, Cossacks of the Escort, soldiers of His Majesty's Regiment hand-selected from the best guards units, even police of the imperial palaces who knew the personal, intimate life of their masters. They vowed allegiance to "the new authority, whose very name they did not know, as if they could not embrace the chains of a new servitude too soon." A count muttered of the desertion of the household troops: "They've seen many things they ought not to have seen. They know too much about Rasputin."

The Okhrana was finished. Vladimir Zensinov, like several Social Revolutionaries the disaffected son of a millionaire and an ex-prisoner, visited its headquarters on Kronversky Prospekt with Maxim Gorky. The windows were broken, the doors torn off. Zensinov could only vaguely recognize the office where he had once been interrogated. While Gorky sifted through documents looking for literary inspiration, Zensinov was more concerned to disentangle the "wily network of provocation." He identified several dozen agents provocateurs from the documents. Among them was the prominent Bolshevik M. E. Chernomazov, an editor of *Pravda*.

People climbed the facades of drugstores and shops that supplied the Romanovs, and threw the wooden double-headed eagles and royal monograms onto bonfires below. Walking in the Summer Gardens on the river bank, Paleologue came across one of the famous "Ethiopians." Four of these gigantic men — one was in fact an American black named Jim Hercules — had guarded the doors to the tsar's study and Alexandra's mauve boudoir, dressed in scarlet trousers, curved shoes, and white turbans. The ambassador watched the man shuffling in civilian clothes, tears pouring from his eyes, a symbol that the old and sumptuous ceremonial dating back to Catherine the Great was now finished.

As if in confirmation, a car with a machine gun mounted in the back drew up, its occupants insisting that the ambassador get in. They drove him to the Tauride, where a boisterous student waved a red flag in his face. "Pay your respects to the Russian Revolution!" he said in excellent French. "The Red Flag is Russia's flag now. Do homage to it in the name of France!" Paleologue, acutely aware that the country was still nominally a monarchy, mumbled diplomatically about the events being a "tribute to Russian liberty."

*   *   *

The monarch was aboard the second of two imperial trains, steaming slowly northeast. For security reasons, a first train preceded the suite train by an hour. On their departure from Mogilev early on Tuesday, the suite train and its companion did not head directly north for Tsarskoe Selo. General Ivanov's detachment to the capital was expected to be followed by other trains bringing in his reinforcements from the front. Traffic on the southern approaches to Petrograd would be heavy. It was decided to route the slow imperial trains on a detour, carrying them northeast from Smolensk through Vyazma to join up with the main Petrograd-Moscow at Likhoslavl. From here, they would steam to Tosno, thirty miles short of the capital, and take a branch line to Tsarskoe Selo.

Nicholas slept until 10:00 A.M. and had a late breakfast. As he passed through Smolensk, the soldiers on a troop train greeted him with the usual "Hurrah." In each successive province, the governor turned out at a station to pay his respects. Nicholas sent the empress a telegram from Vyazma at 3:00 P.M., saying that he was sending "many troops from the front" and that the weather was marvellous. The first intimation that the Duma provisional committee had replaced the government in Petrograd came when the train arrived at Likhoslavl at 9:00 P.M. The Duma deputy who had been made responsible for transport, Alexander Bublikov, was using the railway telegraph network to transmit appeals by the committee. It was feared that Bublikov had ordered railway workers to reroute the trains to go straight on from Tosno to Petrograd instead of branching off to Tsarskoe Selo.

There was some discussion about altering course at the Bologoye junction, and steaming east to Pskov where the headquarters of the northern front would offer the tsar protection. No decision was reached and the trains passed through Bologoye at midnight. At 2:30 A.M. the suite train crossed the two-hundred-foot-deep ravine of the Msta river to reach the small station at Malaya Vishera, ninety miles short of Petrograd. The security train had halted here. An officer in a railway regiment, who had fled on a railway trolley, warned that the next station up the line had been seized by mutineers. The tsar was woken and he agreed to backtrack to Bogoloye and head for 220 miles to Pskov. At Malaya Vishera, in the early hours of Wednesday, March 1, Nicholas was finally fleeing from his people.

Alexander Bublikov, following the progress of the ghostly train over the telegraph network from the transport ministry, was asked to stop it at Bogoloye; Mikhail Rodzianko wished to meet the tsar for discussions there in his capacity as Duma chairman. Instructions were telegraphed to railway workers but the trains slipped through the junction at 9:00 A.M. on Wednesday. Bublikov now wanted the trains stopped at Dno, the last major station before Pskov. The trains passed along the southern shore of Lake Valdai, in rolling country with three wooded islands, on one of which lay the Iverski convent, a popular place of pilgrimage. It was a leisurely journey. At Staraya Russa, a spa town with salt baths, a large crowd, including nuns from a local convent, hurried to the station to catch sight of the tsar. "Many took their hats off and bowed," said a member of the suite. "They were expressing their pleasure at seeing the emperor, if only through the window. Perfect order prevailed everywhere."

Rodzianko was unable to keep his rendezvous at Dno. Conditions in the Duma were chaotic on Wednesday morning, March 1. The committee had moved to two small rooms facing the library at the end of the Catherine Ballroom. Kerensky burst in, followed by two armed soldiers and a man holding a bundle. Interrupting a report by Vasily Shulgin, Kerensky hurled the package on a table.

"Our secret treaties with the Allies. . . . Hide them," Kerensky ordered and disappeared as dramatically as he had entered. What should be done with these pieces of paper, which contained the detailed aims for which Russia was fighting the war? There was no cupboard in the room. "Throw them under the table," someone said. "Nobody is going to see them there. Look." They were kicked under it. A little later, Kerensky reappeared with another bundle. "Here are two million rubles . . . brought from some ministry," he said. "This can't go on. We have to appoint commissars."

Rodzianko was equally convinced that a formal government had to be named. For this to be constitutional, the position of the tsar had to be resolved. Rodzianko was in touch with General Alexeev, the commander in chief in Mogilev, warning him that the Soviet was sitting alongside the Duma committee and threatening to undermine its authority. Exceptional steps would have to be taken. A responsible ministry might have done the trick on Tuesday, Rodzianko said, but by now it was clear that only an abdication would save the dynasty.

The Duma chairman planned to meet Nicholas to urge him to accept a constitutional monarchy on British lines, and to stand down in favor of his son. A special train was standing by to take him, but Rodzianko's relations with the Soviet were deteriorating fast. He had gone to the Soviet to greet a delegation of sailors and returned to the Duma offices near speechless with rage about "*them* . . . how do you call them? . . . those sons-of-a-dog deputies from the Soviet committee . . . you know, that *riffraff*." He used *sobachie deputaty*, "dog deputies," as a biting pun on *rabochie deputaty*, "workers' deputies."

Still shaking, Rodzianko explained that he had been cheered when he made a welcoming speech to the sailors about not letting the enemy, "the damned Germans," destroy Mother Russia. But then a member of the Soviet had opened up on him. "The president of the Duma calls on you, comrades, to save the Russian land," the Soviet man sneered. "That is easy to understand. Mr. Rodzianko has something to save. He has a considerable piece of the Russian land, in Ekaterinoslav province. And what land! . . . You see, Rodzianko and the rest of the landowners in the Duma have something else to save — their estates, princedoms, counties, and baronies. They are calling on you, comrades, to save it. Suppose you ask him if he would be as keen on saving the Russian land if it became yours?"

Rodzianko, broad and bearlike, banged the table with such force that the secret treaties beneath it jumped. "The scoundrels!" he roared. "We offer up the lives of our sons, and that riffraff thinks we begrudge our land. Damn the land! What good is it to me if Russia perishes? Dirty *scum*! Take my shirt but save Russia. That's what I told them."

"They," the Soviet, were equally irritated with the Duma territory in the Tauride. Sukhanov felt it to be altogether too seemly. Hall porters in full livery, solemn young officers, and "men in morning-coats, beaver collars, and handsome liberal faces" were darting about. The Soviet executive committee suspected that Rodzianko was plotting a promonarchist coup. When the committee got wind of his proposed trip to meet the tsar, it used its influence with the railwaymen to block his train from leaving.

Kerensky burst into the committee room. "How could you?" he asked in a broken whisper. "You won't provide a train! Rodzianko was supposed to go to make Nicholas abdicate and you've ruined everything. . . . You've played into the hands of the Romanovs. It'll be your responsibility!" At that, exhausted by three nights of catnapping, Kerensky fell half-swooning into a chair. His collar was loosened and water was sprinkled on his face. The sight sickened Sukhanov. It was bad enough that Kerensky had been weakened to "banal hysteria." Worse, he was appearing on the left wing as the "direct if unwilling mouthpiece" of the Rodziankos on the right.

The Soviet committee was more impressed by Kerensky's histrionics, and reluctantly voted to give Rodzianko his train. Its permission, however, was hedged with conditions. The committee insisted that Nikolai Chkheidze and a battalion of revolutionary soldiers should accompany the Duma chairman. "Imagine what they would have done," Rodzianko exploded. "With that cattle . . ." The stationmaster at the Warsaw Station at the end of the Izmailovsky Prospekt telephoned throughout the afternoon to see if the waiting special was needed. It was not, Rodzianko staying put.

The ambivalence at the core of the revolution was disturbing. Zinaïda Gippius found the Soviet to have the "will to action and power, and this is set over against the tender lack of authority of the Duma deputies. . . . There will be more fighting — Lord! Save Russia!" Maxim Gorky, dining with Nikolai Sukhanov after his excursion to the Okhrana headquarters, gloomily predicted that it would all end up in "Asiatic savagery."

Nicholas, who had spent the afternoon on the train discussing constitutional concessions with his suite, reached Dno at 6:00 P.M. General Ivanov's train had passed through the junction early that morning. Ivanov found it full of drunken soldiers who had arrived from Petrograd in trains with smashed windows. He had restored order — remembering the old days in Kronstadt, and armed only with his enormous spade beard, he had successfully bellowed "On your knees!" to a mutineer who was making for him with a saber — and the town was calm by the early evening. The railwaymen at Dno confirmed with Petrograd that, although the special train was still in the Warsaw Station with its boiler fired, there was no sign of Rodzianko. The tsar telegraphed Rodzianko that he was moving on to Pskov and would receive him there.

Shortly after 7:00 P.M. on March 1, thirty-eight hours after his meandering journey had started from Mogilev, the tsar arrived in the "safe haven" of Pskov. Only the governor and a few officials were on the platform. There was no guard of honor. The tough commander of the northern front, General Nikolai Ruzsky, arrived late in a somber mood and wearing galoshes.

VIII
No Tsar in Russia

DNO WAS NIKOLAI IVANOV'S ONLY ACHIEVEMENT. After Dno, the general steamed on slowly north, attaching a second engine to the back in case he was forced to retreat. When he arrived in Tsarskoe Selo shortly before midnight on Wednesday, none of the promised reinforcements from the northern and western fronts were waiting for him; troopers of the Fifteenth Cavalry Division had found their trains held up by railwaymen acting on Bublikov's orders. "They mysteriously double-checked everything and said they could not help in any way," the commanding officer complained.

Armored cars manned by mutineers were roaming the streets of the town. The palace police had gone over to the revolution and the tsar's railway regiment had murdered two of its officers. Ivanov had a short audience with the empress. She thought that the revolution could still be checked with a show of authority. Ivanov, the illegitimate son of a Siberian convict and a man who had made his career on blunt force of character, could not understand her "mystic optimism." He realized that his men would be annihilated if he continued his mission.

To his relief, Ivanov escaped the dilemma. The tsar dined with Nikolai Ruzsky in Pskov on Wednesday evening. The news was grimmer than ever; the commander of the Moscow military district, General Mrozovsky, reported that "total revolution" had gripped the city and that the garrison was siding with the people. Sailors at Kronstadt had mutinied.

Nicholas was particularly shocked by the desertion of his personal guard in Tsarskoe Selo. He asked Ruzsky to contact Rodzianko on the Hughes wire in Petrograd. Ruzsky was to offer him a government acceptable to the Duma under a premier, presumably Rodzianko himself, who would have full authority over internal affairs. Nicholas still wanted to maintain personal influence over foreign and defense affairs. Hopeful that a constitutional settlement would be reached, the tsar cabled Ivanov at twenty minutes past midnight: "I request you to take no measures whatever before my arrival." With that, he went to bed.

Ivanov, the would-be dictator of Petrograd, thankfully quit Tsarskoe Selo and steamed at full speed back along the line to Vyritsa. As it had escaped Kutepov's internal counterforce, so Red Peter was now safe from external loyalists.

Ruzsky spoke with Rodzianko over the laborious Hughes wire for almost four hours from about 2:30 A.M. on Thursday morning, March 2. A special link connected Pskov to the Duma president in the Tauride. Rodzianko was surrounded by a throng of deputies, shouting advice and instructions. Ruzsky told him the tsar's suggestion. "It is obvious that neither His Majesty nor you realize what is going on here," Rodzianko replied. "Anarchy grew to such an extent that the Duma, and myself in particular, had no alternative but to take the movement into our own hands and to head it."

He was, however, far from thinking that he had succeeded. Rodzianko warned Ruzsky that loathing of the empress had reached the "utmost limits" and that he had been forced to put the ministers in the Peter and Paul Fortress for their own protection. "I am afraid that the same fate awaits me, because everything that is moderate is hated," he confessed. "I am hanging by a thread myself, power is slipping from my hands. What you propose is not enough. . . . The dynastic question must be decided immediately."

Rodzianko read his own position clearly enough. The Soviet was still attempting to steal a march on the Duma committee. A few hours earlier, it had produced its "Order Number One," which, among other things, instructed all soldiers only to obey commands issued by the Soviet. It had been set in train, according to Rodzianko, by an unidentified soldier who saw Colonel Engelgardt in the military commission office during the evening and demanded that an order should be written out to set relations between officers and men on a new basis. Engelgardt told him sharply that this was inadmissible. "Very well," the soldier said. "If you don't want to, then we can dispense with you."

A little later, Sukhanov said that he looked into Room 13 at the Tauride, where the Soviet executive committee had been meeting. He saw the Social Revolutionary Nikolai Sokolov sitting at a writing table, his straggling beard spread out over his waistcoat, his lawyer's frock-coat creased, surrounded by soldiers. They were leaning over him to suggest things that he was writing down. Sukhanov was reminded of how Tolstoy had taken down the stories told him by children at the village school on his estate. Everyone was "talking, completely wrapped up in their work. . . . When they had finished their work, they put at the top of the page the heading: Order Number One."

The document was too measured to have been drawn up in such a haphazard way, although Sukhanov's scene was taken at face value in revolutionary folklore. Some soldiers may have looked curiously over Sokolov's shoulder as he wrote it down, but it was drawn up by socialist civilians anxious to establish Soviet control over the garrison. The Order reflected the rumors current among soldiers on Wednesday that some officers were disarming their regiments. Engelgardt's declaration that the military commission would send any such officer to the firing squad did not calm them, any more than the renaming of the Soviet of Workers' Deputies to include "and Soldiers' Deputies." Order Number One was designed to ensure that neither officers nor the Duma would be able to turn the garrison troops against the Soviet.

The order instructed all garrison units to elect committees among the lower ranks and to send one delegate per company to the Soviet. The political activity of all units was to be subordinate to the Soviet; no orders of the Duma committee were to be obeyed if they clashed with Soviet orders. All kinds of arms — "rifles, machine guns, armored automobiles, and others" — were to be controlled by the soldier committees. Military discipline would be observed on duty, but soldiers were otherwise free to enjoy full civil rights. Off-duty saluting was abolished. Rudeness toward soldiers, and "especially calling them 'ty' " — "thou" — would not be tolerated.

"It was," Shulgin thought, "the end of the army." It enraged Rodzianko. "Who wrote this?" he bellowed. "Of course, *they*, the scoundrels. It has been done purposely to help the Germans. . . . Traitors." It did, however, spur the Duma men to name a formal Provisional Government.

Amid deputations, speeches, telephone calls, and the "growing insolence of the Soviet executive committee," Pavel Miliukov squatted on the corner of a table and wrote down the list of ministers. Miliukov was to be foreign minister, Kerensky justice minister, and Alexander Guchkov minister of war. Though Miliukov and Guchkov were hostile to the revolution, both were leaders of political parties, respectively the Cadets and Octobrists. Like Kerensky, they had political experience.

That was far from true of two other key posts. Mikhail Tereshchenko, a young Moscow sugar king with a fortune put at eighty million rubles, inherited the inflation crisis as the new finance minister. At thirty-two lively and charming, an aesthete who had commissioned ballet scenarios from

Alexander Blok, Tereshchenko was "very dashing and talkative" but a "political parvenu" with no administrative experience. The Soviet refused to join the government, but it was able to block the appointment of Rodzianko as premier. Prince Georgy Lvov was named in his place, a comfortably off landlord and a liberal but almost heroically inactive. On seeing Niagara Falls, he had said, "A river flows and drops. That's all." Lvov viewed the revolution with the same sluggish nonchalance.

Rodzianko's influence, as he had predicted, was waning. While he continued to talk to Ruzsky, Miliukov was patiently negotiating with four exhausted members of the Soviet committee. They were slumped in armchairs, Sukhanov's head "swimming and tormented with hunger" as Miliukov carefully wrote out an agreed statement in pencil. A Constituent Assembly was to be elected by universal, direct, equal, and secret suffrage. The assembly would settle a permanent form of government to take over in due course from the Provisional Government. All nationalities of the empire were to be equal and soldiers were to enjoy civil rights. The Petrograd garrison was to be allowed to remain in the capital. None of its units would be sent to the front.

Ruzsky meanwhile pressed Rodzianko over the Hughes wire from Pskov for details on what was proposed for the dynasty. "The empress has taken on a heavy responsibility before God in turning the emperor's heart away from his people," Rodzianko replied. "The threatening demands for an abdication in favor of the son, with Mikhail Alexandrovich as regent, are becoming quite definite." Dawn was already breaking when the two men finished their telegraph conversation and Ruzsky took a nap.

New emissaries, unknown to Ruzsky, were planning to come to Pskov. Alexander Guchkov burst into the Duma committee room at 4:00 A.M. on Thursday. A rich young landowner, Prince Dmitri Vyazemsky, had just been shot dead next to him in an automobile, apparently for no better reason than that he was wearing an officer's uniform. "Similar acts take place elsewhere," Guchkov said. "There are officers hiding in the Duma. They pray to us to save them. We must do something. . . . We must above all save the monarchy. Russia cannot be without it." He spoke of the danger of the "riffraff" settling the question of the monarchy in its own way.

"We must put a fait accompli in front of them," Guchkov went on. "We must act quickly and secretly and give Russia a new emperor and rally round him." Vasily Shulgin agreed to go with him to Pskov to persuade Nicholas to step down. At 5:00 A.M., they got into Guchkov's bloodstained automobile and drove to his house where, completely exhausted, they scribbled out a draft act of abdication. As Ruzsky dropped off to sleep in Pskov, Shulgin and Guchkov drove on through the dawn streets to the Warsaw

Station, finding to their relief that "the revolutionary people were still asleep." No one stopped the stationmaster from making up their train, a locomotive and one carriage, for the journey to Pskov.

The telegraph tape of Ruzsky's conversation was meanwhile being re-transmitted to the Stavka in Mogilev. Alexeev, feverish from flu, summarized it and dispatched it to the commanders of all fronts at 10:15 A.M. Alexeev added his own comment. He said that there was no alternative to an abdication; the army and the railways "are actually dependent on the Petrograd Provisional Government"; an abdication decision would spare the army the temptation to take part in a coup d'etat, which "will be less painful if effected from above."

Ruzsky woke and returned to the imperial train in the southern outskirts of Pskov. He gave the tsar the record of his conversation with Rodzianko. Nicholas read it and a copy of Alexeev's cable to the commanders in the field. He spoke quietly of abdication, recalling that he had been born on the name-day of suffering Job. He walked with Ruzsky on the station platform and took lunch.

In Petrograd, Kerensky was justifying his acceptance of the justice portfolio to the Soviet. He was as white as a sheet, so agitated Arthur Ransome thought he was about to burst a blood vessel in his brain. "Comrades, do you trust me?" Kerensky started. "I speak, comrades, with all my soul — if you don't trust me — here and now — before your eyes — I am ready to die." He explained that he had been offered the justice ministry in the early hours, with no time to ask the Soviet's approval. But his first act had been to order all exiles to be returned from Siberia with special honors. He knew that the Soviet was not joining the Provisional Government. "If you want me to resign — I will," he said. "I will remain if the Soviet wills it."

"We do! We do!" the delegates shouted, urging him to remain on the Soviet committee. As Kerensky went off, surrounded by admirers, he paused to speak to some British officers. "Look at that now," thought Sukhanov, spitefully watching the new minister. "Time enough now to pay attention to our gallant allies." There were further unpleasantnesses when Miliukov read out his ministerial list to the Soviet. A roar of laughter greeted the naming of the millionaire Tereshchenko as finance minister. Guchkov's appointment was hissed. "Prince Lvov — that's another joke on us," a soldier said when the new premier was announced. " 'Tsar' has something about it and 'emperor' is even better. But 'prince,' that just isn't the same thing."

To insistent shouts about the dynasty, Miliukov replied that the "old despot who has brought the country to utter ruin" would abdicate or be deposed in favor of his son. "We conceive of the State as a parliamentary and constitutional monarchy," said Miliukov. "If we quarrel about this instead of deciding at once, then Russia will be in civil war." The booing only changed to cheers when he went on to promise that the Constituent Assembly would be elected as soon as order was restored.

Serge Mstislavsky felt a familiar aversion sweep over him. He thought the Soviet executive committee was frightened of the bourgeoisie and the Cadets and Octobrists. The Soviet saw the *burzhui* groups as "masters of the art of government, technicians who possessed the secret of the governing mechanism" that eluded mere socialists. Mstislavsky was sure that the bourgeoisie had no fear of taking power — they were "longingly waving their tentacles" around it — but they were frightened of the masses. The socialists were the lightning conductor the bourgeois parties needed for the mob. In order to survive, both sides had to stick together — "for the moment," Mstislavsky added.

The only unanimity to be displayed in the Tauride on Thursday came when a Menshevik deputy waved a copy of the newspaper *Russkoe Selo* in his hand. Amid a hurricane of applause, he announced that a revolution had broken out in Germany and that the kaiser was deposed. The "indescribable excitement" that this caused was premature by almost two years. *Russkoe Selo*, like many of the new newspapers being founded — four that day in Petrograd — was already running illusion in place of fact.

Replies from the commanders were forwarded from Mogilev to the Imperial train in Pskov station at 2:00 P.M. They were regretful, but all the commanders agreed that the tsar must abdicate. Admiral Nepenin, who would be murdered by his men within forty-eight hours, was urgent: "It is only with the greatest difficulty that I keep the troops and fleet under my command in check." Nicholas got up, walked to the window of the carriage, turned, and made the sign of the cross. "I have decided," he said. "I will give up the throne in favor of my son." The generals crossed themselves.

The tsar thanked them for their loyal service, which he hoped "will continue under my son." He went to his private compartment and wrote out two short telegrams of abdication, one addressed to Rodzianko as chairman of the Duma and the other to Alexeev. They were timed at 3:00 P.M. Then Nicholas took his afternoon walk between the two imperial trains. General Dmitri Dubensky, attached to the tsar as official war historian, caught his eye as he passed his window. Nicholas smiled and waved a hand. "He was such a fatalist," Dubensky wrote. "I can't even imagine it."

An attempt was made to withdraw the telegram by shocked members of the tsar's personal staff. "How is it possible to give up the throne just as if one was handing over the command of a cavalry squadron to another officer?" a general asked. The staff blamed Ruzsky for pressuring the tsar. Ruzsky agreed to hold the telegram to Alexeev until Shulgin and Guchkov arrived; they were due at 7:00 P.M. It appeared that the copy to Rodzianko had already been sent.

During the late afternoon, Nicholas had a heart-to-heart talk with Dr. Serge Fedorov, his personal physician. He assumed that he would be able to retire with his family to the Crimea, where he would devote himself to educating his son. The doctor said that it seemed politically impossible for a man who had abdicated to bring up the new monarch. The tsar was startled. He raised the matter of the tsarevich's health. Rasputin had predicted that if young Alexis survived to seventeen, he would be healthy thereafter. "Is that right? Can he become healthy?" Fedorov told him gently that only a miracle could cure hemophilia in the present state of medicine. "It is incurable," he said. "He may live to old age or he may die from the simplest accident. He will need constant treatment and care."

"Then I cannot be separated from Alexei," he said. "It is beyond my strength." He began to cry. Then he took afternoon tea.

The train carrying the Duma monarchists was two hours late on its journey across the featureless and snowy plains. "We traveled like the doomed," said Vasily Shulgin. But he consoled himself that "the resignation must be in the monarchists' hands to save the monarchy. . . . If the abdication took place there would be no revolution. The sovereign would willingly step down, power would pass to a regency which would appoint a new government. In a juridical sense, there would be no revolution." As the train slid into Pskov station at 10:00 P.M., a thought bothered him: "It was awkward for me to appear before the tsar unshaven, in a crumpled collar and jacket." Shulgin's thin, curly blond hair and "his stiff, starched, ridiculously high collar" were a caricaturist's dream.

Blue lanterns lit the platform. The two Duma men went across the tracks to the suite train and were shown into the drawing room car, hung with green silk. The tsar was wearing a simple gray uniform. He shook hands in a friendly way and waved them to a seat. Guchkov launched into a long explanation of why the abdication was necessary. "Literally no one tried to block us, literally no one supported the tsar," Guchkov wrote, the old plotter now feeling pity for his prey. "Total emptiness surrounded the throne." The tsar listened impassively. The only thing that Guchkov could read on his face was that the length of his speech was unnecessary.

"Until three this afternoon, I was thinking of abdicating in favor of my son," Nicholas replied. "Now I have reconsidered. Because of his illness, I must abdicate at the same time both for my son and for myself, in favor of my brother Mikhail. I trust you understand a father's feelings." This was unconstitutional. Nicholas had no legal right to renounce the throne on his son's behalf. The boy had not been consulted — he was sick with measles in Tsarskoe Selo — and he was a minor. "How could we have disagreed?" Shulgin observed. "We had arrived to tell the tsar the Duma committee's opinion. . . . Whether Alexei or Mikhail would be tsar was, in the last analysis, a mere detail."

The tsar went to his private car and returned with the act of abdication. A phrase was added to it stating that the new emperor would govern in "full and inviolable union" with the people's representatives. A fresh copy was typed out. Nicholas signed it in pencil. It was "as if he were so indifferent to it all, as others are when they scribble notes in pencil to a friend or make a list of dirty laundry."

It was over. Nicholas asked who should become the new premier. Shulgin and Guchkov named Prince Georgy Lvov. "Very well . . . Lvov," Nicholas replied. The document was dated 3:00 P.M. on Thursday, March 2, although it was now almost midnight. The Duma men did not want it said that they had pressured the tsar — the empress had written to her "holy sufferer" earlier that day, though he never received the letter, to say that "they" would want him to sign "some kind of paper, a constitution or something of that nature" but that he was not obliged to honor anything extorted under duress.

Varnish was coated over his signature. At 1:00 A.M. on Friday, March 3, the ex-tsar's train steamed for Mogilev. "I leave Pskov with heavy heart," he wrote in his diary, before falling into a long and deep sleep. "I am surrounded by treason and cowardice and fraud." Dmitri Dubensky, with a military historian's bluntness, wrote in his diary, "A weak, indecisive but good and clean man, he was destroyed by the empress and her senseless attraction to Gregory [Rasputin]. Russia could not forgive this."

The dynasty had only the briefest postscript. On their return to Petrograd to proclaim the new tsar on Friday morning, Shulgin and Guchkov were caught up in a rally of railway workers at the station. The men were angry at the list of Provisional Government ministers. "Prince Lvov . . . prince!" a speaker said. "Who is our new finance minister? Maybe someone who knows first-hand how the poor live? No, our new finance minister is Mr. Tereshchenko who owns ten sugar mills, and a quarter of a million acres of land."

Another railwayman turned on the delegates. "They've arrived back from Pskov," he yelled. "Who knows what they've brought back with them? Maybe they've brought what the revolution doesn't need. On whose behalf did they go? The Soviet? No, the Duma. And who belongs to the Duma? Rich landowners." Shulgin thought it best not to mention Tsar Mikhail. "Maybe the decisions taken will please everyone," he said. "In any event, Alexander Ivanovich and I must leave at once." They scuttled off.

Mikhail had little advance warning that he was to become tsar. Indeed, the day before the Soviet had denied him the use of a private train from Tsarskoe Selo, Sukhanov saying that "Citizen Romanov can go to the railway station, buy a ticket, and wait for a public train like anyone else." Mikhail received a cable from Nicholas telling him of his elevation at 11:00 A.M. Alexei Bobrinskoy saw him driving along the Nevsky in a black limousine. As the grand duke returned his salute, Bobrinskoy had a glimpse of "large gray eyes tense with anxiety, in a face of extraordinary pallor." The cry of "No more Romanovs!" was being taken up in the Soviet and the streets.

Wisely, the new tsar tucked himself away in the apartment of his friend Prince Putyatin on the Millionnaya a few hundred yards from the Winter Palace. There, a pale, youngish man in an armchair whom Shulgin thought was the "very picture of fragility," Mikhail received a deputation from the Provisional Government. Only Pavel Miliukov, his face "purple from sleepless nights" and his voice raw from speeches, croaked out a last appeal for the monarchy: "If you refuse, anarchy will set in . . . chaos, bloody confusion . . . Russia will lose the symbol that holds it together."

Miliukov still hoped that the monarchy could be salvaged. The revolution might be bought off by the abdication of Nicholas, leaving his brother Mikhail on a less autocratic but still intact throne. A second abdication, within a few hours of the first, would ruin this chance. There was no realistic alternative to Mikhail. If he went, Russia would, at a time of external war and internal mutiny, be without its royal symbol for the first time since Ivan the Terrible had been crowned Tsar of All Russia in 1547. Kerensky, almost beside himself with fury, begged Mikhail to abdicate. "I implore you in the name of Russia to make this sacrifice," he said, adding: "I cannot vouch for your safety, Your Excellency."

Mikhail asked for a moment or two to think things over. "Promise us not to consult your wife!" urged Kerensky, for she dominated her husband and, a divorcée, was thrilled at the prospect of becoming consort to an emperor. Mikhail assured him that she was at home. He returned and said, "I have decided to abdicate." Kerensky was overjoyed: "Sire, you are the noblest of men!" Miliukov was worried that the second abdication would make the new government appear to be the creature of the riots of February 27, rather than the legitimate result of the document signed the evening before in Pskov. It was, Miliukov said, the "worst of beginnings," but the revolution had left the main participants too physically exhausted to bother much with legal niceties.

A proclamation was drafted at a school desk in the study of Prince Putyatin's daughter. It was written in a school notebook and the hours-old tsar signed it, and then sat down to lunch with the Putyatin family and Vasily Shulgin. The Romanov dynasty was at an end. That afternoon, an extra edition of *Izvestiya* came out with banner headlines: "Abdication from the throne. . . . The sovereign Nicholas II has abdicated in favor of Mikhail Alexandrovich, who in turn has abdicated to the people. Grandiose rallies and ovations take place in the Duma. Rapture defies description."

Alexandra had heard nothing from Nicholas for two days. Grand Duke Pavel, his uncle, called on her at Tsarkoe Selo later in the afternoon with a copy of *Izvestiya* in his pocket. He read it to her. "It isn't true!" she burst out. "It's another newspaper lie! I believe in God and trust the army. Neither can have deserted us at such a moment." Seeming, Grand Duke Pavel thought, to "realize all that she, Grishka Rasputin, and Protopopov had done to the country and the monarchy," she burst into tears.

The soldiers milling on the streets of Petrograd were pleased but puzzled. "What we want is a republic," Meriel Buchanan heard one say. "Yes," his companion replied. "A republic — but we must have a good tsar at the head of it."

At Zinaïda Shakovsky's school for young noblewomen, a senior pupil read out the morning prayer on Saturday. For the first time in three centuries, the prayer for the tsar and his family was omitted. The girl stumbled over her words and was unable to pronounce properly the phrase "Let us pray for the Provisional Government." She started to cry. The teachers and mistresses took out their handkerchiefs and "soon about four or five hundred of us were sobbing over something that was lost forever."

It was gloomy and dark outside, impossible to see more than twenty paces in the thick snow. Zinaïda's mother came to take her away from the capital. There were few carriages about, and only a handful of "gloomy civilians scurrying along." The sledge driver kept saying, "Let's hurry, let's hurry before the shooting, God forbid, the shooting starts again."

IX
Exiles

FOREIGNERS KNEW of the revolution at once, the Americans hailing it as a "fitting and glorious successor" to their own. Ambassador Francis cabled the State Department on March 5, praising the "most amazing revolution in history" and urging U.S. recognition of the Provisional Government as the realization of an American dream — "I mean government by the consent of the governed." Francis thought that American recognition "will have a stupefying effect, especially if given first."

The French and British were as enthusiastic, for the promised democracy removed the stain of alliance with an autocracy. Russian shares were up. The London *Financial Times* told its business readers that it was one of the most important events in world history. Its report was headlined "Dawn of a New Era," with a story on "How British Traders May Profit." Russian stocks climbed on the London market.

The big cities accepted the abdication joyously and with few incidents. In Moscow, a crowd of demonstrators had run into a formation of troops. Everything, Bruce Lockhart recalled, had "stilled as a cat freezes, swaying imperceptibly from side to side, flanks trembling as it collects strength to leap and kill. . . . Suddenly both crowds flung themselves forward — *on*, and not *at*, each other." He remarked on the warmth and friendliness of the surging mob that then took the city unopposed. The British consul was the first foreigner into the town hall, where he found "hot, greasy, and officious" soldiers, raucous students, and gray-haired revolutionaries who had come out of their "mouseholes" to celebrate their triumph with "trembling knees and a strange light in their eyes."

The dead were mainly restricted to the 1,224 people listed as killed and wounded in Petrograd, and to officers and petty officers murdered in the Baltic Fleet. Towns along the railway tracks had been kept aware of events by the energetic use of the railway telegraph network by Alexander Bublikov at the transport ministry. Five percent of the Petrograd garrison were given special leave to inform their home villages, but many Russians did not hear the news for weeks.

Alexis Babine, an education inspector making a long tour of country schools by sled, was at a relay station for fresh horses in Vologda province on March 19 when an excited man with a Polish accent burst in and said that Nicholas had abdicated. Babine, a monarchist, did not believe it. He traveled on — "sleeping in my sleigh at night, snug in my fur coat, my dog robe, and a big dog fur blanket, with my faithful spaniel buried at my feet" — until he reached a town, Totma, on March 27. Here he had incontrovertible proof of revolution. Agitators were holding meetings in the school, which previously they "would never have dreamed of doing without my permission."

A sled ride was also necessary for Boris Pasternak, a young poet. Pasternak was at a remote chemicals plant in the Urals, where he was responsible for deferring workers from military service. He muffled himself in three sheepskins and bounced in a troika sleigh through a night and a day for a hundred miles to the nearest railhead. When he got to Moscow, Pasternak wrote only half a sentence — "Just fancy! When a sea of blood and mud starts secreting light . . ." He was unsure what the revolution meant.

Early spring thaws elsewhere brought liquid mud and *bezdorozhie* — "roadlessness" — cutting communications with remote villages. Areas round Pskov were unaware that Nicholas had abdicated in the provincial capital until the end of March. A textile salesman struggled through mud that came over the top of his boots to a small Ukrainian town, Bershad. Nadezhda Ulanovskaya was in her father's shop when the man said casually, "Did you know there's been a revolution? The tsar has abdicated." She thought it was a provocation. "Rubbish," she said. "That's not how it works. Revolution means barricades and shootings."

Nothing had happened in Bershad for centuries. The only important event Ulanovskaya could remember was the bankruptcy of the family who had once owned the town. Only when the newspapers arrived at the end of the month did the festivities start. Ulanovskaya heard the Zionist anthem *Hativka* for the first time as Russians, Ukrainians, and Jews celebrated together.

Officials in the province of Kazan refused to have any truck with the Provisional Government until well into April. The "whole phalanx of the old power," a Duma report said, from rural police inspectors to petty gendarmes, remained at their posts. Petrograd was urged to withdraw stamps and coins with the tsar's head on them because they were being used as evidence that Nicholas still reigned. Though the Holy Synod abolished the standard prayer for the sovereign, parishioners in Archangel were interceding with the Almighty on his behalf in late April.

Villagers singing the "Marseillaise" and carrying red flags congratulated Felix Yusupov, exiled to his estate in the Crimea, on his part in the revolution. He found life "peaceful enough," although he was running short of funds and returned to Petrograd to pick up a couple of Rembrandts. *Man in a Large Hat* and *Woman with Fan* had more solid value than inflated rubles and, rolled up, were almost as easy to carry.

A thousand miles away, in Kazan, there was less goodwill toward landowners. *Muzhiks* seized *pomeshchik* estates and beat up officials who were requisitioning hay and grain. The agent on an estate belonging to Zinaïda Shakovsky's family near Tula reported that peasants came in force as soon as the revolution was confirmed. They broke the seals on the vodka stores, impounded in the estate distillery since 1914. "They went for the liquor," the agent wrote to Prince Shakovsky. "Some of them drowned in the huge containers but the rest went on with their drinking spree, and upon leaving said they would come back and burn everything." Taking them at their word, the agent fled.

The news was heard most eagerly by the political exiles in the vast Siberian territories arcing round Irkutsk, the main Siberian city, from which gold miners, engineers, fur traders, and the exiles fanned out into the wilderness. Irkutsk reminded the American Basset Digby of San Francisco in 1849, a "gilded Gomorrah" where "peroxide blondes in tight blue knickerbockers" went through double shuffles "with an incompetence that would leave a Bowery amateur night audience dumb with scorn."

The geographic extent of internal exile was colossal. Some politicals held on the lower reaches of the Yenisey and Lena rivers were more than seven hundred miles from the nearest railhead. The number of exiles was not on the same scale. Revolutionary movements had been quiescent and submissive since the start of the war. After an initial roundup in late 1914, there had been few fresh exiles. Low-level agitators in factories were more easily dealt with by enforced conscription.

Escape, commonplace before the war, was rare since it was now punishable under martial law. Debates between the politicals, for which they had once traveled hundreds of miles by reindeer sleds and riverboats, had dwindled as they lost interest in an outside world dominated by war. Joseph Stalin, a thirty-seven-year-old Bolshevik veteran, found himself overcome by a "silly longing" for picture postcards showing any landscape but the Arctic flatness that surrounded him. If he had any political thoughts, he no longer bothered to write them down. The lethargic exiles were so unimpressive a danger that the authorities had begun to call them up for army duty. When the revolution broke out, Stalin had been taken from the wilderness of the Yenisey by reindeer and dog sled to the railhead town of Achinsk. He had just failed his army medical, due to a childhood stiffening of the left arm.

News reached Irkutsk on Thursday, March 2. The town blossomed with red flags and songs. Most householders had revolvers — Basset Digby complained that it was difficult to sleep because of their habit of firing them out of the window before they went to bed to frighten off burglars — and there were volleys of shots. Messengers were sent to distant settlements with Alexander Kerensky's order made that day for the release of all those convicted of political and religious crimes. The new justice minister said that he was holding the Irkutsk governor-general personally responsible for ensuring their immediate "honorable return to Petrograd." One exile, V. V. Voitinsky, had to plead with a police officer to let him stay on for a few days since he was ill with flu.

The shock of events was too much for some. Telegrams announcing the revolution were read out in the town theater at Minusinsk, southwest of Irkutsk. Many of the politicals became hysterical when they went on stage to speak. N. R. Shagov, a Bolshevik deputy in the Duma exiled shortly after the start of the war, walked all night from house to house, screaming, "How can you sleep? How can anyone sleep now that the revolution is here?"

It was a three-hundred-mile journey, skirting the banks of the Yenisey, to the nearest trans-Siberian station at Achinsk. Peasants greeted the exiles with traditional gifts of bread and salt. The politicals replied with speeches about the meaning of the revolution, which baffled their simple hosts; some of the peasants seemed to think that *Revolutsiya* was a person, successor to the tsar. The roads were bad, with the snow melting under a weak spring sun, but the villagers were eager to lend the exiles horses. "The entire way was a triumph for us," wrote S. Samoilov, a former Bolshevik deputy, "were it not for Shagov, who gave evidence of progressive mental illness."

The train at Achinsk was full of other exiles from farther east. It was met at most stations by crowds and soldiers playing the "Marseillaise." The trip turned sour. "Many of us lost our voices from uninterrupted speaking, fell ill, and no longer left the carriages," Samoilov reported. "Even inside the train people would not leave us in peace. When they learned we would not come out, they burst in with flowers and asked us about our health."

When the train at last reached Petrograd, Shagov collapsed. Speaking in Moscow on March 7, Kerensky said that his first task was to look after the mental and physical health of the returning exiles. Donations flowed into a special fund. A consortium of Petrograd banks made an immediate donation of half a million rubles for the welfare of the ex-terrorists, many of whom were committed to overthrowing the banking system. The pianist and composer Serge Rachmaninov donated his thousand-ruble fee for a recital in Moscow to the politicals.

The early arrivals were triumphal. Yekaterina Breshko-Breshkovskaya was known as "Babushka," the seventy-three-year-old grandmother of the revolution. The daughter of serf-owning landowners, she became the first woman to be sentenced to hard labor in Siberia for terrorism in 1874. The American journalist George Kennan visited her in 1885, making an international scandal of her suffering. Released, she made a spectacular coast-to-coast tour of the United States, fund-raising for the Social Revolutionaries. She was rearrested after the 1905 revolution and sent into perpetual exile. Kerensky had met her in Siberia, and they had close and affectionate ties. Two years before, she had fled for six hundred miles from exile north on the Lena river before being picked up on the outskirts of Irkutsk.

Breshko-Breshkovskaya took one of the flag-bedecked "revolution specials" on the trans-Siberian to Moscow. Crowds carefully carried her from the platform and escorted her through the streets in a gilt-and-white imperial coach. Her impression of the journey was different from Samoilov's: she had noticed only "the groan of the people at every junction for books and teachers." At Petrograd, Babushka was welcomed in the tsar's waiting room at the Nikolaevsky Station with flowers inscribed to "Dear Grandmother" and "Our Heroine."

In this honeymoon period, the writer Alexander Blok found an "extraordinary feeling that nothing is forbidden — menacing, breathtaking, and terribly exciting." The gutted facades of the Litovsky Prison and the High Court building in Petrograd seemed to have been licked clean by the flames. They had become beautiful, he noted in his diary, because "all the foulness that made them so hideous within has been burnt out."

At Chita in Siberia, the Social Revolutionary terrorist Maria Spiridonova blew up the prison where she had been serving a life sentence for the murder of the tsarist police official in Tambov. She was then elected mayor of the city. She had been gang-raped by Cossacks after her arrest and had attempted suicide, and an observer who saw her after her release thought that the "earnest, almost fanatical expression in her eyes" showed that her sufferings had affected her mind.

Miracles were taking place aboard the trans-Siberians. Joseph Stalin, sometimes shunned by comrades for his "ill temper and vile tongue," was aboard one moving west from Krasnoyarsk. Stalin was in unusually good humor. He was traveling with his colleague Lev Kamenev, a sharp contrast in personality to Stalin, a quick-moving little man with a wide, vivacious face set close to his shoulders.

At one Siberian halt, the notoriously tetchy Bolsheviks found themselves speaking from the same platform and celebrating with liberals, Social Revolutionaries, and Mensheviks. Kamenev even joined in sending a joint telegram to Grand Duke Mikhail to congratulate him for refusing the throne. The uncharacteristic harmony persisted after they reached Petrograd on March 12. Stalin and Kamenev took over the editorship of *Pravda* three days later. The Bolshevik paper had been closed at the start of the war and was revived on March 5, with the help of a three-thousand-ruble loan from Maxim Gorky. Its twenty-seven-year-old editor, Vyacheslav Molotov, had attempted to stick to a Leninist line. Molotov thought, correctly, that this would involve outright hostility to the Provisional Government, contempt for the majority Social Revolutionaries and Mensheviks in the Soviet, and opposition to continuing the war.

The returning Siberians shifted *Pravda* toward compromise and defensism. "The mere slogan 'Down with the War' is absolutely impractical," Kamenev wrote on March 15. "As long as the German army obeys the orders of the kaiser, the Russian soldier must stand firmly at his post, answering bullet with bullet."

Kamenev was a natural conciliator, a man who "lacked sharp edges" and who, if it was always necessary to take him in tow, would never balk too violently. He jibbed at extremism at the beginning of the revolution, as he was to jib at the terror at its end. "But — he always surrendered on all points," Sukhanov observed. Kamenev represented one element in the party. Under his real name of Rosenfeld, he had read law at Moscow University and despite his police record and alias he remained unmistakably an intellectual, highly strung and cerebral in homburg and dark overcoat.

Stalin, in a black leather jacket, was made of baser and less brittle metal. He was swarthy, born in a one-room hovel to a drunken Georgian cobbler, and the marks of childhood smallpox were evident enough for his police nickname to be *"Ryaboi,"* the pockmarked. "Illegals" like Stalin formed the in-country core of revolution. He had worked run-down halls in the slums of Batum, the hot, grimy half-Turkish city on the Black Sea, hand-setting strike calls on a crude flatbed press until informers came calling with the police. He was a linkman between the party in the Caucasus and the fighting squads of idealists, crooks, and adventurers who had replenished funds with attacks on armored cash transports and banks. Rootless, shifting from lodging house to railway station, Stalin had used twenty aliases in fifteen years.

Tsardom was squeamish when it came to the intellectuals, rebels with a background identifiable within Russia and abroad who played on its developing sense of shame. The autocracy had sentenced Lenin's brother to death with embarrassment. It was happy to let the "dazzlers" escape abroad. Stalin and his ilk were tiny irritations that a provincial governor and his hangmen could deal with at will. To be jailed in the Schlüsselburg or the Peter and Paul was a battle honor, a mark of respect. Stalin had been stashed away with common criminals in an obscure prison at Bailov, built for four hundred but holding fifteen hundred thieves, murderers, and rapists.

To him, an emigré intellectual with the glamor of a Trotsky was "beautifully useless." Stalin made little impact himself, Sukhanov thinking of him as a "gray blur, looming up now and then and not leaving any trace." Bruce Lockhart remembered only his "sallow face, black moustache and heavy eyebrows. . . . I paid little attention to him." Stalin was not the sort to give the rich sleepless and guilty nights.

Those who did were displayed in the Maryinsky Theater at a gala concert in mid-March. The famous exiles — Vera Figner, abettor of the murder of Alexander II and the *grande dame* of terrorism prominent among them — stood to the public applause in the great imperial box, shorn of its double eagles and monograms. "I shivered to think of all that little party stood for in the way of physical suffering and moral torment, borne in silence and buried in oblivion," said Maurice Paleologue. "What an epilogue for Dostoevsky's *House of the Dead*!"

For the time, however, moderation was the order of the day. Stalin expanded the defensist heresy, the line he and Kamenev were taking in *Pravda*, in the Soviet on March 16. He said that the Bolsheviks would support the Provisional Government "to the extent that it fortifies the march of the revolution." This conciliation amazed the Social Revolutionaries and Mensheviks. When *Pravda* appeared, the Tauride "buzzed with only one item — the triumph of the moderate and sensible Bolsheviks over the extremists."

Fashionable Petrograd recovered its nerve. At a tea party on the Sergievskaya, the hostess, in a tailored suit and toque, asked the assembled generals and princes, "What will become of us without our rent rolls?" A Horse Guards lieutenant, a red favor on his tunic, reassured her: "The *muzhiks* can take the Crown and Church lands. That'll be enough to keep them quiet."

A small black-clad agitated figure, and her theatrical agent, a man with magnificent mustaches and a "commercial traveler's face," came to see Nikolai Sukhanov. Mathilde Kshesinskaya pleaded for the return of her palace from the Bolsheviks, who had requisitioned it as their party headquarters. Sukhanov told the ballerina that it was unlikely that the party of the pro-

letariat had moderated enough to agree to a request from an ex-mistress of
the tsar.

The exile glamor rapidly wore off. When the Mensheviks Irakli Tsereteli
and Fedor Dan arrived on another train in Petrograd on March 20, they
were met only by a few members of their families. The return of the first
major external exile, Georgy Plekhanov, the man who had first urged Russians to examine the newfangled "scientific socialism" from their own viewpoint thirty-five years before, was a flop. "A martyr, plagued by doubt, by
inner division, having lost his way," a colleague noted. "An eagle with
broken wings." Plekhanov was exhausted by the journey from Paris, and by
tuberculosis, and had no influence on the younger revolutionaries he had
once inspired.

Lenin was rarely mentioned by the Bolsheviks themselves. The articles he
was frantically sending to *Pravda* from Switzerland seemed so muddle-
headed that Stalin and Kamenev were cutting them to ribbons to spare the
party from ridicule.

Vladimir Lenin was told of the revolution in the early afternoon of March
2 in his walk-up apartment on the Spiegelgasse in Zurich, a dismal place
rancid from the smell of a neighboring sausage factory; the windows could
only be opened when the factory closed down for the night. Lenin did not
believe the news until he had scanned the front pages of the evening papers
displayed on notice boards in the snapping wind on the lakefront. At forty-
six, Lenin looked older, subject to headaches and insomnia; his nickname
was Starik — "Old Man."

Short and rather stout, with a bull neck, a round and red face, and a high
forehead, his nose was slightly turned up above a brownish mustache and a
stubby beard — the unremarkable face of "any north Russian merchant."
But even as a schoolboy, a classmate had noticed his "fierce little brown
eyes." With maturity they had become "quizzing and half-contemptuous,"
revealing "confidence and conscious superiority." The son of a senior civil
servant in Simbirsk, he had been brought up in an eleven-room house with
a garden of poplars and fruit trees and an odd-job man, cook, and nurse.

Simbirsk, its "very courtyards overgrown with grass," sat quietly above
the mile-wide Volga. Over it, the novelist I. A. Goncharov wrote, lay the
"torpidity of peace, the calm on land which is found at sea. . . . Here and
there someone sticks his head out of a window, looks around, gaping in
both directions, spits, and disappears." In this landscape Goncharov set his
heroically idle character Oblomov, the symbol of Russian lethargy. Lenin
remembered Oblomov only to say that "we must cleanse him, shake him,
and thrash him." The town had another side. Alexander Kerensky remem-

bered the carriage with drawn blinds that drove through Simbirsk at night and "took people into the unknown at the behest of Sonia's stern father." Sonia was Kerensky's childhood playmate, her father the chief of the town Okhrana. Lenin's early exposure to the political police through his brother Alexander's arrest was more brutal. Vladimir was an intelligent, lively but rather aloof boy. His schoolmates called him the "walking encyclopedia," who always used the formal *vy*, never the usual and more affectionate *ty*, "thou." "He was extremely secretive and cool," one of his classmates, Alexander Naumov, recollected. "I do not remember one time when he allowed himself to unbend."

Until his brother's execution, Vladimir's childhood on the Volga was comfortable and secure. The family spent their summers on a cousin's country estate, swimming and rowing, playing billiards, and collecting mushrooms. They had a croquet lawn in the garden at Simbirsk and the children played elaborate games of soldiers. Alexander represented Garibaldi and the Italians, while Vladimir posed as Lincoln, using other boys or cutout figures of Grant and Sherman to lead his troops. They read the great Russian writers, *Ivanhoe*, and *Uncle Tom's Cabin*. The Ulyanovs were loyal, quiet, and industrious. Yet Alexander was politicized with such speed and fury at Saint Petersburg University that, less than two months after meeting some of his fellow middle-class students, he was plotting with them to assassinate the tsar.

It was a phenomenon that worried parents, university teachers, and the security police — particularly in the drowsy and respectable towns of the Volga, which were often the curious breeding grounds for student terrorists — and that they did not understand.

After Alexander was hanged in the spring of 1887, Lenin reread Nikolai Chernyevsky's political novel *What Is To Be Done?* Alexander's favorite book, it convinced Vladimir that "any correctly thinking and truly honest person must be a revolutionary." He had contained the earlier shock of his father's death, and he did the same with his brother. Later in the year, he graduated top in his class from high school. He scored perfect marks in all subjects except logic. "Very gifted, always neat and assiduous," the school director, Kerensky's father, wrote generously. "First in all his subjects, and upon completing his studies received a gold medal as the most deserving pupil with regard to ability, progress, and behavior. . . . Religion and discipline were the basis of this upbringing."

The model student soon lapsed. Vladimir was expelled from university in Kazan, where he was reading law, for his part in student demonstrations. His mother, worried that he would go the same way as Alexander, sold up in Simbirsk. She bought a small estate near Samara and encouraged him to

Nicholas and Alexandra.

Left: The Tsar's sledge-automobile, converted for winter use and seized by revolutionary troops at the end of February.

The demonstration that started the revolution: marchers on Women's Day in Petrograd, February 23, 1917.

"The House of the Russian Tsars." A cartoon from March 1917 shows Rasputin dominating Nicholas and Alexandra.

Felix Yusupov, transvestite and killer of Rasputin, with his wife, Princess Irina.

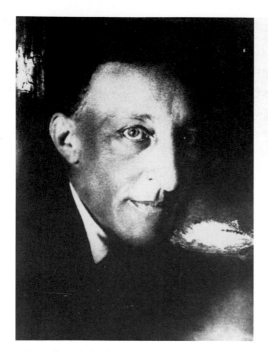

Alexander Blok, the poet whom revolutionary Russia "gulped down like a sow her piglet."

Maxim Gorky, chronicler of slum life who turned on Lenin as a "cold-blooded trickster."

Mikhail Rodzianko, the "bearlike" Duma chairman who, though a monarchist, urged Nicholas to abdicate.

Alexander Kerensky, the man who "emerged from the mud" to lead the revolution, sitting at the Tsar's desk in the Winter Palace a few days before his overthrow.

General Kornilov and his staff.

The terrorist-turned-moderate Boris Savinkov (*seated, extreme left, with number 1 written on his breeches*) with a group of Provisional Government military commissars. Winston Churchill thought Savinkov "one of the most interesting men alive."

Above left: The Menshevik Nikolai Chkheidze, the weak Soviet chairman with "every talent for being led in a halter."

Above: A naval officer saved his life during the Baltic Fleet massacres by allowing a sailor to cut off his badges of rank.

Left: General Mikhail Alexeev, long-suffering commander in chief of Russia's disintegrating armies.

Crowds celebrate the first May Day of the revolution in Petrograd, angered by the publication of "aggressive" Russian war aims.

A furious crowd attacked the huge statue of Alexander III in Moscow, scornfully leaving the head in the gutter.

farm. "In a sense, I too am a scion of the landed gentry," Lenin said. "I lolled about in haystacks, though I had not made them, and ate strawberries, although I had not planted them." He saw no moral problem in this — the fact of his views released a revolutionary from the shame of a comfortable childhood. He enjoyed country life but he had no intention of following it. Graduating as an external student in law, he started practicing in provincial Samara. Though academically brilliant, he did not have Alexander Kerensky's persuasive skills as an advocate. He defended peasants and workers in a dozen cases and lost them all.

Moving to Saint Petersburg, Vladimir was involved in Marxist groups and met his future wife, Nadezhda Krupskaya. She was middle-class like himself, the daughter of a factory inspector. Known as "the Fish" because of eyes that bulged through thyroid trouble, plainly dressed and severe, Krupskaya had the loyalty and patience needed to support the obscure theorist. Her earnestness suited a prematurely serious man in his midtwenties whom a contemporary thought was "only young according to his birth certificate. . . . The face withered, the head almost bald and . . . an unyouthful, coarse voice."

In 1895 Lenin took the Grand Tour — Austria, France, Germany, and Switzerland, with the obligatory visit to the grand old man of Russian Marxism, Georgy Plekhanov — typical of the better-heeled Russian revolutionary. He returned to Saint Petersburg with the bottom of his trunk stuffed with revolutionary propaganda. Krupskaya thought him a born conspirator. He used over a hundred aliases, or *klicki*, during his career; Lenin, taken from the Lena river, was the one that stuck. He studied the tools of his revolutionary trade, secret inks and aliases, and was "a skilled hand at giving the police-spies the slip." A local dentist, however, penetrated his little group on behalf of the Okhrana. The police raided a meeting at the end of 1895. Lenin was arrested and charged with subversion. He kept himself fit in prison — gymnastics every day and a rubdown with a wet towel — and alert by reading and translating. He was sentenced to three years' exile in Siberia.

Exile under the tsars was not what it would become under Leninism. Lenin was sent to a village near the Mongolian border, where he hunted for duck and snipe with his setter Pegasus, wrote his book *The Development of Capitalism in Russia*, and carried on a lively correspondence with other Marxists. Many exiles — Trotsky, Stalin — fled from Siberia. It was not difficult. Lenin was not an escaper. He married Krupskaya — in a church wedding, an embarrassing detail the Bolsheviks later suppressed — and the newlyweds skated on frozen lakes and translated the Webbs' great tome on trade unionism. Friends came at Christmas to "skate, play chess, sing, argue." Lenin had a state allowance of eight rubles a month, enough to hire a daily help and have the laundry done, and spun out with payments for his writing. His mother sent him remittances from her state pension.

Their Siberian idyll ended in 1900. Lenin and Krupskaya began a long circuit of those cities in Europe that would tolerate them — Paris, Geneva, Zurich, and London, where they worked in the British Museum and saw the sights from a double-decker bus. Dogmatic, ferociously self-confident, Lenin was soon at loggerheads with Plekhanov. In 1903, Lenin forced the split between his Bolsheviks and Martov's Mensheviks during the Social Democrat party congress in Brussels and London.

"We ought to pin an ace of diamonds on them," Lenin said of his socialist opponents, referring to the diamond-shaped badges sewn onto tsarist prison uniforms, "without ever looking into their cases. . . . When you find a stinking heap in your path, you don't have to dig your hands into it to know what it is. Your nose tells you it's shit, and you pass by." The one pleasure Paris gave him was watching French politicians who "knew how to smear an opponent's mug so he couldn't clean it for a long time."

Lenin was still consumed with vitriolic infighting as Bloody Sunday rolled out its afterbirth in 1905. The seismologist of social upheaval neither predicted the revolution nor influenced it.

From Geneva, an "awful hole," he fumed in frustration. "It horrifies me to find that there has been talk about bombs for *over six months*, yet none has been made!" he wrote. "Form fighting squads *at once* everywhere." He wanted small workshops to be organized for bomb-making, and read up the tactics of street fighting in the library of the Geneva Readers' Society. He was appealing to a phantom force. The Bolsheviks played almost no part in the 1905 revolution. Lenin did not return to Russia until November. He made no impact. Short of funds, the Bolsheviks fought squalid little battles with the Mensheviks over gifts and legacies.

"Expropriations," such as an armed raid on the post office in Tiflis organized by Stalin in 1907, provided some cash. Most of the 341,000 rubles netted were in 500-ruble notes, easy to trace, and Bolsheviks were picked up in Paris, Berlin, and Munich as they tried to change them. A future foreign minister, Maxim Litvinov, was arrested in Paris with twelve of them. Some "party" men were professional gangsters. It did not worry Lenin. "Ours is a big business," he said. "We can use all kinds of trash." When evidence of personal squalor came up, he dismissed it as *Privatsache*, a private thing — "it doesn't mean anything to me." As to violence, he thought it a "sacred duty" to "pay for the spilled blood of the people with the blood of its oppressors." By the end of 1907, the police closing in on him, he was back in Switzerland.

The small organization surviving in Russia was riddled with informers. The head of the party's foreign bureau, Dr. Y. A. Zhitomirsky, was an Okhrana agent, as was the man charged with smuggling Bolshevik literature into Russia. Roman Malinovsky, a man whom Lenin "trusted above all others" and the leader of the Bolshevik faction in the prewar Duma, had been turned by the Okhrana in 1910. Malinovsky supplied the secret police with more than fifty reports detailing the location of party meetings, storage sites for party literature, and the pseudonyms used by the leadership.

Malinovsky was the Okhrana's highest paid spy, with a monthly stipend of five hundred rubles and an expense account in which he entered his contributions to party funds. The Okhrana ensured his election to the Duma by arresting rival candidates. His rousing speeches — Malinovsky was a fine orator with flashing mustaches and a florid drinker's face — were edited both by Lenin and by his Okhrana contacts. The interior ministry, worried at the potential scandal of running a Duma deputy, and perhaps concerned that Malinovsky was doing too well at popularizing the Bolsheviks, ordered him to resign in 1914. The Okhrana paid him off with six thousand rubles and a passport. He fled to France, where he served in the French army before being taken prisoner by the Germans in 1915. Despite his treachery, Krupskaya sent food parcels to Malinovsky in his prison camp.

The Okhrana's informers were "not the old type of spies who used to hang around street corners," Krupskaya admitted. "They held high party posts. Arrests were no longer done haphazardly. They were carefully planned."

Lenin exhausted himself with feuding. "He looked awful," Maxim Gorky said after a visit to Switzerland. "Even his tongue seemed to have turned gray." In a Geneva café, Krupskaya saw two revolutionaries arguing until one snatched some papers off the table and stormed out. She almost burst into tears; the incident was so typical of their emigré life that it "wasn't even funny." Lenin squabbled with Plekhanov, with Gorky, with the Mensheviks, and with his own followers, attacking them with a peculiar violence in which former friends became "ugly scum . . . blisters . . . pus."

The outbreak of war increased his isolation and irrelevance. A conference of antiwar socialists was held in 1915 in Zimmerwald, a village in the mountains south of Berne. Thirty-eight delegates turned up, aware that half a century after the founding of the First International, they could all be fitted into four horse-drawn coaches. Within this tiny band, watched with amazement by curious villagers, Lenin was a "minority of one."

He had no time for pacifism. "Socialists cannot, without ceasing to be socialists," he said, "be opposed to all war." They were obliged to fight a civil war against the ruling classes. But in the current war between governments, one "must *welcome* the defeat of one's 'own' country." Military reverses at the front made it easier to overthrow a government in internal, civil war. Lenin's "revolutionary defeatism," in which national defeat would lead to successful civil war, was rejected as childish and dangerous by the other delegates. A French delegate said scornfully that much of the French proletariat was in the trenches, and that it would be difficult to convince them that their interests would be best served by the victory of German imperialism.

Already at loggerheads with foreign socialists, Lenin fell out with his own party. He would fly into violent tempers — Krupskaya, using the French word, called them his "*rages*" — and then relapse into fatigue and sleeplessness, tormented by headaches while the "light died in his small Mongol eyes." Moscow Bolsheviks warned that the advice to "sell the house," the code for defeatism, was odious. Some exiled Bolsheviks in France volunteered to join the French army. "Look at my fate," Lenin grumbled at the end of 1916. "One militant campaign after another — against political stupidites, banalities, opportunism, etc. This since 1893. And the hatred of the vulgar people in return." But the ego that would so impress observers — Paleologue called him "crazy with vanity" — was intact. "I still would not change this fate for 'peace' with the vulgarizers," Lenin added.

By 1917, he was impoverished. "I need to earn. Otherwise we shall die of hunger, really and truly!!" he wrote. The Bolshevik treasury dipped as low as 160 Swiss francs. The party journal appeared irregularly, because it could only afford the services of an alcoholic emigré printer. As the Women's Day marches began in Petrograd, he was complaining, "the cost of living makes one despair and I have desperately little capacity for work because of my shattered nerves." He was so depressed that he found it difficult to get through a meeting. "They tire me," he noted. "Nerves no good at all; headaches; left before the end." Krupskaya called theirs a "quiet, jog-trot life" — "out there, the revolutionary struggle was mounting, life was seething, but it was all so far away."

Lenin was rarely in direct contact with Russia, where he remained almost unknown. Since the turn of the century, he had spent only a few months there. His habitat was the libraries and progressively cheaper lodgings of foreign cities. He was losing interest in Russian politics.

He had good reason. The Bolshevik's Petrograd committee had been ravaged by well-informed Okhrana arrests in 1914, in April and July of 1916, and again in January and February of 1917. Alexander Shlyapnikov, the main Bolshevik figure in the capital, estimated current party membership at the beginning of 1917 at a maximum of three thousand. Hopes of recruiting sailors to boost numbers were dashed when V. Shurkanov, the Bolshevik entrusted with establishing links with the Baltic Fleet, turned out to be another Okhrana agent. Funds were so low — Shlyapnikov recorded that 1,117 rubles and 50 kopeks entered party coffers in the two months to February of 1917 — that the Petrograd Bolsheviks could not afford to send anyone to the provinces and had to rely on people visiting relatives or traveling for their employers.

On February 27, two days after the latest Bolshevik committee had been rounded up by the Okhrana in Petrograd, Lenin was railing against the leader of the German Social Democrats: "I hate and despise [Karl] Kautsky more than anyone, with his vile, dirty, self-satisfied hypocrisy." When the news of the revolution came through, he was about to leave his rooms for the Zurich public library, where he was gathering material for another attack, this time on the Swiss Social Democrat Robert Grimm.

So suspicious was Lenin of "provocations" that he first thought that the headlines on March 2 might be "German lying." His next reaction was to claim that he had foreseen events. "That Russia has for the last few days been on the verge of revolution is beyond doubt," he wrote that evening. Nothing he had written or said for months past reveals the slightest premonition. Indeed, on the anniversary of Bloody Sunday in January, he had told a group of young Swiss socialists, "We of the older generation may not live to see the decisive battle of the coming revolution." Given his life expectancy of a further twenty years or so, this implied that he did not expect a revolution until 1937 at the earliest.

"On tactics — no trust in and no support of the new government," he cabled Petrograd on March 5. "Kerensky is especially suspect — arming of the proletariat is the only answer — no rapprochement with other parties." The message created such resentment when it arrived eight days later that he was obliged to qualify it as a personal rather than a party view.

Russia's mood was rhapsodic and far from the civil war against the bourgeoisie implicit in arming the workers. Not one voice in the Soviet executive committee, which included three members of the Bolshevik's own central committee, had been raised against the takeover of power by the Provisional Government. But it was Lenin's assumption that his party was a functioning entity, capable of independent action, that most alarmed the Bolsheviks on the spot. In fact, of 27,000 Putilov workers, barely 150 were Bolsheviks in a sea of Social Revolutionaries and Mensheviks. The party had 500 members in the Vyborg district, its supposed heartland. Of the 1,500 delegates crowding into the Soviet, only 40 or so were Bolsheviks. The party was too marginalized to be able to indulge in overt hostility to others.

Lenin, for his part, was infuriated by the scanty reports he began to receive in mid-March of the shift from defeatism to defensism in Lev Kamenev's new *Pravda*. "I personally will not hesitate to declare that I prefer even an immediate split with anyone in our party, whoever it may be," Lenin thundered from Zurich, "to making concessions to the social-patriotism of Kerensky and Co. or the social pacifism and Kautskianism of Chkheidze and Co." The epithet "Kautskianism" was so arcane as to be unintelligible, and the veiled threat to resign was ignored.

Seething, Lenin began writing five "Letters from Afar" for publication in *Pravda*. Kerensky was dismissed as a "*balalaika*" and leading Social Revolutionaries as "traitors" plotting to bring back the monarchy. The first letter described the revolution as a "plot against Nicholas Romanov" organized by the "billion-dollar firm 'England, France and Co.' " and their Russian agents. The second letter was written as a rebuttal to a report in the *London Times*. Ignoring the fact that few, if any, members of the Russian proletariat were *Times* subscribers, Lenin lambasted the newspaper's Petrograd correspondent as a "poor English Guchkovite."

The third letter maintained the bizarre standards of its predecessors. It urged the workers to "smash the 'ready-made' state machine" and substitute a new one by "*merging* the police force, the army, and the bureaucracy with the *entire armed people*." Once a fortnight, each individual would stand guard over a republic thus miraculously freed of the need for soldiers, civil servants, and gendarmes.

Peace was addressed in the fourth letter. To urge the "landlord and capitalist" Provisional Government to conclude peace, Lenin said, "is like preaching virtue to brothel keepers." Lenin proposed that a government of Russian workers and peasants should "publicly call upon *all* the belligerent powers to conclude an *immediate armistice*." This new government would insist on the liberation of all colonies and oppressed nations; appeals would go out to workers in all countries to overthrow their bourgeois governments. The final letter dealt with the "transition to socialism," the control of production and the introduction of "universal labor service."

The claim that the revolution was the work of imperialist British and French agents was absurd. The insulting references to other socialist leaders were dangerous at a time of Bolshevik fragility. The notion of an armed militia taking over the functions of the state — down to providing "milk for babies, palaces for the proletariat, and security on the streets" — seemed as utopian as the notion that English workers were about to overthrow their government and liquidate the British Empire.

The editors of *Pravda* were shocked. They cut the personal insults and the reference to the Anglo-French conspiracy from the first letter; not a word of the others appeared.

Lenin's attempts to get back to Russia were as unrealistic. Krupskaya said that he could not sleep for "making up all sorts of incredible plans." He dreamt in "the semi-delirium of the night" of traveling by aircraft, ignoring his lack of funds and the hostile airspace that surrounded Switzerland. He sent his photograph to a Bolshevik in Stockholm and asked him to find a Swede who looked like him and take his passport. Lenin spoke no Swedish, but thought he could pass himself off as a deaf-mute. Krupskaya worried that he would fall asleep, "see Mensheviks in his dreams," and give himself away by shouting "scoundrels, scoundrels" in Russian.

The only realistic plan seemed an approach to the Germans. "Revolutionary defeatism" would knock Russia out of the war. The French and British had no interest in allowing its principal proponent to return over their soil or in their ships. The Germans were in an altogether different position.

Other external exiles were in New York. There was a large Russian colony in the city, enough to support two daily newspapers in Russian and others in Yiddish. Among them was Leon Trotsky, now thirty-eight years old, still dimly remembered in Petrograd for the part he had played in the 1905 Soviet. He had been born Leon Bronstein, the son of a rarity, a landowning Jew with a small estate in the southern Ukraine, in 1879. Schooled in Odessa, with its light seascapes of the Black Sea, he was intelligent, sparkling, and precocious — "for several months I was in love with a coloratura soprano." He entered Odessa's university in 1897, his early passion for the theater and pure mathematics giving way to politics.

His credentials included periods of Siberian exile and escapes. His first stint in Siberia began in 1899. He used it to read hungrily, a gluttonous diet that included the future Fascist heroes Friedrich Nietzsche and Gabriele D'Annunzio as well as the socialists' Emile Zola. "The spiritual estate of man is so enormous and so inexhaustible in its diversity," he wrote, less self-obsessed than Lenin, that one should "stand on the shoulders of great predecessors." He escaped under the hayload of a peasant cart. Boarding the trans-Siberian express at Irkutsk, he wrote the name of one of his former jailers in his false internal passport.

Bronstein was now Trotsky. He relaxed on the westbound train by reading Homer's hexameters. In the autumn of 1902, the Siberian fugitive was in lodgings near King's Cross Station in London, close to the one-room-and-a-kitchen apartment Lenin shared with Krupskaya. The relations of the two men were volatile. As a Menshevik, Trotsky attacked Lenin after the split with the Bolsheviks as "hideous . . . dissolute . . . malicious and morally repulsive."

Trotsky moved on to Paris, a city that more suited his vivacity and style. The 1905 revolution tempted him back to Russia more than six months before the reluctant Lenin. Witty, literary in the cascade of his speeches, he dominated the Soviet, the workers' council, during its fifty-day lifespan in the capital. His attractive insolence allowed him to debate with all classes of society. Speaking to a group of Guards officers at a political soirée in the house of a baroness — "the butler waited for my visiting card but, woe is me, what visiting card should a man with a cover name produce?" — he told them that it was their duty to hand over the keys of the arsenals to the people.

Whatever amusement their officers got from flirting with Trotsky, the mass of guardsmen, Cossacks, and peasant infantrymen stayed loyal to the tsar. Trotsky was back in prison by the end of 1905, first in the Kresty and then the Peter and Paul Fortress, lying on his cot, reading French novels with "the same physical delight with which the gourmet sips choice wine or inhales the fragrant smoke of a fine cigar."

Sentenced to exile for life in Siberia, he had a false passport and money concealed in the sole of his boot as the Trans-Siberian deported him east early in 1907. It was not thought good form for prisoners to escape on the train, as it got the escort into trouble. By mid-February Trotsky arrived in Berezovo before the final leg to the penal colony at Obdorsk, on the Arctic Circle in empty *taiga* a thousand miles from the nearest railhead. He left Berezovo at night, after an evening watching an amateur production of a Chekhov play. The guard was lax. February is a blizzard month in the *taiga* and his escape route took him across roadless wilderness to a gold-mining settlement in the Urals with a single-track railway. A local Zyrian, so drunk that Trotsky had to kick him and take off his fur hat to keep him awake, guided his reindeer-drawn sledge.

This odd couple — the drunken native and the liquid-eyed revolutionary, taking notes on the tracks of ermine, wolf, and fox and on the social habits of the few raw-fish-eating inhabitants as he passed — sped for a week over a landscape "which nobody had measured except for the archangel Michael." They reached the railway at Bogoslovsk, where Trotsky explained variously that he was a polar explorer or a merchant.

A train returned him west to Saint Petersburg. From there, he did the revolutionaries' circuit — London, Berlin, and Vienna — before settling in Paris after the outbreak of war. He became a war correspondent for the underground journal *Slovo — Our Word* — run by a former tsarist officer, Vladimir Antonov-Ovseenko, sentenced to death in absentia for joining the rebels with his unit in 1905. Trotsky was deported from France after the paper was banned in September 1916. Arriving in Spain, he was shipped out to the United States from Barcelona with a boatload of rich deserters from the Western Front and other undesirables. The ship docked in New York on a rainy Sunday in January of 1917. "It is dark. Cold. Wind. Rain. On land, a wet mountain of buildings," he wrote. "The New World!"

Many Russians were unnerved by New York. Alexander Shlyapnikov found it a "monstrous city, resembling a huge workshop. America is steeped in hard-headed business. . . . Everyone lives only to get rich quick or to dream of doing so." Shlyapnikov preferred to return to the dangers of an underground existence in Petrograd, taking with him $250, the fruits of two months of fund-raising in the late summer of 1916.

Trotsky, open and imaginative, was fascinated by the United States — "the foundry in which the fate of men is to be forged." But he was as uncertain as Lenin over his future. He looked "haggard, he had aged, there was fatigue in his face," said a Russo-American communist, M. Olgin, who had known him before. "His conversation hinged around the collapse of international socialism." He gave lectures on its failure in New York and Philadelphia. News of the revolution came to him in the $18-a-month apartment he was furnishing on the installment plan on 164th Street in the Bronx. For the first time in his life, he had a telephone. He was working on the Russian émigré daily *Novy Mir — New World —* edited by the Bolsheviks Nikolai Bukharin, a short, literary twenty-nine-year-old, and Alexandra Kollontai, a forty-five-year-old general's daughter and an energetic feminist. It was Trotsky's first intimate contact with Bolsheviks since the London split.

Trotsky had his doubts about Nikolai Bukharin. "You must always keep your eyes on him," Trotsky said, "or he will succumb to the influence of someone directly opposed to you, as other people fall under an automobile." He was not overimpressed, either, by the American socialists he met, "semi-successful doctors, lawyers, dentists, and the like." Trotsky thought they were elected to important left-wing committees "purely because they have automobiles." When he told them that the proletariat would gain power in the second stage of the Russian revolution, it produced the same impression as a stone thrown into a "puddle alive with pompous frogs."

But American journalists queued at the *Novy Mir* offices in Saint Marks Place to interview him. Trotsky had charisma, and he quoted well. "Europe is a powder magazine of social revolution," he told American readers. "The Russian proletariat is now throwing a flaming torch into it. To suppose that this will cause no explosion is to think against the laws of historic logic and psychology." He intended to take part in the explosion. On March 14, after a boisterous send-off party, he and his family sailed from New York aboard the ten-thousand-ton Norwegian ship *Christianiafjord.*

He left with some regret. His young sons had been completely won over by New York, and were under the spell of the electric light, telephone, service elevator, and garbage chute in their apartment. Trotsky thought New York was the "city of prose and fantasy, of capitalist automatism, its moral philosophy that of the dollar." It represented to him the "fullest expression of our modern age," so vigorous that Europe might by contrast "sink into nothing but a graveyard."

X
"Look in His Eyes . . ."

WHEN PAVEL MILIUKOV HAD READ OUT the list of new ministers in the Soviet on March 2, 1917, a soldier yelled at him, "Who chose you?" Miliukov made no reference to the Duma or any other elective body. "We were chosen by the Russian revolution," he blustered. "A small group of men was at hand whose past was sufficiently known to the people, and against whom there could be no hint of objections." It was an emotional moment, and Miliukov was cheered, but the statement would not have passed legal scrutiny.

Since Nicholas had had no right to renounce his twelve-year-old son's claim to the throne in favor of Grand Duke Mikhail, Mikhail could not legitimately pass authority to the new government. Mikhail's abdication act, scribbled out in the exercise book in Prince Putyatin's house, requested all Russian citizens to obey the Provisional Government, which "came into being at the initiative of the State Duma and is vested with all the plenitude of power," until the Constituent Assembly was convened "in as short a time as possible."

The original draft had referred to the Provisional Government having arisen at the "will of the people." Kerensky refused to accept this, pointing out that "the people" had had nothing to do with forming a government largely composed of landowners. But the reference to the "initiative" of the Duma was equally false. The Duma had not agreed to the formation of the Provisional Government. It had neither elected nor chosen the ministers, some of whom, including the premier, were not deputies and held no elective post.

The new government, as its "provisional" tag implied, had two additional flaws. Although its burgeoning pronouncements used the formula "vested with all the plenitude in power," the government constantly referred to the Constituent Assembly as the "real master of the Russian land." The assembly did not exist, and there was no urgency to hold the elections that would bring it into being. For months to come, the "small group of men" calling themselves the Provisional Government were to take decisions that they admitted should have awaited the calling of the Constituent Assembly. The consciously temporary government was involved in power-sharing with the Soviet, whose legal status was equally unclear but which was already sharply to its left. Russia had no "real master."

As to the cabinet, the true answer to the soldier's shouted question — "Who chose you?" — was that the ministers had chosen themselves, and oddly at that. Prince Georgy Lvov was personally little known even in the Duma, although, as Soviet delegates jeered, he was undoubtedly "*Tsensovogo!*" — "privileged class." On his appointment, Lvov spoke of his faith in the "political wisdom of the Russian people and the greatness of its soul." He believed that democracy would flow from the goodwill of the people and avoided personal decisions where possible, leaving them vaguely to the "people itself" to sort out. The new cabinet secretary Vladimir Nabokov could not remember any occasion when the new premier used a tone of authority or spoke out decisively. Why had Lvov been chosen? Miliukov himself did not know — he was appalled by Lvov's handling of the Provisional Government's first cabinet meeting, describing the premier as "a drip."

Miliukov was as energetic as Lvov was idle, but the new foreign minister had no affection for the revolution and little intuition of what fueled it. The Soviet did not forgive his monarchism. The finance ministry was expected to go to the experienced chairman of the Duma budget committee, Andrei Shingarev. The appointment of Mikhail Tereshchenko — thirty-one years old, unqualified, facing huge inflationary pressures, and not even a Duma deputy — was met with howls of "And who is he?" All most Russians knew was that Tereshchenko was famously rich. His mother had dipped into his late father's sugar fortune before the war to buy him a 500,000-ruble yacht. The Tereshchenkos were charitable — the yacht had been converted into a hospital ship in 1914 — but their fortune rankled.

The appointment also involved freemasonry. Tereshchenko was a mason and the new cabinet was seen to have a strong masonic bias. Shingarev went reluctantly to the agriculture ministry, convinced that "occult forces" had kept him out of finance. The mason Nikolai Nekrasov was named transport minister over the head of Alexander Bublikov, who had kept the railways running with great efficiency during the first days of the revolution.

Both trade and justice went to masons. Alexander Konovalov's experience as a major industrialist qualified him for the trade post. Kerensky, vigorous with his cropped, flat-topped hair, was popular enough. But tensions were certain to arise from the presence of a revolutionary in a cabinet whose primary wish was for the revolution to end. How, it was asked, could he cohabit with Alexander Guchkov, the right-wing monarchist at the war ministry?

Heart problems dogged Guchkov, and the cabinet often had to meet at his bedside. He irritated the Soviet with his strident support for the war, and the military were alienated by his sacking of officers whom, often on flimsy evidence, he thought unreliable. One of his victims was the popular commander of the Russian bomber fleet, General M. V. Shidlovsky. Morale in the squadrons sagged when Shidlovsky, in tears, told his crews that the new war minister found him "harmful."

The church fared no better. Vladimir Lvov — no relation to the prince — was named to supervise church affairs as procurator of the Holy Synod. He so tyrannized the bishops and clergy that some sought the protection of the Soviet. The Metropolitans of Moscow and Petrograd, Orthodox archbishops, fled to Siberian monasteries. Lvov's colleagues found his mixture of jingoism and revolutionary fervor amusing, though they were appalled by his "striking naïveté and unbelievably frivolous approach to business."

It was, nevertheless, possible for a newspaper to be able to claim within a fortnight that Russia "has joined the advanced democracies of the world." On one day, March 4, while Lenin was still coming to terms with the fact of revolution, the cabinet dealt with more than a dozen issues between 7:00 and 11:00 P.M., covering religious, educational, and property rights.

Kerensky — "the man with one kidney, the man who had only six weeks to live" — was hyperactive at the justice ministry. The same day, the Okhrana, special gendarmes, and the railroad police were abolished. So were the secret funds that had been used to penetrate revolutionary cells. The Supreme Criminal Court and other special civil courts, tarnished by their use in political suppression, were scrapped. The general political amnesty already introduced by Kerensky was confirmed by the cabinet two days later. It was extended from sedition and subversion to cover criminal acts perpetrated for political motives. Full civil, political, and property rights were restored to all those amnestied.

Fueling himself on bits of chicken, coffee, and brandy, snatching four hours of sleep a night, Kerensky was driving through major legislation each day. He found the tensions of work "unendurable," but "I was living ecstasy." An admirer wrote a couplet that families wrote in their commonplace books:

Russia's heart will never forget him
Like a first love.

The correspondent of the *Daily Telegraph* assured his readers in England that Kerensky "is fired by a fervent and profound belief in the religion of freedom."

The death penalty was abolished. Criminals languishing in more than five hundred condemned cells were reprieved, the penalty commuted to hard labor. Moral opposition to execution — "this worst type of murder," Vladimir Nabokov called it in the Cadet newspaper *Rech* the following morning — had a particular "shattering force" to a Russian public brought up on the abolitionist novels of Dostoevsky and Tolstoy. *Novoe Vremia* found it difficult to "express the whole colossal majesty" of the act of abolition. It was a time when "one item of good news follows the other" and the Petrograd editorialists were certain that this act sealed the "straightforward nobleness" of the Provisional Government.

Protopopov, Stürmer, and the other symbols of tsardom were still alive. "Where," *Novoe Vremia* asked, "is the axe of the guillotine? Where are the blood-smeared heads on the spears of the cannibals? Where are the maddened furies?" On the contrary, the guilty had magnanimously been granted life. Far from a Leninist civil war, Nabokov felt that "the people do not want bloody retributions against anyone, not even against its worst enemies."

Kerensky had begun to think that Nicholas and Alexandra were themselves "victims of tsarism." He went to Tsarskoe Selo out of curiosity — he had not forgotten his glimpse of the tsar on the Winter Palace balcony thirteen years before, and his belief that their paths would cross. He found Nicholas to be a "pleasant, somewhat awkward Colonel of the Guards, very ordinary except for a pair of wonderful blue eyes." He was more impressed by Alexandra, a "born empress, proud and unbending, fully conscious of her right to rule." Critics were noting an imperiousness in Kerensky himself, and his sympathy for the Romanovs was to develop a certain fellow feeling.

Brutal prison practices — "whipping and the use of irons or fetters and straitjackets" — were deleted from the prison code of regulations. It was recognized that the tsarist warders had been "brought up in an atmosphere of lawlessness and disrespect for human dignity." They were to be replaced wherever possible by disabled ex-soldiers.

All restrictions based on religion and nationality had gone by mid-March, a severe blow to officials who had made their living from the bribes levied for their evasion. The roll call of the "pariahs of Russian legislation" had been long. The revolution was particularly welcome to Jews, forced to live in the pale of settlement and outside the law, "against whom everything was permitted, everything was possible."

At the turn of the century, the Russian empire had the largest Jewish population in the world, more than five million. A million and a quarter had since emigrated, largely to the United States, speeded on their way by pogroms. Violence against Jews was almost casual. As a child, the painter Marc Chagall "felt at every stage that I was a Jew — people made me feel it." He described a pogrom. "The street lamps are out," Chagall wrote. "I feel panicky, especially in front of butchers' windows. There you can see calves that are still alive lying beside the butchers' hatchets and knives." A gang of five or six looters came round the corner, armed with knives. "Jew or not?" they asked him. "My pockets are empty," Chagall wrote, "my fingers sensitive, my legs weak, and they are out for blood. My death would be futile. I so wanted to live." He denied his heritage, and gruffly the men shouted, "All right! Get along!"

A survivor of the great Kiev pogrom of 1905, the banker Alexander Gunzburg, recollected shouting at the mob, "Have you no fear of Christ?" Then he was beaten with blows "so powerful that my head was almost driven into my shoulders and my front teeth split." Gunzburg escaped to the house of the British consul next door. The authorities did little to control pogroms; they were a safety valve to take people's minds off the regime.

For the Jews of Poland and Lithuania, the war was "one of the greatest disasters they had known." Several hundred thousand had fled from the combat zones, and were seen "wandering over the snows, driven like cattle by platoons of Cossacks, camping in the open round the towns, and dying of hunger, weariness, and cold." Maurice Paleologue reported that "not a day passes in the zone of armies without a number of Jews being hanged on a trumped-up charge of spying. . . . And yet there are 240,000 Jewish soldiers fighting, and fighting well, in the ranks of the Russian army." All publications in Hebrew characters were banned in 1915 and correspondence in Yiddish prohibited. With such persecution, it was remarkable that — although Nicholas had claimed in a letter to Alexandra that "nine-tenths of the troublemakers are Jews" — only around one in ten of the Russian revolutionary leaders, at a rough estimate, were Jewish.

There were also Dukhobors and other Russian sectarians who suffered "oppression, violence, and disfranchisement"; Moslems whose mosques were desecrated; Galicians "treated as serfs." The Provisional Government now freed all to travel and live where they pleased, to engage in any business or profession, to hire workers and apprentices, to be admitted to civil and military state service, to vote, and to hold "any office in government and public establishments." The ban on non-Russian languages and dialects in schools and business, a powerful weapon against minorities, was lifted.

Public reaction was euphoric. To the liberal newspaper *Russkiya Vedomosti*, another "survival of barbarism." had fallen. The Menshevik daily *Den* declared "a feast of the revolution. One of its greatest conquests has been given legal form and expressed in official terms. With this victory we congratulate the revolutionary nation and the Provisional Government." "Roads, trees, and stars seemed to be holding meetings," Boris Pasternak wrote, "and delivering orations along with humans." The poet was enraptured, like most of Russia, by the justice minister:

> *This is no night, no rain, no choral recital*
> *exploding "Kerensky, hurrah!"*
> *It is the blinding march into the forum*
> *from the locked catacombs of yesterday.*

Foreigners were equally pleased. The United States was the first nation officially to recognize the Provisional Government, at 4:00 P.M. March 9, to the great delight of Ambassador Francis. The British and French followed two days later. The *Financial Times* in London thought that "everything now points to an immense development in Russian trade." The bellwether stock on the foreign exchanges, Russian 5 percent, held by thousands of small investors in the United States, Britain, and France, had put two points on its prerevolution price, to eighty-two.

The Soviet was less generous toward the "former people" than the Provisional Government. Tension between them ran high over "bloodstained" Nicholas and "traitress" Alexandra. Cheap newspapers, reveling in their freedom to peddle scandal, were recharging hatred for the empress with a string of invented "exclusives" on her sexual escapades with Rasputin. On March 7, the cabinet bowed to Soviet pressure and agreed to arrest the imperial couple.

In Mogilev, red flags were flying opposite Nicholas's windows at the Stavka and his aides had hastily cut his initials out of their epaulettes and ripped off their golden shoulder knots. Alexandra was in the Alexander Palace in Tsarskoe Selo. The Guards had taken advantage of Order Number One to vote out their commander, General Ressine. Untidy and quarrelsome troops roamed the darkened rooms and shot the tame deer in the park. The palace deacon had been arrested for praying for the tsar, the congregation hissing at Nicholas's name.

A Duma delegation arrived at Mogilev at 3:00 P.M. on March 8. The tsar was with his mother on the platform. He submitted quietly to arrest by four Duma deputies. As his train moved out for Tsarskoe Selo, Nicholas waved to the dowager empress from the window. He did not see her again. The same day, Alexandra was arrested by a tough combat general, Lavr Kornilov, in the green drawing room of the Alexander Palace.

A rumor swept Petrograd on March 9 that the Provisional Government was about to evacuate Nicholas from Murmansk to England aboard a British warship. The Soviet executive committee convinced itself that the cabinet had ordered the arrests to "lull our suspicions" and that a plot to restore the monarchy was underway. It summoned Serge Mstislavsky from the Soviet military section. The mood in the executive committee was excited. Sukhanov was there, his "yellow-gray browless face" set in a dry and acid smile. Nikolai Chkheidze presided, "lurid" with anger.

"All the 'dangerous' Romanovs must be in the hands of the Soviet," Chkheidze said. "Our hands, not those of the 'provisionals.' "

Nicholas arrived in Tsarskoe Selo in the morning of March 9. When he tried to take his afternoon walk in the park, soldiers blocked him with their gun butts, shoving him around "as if he was some wretched vagrant on a country road." Chkheidze ordered Mstislavsky to check that "citizen Romanov" had indeed arrived. A special train was readied for Mstislavsky and a party of machinegunners. At the Tsarskoe Selo station, Mstislavksy commandeered a car and ordered the driver to take him to the Alexander Palace — "Step on it, comrade chauffeur."

The commander of the palace guard said that he was under the strictest orders from the "legal government" not to allow anyone to see the tsar. "So, Captain, in your opinion is the Soviet not legal?" said Mstislavsky. The captain shifted uneasily, his fat jutting out from under his short-cropped Uhlan jacket. "I must make certain that the beast is indeed here," said Mstislavsky. "You must show me the prisoner."

The court master of ceremonies, Count Benkendorff, was summoned. The count's exquisite manners deserted him when he saw the Soviet representative. "You wish to 'inspect' His Majesty . . . what insolence!" he shouted. "And who are you, a mere rebel! Let's call things by their proper name." Mstislavsky retorted that the Soviet had the real power and that the count was in danger of "breaking his fingers" if he tried to hold back the wheel of history.

It was agreed that Mstislavsky would be given a glimpse of the former tsar. The palace officers hastily buttoned their gloves. Mstislavksy, in a rough sheepskin coat with bits of straw sticking out of it, his hair uncombed, did not bother to remove his Cossack hat. Nicholas approached, his face puffy and red, with swollen eyelids making a frame for "dull, bloodshot eyes." He had broken down a few hours before when he had been reunited with Alexandra. Nicholas looked at Mstislavsky, or so the latter claimed, with the look of a "tired hunted wolf." Then he turned and walked rapidly away.

"Well, watch out now," an officer said to Mstislavsky. "If the Romanovs ever get back into power they won't forget *you*. They'll find you at the bottom of the sea, if need be." There was, Mstislavsky thought, little doubt where the loyalty of the officers lay. The army was in for a bumpy ride, torn between government and Soviet . . .

When Mstislavsky returned to report to the Soviet in Petrograd in the late evening, he was told that the Provisional Government had reluctantly agreed to place the imperial prisoners under a specially appointed Soviet commissar.

That night a band of soldiers broke into the small chapel in the imperial park in Tsarskoe Selo. They exhumed Rasputin's coffin and took it to a clearing in the Pargolovo forest. After forcing the lid, they used sticks to hoist the putrefying corpse onto a heap of logs. They drenched it in gasoline and set it on fire. The grisly process of cremation lasted for six hours until dawn. In spite of an icy wind and the clouds of "pungent and fetid smoke" which rose from the pyre, groups of *muzhiks* emerged from the forest and gazed in "horror-stricken stupor at the sacrilegious holocaust" as it slowly consumed the empress's Friend.

If the cabinet mistrusted the Soviet, it was also at odds with itself. Chaos and fatigue lay under the surface activity. Meetings were held when there was a quorum, often after 1:00 A.M., the makeup shifting as ministers came and went. Sir George Buchanan found only Guchkov and Kerensky to be "really strong men." Of these, Guchkov was often ill and deeply pessimistic, complaining that Russia now had two governments and that the Soviet "interferes in everything we do."

The French ambassador was more selective than his British colleague. Comparisons with the figures of the French Revolution were already in vogue — every book on the subject had been borrowed from the Imperial Public Library on Alexandra Square. Maurice Paleologue said that Kerensky reminded him of Saint-Just, the brilliant orator executed at twenty-seven with Robespierre in 1794. Only Kerensky, Paleologue said, was a "man of action, by his energetic figure, his dry gestures, by something fanatical and clear-cut. . . . He is certainly the real head of the Provisional Government."

Relations within the cabinet were brittle. Pavel Miliukov at foreign affairs regarded Nikolai Nekrasov at transport as "simply a traitor." Alexander Konovalov described Mikhail Tereshchenko, whose finance ministry took precedence over Konovalov's trade and industry department, as a "bungling amateur." Nonmasons were jealous of the "magic circle"; Miliukov said that Nekrasov and Tereshchenko owed their position to their "special intimacy with conspiratorial circles."

Kerensky and Miliukov disliked being in the same room. The foregin minister baited Kerensky by wondering aloud in a cabinet meeting at the part played by German agents in the revolution. "After Mr. Miliukov has dared to slander the sacred cause of my presence," Kerensky said, "I do not wish to stay here for a minute more." With that, he walked out of the meeting, leaving Miliukov to mutter, "That's his usual style. He's always pulling tricks like that."

The justice minister's colleagues thought that he was behaving as a surrogate premier. Kerensky got up early in his apartment in the ministry to read a digest of the press, alert to his own image in it. Both his estranged wife, Olga, and his mistress, Lilya, visited him in the apartment, but he was sleeping alone for the moment. Over breakfast, with the ex-terrorist Vera Figner acting as hostess after her return from Siberia in place of Olga, he spoke with allied diplomats and civil servants from his own and other ministries. Breakfast was the only slot where they were sure of seeing him; Kerensky set in motion sixty separate acts of legislation over early coffee and cakes. He then moved to the ministry reception hall to receive a string of petitioners, admirers, foreign journalists, and relatives of figures of the old regime pleading for clemency. Kerensky's Okhrana file was prominently displayed on a lectern so that his visitors had firsthand proof of his revolutionary purity. In the afternoons, he gave more interviews and attended government meetings. When these finally wound up, he moved on to the Soviet executive committee, where he retained his seat.

Kerensky fell out with Miliukov most publicly over war aims. Although Kerensky went far beyond most of his socialist colleagues in his support of the war, he was against Russian seizure of Constantinople and the Straits, the link between the Black Sea and the Mediterranean. On March 22, Kerensky declared that he favored the internationalization of the Straits. Miliukov promptly arranged an interview with the Cadet paper *Rech* to stress that, whatever Kerensky said, the government intended to pursue all the original aims agreed with the Allies, including the conquest of the Straits.

The next day, Kerensky rushed into a cabinet meeting, waving a copy of *Rech* and shouting, "This can't go on!" When Miliukov protested, Kerensky spat at the monarchist, "We are your Sovereign Emperor now." Kerensky's popularity made him essential to the government. Neither, for the moment, could the Soviet do without him — "Either exclude me or trust me unconditionally," he asked it on March 26, to be rewarded with cheers as the "leader of Russian Democracy." Prince Lvov found it impossible to live "without a belief in a miracle"; Kerensky provided it.

The revolution had raised huge expectations of miracles. Konovalov at the industry department complained that demands by workers were making it impossible to maintain war production. A few managers were murdered in early March; the director of the Putilov works and his assistant were killed and their bodies tossed into the Obvodnyi Canal. "Carting out," more common, continued: unpopular managers and foremen were taken out in wheelbarrows and dumped in the street, a ritual humiliation which the employers' newspaper *Torgovo-Promyshlennaya Gazeta* compared to ripping off officers' shoulderboards. The head of the Black Hundreds in the Putilov engine assembly shop suffered the added indignity of having red lead poured over his head before he was consigned to the barrow.

Under this pressure, employers conceded an eight-hour day with no loss of pay on March 10. Workers in Finland were more direct. They discovered that Finnish employers were meeting in a private house in Helsinki. Backed by workers from the Baltic Fleet, the men broke in and "brandishing their revolvers demanded the immediate introduction of the eight-hour day." The employers, "quietly sitting in their soft armchairs," agreed.

Russians were not the slave laborers of Bolshevik myth. In the country at large, 79 percent of all male and 44 percent of female factory workers were literate. In Petrograd the figures increased to 89 percent and 65 percent. Only 8 percent of workers in the big Petrograd plants were under eighteen years old, and none was less than fifteen. Workers in German and British war industries were working longer hours, and they worked them more often. The numerous religious holidays had not been abolished, and they kept Russian industry down to a 270-working-day year — 20 to 30 days fewer than in Britain and the United States.

Nevertheless, by March 20, the Skorokhod works in Petrograd was back on strike, this time for a one-and-a-half-hour dinner break, double pay for overtime, and back pay for the February strikes — "for our work in throwing out the Romanovs," as the workers put it. Students were also out, demanding the right to elect their teachers and calling for the wholesale sacking of "reactionary" teachers, including half the law faculty in Petrograd.

The most serious problems for the new government lay where the majority of Russians were living, in barracks and trenches and on the land. "The *muzhik* is glancing around, he is not doing anything yet," a Moscow newspaper had warned on March 8. "But look in his eyes. His eyes will tell you that all the land around him is his land."

Land seizure was the one real gain that the peasants expected of the revolution. In some places, as the Shakovsky family had discovered, they were already helping themselves. The government recognized that this was its "first and foremost" difficulty, but its attitude was ambivalent. Guchkov told a cabinet meeting on March 9 that the use of military force to put down the disorders was "inadmissible." He then charged Kerensky with prosecuting plunderers for criminal action, ignoring the fact that the cabinet was about to abolish the police force.

The estates used to maintain the imperial family were transferred to the state on March 16. The following day, the tsar's personal land and properties were confiscated. The newspaper *Novoe Vremia*, though supporting this move, felt all properties should be distributed to the people. The newspaper claimed that the peasantry "has the full right — human and divine — to this land." The *muzhiks* needed little encouragement. They began burning the manors of landowners with German names, maiming pedigreed stock or leading it off to slaughter. Timber was "liberated" by the cartful. A government declaration on March 19 warned that "seizures, violence, and robbery" were the "worst and most dangerous expedients." The declaration confirmed that a land committee was being formed. The committee's proposals, however, would not be put to the Provisional Government, but would await the Constituent Assembly. The cabinet thus admitted itself to be noncompetent to deal with the country's most pressing question.

The Soviet newspaper *Izvestiya* called aggressively for the takeover of the remaining *pomeshchik* landlord estates in an editorial on March 26. The Soviet had already insisted that the political amnesty announced by the government should include "terrorist acts, military revolts, and agrarian offences, etc." At the same time, the cabinet agreed to replace the police by a popular militia with elected officers. The peasants were apparently legally immune from "agrarian offences" and were no longer faced by a centralized police force. *Izvestiya*'s incitement further encouraged the drift into anarchy.

Sailors were relieved by the amnesty on military revolt. The Baltic Fleet mutinied after the abdication in what a survivor called a "Golgotha." Discipline in the imperial navy was brutal, and naval officers paid a terrible price, flung to drown in holes in the ice, tortured, and shot. The captain of the cruiser *Aurora* was the first to be murdered. Admiral Robert Viren, commander of the Kronstadt base outside Petrograd and a "whip-wielding martinet," and the Baltic Fleet commander Admiral Nepenin followed. Eighty-eight officers and petty officers were killed aboard the battleships *Pavel I* and *Andrei Pervozvanny* in Helsinki's harbor.

At the Helsinki funeral of one officer killed by his crew, Lieutenant Commander Polivanov, a mob of sailors broke into the church and filed past the coffin spitting in the dead man's face. They then turned the coffin upside down, emptied out the corpse, and left bawling the "Marseillaise."

The Bolsheviks made a particular propaganda effort with the Baltic Fleet. Alexander Ilyin Genevsky, a party member and a lieutenant in a chemical warfare battalion, went to Helsinki to bring out a naval newspaper called *Wave.* Men on the *Pavel I* raised a thousand rubles from their mess fund to pay printing costs and sailor-newsboys sold copies at three kopeks apiece on ships. Genevsky was put up in a bunk aboard a naval transport. He was "sole editor and staff, publisher, and proofreader," writing half its articles under various pseudonyms and locking himself up in a lavatory to get some peace. Though Genevsky admitted that it was an amateur product, with "nothing in it but political articles," it sold out because the sailors were anxious to read about their new rights.

Order Number One, the "cancer in the army" Rodzianko had so violently objected to, applied in its original form only to the Petrograd garrison. The thousands of copies that reached the front deleted the reference to the garrison, and included Guchkov's signature as war minister; the order thus appeared to be an official document applying to the army as a whole. In fact it had no official Soviet sanction, and Alexander Guchkov was opposed to it. Nevertheless, the Soviet refused to renounce it and the minister dared not disagree. "We could formulate policy only if we tried for agreement with the Soviet," Guchkov wrote. "Of course, I could have used my authority as minister of war to cancel the order, but it wouldn't have had any practical result."

The cabinet agreed that some concessions were necessary. A meanness had hung in the relations between officers and men. Soldiers on leave were beneath society, forbidden to enter first- and second-class compartments on trains, kept to the lower decks on steamers, barred from theater stalls, restaurants, and cafés. Though a prince, Serge Obolensky was also a trooper and as such could not ride in an automobile. Civilians and superiors addressed the men in the familiar, *thou,* as they would a child or pet. Officers called them fool, idiot, pig, or dog to their face. Young Arvids Jurevics saw an officer walking with his girl on a fashionable Petrograd boulevard when a soldier failed to salute him. "The officer grabbed him, hit him, pushed him into the roadway," Jurevics recalled. "He hit him a couple of times until the man apologized and saluted, then went back to the girl."

NCOs beat men on parade with incessant flicks of their swagger sticks, a ritual compared to a valet beating dust from a curtain. If Red Peter was literate enough, the peasant conscripts were not. The average literacy rate in the country was only 30 percent, lower than in mid-eighteenth-century England. The better-educated artillery treated infantrymen with contempt. The Germans frequently captured thousands of infantrymen without taking any guns, evidence that the gunners had left the "cattle" to fend for themselves.

For their part, the men often despised their officers. General Alexeev was told by his son, an infantry officer, that the men thought their commanders were "imbeciles" and that there was hardly a general who was popular with his men. The collapse in morale showed in desertion, lengthening sick lists, and a readiness to be taken prisoner. Perhaps two million had been taken prisoner — nobody in Mogilev knew for certain. They accepted capture with such passivity that a Russian attack was halted east of Lodz because a large mass of Russian prisoners in the enemy rear were assumed by their orderly and docile manner to be German reinforcements. "We throw our rifles away and give up," a prisoner explained, "because things are dreadful in our army, and so are the officers."

The rot was worst with the reserve troops, crammed into barracks and warehouses in the big cities. The whole country was "swarming with soldiers." Besides Petrograd, there were 150,000 men apiece in Kiev, Helsinki, and Tiflis, 70,000 each in Saratov, Samara, Tambov, and Omsk. Moscow, the biggest medical center, had 30,000 convalescent troops, a "wild crowd of libertines knowing no discipline, rough-housing, getting into fights with the police, rescuing arrested men, etc."

Casualties were sustainable. Cannon fodder the *muzhik* might be, but he was being fed to the guns at a proportionately much lower rate than French *paysan* or German *bauer*. The total number of men called up, about thirteen million, was marginally less than in Germany, which had not much more than a third of the Russian population. The fronts were quiet for months on end as the Germans attended to business in France. The number at the front, in trenches in alder-grown marshes, in huts and barns in freezing fields and lice-ridden billets in small towns, was seldom more than two million. If the Russians had matched the French in the proportion of adult manpower deployed in the trenches, the figure would have risen tenfold.

It was the manner in which casualties were taken that was unnerving the men. In per capita terms, with its military connotations of literacy and organizational skill, the German had an income of $184 against the Russian $41. The Russians performed well against Austro-Hungarians, whose $57-a-year income was not much greater than their own, but the gap with the Germans was unbridgeable. It was compounded by weaknesses in training and tactics.

The gigantic army had only 162 training battalions, each of which could take only one or two thousand men for a six-week course. Thousands of conscripts were sent to the front barely knowing how to fire their weapons. They often arrived in a state of shock. "Many had never seen a railroad car before, and the long ride down seemed to have unbalanced them in some peculiar way — for when they arrived they were little short of demented," a Cossack said. "It was not that they screamed or gibbered or did anything violent. They simply marched into camp, shoulders hunched, heads down, and if they looked up as they passed, their faces wore a vacant expression that is the beginning of insanity."

There were too many men for the officers to deal with. "What in hell shall we do with them?" a captain said. "No buildings for them, no hospitals, no way of sending them back — which is what we ought to do for all the good they are." Another officer replied, "Keep a heavy guard over them until we go into action. They will be the first meat."

General Dolgorousky, the myopic commander of the Horse Guards, refused to let his men take cover under fire. He insisted they stand up, shouting, "The Horse Guards do not lie down!" The general held his riding crop perpendicularly against his eye to improve his vision whenever there were Germans about. If he saw them, he shouted, "*Je les vois*" in French and ordered an immediate attack. Climbing on the roof of a barn, a difficult exercise due to his bulk, he made out a German battery. He could not, however, make out the intervening barbed wire, and the squadron ordered to attack took 30 percent casualties.

In its last major offensive before the revolution, twenty-nine infantry and twelve cavalry divisions assaulted a third of that number of German and Austrian divisions in the area round the Pripet marshes. They came in thin lines across swampy ground, officers at the head, sergeant majors in the rear to deal with deserters. No effort was made to maneuver or to use the assault troops in smaller groups who could give each other covering fire, now standard practice on the western front in France. Guards regiments, including the Preobrazhenskys, whose restless reserves were garrisoning Petrograd, took part in seventeen such futile attacks.

The dead were so thick on the ground that, though they gave off a terrible stench of putrefaction, the Germans refused a truce to bury them since they constituted a physical obstacle to advance. Some were slowly swallowed in the quicksands. Two months later, Prince Obolensky found that "still above the sand one could see the tops of their bayonets." By the time that Alexeev called off the offensive, Russian artillery was bombarding its own forward trenches to force the terrorized infantry back into the attack.

*   *   *

The Petrograd mutinies had created the revolution. The cabinet needed to treat an army so nervous and dangerous with extreme care. It was, in particular, well advised to listen to the views of the commander in chief. Short, with a gray handlebar mustache, Mikhail Alexeev was a shy man, embarrassed to be saluted in the street, with a weak eye muscle that had caused the tsar to call him "my cross-eyed friend"; nevertheless, Alexeev was "dogged, calm, and reasonable."

Alexeev was unhappy. The pledge in Order Number One not to transfer the Petrograd garrison to the front rewarded men who had tasted the fruits of indiscipline. An officer wondered whether the order would be remembered in the same way that the French celebrated the storming of the Bastille. "Perhaps," a colleague replied, "it is now we who are the prisoners in the Bastille."

The Egersky Regiment refused to have "officers hung around our necks once more." Another insisted that it should choose them: "Those who bashed us in the snout, sympathized with tsars and princes, and those who want to open up the front against the Germans — those we don't want." Alexeev wanted summary courts-martial to deal with deserters on the spot. He was alarmed that he had received no oath of allegiance from the new government to administer to the troops, who had technically owed loyalty to no one since the abdication. He complained, in an urgent wire, at the confusion created by conflicting orders from the Soviet and the government. Guchkov took three days to respond with a vague appeal for "solidarity" between officers and men.

Kerensky had also convinced himself that nothing was seriously amiss. He toured the front and men pumped his hand so hard that it was scratched and infected. He had taken to carrying it, theatrically, in a black sling. "The whole army, from the commander down to the last soldier," he told an Associated Press correspondent, "is eagerly devoted to the continuation of the war." It was what American readers, and Kerensky himself, wanted to hear. But it was nonsense.

Officers on the northern front were so frightened of their men that they had them parade unarmed, looking a "disorderly collection of ragtag and bobtail men," their uniforms disheveled and boots filthy. Only the cadets, ensigns, gunners, and field gendarmes looked normal. Two Duma deputies who toured the front in the first half of March found that clarification from the Provisional Government was needed "more than ammunition." They were kept up until two in the morning with questions. There was a "terrible thirst for news," the men kissing their hands in gratitude when the deputies arrived and carrying them from their sleighs. Was Russia a republic or a monarchy? The Duma men replied that the Constituent Assembly would decide, but "both officers and men have no clear idea of what the Provisional Government or the Constituent Assembly is."

On the sectors where confusion and lack of leadership were worst, men were decamping in a body as soon as they reached the rear. "The movement was something elemental," the British observer Bernard Pares noted. "They packed even the roofs of the railway carriages." The London *Daily Mirror*, unwilling to believe that the gallant Russian steamroller could have run so amok, published a picture of a train swarming with deserters under the caption "Russian Troops Hasten to the Front." Alexis Babine, still on his two-thousand-mile inspection tour of schools, found that "straggling, shabbily clad soldiers are beginning to line the road," with half-empty rucksacks on their back, going home.

The root of the mischief, Bernard Pares was sure, lay in Petrograd and the cabinet. "My hope that the army would serve as a support of order had already been ruined," he wrote. "Not at the front itself but from the rear."

On April 15, the Bolsheviks launched *Soldatskaya Pravda*, a soldiers' edition of *Pravda*. Alexander Ilyin had returned from Helsinki to Petrograd to work on its editorial board. The new paper was written in a "very colloquial style" to win the hearts and minds of ill-educated troops. Articles "always started with the ABC of any question and hifalutin' words were absolutely taboo." Because Ilyin's chemical battalion was a technical unit, it was asked to provide officers to do clerical work at the war ministry.

Ilyin became one of Guchkov's secretaries. By day, his job was to reply to all telegrams sent to the minister. In the evenings, he helped edit *Soldatskaya Pravda*, which, with its constant attacks on the war, "strenuously fought the same Guchkov."

XI
The Plague Bacillus

THE GERMANS were eager to add to Russia's military woes by aiding the leading defeatist to return to his homeland. The Auswätiges Amt, the foreign ministry in Berlin, had been funding revolutionary groups in Russia and abroad since early in the war in order to destabilize the Russian front from the rear. Vladimir Lenin had been in touch with German agents since 1915; it was a simple matter to speed the rot by transferring him across Germany to neutral Sweden and on to Petrograd.

To the penniless Bolsheviks, the Germans represented a source of party funds as well as a means of transport. For Berlin, an investment in Lenin could bring the double dividend of sowing social upheaval and defeatism among the enemy. The main difficulty was that, for all their obsession with wigs and false papers, the Bolsheviks were amateur conspirators.

Looted Okhrana files were showing how easily Bolshevik cells were penetrated. Lenin's plan to return was no more secret, and that it was soon known to depend on German help was no great surprise: if so many party members had been compromised by the Okhrana, why should the leader not fall in with the foreign enemy? Miliukov, as foreign minister, got wind of the plan and threatened to charge any emigré returning through Germany with treason. The Bolshevik leader's collusion with an enemy power was undoubtedly high treason, and he would have faced hanging under the law of any of the belligerent nations save one. The exception was Russia, where the government he wished to overthrow had abolished the death penalty.

Fortunately for Lenin, in any case, Miliukov took no practical steps to back up his verbal threat. The Provisional Government did not regard Lenin as a serious threat. His party was small and the *Pravda*'s new defensist line suggested that his hold on it was evaporating. The "party records" that Krupskaya was neatly packing in Zurich were yellowing with age as far as activity in Russia was concerned. Lenin had not addressed a meeting in Russia for ten years. The fresher press clippings and documents reflected the irrelevant disputes in exile.

The Germans had already distributed between two and three million marks to Russian radicals through Alexander Helphand, an ex-revolutionary who advised them on Russian internal affairs. Russian-born and known as "Parvus," he had been a brilliant young Marxist journalist who played a major part in the Petrograd Soviet of 1905 with his friend Trotsky. Parvus was arrested in 1906 and escaped from Siberia to Germany. He moved on to Constantinople, making a prewar fortune dealing in the shadow ground where politics, espionage, and high finance meet. He became grotesquely obese — his stomach "vibrated like a sack of grain" — and shocked his socialist collaborators with his champagne breakfasts and gaudy mistresses. But he remained a revolutionary and stayed in touch with emigré groups, including the Bolsheviks.

Parvus became convinced during the war that the "interests of the German government are identical with those of the Russian revolutionaries." He wrote an eighteen-page blueprint on how Russia could be destabilized by using radicals to raise mutinies, inflame minorities, inspire rail strikes, and sabotage oilfields, which he put to senior officials at the foreign ministry on the Wilhelmstrasse in Berlin in 1915. The Wilhelmstrasse developed a policy of "revolutionizing" to weaken enemy states — Sir Roger Casement, the Irish separatist executed by the British, was a client — with Parvus orchestrating antiwar radicals with German money. Not an impoverished, run-of-the-mill radical, Parvus's bulk reflected his great wealth — his neck had disappeared beneath his chins, his "small lively eyes were deeply embedded in fat," and when he walked, on short legs barely strong enough to support him, he seemed to use his arms to stay on an even keel. The Germans were impressed, advancing him one million marks to invest in the disintegration of Russia.

Parvus considered Lenin to be a key element — he assured the Germans that Lenin was "much more raving mad" than other revolutionaries — and he dined with the Bolshevik leader in Switzerland in May 1915. Although Lenin claimed that Parvus "ate without salt," meaning that he achieved nothing, the obese agent remained in contact with the Bolsheviks from his new base in Denmark. Wartime Copenhagen was a place of black marketeers and easy money. Here, Parvus dealt in military contracts, pharmaceuticals, contraceptives, and loyalties, working for governments and movements on many sides of many fences, but chiefly for Berlin. Lenin was also in contact with Alexander Keskula, a former Bolshevik who had thrown in his lot with Berlin to further Estonian independence from Russia. Keskula subsidized Bolshevik publications; in return, Lenin supplied Keskula — and, through him, the Wilhelmstrasse — with confidential party reports on the internal situation in Russia.

Within a few days of the revolution, the German ambassador in Copenhagen, Ulrich von Brockdorff-Rantzau, was writing to Berlin at Parvus's suggestion: "We must create as much chaos as possible in Russia." Everything should be staked on "deepening the antagonisms between the moderate and the extreme parties in secret." If the extremists got the upper hand, then within three months "in all probability the disintegration will be far enough advanced to guarantee the collapse of the Russian power through a military intervention on our part."

Lenin took the initiative in approaching the Germans. The German minister in Berne told the Wilhelmstrasse on March 10 that "leading Russian revolutionaries here wish to return to Russia via Germany," adding that "they are afraid to travel via France because of the danger from submarines." This was an understandable precaution; one group of returning exiles had been drowned when the steamer *Zara* was torpedoed on passage from England to Norway. The German foreign minister, Arthur Zimmermann, agreed that it was in German interests for the "radical wing of the Russian revolution to prevail."

Travel arrangements were made by two Swiss Social Democrats, Robert Grimm and Fritz Platten, who opened formal negotiations with the German minister in Berne. On Wednesday, March 22, Lenin and Krupskaya traveled from Zurich to Berne to agree to final German conditions. As they negotiated, German troops were smashing a Russian bridgehead on the west bank of the Stokhod River. The Russians were cut off by the snowmelt floods at their backs. Shelled and caught in machine gun cross fire, ten thousand surrendered and the gray-coated bodies of the dead were swept into the Baltic. The attack disabused frontline Russians of German goodwill and pepped up their fighting spirit. Berlin ordered the High Command to play down the victory and to cease offensive operations on the eastern front.

Lenin tried to spread the political risk of cooperating with the enemy by getting other émigré socialists to join the trip. He failed, while ruining any secrecy the journey might have enjoyed; a defensist émigré, Gregory Alexinsky, outraged that Lenin was dealing with the enemy, spread the word among the Zurich cafés on March 23.

The basis of the agreement was straightforward. Lenin needed, desperately, to get to Petrograd if the party was not to miss out as badly on the opportunities of 1917 as it had in 1905. The defensist views of the Bolsheviks made them, as one of them put it, "living bombs," who would disrupt the Russian war effort. Berlin considered that this alone justified the provision of a special "sealed" train. The Germans were protective toward their potential passengers. No mention of the journey was to appear in the German press. Should this become unavoidable — the British foreign office was already sending details of the trip to Miliukov in Petrograd — no German motives should be given "such as might compromise the émigrés."

The agents of all the belligerent powers, along with café habitués like the writers Stefan Zweig and James Joyce, soon learned of the arrangement. "It sounds like the Trojan horse to me," said Joyce. As negotiations continued, the revolution was burying its dead fourteen hundred miles away in Petrograd. Under a snowy and wind-lashed sky, 184 red-painted coffins were collected from hospitals and carried to a long trench dug on the transverse axis of the parade ground on the Champs de Mars. A million mourners marched through the city, even the anarchists bearing black banners and Colt revolvers maintaining perfect order. The guns of the Peter and Paul Fortress boomed at one-minute intervals. No priests were present, no hymns sung beyond the "Marseillaise." The Cossacks alone remained in their barracks, their conscience forbidding them to attend any funeral at which the figure of Christ was not displayed. As the light waned and the square slowly emptied, a dismal and icy mist rose from the Neva. It was, Paleologue thought, one of the most considerable events in modern history — for "what has been buried in the red coffins is the Byzantine and Muscovite tradition of the Russian people, the whole past of Orthodox Holy Russia." Along with its autocrat, it seemed, had gone the great empire's religion.

The Germans agreed to provide a train from the Swiss border to the ferry port at Sassnitz on the Baltic with extra-territorial rights, which would be sealed throughout the journey — Lenin, as Winston Churchill was to put it, would be transported like a plague bacillus in a test tube. A French newspaper had reported Miliukov's threat to arrest émigrés who had dealt with the Germans. Berlin insisted that everyone aboard the train sign a formal statement confirming that they understood the transit conditions — they were not to leave their carriage and were to speak to no one — and that they accepted responsibility for whatever reception awaited them in Petrograd. In return, Lenin signed an assurance that he would make every effort to obtain the release of Germans and Austrians interned in Russia.

Thirty-two travelers, Bolsheviks and their children. assembled at the Volkshaus in Berne early in the morning of Monday, March 27. They included two of the people closest to Lenin, Gregory Zinoviev, traveling with his wife and nine-year-old son, and Inessa Armand. Zinoviev, an earnest thirty-two-year-old, was the party leader's chief aide, a good organizer, rather plump with a pallid skin that hinted of ill health, and an odd, high-pitched voice.

Inessa Armand was a more exotic figure, a near-beauty with chestnut hair and gray-green eyes. The daughter of a French vaudeville actor, Inessa had been brought up in a family of wealthy textile manufacturers in Moscow, married a son of the family, and had five children by him before devoting herself to revolution and women's rights. She was arrested after the 1905 revolution and served three years in Siberia before escaping abroad. Devoted to Lenin, Inessa translated for him and lived almost in a *ménage à trois* with him and Krupskaya.

Though the Bolsheviks had no moral objections to free love, the nervous way the party played down her role indicated that she was his mistress. He wrote to her frequently, in letters that were later carefully edited, and allowed her to play the piano for him, a "soft luxury" he normally denied himself. Inessa was one of a tiny circle whom Lenin addressed in the intimate *ty* in letters. A French socialist had noticed how, during their time in Paris, Lenin would take Inessa alone to cafés and "with his little Mongol eyes gaze all the time at this little *Francaise*."

Several of the party were late at the Volkshaus rendezvous as Platten made a head count. The émigrés took a normal passenger train to Zurich, arriving in time for lunch at the Zahringerhof Hotel. During the meal Lenin read out his "farewell letter to Swiss workers." The others were in bubbling high spirits, but Lenin warned that "Singlehanded, the Russian proletariat cannot bring the socialist revolution to a *victorious* conclusion." At 2:30 P.M. they went to the central station where they were met by angry demonstrators alerted by the defensist Alexinsky. The émigrés left Zurich at 3:10 P.M. on the short trip to the border at Schaffhausen, with insults ringing in their ears: "Traitors! . . . German spies!"

The Swiss waived exit formalities for the revolutionary package group, the men in waistcoats and ties, the women in picture hats, unusual only for the large amount of luggage they carried. Platten hustled them aboard the sealed train — a locomotive, a single green carriage, and a baggage car drawn up on the German side at Gottmadingen. A six-day journey lay ahead.

Lenin was tetchy. Tobacco fumes upset him and he restricted smokers to the lavatory. This led to a queue and the discomfort of those who wanted to use it for more pressing reasons than nicotine withdrawal. Having created the problem, Lenin attempted to regulate it by issuing passes. Irritated by laughter and chat coming from the next compartment, he identified the culprit and banished her down the corridor. He was, however, well pleased with the food provided by the Germans. They were "good square meals," said Krupskaya, much better than the impoverished revolutionaries were used to. Krupskaya had aged badly in exile and at forty-eight, a year older than her husband, her round face had become pinched and her hair was lifeless and heavily streaked with gray.

As the Swiss guarantor of the group's conduct, Platten was able to use the one unlocked door to get off the train at Frankfurt and buy beer and newspapers. German soldiers helped him carry them back to the carriage. One member of the party could not resist chatting to them. Karl Radek, high-spirited and a mimic, a "little revolutionary goblin of incredible intelligence and vitality," was Polish-born and an Austro-Hungarian subject. He was technically a deserter from the Austrian army, and he found the conversation piquant.

This was the only breach of the agreement. German Social Democrats who greeted the train when it stopped for several hours in Berlin were not allowed to speak to the passengers. The Germans fulfilled their side of the bargain to the letter, delaying a train with the crown prince aboard for a couple of hours to give Lenin priority. Even so, it was late on Wednesday evening when they reached the Baltic ferry port at Sassnitz. Excitement had dissipated in long waits in sidings and fitful sleep.

The sixty-mile crossing to Sweden was rough. Lenin's man in Sweden, Jacob Ganetsky, who worked for a Parvus company that was running German pharmaceuticals into Russia through Sweden, was at the dockside in Trelleborg to meet them at 6:00 P.M. on Thursday. Genetsky had arranged another special train carriage for the group.

After dining in Malmö, the Bolsheviks traveled overnight to Stockholm. Newsreel cameramen and reporters were waiting for them. The sealed train and its exotic occupants were becoming a front-page story, although Lenin had no wish to play up his German connection and avoided interviews. Parvus was anxious to talk with Lenin on behalf of the Auswätiges Amt. Jacob Ganetsky put the request to Lenin. The danger of being further compromised by the Germans was so clear that Lenin made sure there were witnesses present when he refused to see Parvus.

Accepting money was a different matter. Karl Radek spent most of Friday closeted with Parvus. Given Parvus's position as a paymaster of revolutionaries, Bolshevik opponents were certain that the two discussed German terms for a large cash injection into the party's meager treasury. Lenin showed signs of suddenly coming into funds. He went to a Stockholm department store to change his shabby derby, threadbare jacket, and hobnailed boots for a smart overcoat, three-piece suit, and shoes. Lenin also stocked up on books and newspapers before settling back on Friday evening to read them on the five-hundred-mile journey around the Gulf of Bothnia.

He was not amused by the handiwork of Stalin and Kamenev when he went through the latest editions of *Pravda*. Krupskaya listened to his angry mutterings about defensism and the Provisional Government with some relief. They would help to make the trip pass more quickly. Early on Easter Sunday morning, April 2, the train reached Haparanda on the Finnish frontier. As it did so, Pontifical Mass was being said at the Nevsky Cathedral in Petrograd by the archbishop of Yaroslavl, the Metropolitan Pitirim already a victim of Nikolai Lvov's purges at the Holy Synod, imprisoned in a Siberian monastery. In the palace chapel at Tsarskoe Selo, Nicholas kissed the officer and men of the guard watching over him at the moment when "Christ is Risen" was said amid the melancholy and magnificent *Raspievy*, the Russian plain chant.

The party crossed the frozen Torne river on sledges, Lenin waving a red scarf tied to an alpenstock as they approached the Tornio customs post in Russian Finland. Miliukov's threat was empty. All the Russians were allowed through, only the Swiss Platten being denied entry. A train from Petrograd had been arranged by Alexander Shlyapnikov, the Bolshevik fixer in the capital. It was drawn up with red flags and bunting and green high-funneled engine in Tornio Station.

Everything was "terribly good and so Russian," Krupskaya thought — the shabby third-class carriages with wooden slat seats, an elderly Russian soldier who held one of the children in his arms and fed him *paska*, Easter cheesecake, the Karelian birches and pines. "Our people were glued to the windows," Krupskaya recollected. "Soldiers stood about in groups. [One of us] put his head out of the window and yelled, 'Long live the world revolution!'" The soldiers stared back in amazement. A pale lieutenant entered Lenin's compartment, followed by a press of soldiers. The lieutenant was a defensist and, as Lenin argued the merits of defeatism, the soldiers gaped at the strange philosopher with open mouths.

Kerensky was also in Finland, trying to snatch a few days rest with his mistress Lilya at the spa of Bad Grankulla near Helsinki. Still weak from his kidney operation, Kerensky had nightmares of separatism, dreaming that the red flag of free Russia was replaced by the yellow and blue banner of a separate Ukraine and the lion and roses of old Finland. He interrupted his recuperation to see groups of Finnish students. Russia was becoming a federal state, he argued, but if the Finns demanded secession too quickly others would follow and revolutionary unity would be wrecked. On the war, Kerensky had gone beyond defensism. He was becoming convinced that only a successful offensive could lance the tensions in Russia. An informant of the Auswätiges Amt reported regretfully, "Kerensky is a solid Russian and *hates* Germany."

The train with Lenin aboard drew into Beloostrov, the crossing point into Russia proper, at 9:00 on Monday evening, April 3. Kerensky was to be held up for a few minutes at the same point two days later on his return from Finland, for, although he was a minister and his carriage was filled with flowers as evidence of his popularity, he had forgotten his identity papers. Lenin had no difficulties. A crowd of workers from the local munitions plant were on the platform with a small Bolshevik welcoming committee, the mustachioed Shlyapnikov, Lev Kamenev, wan and his eyes nervous behind steel-rimmed spectacles, and Fedor Raskolnikov, a young naval officer of good family, victim of a nervous breakdown during a prewar stint in solitary confinement and now the leading agitator of the violence in the Kronstadt naval base.

After an impromptu buffet of beer and sandwiches, they reboarded the train for the run into Petrograd. They had hardly sat down, Raskolnikov recollected, when Lenin was snapping at Kamenev. "What's this you're writing in *Pravda*?" he said. "We saw several copies and really swore at you."

At 11:10 P.M. on Monday night the Swiss exiles arrived in Petrograd. No newspapers were published on Easter Monday, but the Bolsheviks had feverishly distributed handbills: "Lenin arrives today. Meet him." Raskolnikov had arranged an honor guard of Kronstadt sailors in striped jerseys and red pompom hats. They commandeered an icebreaker to cross the frozen gulf, disembarking at the Liteiny Bridge a few minutes before the train reached the Finland Station. A brass band played the "Marseillaise." Lenin, his Swedish overcoat flapping, preoccupied with finding a cab near midnight, was striding toward the exit when he ran into a dense crowd on the concourse. Alexandra Kollontai, the tubby feminist, pressed a huge bouquet of flowers into his chest and he held them awkwardly as he was led to the imperial waiting room to meet the welcoming committee.

Nikolai Chkheidze greeted him in the name of the Petrograd Soviet, glumly, Sukhanov thought, and in the tone and spirit of a sermon. No love was lost between the Menshevik leader and his Bolshevik rival. Lenin had been keeping a file on Chkheidze for two years to gather evidence of the Menshevik's "chauvinism" and "opportunism." Chkheidze saw Lenin as a "mischief-maker." Chkheidze said that his main task as the chairman of the Soviet was to defend the revolution from within and without. "We consider that what this goal requires is not disunity but the closing of democratic ranks," he went on. "We hope you will pursue these goals together with us."

His face "looking frozen," Lenin fidgeted with his bouquet and examined the gilded plasterwork of the ceiling while Chkheidze finished his speech. He turned to address the crowd. "The piratical imperialist war is the beginning of civil war throughout Europe," Lenin said. "The hour is not far distant when . . . the people will turn their arms against their own capitalist exploiters. The worldwide socialist revolution has already dawned. Germany is seething. . . . Any day now the whole of European capitalism may crash. Long live the worldwide socialist revolution!"

It was, Sukhanov said, "very interesting!" Lenin had turned his back away from Chkheidze, away from internal unity and the external defense of the fatherland, and had appealed directly for civil war and international revolution. The troublemaker had not reformed.

Lenin underlined his message with a harsh speech to Raskolnikov's sailors. "I don't know yet whether you agree with the Provisional Government," he said. "But I know very well that when they give you sweet speeches and make many promises they are deceiving you and the whole Russian people. The people need peace. The people need bread and land. And they give you war, hunger, no food, and the land remains with the landowners. Sailors, comrades, you must fight for the revolution, fight to the end."

Those who had been swallowed up by the drudgery of the revolution, Sukhanov thought, were suddenly faced with "a bright, blinding, exotic beacon. . . . Lenin's voice, heard straight from the train, was a 'voice from the outside.' " Sukhanov found it "novel, harsh, and somewhat deafening." There were not many to listen to it. The train was late. Kollontai's bouquet had wilted and much of the crowd had drifted away.

Lenin was hoisted onto an armored car by those who remained and driven across the Sampsonievsky Bridge to Kshesinskaya's mansion on the Petrograd side. At times the slab-skirted car was caught in the searchlights of the Peter and Paul Fortress, revealing Lenin in his blue peaked cap atop it.

The Provisional Government was, whatever Lenin said, visibly fighting injustice, and he drew immediate hostility for attacking it. On his arrival at the Kshesinskaya palace, the crowd outside demanded a speech. Lenin addressed it from a wrought iron balcony: "Capitalist pirates . . . defending the fatherland means defending one set of capitalists against another." Sukhanov overheard angry mutters. "Ought to stick a bayonet into a fellow like that," a soldier said. "The things he says!" said another. "If he came down here we'd show him! Must be a German."

Party members gathered in the ballroom for tea and sandwiches. Kshesinskaya's furniture had been looted, but the room retained its gilt-and-white elegance. Chandeliers with crystal swans as mementoes of the ballerina reflected in the light oak floor and the radiators had brass art deco panels. Lenin spoke from the marble fireplace with its blackamoor supports, his words clashing with the cool beauty of the palace and the charitable enthusiasm of his audience.

He flailed at *Pravda*'s defensism. The government was the tool of the "imperialist bourgeoisie," and all other radicals and socialists were "traitors, fools, and its lackeys." The very name "Social Democracy," he said, was so "desecrated by treason" that the Bolsheviks should call themselves "Communists." Peasants should seize land in the countryside without waiting for any sanction. Armed workers should patrol the cities. Troops should bring about peace by fraternizing with German regiments. "We don't need a parliamentary republic," he said. "We don't need bourgeois democracy, we don't need any government except the Soviets of Workers', Soldiers', and Peasants' Deputies!"

What he called for was already happening spontaneously in the army and on the land. Men of the Twentieth Corps were accepting gifts of bread and sausages from the enemy. On another section of the northern front, artillery units from the second Grenadier Guards Division opened fire on their own men, who had gone out to meet the Germans in no-man's-land.

All the horses had been driven off Prince Obolensky's model estate. Countess Lamoyska, a wealthy landowner, dared not return to her estate in Podolia. "We see the peasants standing about at the castle gate," she told Maurice Paleologue, "pretending to divide up our land in dumb show. One of them affects to want the woods by the river, another puts in for the gardens. . . . They go on talking like that for hours on end and do not stop when I go up to them." The peasants felt they were close to the old *muzhik* dream of *tcherny peredel*, the "black partition" when all land would be divided out.

These sentiments were independent of Lenin, whose name was almost unknown in the villages and at the front, but he was the first to express them. Nobody, Sukhanov said, had ever heard anything like it. It was "as though the spirit of human destruction, knowing neither barriers nor doubts," was hovering over the heads of the bewitched disciples. Nobody before had thought parliamentary democracy to be contemptible. Nobody had dreamed of the Soviets as organs of state power. But Sukhanov noted that Lenin made no mention of the economic crisis, nor did he explain how the Soviets — representing a tiny minority, having "no stable bonds or the most primitive constitution" — could create a government.

V. V. Voitinsky, a sober Menshevik and a Siberian returnee, said that Lenin was out of touch with Russian reality. He accused him of substituting catchphrases for thought and fact, of not thinking through the complications of the war. "You are mistaken to say that I am unfamiliar with conditions in Russia," Lenin retorted. "On the way through Finland to

Petrograd I shared a compartment with a soldier from the front. He told me all I need to know about the war." Lenin's formulae, Sukhanov thought, fired off without any commentaries, were pure anarchism. His speech had no pathos, no wit, and its concepts were simplistic. But Lenin had the gift of "hammering and hammering [ideas] into the heads of his audience until he took them captive."

For the moment, it worked only with the faithful. Lenin frightened his listeners but some already "felt themselves to be devoted servitors, knights of the Holy Grail." The applause was rapturous, giving way to revolutionary song singing as the Tuesday dawn broke. Sukhanov caught Kamenev's eye. The *Pravda* moderate shrugged and said, "Wait, just wait."

Within a few hours, the general enmity to Lenin's arrival was manifest. The honor guard of Baltic sailors passed a resolution expressing their "profound regret" at participating in his welcome. Had they known that he had returned by kind permission of the German emperor, they said, their hurrahs would have been replaced by a simple exhortation: "Away with you! Back to the country you passed through!" Kerensky deplored the presence of "the anarchist socialist Lenin," but added that it would have been morally wrong for the government to have prevented his return. It was not in character for Lenin to reciprocate such magnanimity.

The Bolsheviks who had cheered him at dawn had second thoughts when he appeared, chauffeur-driven in a commandeered Renault, at a joint Social Democrat meeting with the Mensheviks in the Tauride later on Tuesday. It was supposedly a "unifying conference," but Lenin harshly stressed irreconcilable differences, on peace and defeatism, on the Provisional Government, and on land. The tireless Sukhanov was present again to note the bafflement and embarrassment of the Bolsheviks at Lenin's "anarchist ravings." The only speaker to support him was Alexandra Kollontai, the highborn convert to revolution, first with the Mensheviks and latterly as a Bolshevik. Her speech produced "mockery, laughter, and hubbub."

"This is the raving of a madman!" the Menshevik B. O. Bogdanov said, shouting Lenin down. "It's obscene to listen to this claptrap." I. P. Goldenburg, once a member of the Bolshevik Central Committee, warned that Lenin was preaching civil war. "It's ludicrous to talk of unity with someone whose watchword is schism," Goldenburg said. "Lenin is making himself a candidate for the one European throne that has been vacant for thirty years — the throne of [the anarchist Mikhail] Bakunin! His new words echo something old . . . primitive anarchism."

Lenin presented a short summary of his views the same day. His "April Theses" were unyielding. There should be "not the slightest concession" to defensism, the Provisional Government, or a parliamentary system. He claimed that the revolution was passing from its first, bourgeois stage to a second stage where power would go to the proletariat and the poorest peasants, ruling through the Soviet. The police, the army, and the bureaucracy should be abolished. All land was to be nationalized, all banks amalgamated into a single national bank controlled by the Soviet.

The theses were published under his name alone, for no Bolshevik group or individual supported them. Lev Kamenev, writing in *Pravda*, found the theses ideologically unacceptable because they assumed that "the bourgeois-democratic revolution is *completed*" when it was not. Gregory Zinoviev, who had joined the *Pravda* staff after his return on the sealed train, was "perplexed." The provincial Bolshevik Lebedev said it seemed "Utopian" and could only be explained by Lenin's "prolonged lack of contact with Russian life."

The anti-Bolsehviks were "full of glee." Viktor Chernov, the Social Revolutionary leader, thought the ideas so extreme that "their dangers will be extremely limited and localized." The party itself rejected them out of hand in a vote on April 8. Bolsheviks in scores of towns were refusing to split from the Mensheviks. The risk of civil war was unthinkable when party support among factory workers was barely 5 percent and among peasants as good as nonexistent. Sukhanov met up with Pavel Miliukov, the two agreeing that Lenin was "a completely lost man" whose views were so unacceptable that he represented no danger at all to Miliukov. "Now he's in Russia," they thought, "he'll learn better."

Hostile crowds collected nightly outside the Kshesinskaya palace, where Lenin's office was in the airy former nursery, hurling abuse at the "German agent" inside. The right-wing press attacked his "plutocratic lifestyle" — the palace, the Renault and chauffeur. "Lenin has been installed in the palace of the mistress of a grand duke," *Novoe Vremia* commented on April 7. "How convenient it is to be friends with the enemies of Russia. The Bolsheviks are given a safe and free-of-charge passage through Germany. In Russia royal waiting rooms are opened for them at railway stations and they live in a luxurious palace — also free of charge."

Soldiers in Moscow appealed for protection from his "German propaganda." On April 19, a huge demonstration of war wounded with armless, legless, and bandaged men, the paralyzed lying in the back of trucks, moved down the Nevsky toward the Tauride. Among banners proclaiming "Our Wounds Demand Victory" were others demanding Lenin's arrest. "Spy and provocateur!" the demonstrators shouted.

Count Alexei Bobrinskoy was unimpressed by Lenin's arrival. "Some workmen greeted him," he wrote, "but on the whole his arrival passed quite unnoticed." Bobrinskoy had tea with the sister-in-law of Mikhail Rodzianko, the Duma chairman. She had never heard of the Bolshevik leader, "like so many others." "Lenin," Madame Rodzianko asked, confident enough that the troubles had abated to slip back into French. "Qui est Lenin? Est-ce qu'il est gentil?" Bobrinskoy thought that she was asking if Lenin was well-bred because she thought he was someone she should ask to a party.

"Non, Madame," she was told. "C'est un de ces affreux revolutionnaires."

XII

"Ready for Murder, Inquisition, and Death"

IT WAS TEMPTING to write Lenin off as a near-lunatic. His conversation was ill-tempered and brutish, cut by a high-pitched and mocking laugh when he mentioned others. Emphases underscored with a narrow-nibbed pen in his writings — "*smashing*," "*pitilessly*," "*crushing totally*" — revealed an obsession with violence. Trotsky had noticed on a bus tour of London years before that he never referred to the sights as "English." They were always "theirs," in the sense of "enemies." People as individuals, Maxim Gorky said, were of almost no interest to him — he thought "only of parties, masses, states."

Another radical, the gentler Peter Struve, thought that Lenin's principal *Einstellung* — mental focus — "was *hatred*. . . . The doctrine of the class war, thorough going, aiming at the final destruction of the enemy, proved congenial to Lenin's emotional attitude." This hatred had "something repulsive and terrible in it," for as well as being animal it was also "abstract and cold like the whole of Lenin's being." It ranged far beyond the autocracy, to embrace liberals, the bourgeoisie, and rival socialists with equal venom.

His intellectual activity, Sukhanov noted, was "extremely limited" and led to a "primitive demagogy unrestrained by either science or common sense." Lenin suppressed an early attraction to music because it led to sentimentality, and "today one must not caress anyone." This applied almost literally, for his marriage to Krupskaya was childless and had little emotional warmth. His one discreet affair was with Inessa Armand, his companion on the sealed train. Inessa was earnest but stylish — "the red feather in her hat was like the tongue of the flame of revolution." Her devotion, a fellow admirer of Lenin noted cattily, made her an ideal Bolshevik prototype of "rigid, unconditional obedience," the "perfect" —

almost passive — executrix of his orders." Inessa had a hard task to humanize a man who described life as a "filthy hell."

He was not physically attractive. Tatiana Alexinsky, the wife of a former Bolshevik deputy, found him repellent — "bald, with a reddish beard, Mongol cheekbones, and an unpleasant expression." She had noticed a personal cowardice underlying his verbal violence when Cossacks charged a Saint Petersburg demonstration during his belated visit to the 1905 revolution. "Lenin was the first to flee," she recalled. "He jumped over a barrier. His bowler hat fell off, revealing his bare skull, perspiring and glistening under the sunlight. He fell, got up, and continued to run."

Certainly, Sukhanov thought, Lenin was "abnormal . . . extremely narrow-minded, with no grasp of the simplest and most generally accepted things." Yet, because of the force of his hatred and his "few 'fixed' ideas," he was irreplaceable. "In the Bolshevik party," Sukhanov wrote, "Lenin the Thunderer sat in the clouds and then — there was absolutely nothing right down to the ground." The times themselves were abnormal and Lenin, navigating them with frantic certainty, was able to concentrate his "super-human power of attack" on his enemies.

The means might be modified, but the aim — the absolute conquest of power — did not vary. Lenin had defined the Provisional Government as the major enemy on his arrival at the Finland Station, and he was already preparing to assault it.

Prince Georgy Lvov was unconcerned. The mother of Zinaïda Shakovsky, the young girl who had been so delighted when the revolution cut short her school term, joined a curious crowd at the Kshesinskaya palace on a trip to Petrograd to listen to Lenin speaking. She did not, she told the premier, "much like what he was saying." Lvov was reassuring. "Do not worry about him," he said. "The man is not dangerous and the authorities can arrest him whenever they want."

The cabinet was busily dismissing the "authorities" who gave Lvov such confidence. No undercover agents now existed to give warning of political plots and there were no uniformed gendarmes to carry out arrests. The tsarist administration was being scrapped, not overhauled or replaced, as if goodwill and committees could replace compulsion. It would have been a dangerous experiment in a small and homogeneous country. In Russia, vast, with war and inflation compounding old ethnic tensions, it was "dream-like." Vladimir Nabokov in the cabinet office felt that "everything experienced was unreal."

A power vacuum was enveloping the provinces. The governor's mansion and the cathedral, old symbols of temporal and spiritual authority, still topped the hills of Simbirsk. But all governors and their deputies were dismissed, though many of them had welcomed the revolution. Asked who would replace them, Prince Lvov said airily: "This is a question of the old psychology. The Provisional Government has removed the old governors and will appoint no one. Let them be elected locally."

When Alexis Babine returned to Vologda after his schools inspection tour, he found that the governor and vice-governor had left the city. Babine went to visit the vice-governor, an old friend, on his country estate, taking forty loaves of scarce white bread with him as a present. He found the vice-governor plowing his land himself. Babine was drafted in to help muck out the stables.

In countries with a tradition of public service like England the richer gentry underpinned provincial stability; in Russia, they seldom played any part in the administration and took little interest in local politics beyond a "discontent so hopeless and insistent as to lead to hysteria." The gentry rarely dabbed in trade and commerce, indolently keeping their surplus cash locked up in government bonds. The autocracy had wanted no local rivals and ensured that the big landholdings were well scattered. The Vorontsov family fortune ran to seven hundred thousand acres. The economic and political clout of this vast holding was dissipated through sixteen provinces.

Peasant resentment against the gentry was accelerating. The Shakovsky family had wisely abandoned their estate near Tula in March after the peasants, not content with their raid on the distillery, threatened to return and burn everything. They moved to a second estate at Epiphan. They were welcomed at the railway station with carriages driven by "our friendly and faithful Austrian prisoners." But here, too, there was an air of menace and the family lived, not in the great house, but on a smaller farm.

A crowd of villagers soon appeared, led by a deserter named Chikin, still dressed in the frayed remnants of his uniform. Chikin said that the forests now belonged to the people. To prevent looting, he wanted the family to stand guard over its former possessions. Young Zinaïda Shakovsky was happy to ride off into the woods, armed with a shotgun and a mother-of-pearl-handled revolver, "feeling like a cowboy."

Chikin returned in mid-April to take the horses and cows and "bid us none too politely to go away." The prisoners of war decided to stay with the family, the Austrian sergeant explaining that "I'd rather be a valet to a gent than a valet to a valet." The family managed to retain some of its livestock, and it set off for a third Shakovsky estate near Matovo, "a little like Noah in his ark under the watchful eye of Chikin."

As the "real master" of Russia, only the Constituent Assembly could deal with the land question. The government had appointed a commission of seventy lawyers on March 25 to work out electoral procedures. The commission had no sense of urgency and an appetite for nitpicking over detail. Jurists were poring over the political systems of Belgium, Switzerland, and the United States, arguing the merits of proportional representation and the relative powers of an upper and lower house. They were concerned, not that the Constituent Assembly should be swift and lusty, but that it be perfect.

Tsarist officials were ignorant and adept at extracting bribes — Blok would look at their smart wives on the Nevsky and think that "behind every Persian lamb coat is a bribe" — but they had at least represented a system of government. The provinces were now largely left to fend for themselves.

What authority did survive — and the system was so confused that the country, having neither president nor tsar and being neither republic nor monarchy, was referred to simply as the "Russian power" — was shadowed by the Soviet. The Soviet took over the whole of the Tauride building in Petrograd, an expansion mirrored in the spread of its influence throughout Russia in April. The government was obliged to move to the Maryinsky Palace.

The Soviet was a bedlam. Meetings ran late into the night. The moderate Vladimir Stankevich complained that important decisions were "often reached by completely accidental majorities. Everyone was physically exhausted. Sleepless nights. Endless meetings. The lack of proper food, people living on bread and tea . . ."

None of this dimmed the ambition of the Soviet. It created its own "commissions" to deal with transport, communications, food supply, and other problems that were being worked on simultaneously by government ministries. It was the Soviet, and not the government, that agreed to the eight-hour day with employers. The Soviet sent its own military commissars to armies and fleets. The commissars were responsible, not to the war ministry, but to the Soviet executive committee.

A "Contact Commission" was set up to monitor government action and to ensure that it met the wishes of the "revolutionary people." There was no means of establishing the will of the people, prior to elections to the Constituent Assembly, but this did not inhibit the Soviet from denying the government freedom of action in the conduct of the war.

Miliukov had ignored his clash with Kerensky over war aims. The foreign minister was particularly pleased at American support. The United States was now a Russian ally, Woodrow Wilson speaking of the "wonderful and heartening things" that were happening in Russia in his address to Congress, which asked for a declaration of war. Overconfident, Miliukov returned to the fray on April 18. He sent the Allies a note confirming that the government would fight for decisive victory and honor all its obligations and aims. He had already assured them that Russia would fight "till her last drop of blood." Alfred Knox, the British military attaché, had "no doubt that Miliukov would, but can he answer for the whole of Russia?"

The Soviet was given a copy of the note the next day. There was particular anger that Miliukov had sent the note on April 18. This corresponded to May Day in the Russian calendar, the first to be openly celebrated with a colossal demonstration on the Champs de Mars, a dozen military orchestras grinding out the "Marseillaise," and dance music. Red-draped trucks were parked at regular intervals, each with orators attacking the war, all "men of the people in workman's jacket, soldier's greatcoat, peasant sheepskin, or Jew's gabardine."

On the evening of April 19, Olga Kerensky organized a concert at the Mikhailovsky Theater in aid of returning exiles. She was still officially recognized as Kerensky's wife, and he attended to listen to Tchaikovsky's Fourth Symphony and an aria from *Tosca*. He was depressed and tired. Though he was applauded when he attacked fraternization with the Germans, he then turned and said, "If the people don't wish to believe and follow me, I shall leave power. I shall never use force to make my opinion triumph." Bolsheviks noted it as an admission of weakness.

The Miliukov note was published in the press on April 20. In midmorning a car raced up to the Soviet with a soldier aboard, warning that a crowd of workers, many armed, was closing on the Nevsky from the Vyborg side. The crowd carried banners: "Hang Miliukov!" and "Down with Aggressive Policy!" Alexander Guchkov, as war minister, was attacked in the same way. A mob of troops from the Finland Regiment made for the Maryinsky Palace where they thought the Provisional Government was sitting. So far as could be judged in the confusion, the men were led by a lieutenant, Theodore Linde, a leftist who thought the Miliukov note was a betrayal of the revolution. A partly armed mass of thirty thousand surrounded the palace.

Guchkov was ill that day with his heart condition and the cabinet was in fact meeting in his office almost two miles away in the war ministry. The Soviet, alarmed that the mob would break into the Maryinsky, dispatched the Menshevik Matvei Skobolev from the executive committee to prevent violence. Skobolev dispersed the crowd with a promise that the Soviet would make an announcement on the issue. The Bolshevik Central Committee was meeting in emergency session. Lenin attacked the government as "thoroughly imperialist" and said that peace was only possible if power was transferred to the Soviet. Bolsheviks turned out on the streets with banners reflecting this: "Down with the Provisional Government!" and "All Power to the Soviets!"

General Lavr Kornilov, commander of the Petrograd military district, asked permission to open fire on the mob if necessary. The cabinet, fearful of Soviet reaction, refused. "The Provisional Government has no real force at its disposal," Guchkov admitted. "The Soviet has in its hands the most important elements of real power, the army, the railways, the post, and telegraphs. It is possible to say flatly that the Provisional Government exists only as long as is allowed by the Soviet."

The Soviet, however, had no intention of making the running. "Why should we take any action at all? Against whom marshal our forces?" Vladimir Stankevich asked a session of the Soviet in the evening. "The sole power that exists is you and the masses which stand behind you. . . . Look there! It is five minutes to seven." He pointed at the clock on the wall and all heads turned to it. "Resolve that the Provisional Government does not exist, that it has resigned. We will communicate this by telephone, and in five minutes it will surrender its authority." The prospect was real but, as the moderate Stankevich intended, frightening. "Who will take the place of the government?" a delegate asked. "We? But our hands tremble . . ."

Counterdemonstrations broke out, with groups of officers and fashionable women running along the Nevsky shouting "Long live the Provisional Government!" and "Down with Lenin!" Heated arguments over the war were breaking out through the city. Caps and the kerchiefs of women workers stood for peace, an observer noted, derbies and bonnets for war. It was suggested that Miliukov could be moved to education; "Constantinople as a topic in schoolroom geography would be less dangerous than in diplomacy."

During the night, S. Bagdaev, a Bolshevik agitator at the Putilov works, printed leaflets calling for the immediate overthrow of the Provisional Government. Nikolai Podvoisky, the head of the Bolshevik's military organization, appealed to party members at the Kronstadt naval base to send squads of sailors to the city. Though Lenin was later to claim that the Bolshevik effort was a "peaceful reconnaissance of the enemy's strength," it had all the outlines of an attempted coup. True to form, Lenin did not venture onto the streets to carry out any personal reconnaissance.

Civil war seemed to have broken out for a few hours on April 21. Sailors arriving from Kronstadt beefed up the troops and armed workers. Miliukov claimed later that those baying for his blood on the streets were "boy workers" paid ten rubles by Berlin's agents — "the idea of removing Guchkov and I was directly inspired from Germany." A journalist on the Cadet daily *Rech* had a different impression. "Their faces amazed me," he wrote. "All those thousands had but one face, the stunned ecstatic face of the early Christian monks. Implacable, pitiless, ready for murder, inquisition, and death."

Pro-Miliukov demonstrations grew larger. Trucks brought in officers and cadets armed with sabers and bayonets to the Nevsky. A mock trial was held in the street and Lenin found guilty of "treason." A crowd of women textile workers marched down the odd-numbered side of the Nevsky. On the other side were well-dressed women, officers, and shopkeepers with placards supporting the government. "Trollops! Rabble! Filthy scum!" a group of millinered ladies shouted. "The hats you're wearing are made with our blood!" came back as the women fought over each other's banners, scratching and screaming.

As the day wore on, U.S. Ambassador David Francis cabled to Washington, the friends of the government "gained courage to such an extent that whenever a Lenin banner appeared it was captured and torn to shreds." Shooting broke out in the Nevsky area as the battles for banners progressed. Gunmen fired from the windows of the Café Empire and the Dagmar Hotel on Sadovaya Street. Crowds fought with clubs and knives, scattering when firing started. The right blamed the riots on the Leninist "horde of outcasts and apaches," the left on former policemen "venting their impotent spite."

The city was pacified by the Soviet executive committee, not by the government. In the evening the committee declared "anyone who calls for armed demonstrations or fires even a shot in the air" to be a traitor. The Soviet forbade any street meetings or demonstrations in the coming days. Both the *burzhui*, the bourgeoisie on the Nevsky, and the workers in Vyborg obeyed. Petrograd was quiet the following morning, the fear of civil war "dissipating like smoke."

The public venting of fury struck Sukhanov as remarkable enough in itself, but he was more impressed that it was liquidated by the Soviet. Two months before, the Soviet had been a shadow dimly remembered from twelve years before. Now "its word commanded the elements." The "April Days" made it clear that, as Prince Georgy Lvov put it, the Soviet was the "power without authority" and the Provisional Government was the "authority without power." Lenin and Lavr Kornilov noted the government's fragility and the premier's tolerance of it. General Kornilov resigned from his post in Petrograd in disgust and was given a combat command at the front. Lenin, also realizing the Bolshevik need for their own combat forces, arranged for armed Bolsheviks to be incorporated into a "Red Guard" on April 28.

Splits opened up inside the Soviet. The moderate bloc included the "populists," Social Revolutionaries, and Trudoviks, and the "opportunist" majority among the Mensheviks. They were committed to defensism and to the support of the government, and they dominated the Soviet as a whole. A smaller group of "Menshevik-Internationalists" stuck to old antiwar principles and would have no truck with a bourgeois government. To their left, the Bolsheviks were the largest opposition group, though it was doubtful whether a third of workers supported them even in "Red Peter." Anarchists camped on the wilder shores of the left, "maximalists" in their Russian guise, swarming in the entrails of revolutionary Petrograd with a "seething nest" among the Baltic sailors.

The street, Nikolai Sukhanov thought, was outstripping the Soviet majority in fervor and radicalism. The April mobs wanted peace, bread, and land. The Soviet leadership would no more slake these gut desires than the government, leaving Lenin free to exploit them.

The government, Prince Lvov and Kerensky realized, would have to broaden its base to survive. They appealed to the Soviet to take a direct part in a coalition government. "All *real power* and *authority* was in the hands of the Soviet," said Sukhanov. "But — the opportunist and defensist majority did not want power and were afraid of it." On April 28, the executive committee voted against joining a coalition.

Two days later, Guchkov quit as war minister, telling Ambassador Francis that he "could not endure the dictation of Soviet deputies to which he was subject." Guchkov said that Russia had become "ungovernable." Miliukov resigned from the foreign ministry. Faced with the collapse of the government, the Soviet reconsidered its position on May 4. During the debate, a figure with "familiar piercing eyes, familiar wavy hair, and an unfamiliar little beard" entered the hall.

Leon Trotsky was back in Russia. The *Christianiafjord* had called at Halifax on its way from New York to Norway. British naval police boarded it and interned Trotsky in a camp at Amherst for captured German U-boat crews. The British, though they claimed that Trotsky was detained because of the shipping difficulties created by the submarine war on the North Atlantic, had no intention of allowing more defeatists to return to Russia. Anti-British feeling ran high in Petrograd, and the Soviet sent telegrams to the British government and press claiming that London was "insulting the revolution by depriving it of its loyal sons." The British released him, to the relief of the camp commandant; Trotsky had been converting the submariners to socialism with enough success for German officers to plead with the commandant to muzzle him. Camp life had become a "perpetual meeting." The British colonel agreed to ban him from speaking. Trotsky left on his interrupted voyage to the cheers of the U-boat men.

No cheers awaited him at the Soviet. Distracted by a shirt cuff that kept shooting out of his sleeve, Trotsky condemned the coalition as a "capture of the Soviet by the bourgeoisie." The socialist ministers were angered at his recipe: "Do not trust the bourgeoisie; control the leaders; rely on your own force." Word was already out that Trotsky, a onetime Menshevik, had grown closer to the Bolsheviks and was "worse than Lenin."

Soviet moderates agreed that "all waverings must be abandoned." The Soviet executive committee reversed its position on a coalition government. All but Bolsheviks and radical Mensheviks now voted to allow their party members to join the cabinet.

The new government was formed at 2:00 A.M. on May 5. Prince Lvov remained premier and the senior of the ten "capitalist" ministers. Mikhail Tereshchenko, whose stint at finance had done nothing to quench inflation, took over the foreign ministry from Miliukov. Kerensky replaced Guchkov at war and the Admiralty. Five other socialists came into the cabinet. The Social Revolutionary leader Viktor Chernov took agriculture, and the "insignificant lawyer" Pavel Pereverzev, justice. Irakli Tsereteli got posts and telegraph, and his fellow Menshevik Matvei Skobolev took his "simple, open, merry face" to the labor ministry. Food supply went to Alexei Peshekhonov.

From the beginning of May, Sukhanov wrote, the "bloc of the big and petty bourgeoisie was completely stable, unshakable, and even formal." Tereshchenko was delighted. "Dual power has disappeared," he said. "The ministry is supported by Cadets, Popular Socialists, Social Revolutionaries, and Mensheviks. Only the Bolsheviks oppose the government." The enthusiasm of the young sugar magnate was premature.

The Social Revolutionaries dominated the petty bourgeoisie, it was true, as the Cadets dominated the *burzhui*. In the cities, the Social Revolutionaries were supported by shopkeepers, minor officials, and the "indigent intelligentsia" as well as non-Bolshevized workers and soldiers. In the countryside, their simple slogan — "Land and Freedom" — had won them the near exclusive control of the dark people. With Viktor Chernov, on the left of the party, as agriculture minister, support in the countryside was firm. Kerensky's popularity on the party right attracted some of the upper bourgeoisie and liberal landowners, as well as "solid masses of military people," regular officers, and even generals. The Social Revolutionaries backed the coalition with apparent fervor — "the loveliest girl in France," Sukhanov said, "could have given no more."

Kerensky, with his "golden hands" and "supernatural energy," was performing well enough. Chernov was another matter. He had been an ideal theorist-in-exile, but was confused by the "din of hammer and anvil" of actual revolution. Sukhanov found him "inwardly feeble and outwardly unattractive, disagreeable, and ridiculous." Chernov barked but did not bite, using his sharp tongue merely to "wash his hands of everything." Without him the Social Revolutionary party "would not have existed any more than the Bolsheviks without Lenin," but he had not the "slightest striking power or fighting ability." At forty-four, Chernov was the leader of the largest party in Russia and his portfolio was one of the most important in the cabinet. He brought, his critics said, a dull and inactive smugness to both.

Chernov was Kerensky's nominal superior in the Social Revolutionary hierarchy. The two disliked one another. Kerensky found "interminable and impractical discussions" of the sort Chernov thrived on to be "repugnant to my nature." When Chernov had returned from exile to the Finland Station, his train was late and Kerensky had made a point of not bothering to wait. Chernov, jealous of the younger man's popularity, seemed better disposed to Lenin than to Kerensky. Chernov was convinced that Lenin's extremism would be tempered by Russian reality. "I am amused by the fears that the reverse will occur, that Lenin will destroy the new Russian life," Chernov declared. It was one of the most flawed judgments of the revolution.

Two portfolios went to Mensheviks. Irakli Tsereteli, the goateed and ox-eyed Georgian whose pale and angular face "radiated energy and integrity," was underemployed at communications. Matvei Skobolev was more usefully placed at labor.

Menshevik commitment to the coalition was less full-blooded than it sounded. Nikolai Chkheidze, the chairman of the Soviet, had said that the Mensheviks would only support the government "for as long as it realizes democratic principles." This little phrase was rich in ambivalence. Worse, Julius Martov, the party's old "begetter, its incomparable, its most authoritative and popular chieftain," was opposed to entry into the coalition. Martov returned from Swiss exile the day after the party conference. Too late to influence the vote, Martov was in good time to split the Mensheviks into a mainstream majority led by Tsereteli and Chkheidze and his own defeatist and anticoalition Menshevik Internationalists.

Martov's body was "unimpressive, puny," his voice muffled and hoarse, his abstract arguments exhausting to a mass audience. At his peak he could give a "dazzling firework display of images, epithets, and similes," so brilliant that the showy Trotsky seemed a dull echo. Sukhanov thought Martov the "most intelligent man I've ever known," a virtue holding the corresponding vice of *"weakness in action."* To "understand everything is to forgive everything," the diarist remarked, and Martov was mild and submissive to opponents. Though he despised the Bolsheviks as would-be dictators, his conscience crippled him from "free and reckless acts of combat" that did not demand reason but only will. Martov suffered from "Hamletism." No one could accuse Lenin of that.

In policy the new government differed little from the old. It remained riddled with internal fault-lines. Its first official statement on May 6 said that the government favored a "general peace without annexations or indemnities," but would continue offensive operations. Why should a soldier risk his life in an offensive when his country was committed to rejecting annexations and the fruits of conquest?

The war inhibited the cabinet from firm action on the land question. If any announcement was made on the breakup of the big estates, ministers argued, the peasant soldiers would desert en masse to be on the spot for the great share-out. But they were already deserting, by the tens of thousands. The defeatist propaganda of Martov and Lenin worked its way to the front, bringing the first instances of grenades being thrown at officers whom their men thought too eager for combat.

As the peace party, the Bolsheviks needed the war because opposition to it set them apart from their rivals. Lenin feared that an "imperialist peace" would leave the Bolsheviks without a platform. But the war continued, to Lenin's immense profit. The new Mensheviks and Social Revolutionary ministers might disapprove of the war, label it "imperialist," and call for it to end as soon as possible. But, through their entry into government, they were now implicated in its daily conduct.

Alexander Blok found it difficult to distinguish between the new coalition, the old government, and tsarism. "I do not even know whether or not there has really been a revolution," the poet wrote on May 12. "It is all in a minor key." Only the Bolsheviks could clearly be identified as distinct, and their support looked flimsy. The "revolutionary people" struck Blok as a rather doubtful concept. The revolution had happened with "utter unexpectedness, like a train crash in the night, like a bridge crumbling beneath your feet, like a house falling down." Most people had been stunned by it and he found it "impossible that they would suddenly become revolutionary."

Blok was himself effectively a deserter from his engineer unit in the marshes near Pinsk, one of the eight thousand a week who were failing to return from leave. He asked Mikhail Tereshchenko, an admirer, to have him transferred out of the army. The new foreign minister, though he carried a slim volume of Blok's poems in his pocket, was hesitant. Ministers committed to continuing the war should not get lieutenants relieved from their posts, no matter how good their poetry. Looking up another contact, Blok got himself appointed as verbatim reporter to the government's Extraordinary Investigating Commission, which was looking into unlawful acts committed by tsarist officials and court dignitaries.

He felt no sense of guilt at not returning to the army. "Let Europe go on fighting if she wants to," he said. "Let her, old exhausted cocotte that she is. All the wisdom of the world will run out through her fingers, soiled by war and politics." He helped to interrogate the "former people" of the old regime, trotting from cell to cell in the Peter and Paul Fortress. Anna Vyrubova was rumpled, half-reclining on her bed recovering from an old injury in a train crash, a crutch pushing up one shoulder. Alexandra's confidante was in fact quite safe — Blok's commission had "no wish to inflict on the prisoners the kind of treatment which 'they' used on us" — but she was fearful. A medical examination carried out to see whether she had been Rasputin's mistress had revealed her to be a virgin.

The former premier Ivan Goremykin had eyes that seemed to be "looking into death." Alexander Sobeshchansky, a once-feared official who had attended tsarist executions, had become a "pathetic, criminal bird." He had a gauze patch on his long neck, and "where there ought to be a forehead is sorrow and anxiety."

Some were made of tougher stuff. Count Vladimir Fredericks, the court minister, was suffering from a bladder disease which obliged him to urinate in front of his jailers. His Petrograd residence had been burnt to the ground by a mob which mistakenly took his surname to be German. But he had kept his dignity, his cane, and his manners. "Charming — of the olden days," Blok noted. "One of the *best* and most characteristic figures. Elegance." Nikolai Markov, ultrarightist and an old Black Hundreds leader, was angry, fit, and tanned. He stroked his mustaches and bared his white teeth as he spoke to his interrogators in a tone verging on insolence.

The garrison at the Peter and Paul Fortress did not trust Blok's commission or the government. The guards refused to give milk and eggs to prisoners who needed a special diet. Blok found it "very, very sad." The commandant at Tsarskoe Selo gave Blok a detailed account of the circumstances of the royal family — lonely walks in the park, surly guards, silence. "That is sad too," Blok wrote. "In fact, everyone is right — the Cadets are right . . . and in Bolshevism there is a terrible rightness. I do not see ahead at all. The 'old' and the 'new' are in us ourselves. . . . And I am suspended in midair; there is neither earth just now, nor heaven. And with all that Petrograd is extraordinarily beautiful again at the moment."

Scarlet trams ran overladen with soldiers. The limes and chestnuts were in leaf in the Summer Gardens. Beneath a "terrible, sharp sickle moon," Blok saw a couple embracing, the woman bent back against the man's shoulder "in a long and languorous curve and does not withdraw her lips."

The talk in the salons was dominated by the troubles in the countryside, and in the English Club by the onward march of inflation. The ruble, 166 to £10 in February, dropped through the 200 mark for the first time. Government 5 Percent, which had put on three and a half points with news of the coalition government, was down seven points at the end of May. "Russia has once more provided something of a wet blanket for stock markets," *The Economist* reported in London. "The problems arising out of the revolution are complex and obscure."

Blok, cuckold and cuckolder as he and his wife Lyuba accelerated their separate affairs, alternated between black moods and elation and prescribed himself narcotics. He found himself "morally off balance. Neurasthenia. Doctor Kannabikh."

In the Crimea on an operatic tour, Fedor Chaliapin sat on a rock looking out to sea. "There's no order," the singer said. "Not a vestige of it. Nothing on earth but speechifying. . . . Absolute chaos. Talking, talking, catching up on a hundred years of lost time."

On the Nevsky, a misshapen dwarf sat on a stout pole held above the heads of the crowds by a sturdy peasant. Passersby, including Somerset Maugham, dropped stamps and kopek coins into the box at the foot of the pole. The dwarf's face had hollow temples and wan cheeks, but the profile was that of a finely shaped young man, who watched the crowds with the "intentness of a bird of prey," his fierce bold mouth "curved into a sardonic smile, aloof, malicious, and yet tolerant." The dwarf, the British secret service agent thought, was "like the spirit of irony watching the human race."

XIII

My Government and I

On June 3, the first All-Russian Congress of Soviets opened in the Nicholas Military Academy in Petrograd. More than a thousand delegates arrived from across the country. They were put up in rows of camp beds, sitting on the red blankets and chattering excitedly like "boys in a gigantic dormitory" amid the snoring of those exhausted by their journey. They were fed in a great refectory in the basement, the sound of their arguments echoing off the low ceiling.

Kerensky was born eleven years after Lenin, too young to have clashed with him in childhood. The two boys from Simbirsk had their first and only head-to-head confrontation on the first day of the congress. Lenin led his small group of delegates to the extreme left of the hall, the preserve of "extremists, irreconcilables, and faddists of all types." The Bolsheviks numbered only 105 out of the 777 delegates with a party affiliation. Their civilian jackets made up a narrow strip in a hall dominated by the soldiers' uniforms and *muzhik* blouses of the 533 Social Revolutionary and Menshevik delegates. The Bolsheviks scarcely outnumbered the "secret Cadets and anti-Semites," the group of junior officers, lawyers, physicians, and officials, sitting on the right.

Lenin spoke first. It was the first time most delegates had seen him. Kerensky cut a dashing figure with his flattop hair, military jacket, and fetching sling, but Lenin wore a drab three-piece suit. His voice was flat and he spoke with soft Rs, reminiscent of the Gallic inflection affected by Polish aristocrats when they spoke Russian. "One of two things is possible," he said, pointing at the benches on the right. "Either a bourgeois government with its paper plans for so-called social reforms, or we have the government for which you seem to long, but have not the courage to bring into existence, a government of the proletariat which has its historic parallel in 1792 in France. . . . Look at what you are doing. Capitalists with 800 percent profits are walking round the country just as they were under tsarism. Why don't you publish their profit figures, arrest some of them, and keep them locked up for a bit?"

It was not a good speech. Having "left his underground cave for the light of day," as Nikolai Sukhanov put it, Lenin was blinking and out of sorts with his audience. His sarcasm was childish — he said that Tereshchenko was no better than Miliukov at the foreign ministry, "just slightly more stupid" — and he appeared absurdly boastful. Why was it said that there was no party that would take the power on itself? he asked. "I answer: there is," Lenin said. "Our party will not refuse it. It is ready at any moment to take over the government."

The claim brought yells from his own side, and catcalls and derisive laughter from the rest of the hall. Who did Lenin, "leader of faddists," think he was? Kerensky was in fine form, the new war minister's eyes "blazing like fiery beads" above his brown jacket and gaiters as he counterattacked. "How did the French Republic of 1792 end?" he asked. "In base imperialism. . . . Our duty is to prevent this happening so that our comrades who have just come back from Siberia shall not have to go back there. And so that *that* comrade," he said, pointing at Lenin, "that comrade, who has been living all this time safely in Switzerland, shall not have to fly back there.

"He proposes a new and wonderful recipe for our revolution. We are to arrest a handful of Russian capitalists. Comrades! I am not a Marxist, but I think I understand socialism better than Comrade Lenin, and I know that Karl Marx never proposed such methods of oriental despotism." Kerensky mocked Lenin's idea that a few friendly meetings between German and Russian troops would usher in the worldwide dawn of socialism. They would wake up one fine day and find that they "are fraternizing with the mailed fist of William Hohenzollern." Bolshevik remedies were "childish — arrest, kill, destroy. Are you socialists or policemen of the old regime?"

Kerensky's voice harshened. "Instead of appealing for reconstruction, you clamor for destruction," he shouted at Lenin, who sat calmly stroking his beard. "Out of the fiery chaos that you wish to make will arise, like a phoenix, a dictator." Kerensky paused, and walked across the platform toward Lenin and the Bolsheviks. "I will not be the dictator you are trying to create." Then he turned his back on them. A resolution of confidence in the Provisional Government was passed against Bolshevik opposition by 543 votes to 126.

Viktor Chernov added a rider that passed almost unnoticed in the applause. "The war," he warned, "is a great pump which sucks out the strength of the country." The Bolsheviks remained the only significant party to propose peace at any price.

Few freshly wounded were arriving in Petrograd, only "train after train of men with scurvy." The Red Cross refused to stop antiwar agitators from working the hospital wards — "We have not the power and can do nothing by force." The British-funded Hospital of Saint George was closed down because it had become impossible to get fit men to leave their beds. Daily, more deserters filtered into the city, slouching down the quays, leaning on the parapets chewing sunflower seeds and smoking cigarettes. They took over trams, going for joyrides and stopping people from getting to work. In provincial towns, deserters "blighted the boulevards and filled all public places."

A demonstration two-thirds of a mile long filed down the Nevsky. Rows of men in "vaguely military uniforms, in deep, glum silence" filed past Sukhanov on the balcony of *Novaya Zhizn*, Maxim Gorky's newspaper: soldiers over forty wanting to be demobilized. They carried no banners but wretched little signs that read, "The land has no one to work it! . . . Our land isn't sown. . . . Let the young men fight!"

Lilya had moved in with Kerensky and the ill will between her and Olga was open. Kerensky began spending more time outside Petrograd.

The front was quiet. "Neither the crack of machine guns nor the exchange of artillery fire," Kerensky reported after visiting the line in Galicia. "The trenches were deserted. With their uniforms in ludicrous disorder, thousands of troops were devoting their time to interminable meetings." Soldiers left their positions, made their way through the wire, and came back loaded down with propaganda newspapers put out by the German High Command. Printed in Russian on bond paper, *Russki Vestnik* told its readers that the British were using the bones of fallen soldiers for fertilizer and that U.S. aid was tied to Russian casualties: "American dollars for Russian blood." The troops "believed this more than they do the Petrograd papers." "*Germani nicht feind*," they shouted from their trenches. "*Feind hinten.*" The Germans were not their enemies. Those were in the rear.

Bomber crews flying missions with the Murometsy near Tarnopol were threatened by soldiers who thought the raids would delay a peace treaty. A bomber was lost and its six crew members killed after a main strut and its cables had deliberately been weakened. Troops were refusing to relieve frontline units because they "hadn't had their baths or the weather was bad." They would not take their rifles into the line with them. "What for?" they said. "We're not going to fight."

Girls were now being recruited into women's "Death Battalions" to shame the men. These units were founded with Kerensky's permission by Maria Bochkaryova, a remarkable twenty-eight-year-old. Daughter of a former serf, she was seduced at sixteen by an officer and, abandoned, drifted into an unhappy marriage with a man who beat her. To save her husband from Siberian exile for sheltering a Social Revolutionary terrorist after the 1905 revolution, she had slept with the governor of Yakutsk. Wishing to rid herself of humiliation, she successfully petitioned the tsar to allow her to join up in 1914.

She was a sergeant, three times wounded, when she persuaded Kerensky to allow her to form the women's battalions in a welter of press publicity. Volunteers were urged to enlist at an apartment on Muitenskaya Street in Petrograd, and a steady stream of peasant girls with "small hands and thick-looking legs" came forward. The better-looking ones were photographed by the illustrated magazines having their heads shaved. The gossips soon added an affair with the handsome Bochkaryova to Kerensky's already embarrassing marital position. Olga Kerensky burst into tears at a recruiting rally after his mistress Lilya said spitefully, "Why do they make all this fuss over you?"

Officers, already bitter at the Guchkov sackings, were shocked that female volunteers were compensating for male cowardice. Their own loss of status rankled. German, Turkish, and Austrian prisoners were demanding that the eight-hour day should apply to their work on farms. But in Revel, a Russian captain was made to put on peasant *lapti* shoes and was led through the streets tied to a rope. In Kronstadt, drunken sailors burst into the cells where naval officers were held and ordered them to "Show us your arse." The generals and the Soviet insulted each other over the need for discipline. Kerensky tried to paper over the cracks: "No one can level accusations at the Soviet," he said. "But no one can accuse the commanders either." He convinced no one.

Kerensky was to tour the front with Viktor Chernov, his fellow minister and Social Revolutionary, but they were barely on speaking terms. Kerensky found Chernov a conceited pedant, "incapable of action." Chernov was so irritated at Kerensky never listening to him that he would ostentatiously start writing in a notebook when Kerensky made a speech.

On the right bank of the Neva, where the river swings ninety degrees to the west, a large park with shaded walks and gardens stretched back from the Palyustrovskaya quay. An ornate villa, built by a former interior minister, Pyotr Durnovo, stood close to the bank. It had been taken over during the revolution by a group of seventy or so anarchists. They stored their black flags and arsenal of bombs and arms in its lofty rooms. Local Vyborg families walked their children in the grounds, and in the evening courting couples held their trysts in its scented rose gardens.

The anarchists emerged spasmodically from the villa with black banners, long-haired, their black clothes festooned with Colt revolvers, bandoliers, and grenades. On one foray, they marched on the U.S. embassy to protest at the death sentence passed on the "anarchist Muni" in San Francisco. This turned out to be the labor leader Tom Mooney, convicted of bomb outrages in California. Ambassador Francis had loaded his revolver before a Cossack unit arrived to disperse the anarchists.

Sometimes they would seize a grand house — anarchists no more stinted themselves with their accommodation than the Bolsheviks in the Kshesinskaya mansion — and turn it into a fresh squat for their followers. Ladies thrilled themselves with salon rumors of happenings behind the high walls of the Villa Durnovo, orgies and free love, plans to murder ministers and blast the *burzhui* with bombs, worship of the "vampires of melancholy." The anarchists compensated for their lack of numbers with the sensual violence of their rhetoric: "Teeth sink with hatred into warm succulent lovers' flesh! Wide, staring eyes follow the pregnant, burning dance of lust! Convulsions — flesh — life — death — everything!"

On June 5, a black band left the villa, flamboyantly armed with automatic weapons acquired from sympathizers in the First Machine Gun Regiment. They filed off to the offices of the right-wing paper *Russkaya Volya*, arrested the managers, and took over the printing presses. "We are liquidating a vulgar rag," they said, "and giving property back to the people." Troops were called in to disarm them. Why, the Cadet paper *Rech* thundered on June 6, had the law not intervened to expel the black nest from the Durnovo?

Lenin's boast of being ready to take power was not empty. As the rich read their copies of *Rech*, the Bolshevik leadership was meeting to discuss Lenin's plan to put forty thousand men — Red Guards and sympathetic troops — onto the streets in an armed demonstration against Kerensky and the Provisional Government. Should resistance be weak, the Bolsheviks aimed to arrest the ministers and proclaim a "Soviet" government which they would dominate. The cautious Lev Kamenev warned that such adventurism would end in the same failure as the April Days. "Lenin proposes a revolution," said V. P. Nogin, a member of the Moscow party. "Can we do it? We are a minority in the country."

The following day, the justice minister Pavel Pereverzev gave the anarchists twenty-four hours to get out of the villa. The Vyborg side was in uproar on June 8. Twenty-eight factories were out on strike. Armed demonstrators demanded that the anarchists be left alone. The Soviet insisted that the government stay firm.

The Bolsheviks replied with a call for a massive antigovernment rally on Saturday June 10. The war, their pasted proclamations said, "is deliberately continued by millionaire bankers." Kerensky was "violating the rights" of the troops. Famine "is ever closer and no steps are taken against it," while "revelry and bacchanalia" were sweeping the rich. "All out in the streets, comrades! Down with the ten capitalist ministers! All power to the Soviet!"

Petrograd was barely functioning. Experienced civil servants who had been too strict or exacted fines had been thrown out of their ministries. Post was taking up to ten days to travel a few streets. Telephones worked only fitfully. The fresh crisis ground at nerves. The Kronstadt sailors and the First Machine Gun Regiment declared that they would join the demonstration with their weapons. Bolshevik agitators were working the Izmailovsky, Pavlovsky, and Moscow regiments. Sukhanov reckoned the rest of the garrison, if not actively pro-Bolshevik, to be "indifferent, neutral, and useless for active operations on the foreign or the domestic front."

The Congress of Soviets could no longer ignore the frantic Bolshevik activity. The poster campaign, the appeals to the machine gunners and sailors, indicated a coup attempt. Sukhanov and Kerensky were certain that Lenin was planning one; not a deeply thought-out affair, but a revolt that would lead to a seizure of power given a "favorable conjuncture of circumstances."

The Soviet sat in emergency session shortly before midnight on Friday. The Bolshevik leaders, absent in their own emergency central committee meeting, were represented by Nikolai Krylenko, an army ensign whom the British diplomat Bruce Lockhart thought an "epileptic degenerate" and "the most repulsive type" of all the Bolsheviks he met. Kerensky was present to deny the Bolshevik-inspired rumors that troops were being brought in from the front to put down the workers. A vote was passed to ban the demonstration. The government warned that any violence would be met with force.

At 3:15 A.M. on Saturday morning, June 10, the Bolshevik central committee voted to call off the demonstration. Surprise had gone and the danger of failure was clear. A messenger was sent to the *Pravda* plant. *Soldatskaya Pravda*, the Bolshevik's army paper, was already being run off the presses with a call to take to the streets. The copies were trashed and the front page remade. The Bolsheviks were shown to remain too weak to deal with an aroused Soviet and government.

On Sunday, the party was flayed at a closed session of all the socialists represented in the Soviet. Lenin, Sukhanov noted sarcastically, "was as ever absent," and Trotsky, though still not officially a party member, had to weather the storm on his behalf. The main Menshevik spokesman, Fedor Dan, the mild-faced and balding chief editor of the Soviet paper *Izvestiya*, said that no party should hold demonstrations or use armed units without the consent of the Soviet.

Irakli Tsereteli went further. "What has happened is nothing but a plot against the revolution, a conspiracy for the overthrow of the government," the Georgian communications minister said, the vein on his temple swelling. "The Bolsheviks know they can never get this power in any other way. . . . It can recur tomorrow. The weapon of criticism is being replaced by criticism with weapons. Revolutionaries unworthy of holding weapons must be deprived of them. The Bolsheviks must be disarmed. We must not leave them machine guns and weapons."

These prophetic words were undone by Julius Martov. Sukhanov had read him right; at moments demanding aggression, the Menshevik Internationalist lapsed into "ultrarefined web-spinning." He attacked Tsereteli, not Lenin, asking him for proof of Bolshevik ill-intention and demanding to know why he wished to strip arms from the proletariat. Tsereteli's amendment was rejected in favor of Dan's bromide. The Bolsheviks were allowed to keep arms they intended for use against the Soviet.

A further resolution was passed to allow an "official" Soviet demonstration on Sunday, June 18. "Now we shall all see whom the majority follow, you or us," Tsereteli boasted to the Bolsheviks. They walked out, to brazenly declare in their newspaper *Pravda* that they refused to submit to any "antidemocratic restrictions." The crisis passed for the minute. But the capital was febrile and unstable, clearly living, Sukhanov said, on the "brink of the volcano."

The Bolsheviks took up Tsereteli's challenge, with every intention of hijacking the coming demonstration. Agitators were busy in the streets. "Don't trust the socialist ministers!" one shouted to his audience. "They are all bourgeois. They've sold out for ten million rubles a man. How are Prince Lvov and Tsereteli any better than Nicholas the Bloody? What's the revolution given you?' Voices echoed back: "The revolution has given us nothing. It was better before."

Alarmed, the government met on June 14 and announced that the elections to the Constituent Assembly would take place on September 17. The cabinet hoped thereby to "remove the sting from Bolshevik agitation . . . paralyze the action of their demagogic poison . . . avert the success of the street demonstration." The chance to hold a snap election while the revolution was fresh had long passed. Impetus had been bogged down in a multitude of questions that allowed for mischief from both right and left.

The Bolsheviks wanted deserters to be able to vote, sensing natural supporters, on the grounds that desertion was a political and not a juridical crime. Hard-line Cadets argued provocatively that the Romanovs should not be disenfranchised. The Bolsheviks, with a young following, wanted the voting age fixed at eighteen, the big Soviet parties, at twenty, the Cadets, at twenty-one.

No one looked to Prince Lvov for clarity; his own office was in "indescribable confusion." The premier's whole conversation, Bruce Lockhart found, was a "confession of the weakness of his position. Everyone seemed to be playing a game of pass-the-parcel to escape from responsibility." When a problem was put to him, Lvov would reply merely with a flickering smile; "his eyes, small at all times, almost vanished beyond his eyelids."

The Bolshevik position, by contrast, was simplicity itself. Lenin insisted that a huge effort be put into the new art of agitation and propaganda, for which the word "Agitprop" was coined. A thousand agitators, many of them sailors from the Baltic Fleet, were recruited during April and carefully trained at the Kshesinskaya palace. They were taught to be brief — Russia was "drowning in pomposity." "A long speech provokes many questions and in the end the soldier's mind wanders," Lenin told agitators going out to win over troops. "You don't need to say much. The soldier will understand in a very few words." Training came under two members of the Bolshevik's military organization, Nikolai Podvoisky, a tall and bearded man of thirty-seven with a "self-consciously hard expression," and Vladimir Nevsky, a stocky figure and a fine orator. Podvoisky drilled his agitators thoroughly in standard slogans and replies to questions on peace and land ownership. On graduation, the newly minted orators were sent out to work in groups.

A role model was provided at the Kshsinskaya, where a continuous flow of propaganda was maintained from the roof of a summerhouse overlooking the street. Each orator was allowed a maximum of thirty minutes, on a rota system, and none was allowed to touch on more than three themes. The major emphasis was soon the party's perceived ace, its peace policy. This, Lenin urged, must be "explained in every square, garden, avenue, street corner . . . from early morning to late at night."

Lenin was himself a summerhouse star, attracting aristocrats as well as workers. "I've been there twice," Countess Irina Skariatina wrote of Lenin in her diary. "He is bald, terribly ugly, wears a crumpled old brown suit, speaks without any oratorical power, more like a college lecturer calmly delivering his daily lesson. . . . Yet what he says drives the people crazy — even more than Kerensky with all his splendid eloquence."

The oral effort was matched by growth in the Bolshevik press. A press bureau was set up under Vyacheslav Molotov, a twenty-seven-year-old from a middle-class background who was helping to edit *Pravda*. By June, the Bolsheviks were publishing over forty newspapers and magazines. Most were giveaways, and the combined circulations were nearing 1.5 million copies a week. *Pravda* and *Soldatskaya Pravda* were being printed on modern high-capacity presses in a new Bolshevik printing plant on Kavaliergradsky Street near the Tauride.

It was a highly expensive business. Funding was a mystery, though in Berlin the German foreign minister, Arthur Zimmermann, took a paternal interest. "Lenin's peace propaganda is growing stronger," Zimmermann noted with pleasure, "and his newspaper *Pravda* is already printing 300,000 copies." Zimmermann was overoptimistic — *Pravda*'s actual daily print run was 85,000 — but for a party that had no press three months earlier to have reached this level was almost certainly a tribute to German money as well as to young Molotov's hard work.

Huge crowds turned out on the Champs de Mars on June 18. The anarchists, still ensconced in the Villa Durnovo, were among them. A search of the villa by the public prosecutor had failed to turn up the rumored bomb factory — instead he had found a bakers' trade union holding a meeting — and they had been allowed to stay put. Their black flags were dots against a red mass of flags where Bolshevik slogans — "All power to the Soviets," "Peace for the hovels, war for the palaces" — predominated. Rattled, the non-Bolshevik leaders went off to the Vienna restaurant to discuss the reasons for Bolshevik strength.

The Bolsheviks were young, the average age of the delegates at their party congress twenty-eight. They were hard men. Less than half had been at liberty at the start of the revolution. Forty-one had been in exile, twenty in prison, others at hard labor or on the run. On average, each delegate had been arrested three or four times, imprisoned for eighteen months and exiled for eight, at hard labor for three.

Adult lives had been spent in Siberian villages or foreign cities. Lenin had never had a nonpolitical job; Trotsky had one, as a clerk, during his first exile, and he had been sacked within a few days for an error in his accounting. Funds had come hand-to-mouth, from kopek donations, German spymasters, the proceeds of bank robberies and terrorism, the sale of postcards of party leaders.

Almost all lived under an alias, or a series of them. Their real names existed only in such police files as had not been burnt. As "Internationalists," they had no native country in the accepted sense. Russia was another stopping place on the jerky and dangerous journey to world revolution. They were not inhibited by any affection for Russia, or even for its proletariat, which Lenin found "less prepared, less class-conscious" than others, particularly the "trustworthy and reliable" Germans. Lenin's responsibilities, as he saw them, were global and not national. The destructive forces at work in the country were to be encouraged, not checked, for they favored collapse and collapse aided extremism.

Contempt for other parties came easily, for only Bolsheviks were "marching with history." So did their characteristic suspicion. The party had been betrayed at every level. Alexander Shlyapnikov, one of the few to survive in the capital, had put the average duration of an "illegal" at three months. Any longer was reckoned as work "in excess of the norm," which brought not praise but further suspicion. Why should that comrade survive when another did not?

Shlyapnikov developed an "incredible sensitivity to being tailed," sensing people watching him at tram stops and bridges and resorting to "all sorts of ruses, using backyards, slipping down other people's staircases and yards." He had the use of eight apartments, scattered through Petrograd, three beyond the Neva Gate, two on the Vyborg side, one apiece in three of the suburbs. A flat on the Steklyanny was particularly convenient, for it was in the same block as a photographic studio and close to a church. Many callers came to the studio and the church and a tram stop attracted crowds in which he could lose himself. Another lay across an orchard. When his followers pursued him late into the night, he would make for it "like a hounded beast." The "sleuths" did not dare cross through the apple trees for fear that he was armed.

His life was a "perpetual wandering. It was hard to write, read and at times even to think. . . . You could survive like that for two or three months but my physical energy did not allow more." Shlyapnikov used a deck of papers — a red Russian passport issued in his own name in 1907, a 1914 French passport in the name Jacob Noé, a membership card of the British Amalgamated Society of Engineers, a Russian carnet in the name Mavritsky, another in the name of a Finn. When the "sleuths" got too close, he ducked out of Petrograd to Copenhagen, with its wartime cargo of spies and profiteers, to Oslo, New York, and London, living off his wits until returning to Petrograd.

Such men were resourceful and dangerous, and the Bolsheviks had more of them than other parties. Kerensky, although confident enough of his own position to speak now of "my government and I," realized that the Bolsheviks were still at work underground. "Bolshevik mole, you are digging brilliantly" was a new party catchphrase. A successful offensive at the front, Kerensky thought, would destroy the attractions of Bolshevik defeatism and reinforce government prestige. A major summer campaign had been agreed on with the Allies before the revolution. Kerensky considered it to be a political as well as a military obligation.

XIV
The Last Offensive

KERENSKY ADMITTED that the new Russian offensive of the summer of 1917 had no military rationale, but was "dictated absolutely by the inner development of events in Russia." Since the government rejected peace, he argued, an offensive was unavoidable. If the troops were not compelled to fight, they would turn into a "meaningless mob" which would threaten the stability of the country. His offensive was necessary "to make the army once more an army, to bring it back to the psychology of action."

In effect, Kerensky was sending a million men into battle for his own psychological and political reasons. The army was to fight because, in Kerensky's analysis, it would cease to be an army if it did not. A German attack would have served much the same purpose, but the Germans would not oblige — they had decided, correctly, that the Russians would rot quicker if they were not provoked. Kerensky's strictly military aims were insignificant. A large-scale assault was planned against the Austrians toward Lvov in Galicia, with smaller operations on the northern front to counter the German threat to Riga and Petrograd.

The Germans were so quiet that Mikhail Tereshchenko thought that peace, far from involving himself as foreign minister, might come about through the "simple cessation of all military action at the front." In parts of Galicia, rye and wheat were growing in half-abandoned Russian positions. Observation posts were blinded by uncut foliage and clusters of lupines. The men had no need to observe. "The enemy here is fine and has told us that he will not attack if we do not attack," they said. "What we want is to return home and enjoy freedom and land. Why should we go on being wounded?"

An offensive was popular enough in the country at large, if not with the troops who would have to fight it. Lenin was careful not to risk public anger by criticizing it too openly. The Soviet backed the offensive, *Izvestiya* saying that it might "stop the disintegration in our army." But there was a deep ambivalence. The socialists were opposed to compulsory overtime being worked in arms plants, and to the reintroduction of combat discipline at the front. They were simultaneously supporting a campaign which needed weapons and discipline. They attacked the war as negative and "imperialist," while expecting soldiers to die in it.

The fantasy in this was recognized by the man whom Kerensky had chosen to lead the offensive. "I could understand the Bolsheviks, because they preached 'Down with the war, and immediate peace at any price,' " said Alexei Brusilov, a general with a "sly foxy face" who enjoyed a higher reputation with civilians like Kerensky than with his military peers. "But I couldn't grasp at all the tactics of the Social Revolutionaries and Mensheviks, who first broke up the army, as if to avoid counterrevolution, and at the same time wanted to continue the war."

Kerensky preceded the offensive with a series of tours to the fronts. He was compulsively energetic, woken at night on his train to be shown off at every station. At times, he was close to nervous collapse. Another deputation would ask to see him, and he would ask his aides, "Why can't you send them all to hell?" and send for his bottle of valerian. The sedative, made from the dried roots of the pink plant, changed his mood. As soon as he stepped down from the train, Kerensky recovered a "joyful and even triumphant sense of himself as the chosen of fate and the protégé of the people."

He enjoyed the adulation but administrative detail bored him. At Rovno he broke off a meeting on supply with senior officers to accept the greetings of the men, returning on their shoulders with a flush of color in his cheeks. He told the officers, "There, now, why do you fear them?" It was only after he had left that they realized they had not returned to the supply problem.

He wore a simple light-colored tunic and soldier's boots, his arm still in its black sling. The familiar flattop hair was hidden under a cap. He traveled with Albert Thomas, the jovial visiting French munitions minister, who was delighted at his commitment to the war. A huge hall at Kamenets-Podolsk was filled with soldier delegates from the front — "weary faces, feverish eyes, extraordinary tension" and the damp smell of greatcoats and chewing tobacco. They cheered the Bolshevik defeatist Ensign Nikolai Krylenko when he demanded immediate peace; they cheered Kerensky when he spoke of war. It was a bravura performance: "Enemies are trying to sow discord. . . . Comrades, fight those who whisper words of distrust. . . . The whole Russian people bows before you. . . . If we are unable to defend

freedom, the red banners will disappear . . . your names will be cursed."
"We will not let this happen!" the troops bellowed.

Kerensky's own changes of mood were as fantastical. The night before, he had asked Albert Thomas on the train why "I should be condemned to have men killed." Now he told those men, "I summon you not to a feast but to death!" Kerensky mastered others, Thomas thought, because he shared his thoughts so intimately with his audience that he was able "to descend into the sentimentality of others, into the little corner of their fear of death." His theatricality was perfect. He caused an angry buzz by bowing low to the front commander, and then turned and delighted the gray mass of soldiers by bowing deeper to them.

By the time Kerensky had finished, the defeatist Krylenko was crying that he would advance alone if his company did not follow him. "They kissed Kerensky, his uniform, his car, the ground on which he walked," noted a British nurse at the front. "Many were on their knees praying, others were weeping." She thought that if there had been an immediate offensive, the men would have fought like tigers. Kerensky could not keep all the armies in a simultaneous state of ecstasy. As his light moved on, it dimmed behind him.

The visits continued in bursts for five weeks, to Helsinki, Riga, Dvinsk, Odessa, Sebastopol, by train, armored car, automobile, horse wagon, as if they were an end in themselves. He had no modesty about their impact. "Rain and storm," he wrote. "Under the terrific downpour, to thunder and lightning, drenched through and through, the thousands did not move, anxious to find in my words faith in the justice of their coming sacrifice of death."

He reached his high point with a speech on suffering at the Bolshoi Theater in Moscow. To Bruce Lockhart, Kerensky embodied that suffering himself — "the deathly pallor of his face, the restless movements of his body as he swayed back and forth, the raw, almost whispering tones of his voice." He tongue-whipped his audience, a favorite device. He was back from the front, he said, where men with lice-ridden heads lived in the mud and dank water of the trenches, and did not complain. It was only in Moscow and Petrograd — from the rich, from those present in the theater — that there was grumbling. How could they betray the front with their languor and apathy? Should he go back and tell the men that their sacrifice was for nothing because the "heart of Russia" — Moscow — was full of the faithless?

When he was done, Kerensky sank back into the arms of his aide-de-camp. Women in a "hysteria of emotion" threw jewelry at his feet for the war effort, an autographed photograph was sold for 16,000 rubles, and the theater "rained roses." As the Bolshevik Krylenko had been swamped by his performance, so General Vogak, a reactionary who loathed the revolution and prayed nightly for the return of the tsar, wept like a child. The speech lasted two hours. It was more impressive in its emotional reactions than anything Bruce Lockhart had heard, or would hear, and that included Hitler. But its effect on Moscow, the diplomat noted, lasted exactly two days.

Marina Tsvetaeva wrote her poem willing Kerensky to become Bonaparte:

> *For someone the thunder rages*
> *— Come, bridegroom, come!*
> *Hot hurricane, young dictator,*
> *He tears along.*

Kerensky denied any such intention but warned, "When trust in me is lost, a dictator will come and then mistrust will be suppressed with bayonets and whips."

Not all were swept along by the war minister. Many officers had no confidence in him — they called him the "little Joan of Arc" or the "Persuader-in-Chief" — and the Bolsheviks were chipping away at him. The party had little broad support in the army, with only fifty delegates out of the seven hundred on the southwestern front's committees. Nevertheless, a Bolshevized Grenadier Guards regiment gave Kerensky a rare setback in Galicia. The guardsmen whistled him off, and said that they would refuse to move up to their positions because "liberty is no good to dead men."

Alfred Knox, the British military observer, was pleased at Kerensky's discomfort. "It's as well it happened to him," he said. "It'll show him the real state of things."

In the real world, Admiral Alexander Kolchak was saying of his Black Sea sailors, "Committees mean more to them than I do, and I no longer wish to have anything to do with them. I do not love them any more." A young officer wrote to his mother that he was leaving his unit and volunteering for a shock battalion: "I had been thinking of the danger of losing my life at the hands of my own soldiers. . . . By joining the Battalion of Death I know that, God willing, I shall be able to render some useful service first." A mob of deserters at Dvinsk turned the passengers off the Smolensk express, smashed the windows, and set off on a five-day jaunt toward Moscow. Troops were being used in Yamburk to track down lepers who had left their colony because they, too, had rights, and would not "remain isolated from society."

Independence movements in the Ukraine, Finland, Georgia, and the Baltic provinces were picking up momentum. At Kirsanov, a former mental patient called A. K. Trounin, a rich merchant and shop owner, declared the town a republic. Troops were being sent, but the illustrated weekly *Iskri* was asking its alarmed readers, "What hope is there for the future of the nation if a man like this, with a background of psychosis, can gain support for independence?"

An officers' congress was held in the small municipal theater in Mogilev. Mikhail Alexeev addressed the congress as commander in chief, the representatives from the soldiers' Soviets lolling impassively in the theater boxes. He warned that the war could not be conducted unless the Provisional Government restored the death penalty and discipline. "Russia is dying," Alexeev said. "She stands on the edge of the abyss. A few more shocks, and she will crash with all her weight into it." Kerensky thought this the work of a "political juggler." Alexeev was curtly dismissed from his post. The general, weakened with fever, a decent man and the best strategist in the army, broke down in tears.

Kerensky named the "foxy" Alexei Brusilov as the new commander in chief. Brusilov's fellow officers thought his reputation overblown and were suspicious of the "over-deliberate egalitarianism" that accompanied his hand-shaking tours of the front.

The government announced new disciplinary measures for deserters at the beginning of June. They were pinpricks compared with the firing squads and military prisons of the other countries at war — loss of electoral rights, deprivation of family food allowances, and the publication of deserters' names. The measures angered the troops, however, and widened the split among Social Revolutionaries. A leftist Social Revolutionary faction emerged, hostile to the offensive and to discipline and resentful of Kerensky as an "idol." Claiming that he was on the verge of reintroducing the death penalty, the Left SRs influenced the party to vote against reelecting Kerensky to the SR central committee. Depressed, Kerensky considered resigning from the government.

It did not take long for the vortex at the top to work its way down to the regiments. A Bolshevik trooper worked a cavalry unit. "Comrades, our officers want to make an end of us. They are the internal enemy," the Kshesinskaya-trained agitator said. He claimed that he had reconnoitered the enemy wire: "I know well there are ten rows of it, with machine guns every fifteen yards. If we advance, we are dead men. . . . Pass this on, comrades." The commissar with the Seventh Army telegraphed Kerensky, "The

Forty-seventh Regiment refuses to go out. The Fifty-first promises to come out tomorrow, and the Fifty-second refused to come out and arrested its officers." Anton Denikin, commander of the western front, his spade beard stained with tobacco and his eyes puffy with exhaustion, told Brusilov, "I haven't the slightest belief in the success of the offensive." Brusilov himself scribbled on a report on the condition of the armies on the western front: "Is it worthwhile to prepare a blow there with such morale?"

Amid the gloomy professionals, only the amateur defense minister was in a mood for combat.

The "Kerensky Offensive" opened at 9:00 A.M. on June 18 after a two-day artillery barrage. As the troops huddled on their startlines — shells burning through the overcast, subalterns unsure whether their men would clamber from the trenches with them — a delegation from the officers' union was meeting with Cadet leaders in Petrograd to see if the offensive could be called off. The union president, Novosiltsev, said that the offensive was pointless and could only result in the "extermination of the best units."

The Russians had overwhelming strength in men and artillery. In parts of the line they outnumbered the Austrians by eight to one and outgunned them five times. Russia had started the war with chronic shortages of machine guns, barbed wire, shells, and field guns. There were so few code books that messages were sent in clear, to the delight of listening Germans. These weaknesses had been resolved in an immense industrial effort that showed how rapidly the economy would have continued to expand in peace. Though the Germans were another matter, Austro-Hungarian morale had frequently been lower than the Russian. The horrors of trench warfare strained French armies to the point of mutiny. The Russians were not alone.

Comparisons with the French Revolution were in vogue. Kerensky was much taken by the way France had rallied to the revolution after the victory over the Prussians at Valmy in 1792. Lack of planning ensured there would be no repeat. The two main fronts were too far apart for any pincer movement between them to be possible. No reinforcements were available to exploit initial successes. No priorities had been set in advance and there was no coordination between the fronts. "The supreme command gave up all idea of planned strategy," said General Denikin, "and had to allow the fronts to begin operations whenever they were ready."

Only the "icons of the tsarina," Trotsky said, were missing in this "blind submission to the will of Providence." A commissar came across a company hiding among the dripping trees at the edge of an immense field that led to the distant breastworks of the Austrian lines. "I understand them," the commissar said. "It's suicide."

Helped by heavy artillery barrages, the armies driving on Lvov took eighteen thousand prisoners in the first two days. This should have produced the increase in morale that Kerensky was banking on. "No such effect can be seen," the commander of the Eleventh Army reported. "The conviction prevails that they have done their work and must go no further." Lavr Kornilov's Eighth Army had similar success when it went in against the Austrians on June 23, capturing forty-eight guns and seven thousand Austro-Hungarians on the first day. But it, too, stopped once it had outrun its artillery support.

Viktor Shklovsky, a poet and literary critic appointed commissar on the Galician front, thought that the men were so cut off from Russia that they had "formed their own republic." He held a rally to inspire them for combat. The men were surly and murderous. "Beat him up," they said. "He's a bourgeois dog, he's got pockets in his field shirt. An officer." Shklovsky was pulled off the rostrum and shoved around to shouts: "Come to stir us up, have you?" A soldier took off his boots and screamed, "Our feet! The trenches have rotted our feet!" They decided to hang the commissar, "as simple as that." Shklovsky was saved by another commissar, who cursed the men and said, "Even with the noose around my neck, I'll tell you you're scum." This amused them and they hoisted the commissars on their shoulders and carried them to their car. The mood shifted again, and Shklovsky and his savior were pelted with rocks as they drove off.

The two commissars passed ravaged, burned-out villages of wattle and thatch, forest that "no longer whispered," chapels burning with yellow flames. The stands of wheat and rye in the hedgeless fields were discolored and dripping with rain. In the starving towns, hunger "creeps into the most private room, there is no escaping from it, for it has a soundless voice, heard in the mind's ear, like the voice of a ghost." The few civilians left had faces "idiotic with fear" and the women snatched their greasy skirts around them when they saw soldiers.

Shklovsky came across a shock battalion of the Seventy-fourth Division, shivering in sodden country near an enemy-held village. The men had thrown away their greatcoats on the march. Someone explained to Shklovsky that the troops "hadn't made up their minds" whether to attack. "Move forward," the commissar ordered. The men were silent. "It was so depressing in that forest, in that deep forest of the revolutionary front." Finally they rushed forward, on a gray day among the wet trees, reckless with fatigue and "hatred for the war and themselves." A German shouted "I give up" and fell on his knees with his hands raised. A Russian ran past him, half-turned, and shot him. The Russians stopped and retreated as suddenly as they had charged. The survivors went to the rear and murdered two Jews they found. "They said they'd been signaling," Shklovsky said. "I'm convinced this wasn't the case. This mixture of cowardice and spy mania was unbearable."

On the northern front, the Germans used gas. "Men in filthy uniforms, their red eyes glaring through the gas mask holes, running forward — hundreds and hundreds of men; the sky above them was brindled with red and green fires." A lieutenant leading a company attack across a swampy field heard a scream and then only the gasp of his panting in the mask. He turned. The headless body of his sergeant major lay red among the potato shoots and in the distant mud he saw the jerky gray backs of his men as they ran.

Kerensky, unaware that the initial successes had been reversed, declared a "great triumph of the revolution" on June 20. He said that the Russian army had proved to the world its "supreme fidelity" and its new discipline. He asked Prince Lvov to allow him to award all the regiments that had started the offensive the style of "Regiments of the 18th of June." Maria Bochkaryova's Death Battalion girls entrained for the front with the blessings of an Orthodox Metropolitan and Emmeline Pankhurst, the British suffragette, ringing in their ears.

Patriotic crowds in their summer best swarmed down the Nevksy, carrying portraits of Kerensky and standing officers drinks all day in the bars of the Astoria. Felix Yusupov made a brief trip to Petrograd with his mother. The family chauffeur thought it prudent to wear a red bow tie as a gesture of the revolution — furious, Yusupov's mother ordered him to take it off. There were worrying signs, as well. Garrison troops appeared on the Nevsky in the afternoon and shouted against the offensive. "Some of the bourgeois took after us with their umbrellas," said one. "We grabbed them and dragged them into the barracks . . . and told them that tomorrow they would be sent to the front."

The men of the battered Twelfth Army demanded that the garrison send reserve units to the front on June 23. The troops in the rear were selling cigarettes, offering their services as porters at the railroad stations, promenading in parks and pleasure gardens. "We demand immediate help," the men at the front wrote. "No delay, no lame excuses." The garrison troops were contemptuous. The offensive was a blow against peace, they said, and the frontline men could fend for themselves.

The offensive turned into a rout when German shock troops arrived on the Galician front to stiffen the Austrians. The Russian Eleventh Army was soon in headlong flight, exposing the flanks of its two neighbors. Three German companies put the 126th and 2nd Finnish Divisions to flight. The only Russian resistance came from a few cavalry and infantry officers supported by individual soldiers. The rest were fleeing, blocking roads and raping and robbing as they forced their way deeper into the rear. On the left flank of the Eleventh Army, twenty Russian divisions — a total of 240 battalions with a hundred heavy guns — were cracked by nine divisions of Germans with 83 battalions and sixty guns.

German aircraft circling the columns of fleeing Russians dropped propaganda leaflets, not bombs. Nikolai Sokolov, sent by the Soviet executive committee to bolster morale, was beaten up by men of the mutinous 703rd Suramsky Regiment. The men of a Siberian infantry company sent a vitriolic letter to Kerensky from Riga on June 26 demanding the release of a Bolshevik agitator, Lieutenant Khaustov. If Khaustov was not returned, the men threatened to send three assassins to Petrograd to deal with the war minister. "You will be killed as a dog, Mr. Kerensky, that has not yet enough gorged with blood," they wrote. "Leave your post before it is too late; for the three, death in a struggle for liberty will be beautiful."

The men torched the manors of Baltic landlords and threatened to storm the front headquarters to murder the generals, "bloodsuckers in zigzag epaulettes." Some stood, their features blackened by the smoke of their arson, along the road from Riga to the front to taunt reinforcements with red banners that read "Peace for the hats [the soldiers], ruin to the palaces."

The degradation of officers was "pitiful." Men stole their horses and "deprived them of food for days because they had spoken in favor of the offensive." The Neishlotsky infantry regiment refused to counterattack on the northern front and prevented others from moving forward by seizing their field kitchens. Commissars reported that for hundreds of miles they could see soldiers streaming away from the front "armed and unarmed, in good health and high spirits, certain they will not be punished."

Shock battalions, slated for the attack, had to be used in the rear to inflict what punishment there was. One battalion moved into Tarnopol, where the streets were clogged with the broken debris of shops, wine cellars and a distillery pillaged by deserters who reeled about stripped to the waist in the summer rain. The shock troops shot thirteen looters by the railway station.

The cabinet was itself in crisis in Petrograd. On June 30, the non-Cadet ministers recognized the Ukrainian nationalist government, the Rada. Feeling this a step toward the breakup of Russia, the Cadet ministers walked out of the cabinet meeting on July 2. "The blood be on your heads," Kerensky yelled at them. "On the front, thousands are giving up their lives — and you here, you desert your posts and smash the government!"

Viktor Shklovsky felt that the offensive might have succeeded. Victory was a less bloody business than defeat. The army "did not die because it took the offensive." It died because it retreated. In Galicia, the commissar saw the wounded fighting for places on the last train as the Germans moved in. "Men on top of the cars, between the cars, men tying themselves under the cars," he wrote. "A tiny locomotive, straining every fiber, pulled at the long line of cars, about to burst asunder . . ."

Regiments dissolved, Shklovsky said, because they "escaped into Bolshevism the way a man hides from life in a psychosis." They were like a sleeping man who hears the doorbell ring. He knows he has to get up, but he doesn't want to. So he makes up a dream and puts it into the sound, justifying his idleness by making it the tolling of a church bell. "Russia made up the Bolsheviks," Shklovsky wrote, "as a justification for desertion and plunder."

The casualties were small by the standards of previous years. In all, 1,222 officers and 37,500 men were killed in the offensive. But they accounted for over two-thirds of the total killed in 1917, showing that little other fighting took place, and the casualties were concentrated among the best units. One division, the 506th Infantry, lost 2,513 killed or wounded out of 3,000. The collapse in morale showed in the ratio of dead to prisoners. In 1916, four and a half times as many Russians were taken prisoner as were killed, 1.2 million to 270,000. That was poor enough in itself — in the British army the position was reversed, with the dead outnumbering POWs by five to one. But in 1917, Russian prisoners outnumbered the dead almost sixteen times, nine hundred thousand to fifty-eight thousand.

Alexander Guchkov saw some of the damage he had inflicted on morale during his brief tenure as war minister on a visit to Kalisch on the southwestern front shortly before the Germans retook it. "One had to see the terrified faces of the inhabitants peering from their cellars . . . to hear the horrors performed by the drunken mob in Kalisch," he said. "Forty and fifty men in turn violated old women of seventy." A nursing child was torn from his mother and the men threatened to throw the baby out of the window if money was not given to them. "Under such circumstances," Guchkov wrote, "the army constitutes a colossal danger."

Shklovsky was evacuated to a hospital in Czernowitz with internal bleeding. A very young officer with a broken back lay on his cot embroidering. Another officer turned to Shklovsky and quietly reproached him "for what we, the politicals, had done to Russia."

XV

"Take the Power, You Son of a Bitch"

As THE OFFENSIVE HAD GONE IN, anarchists from the Villa Durnovo in Petrograd raided the Kresty Prison and released seven prisoners. The government retaliated with a predawn raid on the villa on June 19. An anarchist called Asnin was shot dead. He was probably killed by an anarchist weapon let off accidentally as the government forces burst in through the windows.

Asnin's corpse, stiff and bloody, was propped up on the entrance steps to inflame the Vyborg crowds who filed into the grounds. Rumors that Kerensky was going to draft garrison troops to the front swept through the barracks. The First Machine Gun Regiment, which already had close links to the Bolsheviks and the anarchists, was emerging as a core of revolt. It was the largest unit in the capital, with eleven thousand men stationed among the seething Vyborg workers, and on June 20 Kerensky ordered it to provide five hundred machine guns and their crews to bolster the offensive. The men voted to refuse to go to the front until a "revolutionary war" was assured by the removal of capitalist ministers from the government.

Bolshevik agitators were urging the troops to "wipe out" the *burzhui*. Anarchists called for pogroms against the rich on the Nevsky. Kronstadt sailors were "boiling like a kettle" and were threatening to liberate the Villa Durnovo.

For the moment, the Bolsheviks held them back from direct action for fear of increasing the public hostility to extremism which the offensive was drumming up. Nikolai Sukhanov spoke of an "orgy of chauvinism, a frenzied war dance of journalists." The cathedral of Our Lady of Kazan was filled with patriotic crowds at a mass for the dead at the front, the men in officers' caps, boaters, and top hats. The illustrated papers were printing pictures of long lines of Austrian prisoners and smiling Russian troops with plentiful artillery support. The Soviet organized a "rally for victory" at the Moscow Hippodrome, with Cossack trick riding and Boy Scouts. A reverse lottery, where the winners had to pay sums to the government, raised 75,000 rubles for the war effort.

Lenin left Petrograd to the patriots on June 29. He arrived without warning at the country cottage of Vladimir Bonch-Bruyevich, a Bolshevik who had trained as a land surveyor and whose keen interest in human behavior had taken him to study the Dukhobor sect in their Canadian emigration. The *dacha* was near the Finnish health resort at Mustamaki on the Karelian Isthmus. Here Lenin slept, read English novels under the lilac trees, sunbathed, and swam, receiving no messages from Petrograd and sending none. He claimed he did nothing because he was exhausted. In fact, he had rarely been seen in public since his return, holding himself aloof, as Sukhanov put it, like "a great noble." Lenin's physical and mental exertions had been restricted largely to private meetings and to writing. They scarcely amounted to a tenth of the effort put in by the kidney-weakened Kerensky. It is not credible that Lenin removed himself from a city on the edge of fresh crisis for no better reason than rest and recuperation. More probably, he suspected that the government had got wind of his continuing financial involvement with the Germans. In Finland, he was safe from arrest.

On the day that Lenin took himself off, a government delegation was meeting with Ukrainian nationalists in Kiev. The huge region of the Dnieper in the south of the Russian plain was to Russia "what Provence is to France," milder and sunnier, with its own softer and more sonorous language. The Ukraine was the richest area of the empire before the war, producing three-quarters of its coal and most of its sugar and wheat exports. The Ukrainians, "little Russians," had long complained that they were being milked by Great Russia, their wealth flowing into central government coffers and Petrograd banking parlors.

The government delegation, hoping to forestall an outright bid for independence, agreed provisionally to recognise the Ukrainian Rada, the semi-autonomous government in Kiev. A clash with the Cadets was inevitable. Pavel Miliukov, the Cadet leader and former foreign minister, attacked the agreement as "chopping up Russia."

On Sunday, July 2, while their comrades at the front were reeling from the German counteroffensive, five thousand machine gunners, whipped up by Trotsky and Anatoly Lunacharsky, held a concert in the big hall of the People's House in Petrograd to make it clear that they had no intention of joining the battle.

"Mild-mannered and silver-tongued," Lunacharsky was forty-two years old, a playwright and literary critic, and a lover of all art and drama, whether *burzhui* or not. He was himself an ex-*burzhui,* the son of a notary, and had studied philosophy at Zurich's university. Lunacharsky had served six years internal exile for his involvement with Marxist groups. He was a friend of Maxim Gorky, and coedited Gorky's newspaper *Novaya Zhizn* on his return. Lunacharsky's interest in Bolshevism went beyond Lenin's narrow social and political limits to a "God-seeking" attempt to satisfy emotional and religious longings. "If Christ was alive today," he was soon to say, "he would have been a Bolshevik." Bruce Lockhart thought him a "man of brilliant intellect and wide culture," and the only apologist for Lenin who struck a chord with the *intelligentsiya.*

Trotsky and Lunacharsky were the two most broad-minded and persuasive speakers on the Bolshevik circuit, and they worked the machine gunners well. A resolution was passed supporting the Bolshevik line that all power should pass to the Soviets, and accusing Kerensky of behaving like "Nicholas the Bloody." The men left the meeting too highly strung to sleep.

The main speaker at an anarchist rally that night was I. Bleikhman-Solntsev, an anarchist recently back from New York, where he had been long enough for his Russian to acquire an American cadence as sharp as vinegar. The anarchists called for a mass demonstration on the next day. Its slogan was to be "Down with the Provisional Government." They planned to turn it into an uprising, with the machine gunners as the catalyst. Kerensky would be arrested, and railway stations, telephone exchanges, and newspaper presses seized.

Maurice Paleologue had proved to be too visibly out of sympathy with the commoners now ruling Russia; Kerensky called him "a society snob who felt he was almost a cousin to all who had royal blood in their veins." He was replaced at the French embassy, much to Kerensky's relief, by the more radical Joseph Noulens, a professional socialist politician. A French journalist, Claude Arnet, briefed the newcomer. Arnet pointed out through the embassy windows across the river to the Vyborg district. "The Bolsheviks rule there and the machine gunners have their barracks," he said. "A thousand weapons and ten thousand men. Neither the SRs nor the Mensheviks can get into their barracks. The remaining regiments are Bolshevik or neutral. If Lenin and Trotsky want to take Petrograd, what can stop them?"

"How can the government tolerate that?" asked Noulens.

"What can it do?" said the journalist. "You have to understand that the government has no power but a moral one, and even that seems to me very weak."

Under the dirty and dilapidated walls of the barracks, the regiments held meetings through which the New York anarchist Bleikhman swam "like a fish in a river." The men were frightened of being sent to the front. "What are the Bolsheviks doing, fast asleep in Kshesinskaya's palace?" they said. "Come on, let's kick out Kerensky." They must carry their arms, Bleikhman said. He was asked about organization. "The street will organize us," he replied.

During the night of July 2–3, the four Cadet ministers resigned over the Ukrainian issue, Kerensky shouting about their "bloodied hands." The crisis deepened fears that the country was disintegrating through nationalisms that the revolution, committed to liberty, would be powerless to halt. Ethnic Russians were in an overall minority, and the loss of thirty million Ukrainians would add to the eight million Poles and four million Byelorussians and Balts now under German occupation. *Iskri* ran pictures of Ukrainian soldiers at a meeting to discuss separation from Russia. "On the one hand they agree that it is not time for 'little Russia' to stab 'Great Russia' in the back," the magazine reported. "On the other, the soldiers want separatism."

Tension grew as it became known that the offensive was in deep trouble. Agitators claimed that the Cadet resignations were the first move of counter-revolution. Miliukov, or so Trotsky claimed, "firmly believed that the situation could be saved with a bold bloodletting." Bleikhman, curly-haired, his shirt open at his chest, worked on the machine gunners. In Kronstadt, a pair of anarchists, wild-haired and festooned with weaponry, harangued a crowd of ten thousand sailors who needed little prompting to do some *burzhui*-bashing in the capital.

By the late morning of Monday, July 3, workers were moving onto the streets. Only twenty-eight factories were on strike, however, and there was little of the intense solidarity of February. Bolshevik agitators paid lip service to party discipline in not openly calling for an armed rising, but made their meaning clear enough. "I spoke in such a way that only a fool could conclude that he shouldn't demonstrate," admitted Vladimir Nevsky, the Agitprop specialist and chairman of the Bolshevik military organization.

Cars full of "delegates, agitators, reconnoiterers, telephone men" sped through the streets. Ensign A. I. Semashko, the Bolshevik leader of the First Machine Gun Regiment, marched half the regiment out of the barracks and toured the city to drum up support. The remainder preferred to wait and see how the young hothead got on. Squads arrived at the Renault works, took over new trucks waiting for delivery and drove them off to the Nevsky. The cockades of tsarist officials, the shiny buttons of students, and the hats of lady sympathizers, prominent in February, were missing. In July "only the common slaves were marching." Bourgeois Petrograd was frightened by their "insane, dumb, beastlike faces," whispering that they were "deceived by spies" and led by fanatics. Fear rayed out from the marching columns like "beams of light." A mob went into a cellar on the Liteiny and dragged out an officer whom they killed on the spot. From the windows and balconies of the Nevsky, thousands of eyes "looked out with no good wishes."

In the early evening, machine gunners were touring in trucks with banners draped on the sides: "The first bullet for Kerensky." An armored car was sent to the Warsaw Station to grab the war minister, but he had already left by train on a visit to the front. A flood of workers and soldiers surrounded the Kshesinskaya palace. The Bolsheviks hesitated, eager to ride mob anger to a putsch, but fearful of being trapped by a patriotic backlash. Kamenev and Zinoviev had written an article against armed demonstrations for the next morning's edition of *Pravda*, arguing that the riots still showed no signs of turning into an irresistible coup.

The bulk of the garrison and the factories were waiting out events on the sidelines, unwilling to get involved in mutiny when the troops at the front were under fierce German pressure. The fighting men despised the garrison units, who "live soft, peddle politics, and do not die," and could be expected to enjoy a punitive expedition to the capital.

Bolshevik speakers tried half-heartedly to get the crowd to disperse. Yakov Sverdlov, a lank little central committee member of thirty-two, his face "black as tar," heard mocking whistles and shouts of "Down with you." "What was to be done?" Trotsky recalled. "Could the Bolsheviks possibly stand aside?" Reluctantly, the Bolsheviks agreed to lead the movement and urged the crowd to go to the Tauride.

At 11:00 P.M., columns of armed soldiers and workers congregated on the palace where the Soviet was in heated debate. Lev Kamenev leapt onto the platform and claimed, "We never called for a demonstration, but the masses themselves have come into the streets to show their will. And once the masses are out our place is with them. Our task is now to give the movement an organized character." Toward midnight, mobs round the Tauride were joined by thousands of Putilov workers with "frightened, fierce faces."

The crowd could have seized the palace had it wanted to — the Soviet was protected by a guard of six men. Nikolai Chkheidze, the Soviet chairman, appealed to the Fifth Army, holding the front nearest to the capital, to send armored cars, cavalry, and an infantry brigade. The government was meeting in the apartment of Prince Lvov, a modest, two-room affair typical of a man who was "more like a country doctor than an aristocrat." Bruce Lockhart's "heart went out to him — he was so forlorn and alone," but the British diplomat thought Lvov was only cut out to be a town mayor and was not the stuff of which revolutionary prime ministers are made; even the impression of cunning he gave was "due actually to timidity." Lvov was reluctant to use force and there was little enough of it as his disposal. Of the huge garrison, the Provisional Government could count only on a company of officer cadets, a hundred guardsmen, and two thousand Cossacks.

Lvov's apartment was undefended. At 9:40 P.M., a truck with a machine gun and ten armed men aboard drove up to the entrance. The men told the hall porter that they wanted the "surrender of all the ministers in the apartment," and that they were confiscating the ministers' automobiles. Irakli Tsereteli went down to speak to them. When the communications minister arrived downstairs, they had already gone, taking his car with them. The motor pool at the Winter Palace was also raided — revolutionaries loved to drive.

The machine gunners had occupied the Finland and Nikolaevsky stations and put squads on the Neva bridges. Demonstrators drove down the Nevsky with three or four machine guns to a truck. Shooting broke out at Gostiny Dvor. Blok's current mistress, the opera singer Lyubov Delmas, telephoned the poet near midnight to tell him that the people were in the streets and that several regiments were advancing on the city center.

A battle was underway on the Nevsky. "Street fighting is a panicky business," Albert Rhys Williams, an American correspondent, wrote. "At night, with bullets spitting from hidden loopholes, from roofs above and cellars below . . . the crowd stampeded back and forth fleeing from the leaden gusts. Three times that night our feet slipped in blood on the pavement. Down the Nevsky was blazed a train of shattered windows and looted shops."

At 11:40 P.M., the weary Bolshevik central committee finally committed itself to a putsch. In order to effect the "transfer of power" to the Soviet, the central committee urged the workers and soldiers to do what they had been doing all day — "at once to take to the streets." The attempt to disguise a Bolshevik coup as a transfer of power to the Soviet was patent fraud, for the Soviet majority was bitterly opposed to the demonstrations. The decision to back a rising was reached too late for the *Pravda* printers to reset the front page. The article written a few hours before Kamenev and Zinoviev, appealing for calm, was pulled out of the matrix, leaving a white space.

Kronstadt sailors were on the move to the capital, despite earlier Bolshevik pleas for them to stay put. The Putilov workers did not bother to go home but bedded down in the Tauride courtyard to be ready for fresh action. The Soviet continued its sitting until dawn. The debate was muddled and morose, marked by the usual socialist reluctance to condemn the Bolsheviks. The famous Social Revolutionary terrorist Maria Spiridonova, back from her Siberian imprisonment, accused government ministers of "preparing to shoot down our comrades, the workers and soldiers," apparently unaware that the reverse was the case. A final resolution was passed that deputies should go to the factories and barracks when the sun was up to persuade them to call off the demonstrations. Nikolai Sukhanov drew a battalion of the Preobrazhenskys.

Lenin was woken at 6:00 A.M. on Tuesday, July 4, by a messenger bringing news of the rising. "It's completely untimely," he told his host, Vladimir Bonch-Bruyevich. He rushed to the nearest station at Mustamaki to get a train to Petrograd, muttering that he wanted the movement stopped "quickly." Or so it was soon said that he said. After the incompetence of April and June, the Bolsheviks had every reason to distance Lenin from the unfolding fiasco of July. If Lenin was truly taken aback by the rising, he had less idea than his sworn enemies in the Provisional Government of what was happening in his own party. Trouble had been in the wind since Asnin's body was first put on display, and government agents had warned on July 2 that a Bolshevik rising was imminent.

As Lenin's train pulled out of Mustamaki shortly before 7:00 A.M., Sukhanov was with his battalion. Conveniently, it had spent the night in the Tauride courtyard. It was still sleepy as a magnificent and clear morning broke. The young officer in charge assured Sukhanov that his battalion was not in a state to do anything. The heavy-set, squat peasant troops mumbled maliciously to Sukhanov about Lenin and the Bolsheviks. Sukhanov, like Spiridonova, found himself defending the Bolsheviks. "They don't know what they are up to!" he said.

The morning papers Lenin was reading on the train showed up Bolshevik isolation. His fellow passengers were angrily blaming the "damned Leninists" for the riots. *Izvestiya* said that the demonstrators were trying to strangle the revolution. The Menshevik *Rabochaya Gazeta* called it a "stab in the back." *Delo Naroda,* the Social Revolutionary paper, warned of civil war and the Cadet daily *Rech* spoke of sheer anarchy. *Pravda* had a large blank space on its front page, where the article urging caution had been pulled out. At the Finland Station, Lenin climbed into a horse cab and made for the Kshesinskaya palace. No trams or motor taxis were running and most shops were closed. Large parts of the city were deserted in the heat.

A third-floor bedroom in the palace served as the Bolshevik operations room. Lenin appeared muddled when he arrived. He was asked whether the day would see the seizure of power — armored cars with pro-Bolshevik crews were already stationed at street intersections with their engines running. "We shall see," Lenin replied. "At present it is impossible to say."

People knew from February that the bridges could turn into sudden killing grounds. Count Alexei Bobrinskoy paid a boatman three rubles to ferry him across the Neva. It was a pleasant fifteen-minute crossing on a perfect day and he was glad he had made it. Three artillery salvoes crashed onto the Liteiny Bridge, scattering a mob of workers trying to cross it. The sound of cannon fire created a panic. Bobrinskoy thought that the salvoes, fired by a Guards artillery battery, saved Kerensky and the government from ruin. There was more to it than that.

Shortly before midday, a flotilla of forty barges, tugboats, and pinnaces dropped around five thousand sailors on the quays alongside the university. They were led by Fedor Raskolnikov, the young midshipman who had welcomed Lenin back to the Finland Station in April. Raskolnikov was unusually amiable, sincere, and open but a "fanatic." He, at least, had no doubt that he was taking part in a Bolshevik coup, having confirmed this with the Kshesinskaya palace by telephone the night before. He marched his men, hung with bandoliers, their caps pushed jauntily back on their heads, to the ballerina's palace. The Bolsheviks were up to their necks in the rising.

Lenin tried to avoid speaking to the sailors but they insisted. He turned on Vladimir Nevsky for encouraging the rising without thinking of the consequences: "You should be thrashed for this." He finally shuffled out on the balcony, complaining that he was not well. Lenin would go no further than to express his confidence that the slogan "All Power to the Soviet!" would eventually win despite the "zigzags of history." Sukhanov thought it a most ambiguous performance. Lenin was himself zigzagging, indecisive over whether to roll with the armed masses in the street below him or to hang back.

Led by Fedor Raskolnikov, a crowd of many thousands set off for the Tauride. Nikolai Podvoisky and Vladimir Nevsky, who were in charge of military planning, followed in an armored car. When they had gone, so Anatoly Lunacharsky told Sukhanov, the Bolshevik leaders agreed to form a "Soviet" government led by themselves. Three ministers were "appointed," Lenin, Trotsky, and Lunacharsky. The first move was to be the immediate announcement of decrees on land and peace to solidify support. In the meantime, the 176th Regiment was to arrest the Soviet executive committee, giving the lie to the Bolshevik banners of "All Power to the Soviet!" The Provisional Government was reckoned so derisory a threat that no special plans were laid for its arrest.

The first shooting broke out on Sadovaya Street and spread to Vasilevsky Island and the Suvorov Prospekt. Incidents started with a stray shot, sparking off panic and a wave of firing. People were carried away in ambulances. The emptied streets were littered with caps and sticks, as armored cars went past firing their machine guns at buildings thought to harbor snipers. Broken chairs and furniture were piled up in a shop front with looted parcels which spilled face powder and ribbons.

A Cossack patrol under an ensign, on its way to defend the Tauride, ran into a crowd of armed workers and soldiers. "A small-sized soldier without shoulder straps turned and fired at me, but missed," the ensign wrote. "The shot served as a signal and rifle fire opened up on us from all sides." His Cossacks slid from their horses and fired back. A worker saw it differently. He claimed that the horsemen started the shooting: "I was hit by a bullet which passed through one leg and stopped in the other."

Seven Cossacks were killed and the bodies of a dozen of their ponies, hay nets attached to the saddles, lay in the street. Six demonstrators died and twenty were wounded. Meriel Buchanan watched "little puffs of hot dry wind" blow up the yellow dust as other Cossacks charged a group of sailors across the Champs de Mars. Both sides were panicky and — apart from the distinctive sailors — found it difficult to tell friend from foe. Passersby got most of the bullets. Using shots fired from houses as an excuse, soldiers and sailors looted food and wine and tobacco shops. A detachment of Cossacks at the Winter Palace ran from time to time to disarm people and stop cars with weapons. They had little idea of whom they were arresting.

Alexander Blok had to walk to work at the investigating commission in the Winter Palace, for the commission cars had been hijacked. When he showed his permit, signed by Kerensky, Blok was told by a soldier, "Kerensky was arrested long ago! You might as well show us a permit from Nicholas II." He worried for his "clients" in the Peter and Paul Fortress, which had been seized by the sailors, but could do nothing.

The physician at the fortress, Dr. Manukhin, had been concerned for several weeks over a possible plot to murder the prisoners. Some sentries' revolvers had gone missing. Manukhin was convinced that Anna Vyrubova, the imperial confidante, was to be the first victim. The doctor contacted his friend Nikolai Sukhanov, who went over to the fortress. There was no sign of anything amiss. When the diarist peered through the peepholes in the Trubetskoy bastion, Alexander Protopopov, the despised former interior minister, was asleep, and the equally loathed ex-premier Boris Stürmer was sitting on his bunk reading a book. Sukhanov arranged to have Vyrubova transferred out of the fortress to a prison hospital, still hobbling on crutches after her railway accident. It proved an unnecessary precaution. The "former persons" remained untouched despite the bloodshed on the streets.

From Kiev, Kerensky sent a telegram demanding that General Polotsev, the Petrograd military commander, put down the mutiny. "I demand the stopping of all further demonstrations and mutinies by armed force," he wired. "The mutiny must be completely liquidated and the guilty ruthlessly punished." It was eerily similar to the diktat sent by Nicholas from Mogilev in February, and Kerensky's own position seemed no more secure than that of the tsar. He left Kiev later in the day, a few minutes before armed Ukrainian nationalists took over the streets and began looking for him.

As the marchers closed on the Tauride, Soviet leaders sent out appeals for reliable troops. Viktor Chernov went out to speak to the crowd. "Take the power, you son of a bitch," a demonstrator yelled at him. "Take it, when it's offered to you." Sailors grabbed him and held him hostage in an open car. Plainly "losing all presence of mind," Chernov waited to be lynched. The agriculture minister was freed by Trotsky, though this rescuer was no more popular with the crowd.

The government could do nothing with a mob which, the justice minister Pavel Pereverzev admitted, could have arrested it "without any risk to themselves if their determination matched even one-tenth their criminal energy." Individual ministers were terrified, and most of them moved to the military district headquarters opposite the Winter Palace for protection. Mutineers put up machine gun posts on the Nevsky without meeting resistance. It seemed the city was theirs. Lenin had moved to the Tauride, remaining inconspicuous, "looking pleased with himself," waiting to declare that the Bolsheviks had seized power.

The head of the Provisional Government counterintelligence service, Colonel Boris Nikitin, said that Bolsheviks, "enjoying complete freedom of action, lorded it over the city." But the colonel noticed that the mutineers had "no concrete orders" to take over telephone exchanges and arsenals, all of which awaited them with "wide-open doors." Units were becoming mixed up with one another, while Lenin continued to fret in the Tauride over the risks of an all-out effort. "The streets flowed with blood," Nikitin said, "but there was no leadership."

Pavel Pereverzev had one last throw, to release the dossier the government had been building up on Lenin's involvement with the Germans. At 5:00 P.M., the justice minister summoned journalists and men from the regiments to his office to leak part of the information. He hoped this would have some effect on the garrison.

The Soviet executive committee continued its meeting inside the palace. Forty armed workers burst into the hall. One, a "classic sans-culotte" in a cap and beltless blue blouse, jumped on the platform, quivering with rage and waving a rifle. "Comrades! How long must we workers put up with treachery?" he asked. "You're all here debating and making deals with the bourgeoisie and the landlords. . . . You're busy betraying the working class. Well, understand that we won't put up with it! . . . Your Kerenskys and Tseretelis are not going to fool us!"

Despite the rifle waving under his nose, Nikolai Chkheidze, the committee chairman, showed complete self-control. He pushed a manifesto into the man's hand. "Please read it and don't interrupt our business," Chkheidze said. "Everything necessary is there." The pamphlet said that all demonstrators should go home on pain of betraying the revolution. Sukhanov thought it one of the finest scenes of the revolution and Chkheidze's calm gesture the most dramatic.

Baffled and embarrassed, the man stepped down from the platform and shuffled off. But he left behind him the shadow of the "will, the longings of the real proletarian lower depths," who scented treachery but were powerless to fight it.

The Bolsheviks were losing their chance. A heavy evening downpour had the mutineers running for doorways "as if under heavy rifle fire." It combined with the "blood and filth of the senseless day" to produce a sobering effect. The majority of the Kronstadt men made their way to the Neva quays, boarded their ships and went home. Some three hundred had been killed and wounded and the rising was crumbling. In the richer areas of the city, shopkeepers began beating up straggling groups of workers. "They attacked us and gave it to us good," said one worker who was set upon. "They were shouting 'Beat the Yids and the Bolsheviks! Drown them!'" Thrown into the Catherine Canal, he was dragged out, bruised and bleeding, by some sailors.

The Soviet executive committee continued sitting into the night, interrupted by alarms when shots were fired in the Tauride courtyard. Rumors had it that Cossacks were charging the palace. In fact, some horses had broken loose and an accidental rifle discharge led to a flurry of shooting into the air, while panic-stricken people in the courtyard smashed ground-floor windows and climbed into the palace for cover. A more solid rumor swept the palace that the morning papers were about to publish documents linking Lenin to the German General Staff. Lenin, tipped off, fled from the palace.

Soldiers slept by their stacked-up arms in the corridors. Putilov workers still wandered through the building. "Irritated with weariness and hunger, we were waiting for something decisive to happen," said a Vyborg man. "At four in the morning on July 5 our waiting came to an end." The noise of tramping feet and the brassy tones of a marching band echoed through the palace. Deputies leapt from their seats in alarm. "Comrades! Be calm! There is no danger," Fedor Dan said with glee. "Loyal regiments have arrived to defend us."

A battalion of Izmailovsky Guards deployed through the building, arresting and disarming the workers and mutineers. The soldiers were dirty, the dust soaked into their uniforms by the rain. They had an active service look with packs on their backs, rolled greatcoats over their shoulders, and mess tins that clanked at their belts. No Bolsheviks were present, and moderate deputies, "choking with delight," linked hands and burst into the "Marseillaise."

The Izmailovsky men had not, as many deputies thought, been sent by Kerensky from the front. They had marched from their Petrograd barracks. Some of the guardsmen had been briefed by Pereverzev at the justice ministry on Lenin's links with the Germans. Pereverzev was persuasive enough for the regiment to abandon its neutrality and come out against the Bolsheviks. The men might not care much for the Provisional Government, but they cared less for traitors. The rising was over. The Soviet finally dispersed. The Tauride courtyard, drenched in the rising sun, was empty and quiet. The demonstrators had gone.

A counterstrike was beginning.

The Bolsheviks spent a miserable night in a central committee meeting. They realized that they had accepted practical responsibility for the rising. Lenin flirted with the idea of continuing it. "Give me an exact account of your strength," he asked the committee. "Name the units which will definitely follow us. Who is against us? Have the Neva bridges been accounted for?" There were no satisfactory answers. It was decided to call the demonstrations off. *Pravda* was to announce that this was because they had already succeeded in pointing up the "danger in which the disastrous policy of the government has placed the country."

There was no *Pravda* in which to run the empty claim. Lenin was in real danger and knew it. "Now they are going to shoot us," he told Trotsky. "It is the best time for them." He went back underground. He spent the rest of the night of July 4–5 with Krupskaya in a friend's flat. Early on Wednesday morning, July 5, as Lenin and Krupskaya moved to another safe house, they passed soldiers on their way to wreck the *Pravda* offices on government orders. Telephones were ripped out, manuscripts torn up, and the rotary presses and linotype machines destroyed. The morning edition of *Pravda* was dumped in the Moika Canal.

The sensational right-wing daily *Zhivoe Slovo* reached the morning news stands with a thick headline accusing Lenin of being a German agent and spy: "Horrors! Petrograd was seized by the Germans!" Gregory Alexinsky, a former friend of Lenin who had fallen out with him, had set out the details in a pamphlet entitled "No Needless Words." It sold out and the editors at *Zhivoe Slovo* battened on the story. It alleged that two German General Staff officers had named Lenin as one of their agents in Russia, and that Lenin was supplied with German money through the Parvus spy ring in Stockholm and Lenin's agent in Sweden, Jacob Ganetsky. Two million rubles had been transferred to the Bolsheviks via Stockholm from the

Disconto-Gesellschaft in Berlin, the money being laundered through a pharmaceutical front company run by one of Lenin's lieutenants, the Polish Bolshevik Mecheslav Kozlovsky. Telegrams between Lenin and Ganetsky were reproduced.

The story convinced even a man as cynical and world-weary as Blok. "Mama, these days there is a revolution in the city," Blok wrote to his mother that evening. "The thought of that German money is in my head." Sukhanov admitted that Bolshevik sources of income could never be satisfactorily explained — "unknown elements, even of German origin" could be gambling on extending Bolshevik influence by "palming them off with some money or other."

More than "some"; perhaps as much as 50 million marks, or up to $10 million in all, was involved. Keeping the party presses going was an expensive business. In addition to *Pravda* and *Soldatskaya Pravda*, the Bolsheviks were publishing "tons" of pamphlets. Richard von Kühlmann, who replaced Arthur Zimmermann as German foreign minister, was to report that it was only when they received a "steady flow of funds through various channels" from Berlin that the Bolsheviks were able to "conduct extensive propaganda" and to "extend the narrow basis of their party."

The detailed evidence of German payments was more damning than the garbled version that appeared in *Zhivoe Slovo*. A French intelligence agent in Petrograd, Captain Pierre Laurent, had obtained copies of telegrams exchanged between Jacob Ganetsky and a relative of his in Petrograd, Eugenia Sumenson, a "lady of the demimonde." Money from Berlin was sent first to Ganetsky's account at the Nye Bank in Stockholm. From there it was transferred to Madame Sumenson's account with the Siberian Bank in Petrograd. She in turn passed the funds, apparently safely laundered, to Mecheslav Kozlovsky's bogus pharmaceuticals company. Laurent provided Russian counterintelligence with coded correspondence — "Nestles sends no flour, Request Sumenson" — exchanged between Stockholm and Petrograd.

Government agents had started shadowing Eugenia Sumenson on June 29, a few hours before Lenin had made his hasty and unexpected exit from Petrograd to the safe *dacha* in Finland.

Tales of treason had a vivid effect on the troops. These "little peasants" were not at all opposed to throwing out the bourgeoisie and grabbing land, Sukhanov thought. But they were "mortally afraid of the Bolsheviks, traitors, lackeys of the kaiser, universal destroyers, atheists," who talked "gibberish" about class war and international proletarian solidarity. They set to their work of arresting Bolsheviks with gusto.

Switchboard operators refused to connect Bolshevik callers. Alexander

Ilyin tried to get through to the *Pravda* plant, not knowing that it had been raided. A girl in the central telephone exchange screamed at him, "You are probably Lenin himself speaking. You spy! You scoundrel!" With that, she cut him off.

Gregory Zinoviev, wretched, upset and in a great hurry, turned up at the Soviet to complain that the "monstrous slander" of Lenin was becoming a second Dreyfus affair. Zinoviev demanded that the executive committee take urgent steps to rehabilitate Lenin. He then scurried off — neither he nor Lenin was to be seen again in public for more than three months.

Young factory workers and Red Guards set off across the Neva in rowboats, with hand grenades concealed in their boots and under their coats, to reinforce the rebels in the Peter and Paul Fortress. But sailors were already abandoning the fortress, slipping out of Petrograd through the back streets. Toward evening, a "huge, gay, bourgeois throng" was parading the Nevsky to celebrate its triumph over the Bolsheviks. Sukhanov thought that the Black Hundreds were behind the looting that continued in parts of the city.

A destroyer, the *Orpheus*, entered the Neva and moored. It had a delegation of sixty-seven sailors aboard who had come to arrest the assistant navy minister, Dudarev. Dudarev had ordered the Baltic Fleet to prevent any men from getting to Petrograd, sinking any ship that disobeyed with submarines if necessary. The confused sailors found the Soviet fulsome in its praise of Dudarev, and were themselves arrested.

Revulsion against Lenin and the "July Days," as the attempted coup was called, was widespread. Stories circulated that the Bolshevik leader had moved into Kshesinskaya's boudoir, while drunken Bolsheviks smashed up the furniture and decorations. "The disgusting scenes of madness which seized Petrograd the day of July 4 will remain with me for the rest of my life," Maxim Gorky wrote in his paper *Novaya Zhizn*. "There, bristling with rifles and machine guns, a truck flashes by like a mad hog; it is tightly packed with motley members of the 'revolutionary army,' among them stands a disheveled youth who shouts hysterically, 'The socialist revolution, comrades!'" Gorky thought the cause was not the Bolsheviks, or the Germans, but a "more evil and stronger enemy — the oppressive Russian stupidity."

Gorky, though now forty-nine years old and a rich man, sad-faced with a walrus mustache, had barely survived a youth of enough real poverty to end any "notions that Russian workers are the incarnation of spiritual beauty and kindness." As a boy, he had worked in an icon maker's shop and as a bargehand before wandering through southern Russia for three years as a tramp. At nineteen, suffering from a "toothache in the heart," he shot himself in the breast, badly injuring his lungs. Five years later, a kindly editor in Tiflis got Gorky to write down his adventures as a wanderer. His play *The Lower Depths* made him the most famous writer in Russia.

Gorky's revolutionary credentials were impeccable — he had been arrested for sedition in 1905, had attacked capitalism on a trip to the United States in 1906, and had met Lenin in London a year later — and he was a soft touch for radical causes. But, though drawn to Bolshevism and to Lenin, he was worried about a dogma that made all proletarians "sweet and reasonable — I had never known people who were really like this." Gorky knew the poor of Russia, "carpenters, stevedores, bricklayers" in a way that Lenin, who had never drudged to earn a wage, did not, and Gorky did not trust them.

A very different writer, more literary and emotional, and the well-heeled grandson of a rector of Petrograd University, Alexander Blok had also had a sneaking admiration for the party. One of his "clients" in the Peter and Paul Fortress, a shrewd and penitent former police chief, Stepan Beletsky, compared the life of the Bolsheviks to those of the early Christians. Now, like Gorky, Blok was not so sure. He felt the movement was non-Russian. "Russian Bolshevism is so permeated, saturated to overflowing by quite foreign elements that it is almost impossible to think of it as a political party," he wrote.

The Bolshevik party, in any case, was in full retreat. A hasty central committee meeting was held in the gatehouse of the Renault plant. Lenin opposed the suggestion of a general strike. In the present mood of hatred, it was not likely to be followed. "What shall we do with this Lenin who's come from Germany?" Krupskaya overheard a working woman jeer. "Should he be drowned in a well, or what?" He moved on continuously, from a flat overlooking the scum-filled and grimy Karpovka Canal to the Vyborg rooms of a worker called Kaurov. "Kaurov's son was an anarchist," Krupskaya said. "Young men were messing around with bombs, so it wasn't up to much as a safe house."

From early on Thursday morning, July 6, troops from the front were arriving at the Nicholas and Warsaw stations. The factories returned to work. A company of bicycle troops was sent to the Kshesinskaya palace. The Bolsheviks had already abandoned it and the troops burst into almost empty rooms, arresting a few people "aimlessly wandering about." The Villa Durnovo was taken in the afternoon, the anarchists leaving a few weapons and much propaganda behind them. The remaining sailors in the Peter and Paul Fortress surrendered without a firing a shot.

At 9:00 P.M. on Thursday evening, Kerensky returned from the front and raced directly from the station to a government session. He ordered the immediate arrest of Lenin, Zinoviev, Kamenev, Lunacharsky, and Trotsky for "high treason and organizing an armed uprising." All the units that had taken part in the revolt were to be disbanded, with their personnel disposed of at Kerensky's discretion.

Eugenia Sumenson was picked up in her apartment. She was "thrilled with her mad adventure" as Lenin's financial go-between, and happily confessed to her interrogators that Ganetsky had asked her to hand over to Kozlovsky any sum he asked for. These were large amounts — 750,000 rubles in June. Sumenson still had 180,000 rubles in her account with the Siberian Bank, and she lived well in prison. She fitted her cell up with pink satin pillows and lace covers on her cot, and had a paper-moon lampshade over the light. In the evenings, she lay back in a pink negligee and discussed art and literature with the admiring warders, "just like a courtesan in the time of the Louis's."

Militiamen broke into Lenin's flat on Shirokaya Street at 2:00 A.M. on Friday morning, July 7, Krupskaya yelling, "Gendarmes! Just like the old regime!" They were three hiding places too late. Lenin was now staying with Stalin's friend, Scrge Alliluyev. Depressed and frightened — "Are they going to do for me?" — he thought of giving himself up. Lenin was, Sukhanov stressed, in no danger of being killed. There was no question of lynch law, the death penalty, or even hard labor. Kerensky had personally defended tsarist prisoners from the mob and the provisional government was treating the mutineers with great leniency. Mensheviks and Social Revolutionaries, if they called the Bolsheviks traitors, still regarded them as comrades and acted as if the coup attempt was little more than an unfortunate misunderstanding.

"Lenin risked absolutely nothing but imprisonment," said Sukhanov. He would have had as much freedom of action in prison as in hiding. His colleagues who were arrested — Kamenev, Trotsky, Lunacharsky — safely sat out their few weeks of imprisonment and went on writing "with martyrs' haloes."

But Lenin's nerve failed. He scribbled a melodramatic note to Kamenev: "If they do me in, please publish my notebook, *Marxism and the State.*" He added, characteristically, that this was vital because he showed up the "falsehoods" of Plekhanov in the notebook. Depressed, he talked of moving the party center out of Russia again to a safer place — Finland, or Sweden. He embraced Krupskaya — "We may not see each other again."

On Sunday, July 9, troops at a roadblock arrested Lev Kamenev in an automobile. Lenin shaved his beard and left the Alliluyev flat that evening. He made his way through the back streets of northern Petrograd to a suburban station on the Finnish line. He waited with Gregory Zinoviev for the

2:00 A.M. "boozers' train" used by revelers coming back from a night in the city bars and restaurants. A group of officers who had been drinking boarded the train. They sang obscene army songs and cursed the Bolsheviks — Lenin lowered his head and swayed as though he was also drunk. Twenty miles out of the city, he hid up in the hayloft of a barn belonging to a party member.

"The shepherd's flight," wrote Sukhanov, "could not help but be a heavy blow to the sheep." As the responsibility for the July Days came down on the workers and Bolsheviks — a word now synonymous with "scoundrel, murderer, Judas, and anybody else it was essential to seize, maul, and beat up" — the real author abandoned his comrades and sought personal salvation in flight.

XVI
"Now It's Back to Work"

IN THE EARLY HOURS of Friday, July 7, a few hours after his return to Petrograd, Kerensky met with the other socialist ministers. They laid out a policy that had, for the first time, two clearly socialist elements. Radical land handouts were promised. A republic was to be proclaimed, formally abolishing the monarchy. Both were measures that should have been decided by the coming Constituent Assembly.

Prince Georgy Lvov argued at a cabinet meeting that started at 8:00 A.M. that the government had no right to preempt the assembly. At 1:00 P.M., failing to make headway, he resigned. Kerensky replaced him as premier, emphasizing his power by retaining the war ministry. It was an amicable enough transfer. Times had become too harsh for what Kerensky called the prince's "gentle manner of governing." Lvov realized this himself. He had aged terribly in office, his "fleshy, well-covered face" now worn and lined around "darkly bagged" eyes. "I resigned because there was nothing left for *me* to do," he told a friend. "To save the situation it was necessary to dissolve the Soviets and fire at the people. I could not do it. But Kerensky can."

An hour after Kerensky took over the government, more firing broke out. A unit arriving at the Nicholas Station from the front was ambushed by unseen machine gunners. They were thought to be Black Hundreds provocateurs, seeking to turn the troops against the left. Kerensky was more frightened of reactionaries than of the fading Bolsheviks, feeling that danger would come from the right, from disaffected army officers and the landowners angrily discussing their pillaged estates in Petrograd salons. The same day that he became premier, fearful that the right was plotting to restore the monarchy, he decided to send the imperial family to Siberia.

The chance to exploit the popular fury against the Bolsheviks slipped away. Kerensky sacked Pavel Pereverzev for leaking a too-flimsy version of the German financial transactions, saying that the justice minister had lost forever the opportunity of "establishing Lenin's guilt in final form." The new justice minister, Alexander Zarudny, patiently collected eighty volumes of evidence against the Bolsheviks. Eugenia Sumenson sang merrily in her satin cell. No court case was opened.

The German connection apart, Bolshevik conduct in the July Days was itself treasonable. Nikolai Sukhanov was told as much by Lunacharsky on July 8. The two met in Dr. Manukhin's rooms, where a sofa was always kept ready for Sukhanov to sleep after late-night executive committee sessions. He found Anatoly Lunacharsky on the sofa. Raising himself from the "blameless sleep of youth," Lunacharsky explained the plan to proclaim the new Bolshevik government, in which he would have been a member, with the help of the 176th Regiment.

A public trial might have finished the party. The American ambassador, David Francis, thought it would be the simplest thing to charge Lenin and Trotsky with treason and to execute them. Francis was a "kindly old gent" of eighty — he amused Petrograd society by carrying a traveling spittoon with him, emphasizing his arguments with a well-aimed gob — and he could not understand the unreciprocated solidarity that still glued Mensheviks and Social Revolutionaries to the Bolsheviks.

The Bolsheviks' socialist colleagues were temperamentally unable to accept that any of their fellows on the left would take German money. Despite Lunacharsky's confession, the Soviet was equally unwilling to believe that comrades had attempted a coup d'état and instead attacked the government for vilifying Lenin. Kerensky could not risk alienating the Soviet, and his persecution of the Bolsheviks was half hearted.

Few things in 1917 were as curious, on the face of it, as the inability of other socialists to realized the fate the Bolsheviks had in store for them. Their reluctance to condemn the Leninists was partly a matter of ignorance. Few had read the works in which Lenin made clear that he saw terrorism and dictatorship as essential parts of revolution. His works had been banned before the revolution. After it, events moved too fast for people to have time to work through the back list of his works. All had had access to *Pravda*, however, from which it was obvious that he regarded socialist as much as capitalist rivals to be candidates for liquidation.

What saved him — and it was a quite crucial stroke of luck — were two strong and intermingled feelings. One was the ideal of solidarity, the other a conviction that the Bolsheviks should not be taken at face value.

Public respect for revolutionaries had run deep in tsarist Russia. "Few of the intelligent families in the Russian Empire are without one or two relatives who have undergone imprisonment for their views," an American correspondent, Basset Digby, had observed before the war. "For this reason, when the 'politicals' have finished their sentences, they are treated kindly by others." Though the Bolsheviks did not believe in the solidarity created by shared persecution, other socialists were happy to extend its courtesies to them. The autocracy had exiled and executed. How could the revolution — whose bloodless treatment of tsarist officials and the tsar himself remained one of its glories — persecute its own?

It was felt, too, that Bolshevik theory would never be put into practice. The totalitarian state — ruthless, politicized and centralized, destructive of the slightest opposition — was still taking shape in Lenin's mind. He was predicting world revolution, governments without officials, societies without policemen, factories without foremen. To take him seriously was to admit to a belief in the millennium.

About eight hundred Bolsheviks were arrested in the immediate aftermath of the rising, and the leadership disappeared underground. There was no attempt to liquidate them as a force. Irakli Tsereteli, the new interior minister and himself a former hard-labor convict, admitted that accusing Bolsheviks of political crimes smacked of autocracy.

The mutineers escaped as lightly. Units were divided into categories according to their degree of involvement in the rising. First-category units were to be disbanded in their entirety, while sections or individuals who had gone over to the Bolsheviks would be routed out of others. The men of the First Machine Gun Regiment were publicly stripped of their arms at a ceremony on Palace Square on July 8. But four of the six first-category regiments were still in the capital two months later, fully armed. No action was taken against second- and third-category units, or against the Kronstadt sailors.

Nevertheless, the July Days cost the Bolsheviks dear. Party agents reported that the mood of the Petrograd works "has turned against us." Morale in the capital was described as a "stagnant swamp." Alexander Ilyin regrouped with a few comrades in the house of another member of the military organization, Genrikh Yagoda. "After the spacious rooms of the Kshesinskaya palace," Ilyin wrote, "we were once more in a small room. The good old days of underground work had returned. It would have been better if they had not."

No printer dared publish Bolshevik papers and leaflets. It was a fortnight before Ilyin found the owner of a small print ship on Gorokhovaya Street who was tempted by a supper party with "plenty of rare liquor on the table" to allow them to share a press with a clergyman who was publishing a weekly called *Free Church*. Neither the owner nor the priest realized that the new customers were atheists and wanted men. Titles were changed — *Soldatskaya* became *Soldat* and *Pravda* was rechristened *Rabochy Put.*

In Moscow, only a third of party members in one district stayed loyal. Others asked, "Where is Lenin? He's beat it, they say. . . . What will happen now?" Agitators were roughed up. In municipal elections in Kiev, the Bolsheviks got 5 percent of the vote, less than the Cadets and a seventh of the Social Revolutionary–Menshevik tally. In Tula, the Bolsheviks won five seats to the eighty-five of the Social Revolutionary–Menshevik bloc. In parts of the southern provinces, Bolshevik organizations disappeared entirely.

The dead mutineers of the July Days went to their graves in secret. The loyal Cossacks killed at the Liteiny Bridge were buried with great pomp on July 15. The service at Saint Isaac's was packed, the cathedral filled with flowers and religious leaders in what was to prove their last major turnout. Kerensky's short speech — "I solemnly announce that all attempts at anarchy, from whatever side they come, will be repressed without pity in the name of the blood of these victims" — was greeted with shouts of joy. He delighted the well-dressed mourners by helping to carry the first coffin. His fellow pallbearers were Prince Lvov and the two men of March, Mikhail Rodzianko and Pavel Miliukov.

Large crowds lined the route to watch the cortege of frock-coated politicians and richly robed clerics follow the coffins on open trucks to the burial in the Alexander Nevsky monastery. Mounted Cossacks with pennants fluttering on their lances stood guard amid ladies in summer hats who cheered "Long live Kerensky!" The Cossacks were less impressed. Meriel Buchanan noted their surly faces; "they had given their lives to save a government that had been overthrown by a horde of rebels, and the government accepted the sacrifice and did nothing to punish the rebels."

Cossacks became the heroes of bourgeois Petrograd. Theaters, movie houses, and public gardens held benefit evenings for the families of the wounded and dead. At the mere entrance of someone in Cossack uniform at a restaurant, a Cossack officer recalled, "all would stand up and greet the newcomer with applause." Alexander Blok walked through the pleasure gardens and saw that the "officers and their tarts in Luna Park were getting bolder." There were rumors that officer cadets were drinking the health of the tsar. The right-wing press, thinking the Bolsheviks to be finished, turned on the Social Revolutionaries and Mensheviks. Sukhanov said that the bourgeoisie — rightly, from their point of view — wanted the Soviets "wiped off the face of the earth."

All processions and street meetings in Petrograd were banned outright, and the government claimed the right to close any private meeting it deemed to be a danger to state security or the war effort. Those guilty of violence designed to "change the existing state structure of Russia, or to sever from Russia any of its parts" were to face hard labor. It was warning as much to nationalists as to Bolsheviks, and it was equally ignored by both of them.

On July 12, the death penalty was brought back in the army. Due to "shameful conduct both at the front and in the rear," Kerensky announced that men in uniform found guilty of "heinous crimes" would be shot by firing squad. This stamped him as a reactionary to the left. Because he was proud of never refusing clemency, however, executions were rarely carried out and his "moral feebleness" undermined him with the right. Military-revolutionary courts, consisting of three officers and three soldiers selected by lot, were to be established immediately. Capital crimes included treason, flight from the battlefield, refusal to fight, surrender without resistance, violent acts against officers, and rape and robbery in the zone of the armies.

The unreality of the exercise, and Kerensky's trick of substituting harsh words for action, was obvious to all. The premier was scorned by senior officers when he arrived at Mogilev for talks on July 16. "What can help?" General Vladislav said mockingly as Kerensky shifted nervously in his seat. "The death penalty? But is it really possible to execute entire divisions? Prosecution? Then half the army would turn out to be in Siberia." The premier found himself friendless in Mogilev — he noted bitterly that Alexei Brusilov had not bothered to go to the station to greet him. He dealt with Brusilov two days later, sacking him as commander in chief and naming Lavr Kornilov to succeed him.

Taking advantage of the swing against the Bolsheviks, Kerensky formed a new government on July 24. Although it had eleven socialists to seven liberals, Pavel Miliukov noted that the real emphasis in the cabinet "unconditionally belonged to the supporters of bourgeois democracy." The new justice minister, Alexander Zarudny, the fourth in five months, was the son of a minister of Alexander II. The deputy premier and finance minister was Nikolai Nekrasov, the Cadet who had floated the idea of handing power to a general during the February revolution. Viktor Chernov, however, unexpectedly returned as agriculture minister.

Trotsky and Lunacharsky were arrested on the night the new cabinet was formed. "Perhaps we made a mistake," Trotsky fretted in prison. "We should have tried to take power."

The Cadets succeeded in having the Constituent Assembly postponed again, this time with elections fixed for November 12. Some hoped that it might be put off sine die, for there was already talk among the Cadets of a strong man who would impose a "bourgeois military dictatorship." In this Mad Hatter world, civilians were encouraged to denounce male deserters while women soldiers fought in the name of a parliament for which they could vote, unlike their sisters in Western democracies, but in elections that were constantly postponed.

In the factories, as at the front, the Bolshevik debacle in the July Days was used to try to restore discipline. "Now it's back to work," the Petrograd Society of Manufacturers declared with premature relief. It declared workers' control to be illegal. Employers made a particular attack on factory committees.

In some plants, where the managers had fled or been expelled, the committees had taken over the administration, attempting to keep the books and to control production, wages, and hiring and firing. The Mensheviks and Social Revolutionaries and the Society of Factory and Works Owners, the big Petrograd employers' organization, at first cooperated. The SFWO agreed to pay workers for time spent in committee. It also undertook to "ensure the future spiritual development of the working class" by providing time off for self-education and union organization. The committees, for their part, worked to prevent unofficial strikes.

Hard-liners on both sides asserted themselves as the early euphoria wore off. Donbass and Urals mine owners, and the harder Petrograd bosses, preferred coercion to conciliation. They closed pits and factories and broke strikes with lockouts, the workers reacting by beating up managers and looting the houses of mine owners. The Bolsheviks had no sympathy for workers' control either, except as a handy slogan, for dictatorship was central to Lenin's thought. But the factory committees were convenient targets for takeover. The Bolsheviks were weak in the rapidly growing national trade unions. In individual plants they led wage demands, sniping at Menshevik and Social Revolutionary moderation, and gained support rapidly.

As committees multiplied in the factories — the Metal Works Company in Petrograd had twenty-eight of them by midsummer, covering food, factory security, wages, hiring and firing, and "culture and enlightenment" — conditions worsened. Absenteeism in the Putilov works, 10 percent in January, reached 25 percent during the summer. From Moscow, the U.S. Consul General Madden Summers reported that "the managers of large factories complain that the workmen are doing what they please and they are managers in name only."

Drinking at work was a chronic problem. "The men drink methylated spirits, varnish, and all kinds of other substitutes," the factory committee at the Atlas metalworks reported. "They come to work drunk, speak at meetings drunk . . . and the result is chaos in the workshops." Courts of honor were set up on some works to deal with drinking, but had little success. In

July, the committee in the Putilov gun shop was faced with the new problem of young workers deliberately smashing their machines. A Menshevik at Putilov found that there was "not even a shadow of discipline left." Professional security guards had been replaced by soldiers who did not know the rules for searching workers coming out of the plant. Worse, he said, was the sharp fall in productivity. Two hundred gun carriages had been produced monthly, but this had slumped to at most fifty to sixty. The works was two hundred million rubles in debt and already in a catastrophic state.

Food was again scarce. The summer bread ration remained at five hundred grams a day, but other staples were now rationed — a kilo of sugar a month, eight hundred grams of meat, six hundred of fats, two hundred of buckwheat, and twenty eggs a month. Petrograd workers in July were getting half the three thousand calories a day that was considered a minimum for those doing medium-to-hard labor. Queues more than offset the cut in the working day. The interior ministry noted that the lines "have in fact turned the eight-hour day into a twelve- or thirteen-hour one, because working men and women go straight from the factory and stand in a queue for four or five hours."

Washington sent a commission under Elihu Root to advise the Provisional Government on labor issues. Its members celebrated the Fourth of July with a dinner at the American Society of Petrograd. To help with the transport crisis, a U.S. railway commission landed at Vladivostok in June. Led by an eminent engineer, John F. Stevens, the commission included men from the Pennsylvania, Wabash, and Baltimore and Ohio railroads. They arrived to a hostile demonstration — Bolsheviks in Vladivostok had been tipped off by Russian exiles living on the East Side of New York.

They found the rail system close to collapse. It was decided that Americans should run the Vladivostok terminal, with U.S. control and expertise to be extended right along the Trans-Siberian to Moscow. A party of two hundred railroad operating men and interpreters was recruited to be ready to leave Seattle for Vladivostok in October.

When food could be found and shipped — factories were sending parties of men out into the countryside to scavenge supplies for works canteens — the prices far outreached pay increases. Wages were up an average of just over half between the revolution and July. The cost of necessities had more than doubled, allowing Bolshevik agitators to claim that the employers were deliberately starving the workers. Alexis Babine, the schools inspector, complained that he was paying 4.5 rubles for the "commonest laundry soap that used to cost fifteen kopeks at most."

Those in the high-wage metals industry struggled to cope. Outside was devastation. Typesetters had been the cream of prewar labor, riding to work by bicycle, wearing starched collars, and going to the theater and race tracks. Their real wages were now cut by a quarter. Shop assistants were laid off from stores that no longer had civilian goods to sell. The *sluzh-aschie,* white-collar clerical workers, slid below metalworkers for the first time.

A textile tycoon, Pavel Riabushinsky, seemed to give the employers' game away when he spoke to a congress of industrialists and stockbrokers in Moscow. He mocked the Provisional Government as a "gang of political charlatans" which possessed only the shadow of power. It was up to the "bony hand of hunger," he said, to "grasp the members of the committees and Soviets by the throat" and make them see sense. Like Marie Antoinette's cake, the "bony hand" entered into the political dictionary of the revolution. Trotsky noted with satisfaction that it "cost the capitalists dear."

The Petrograd bourse was booming in apparent confirmation of heady profitability. The outcome of the July Days, the London *Economist* reported, had "certainly had the effect of unloosening the investors' purse strings." Russian Petroleum and the big Russo-Asiatic Consolidated reached record highs, Government 5 percent was up 4 points to 78; and the ruble recovered from 212 to 203 to £10. Paper money flooded off the presses, 476 million rubles in April, 729 million in May, 869 million in June, a billion in July. But inflation and the drop in productivity were crippling real profits. Employers, faced with unit costs that had quadrupled in a year due to the cut in working hours and the fall in output, were going bankrupt. It was not necessary to resort to lockouts to reinforce their message. Factories, the SFWO warned, would close down "inevitably and gradually, so to speak, one by one."

Firms employing more than a hundred thousand workers had closed their gates since the revolution. Fuel shortages were so bad by July that Petrograd plants were sending *tolkachi* — fixers — to the Donbass to search for coal supplies. Some managements concealed supplies to put pressure on workers, who began to search factories. Workers at the Rosenkrantz plant in Petrograd discovered 140,000 pounds of hoarded metals on July 14. It was found that managers at the Duflon and Nevsky works had sold off metal stocks at high prices prior to closing down.

Menshevik factory committees passed resolutions to use fines and dismissal to eliminate the "unserious approach to work." This was unpopular and more factory committees fell to the Bolsheviks, who accused employers of going on "investment strike" by refusing to accept new contracts or to repair machinery. "From you, capitalists, weeping crocodile tears, we demand you stop sniveling about the chaos you have yourselves created," Bolsheviks in the Putilov works menaced. "The cards are on the table. Go off and hide. Think your own thoughts and don't dare show your noses, or else you'll find yourself without a nose, and without a head to boot."

The Bolsheviks had raised their own militia, the Red Guards, although these were too inefficient to play much part in the July Days. They also kept their distance from other socialists in cultural enlightenment — "Prolekult" in revolutionary newspeak. Non-Bolsheviks entertained workers with popular operas and taught them natural sciences and math at evening classes. The Bolsheviks insisted on a diet of politics, teaching illiterates to read with party slogans chalked on blackboards. "We do not exist to amuse," the Bolshevik theater group at the Nobel works declared, "but to foster spiritual growth . . . to unite individual personalities into one gigantic class personality." The only aim of culture was to prepare "fighters for the class war." In the theater and ballet, artists "went out of their way to bring 'Comrades' into conversation." Every dance troupe had a committee, and the prima ballerina Tamara Karsavina complained that the "youngest dancers claimed a rise of salary and promotion on the grounds of justice and equality."

Matvei Skobelev, the Menshevik labor minister, issued circulars to boost management control. He emphasized that the right of hiring and firing "belongs to the owners." All factory committee meetings were to take place out of working hours. "It is the duty of every worker to devote his energies to intensive labor and not to lose one minute of working time," Skobelev said. Management had "the right to deduct pay for loss of working time." The committees were instructed to disband all workers' militiamen and Red Guards, giving them the choice of going back to their benches or of joining the civil militia for a miserly 150-rubles-a-month pay.

The government was easily mocked. It was unreal to insist on squeezing the last minute of labor out of workers who were idled for days on end by shortages of raw materials, and whose pay left them prey to hunger. The leadership at a conference of factory committees, which met in Petrograd on August 7, was solidly Bolshevik. The conference had no interest in liquidating the Red Guards or in increasing production for a war effort in which it did not believe. Many delegates shared Lenin's ambition that the factory committees "must become the organs of insurrection."

Kerensky was more concerned with the threat from the "dark forces," the monarchists and reactionaries, than with the raggle-taggle Red Guards whose leaders were in prison or underground. Shortly before midnight on July 31, he left a cabinet meeting for Tsarskoe Selo to finalize the secret transfer of the imperial family to Tobolsk. A monarchist coup, Kerensky hoped, would be less likely with the ex-tsar safely in Siberia.

The guards at Tsarskoe Selo were restless and reluctant to leave for

Siberia. "No hitting a man when he is down," Kerensky told them. "Behave like gentlemen, not cads." The men refused to carry the family's trunks and packing chests from the palace without special pay. The premier watched as Grand Duke Mikhail said goodbye to his elder brother. "The brothers were most deeply moved," Kerensky said. "They stood opposite each other, shuffling their feet in curious embarrassment, sometimes getting hold of one another's arm or coat button."

The empress was tired and worried. For the first time, Kerensky saw her "weeping like any other woman." He found her unbalanced and hysterical, but also sensed that she had about her something "strong, earthy, passionate and proud." When the tsar asked a group of officers for a cup of tea, they stood and said they would not sit at the same table as Nicholas Romanov, but when their men were out of earshot the officers apologized and told Nicholas they were afraid of being branded counterrevolutionaries. Suspicious railwaymen refused to couple the cars of the special train ordered for the trip and Kerensky had to telephone the marshaling yards himself in the early hours.

At dawn the train was ready. Kerensky said his farewell, having assured a member of the entourage that Nicholas would be free to return to Tsarskoe Selo once the Constituent Assembly had met in November. The family was driven to the station with an escort of Cossacks. The carriages had no steps and Alexandra and her daughters were lifted aboard. The train headed east. To forestall rescue attempts by monarchists or assassination by deserters, the train carried the flag of the Rising Sun and was boldly marked "Japanese Red Cross Mission."

XVII
Black Earth, Red Fire

THE "JAPANESE" TRAIN crawled eastward with drawn blinds through European Russia and across the Urals for four days before it reached the railhead at Tyumen, a thousand miles east of Moscow. Here the imperial family transferred to a steamer for the two-day river journey to Tobolsk. The family went on deck to watch Rasputin's home village, Pokrovskoe, drift by on the shore. Kerensky's writ did not run in the countryside through which they passed. "Russia," said the Cadet newspaper *Rech,* "is turning into a Texas, into a country of the Far West." From those who had fled, Sukhanov heard of burning country houses, lynch law, unauthorized arrests, and herds of stolen cattle.

"The state was falling to pieces like a handful of wet mud," the journalist Konstantin Paustovsky wrote. "The provinces and districts of Russia were no longer ruled by Petrograd and no one knew what they lived on or what was seething inside them."

When Paustovsky went home to find out, the countryside was so dangerous that his mother would hardly let him out of her sight. The man who drove him home asked when the peasants would be allowed to take the land and "to drive out all the big Pans and the little Pans with our spades, straight to the devil's mother." Paustovsky visited a small monastery a few miles away. Only a few aging monks were left, occasionally ringing the bell so gently that a crow in the belfry did not fly away. There were bandits in the woods, who later looted the monastery for silver, shooting the monks and firing the church.

A landowner, Pyotr Shilovsky, set off for his estate in Ryazan in the summer. His butler in Petrograd had given notice that he did not want to serve "capitalists," and the cook had taken to going off to the Kshesinskaya mansion in the evenings to listen to the Bolshevik speakers. Shilovsky realized that things were worse in the provinces when he arrived at the governors mansion in Ryazan.

His wife had grown up in its elegant rooms. Now the fine furniture, carpets, and mirrors had gone. The parquet flooring was spattered with spittle and cigarette ends. A few ragged armchairs stood against the walls, together with benches brought in from the garden. In the dining room, "two or three good-looking Jewesses were carrying on a lively trade in cigarettes and sandwiches." Scruffy soldiers and some strange civilians sprawled on the seats or rushed about. A colonel from the front, with wound stripes on his sleeve, walked in uncertainly. "Nobody paid the slightest attention to him," Shilovsky said. "We looked at each other in silence." To his astonishment, Shilovsky was given a check by an official for twenty thousand rubles as payment for oats supplied to the War Office. It was the last income he was to get from his estate, however, and he found it clear that authority was "simply disintegrating without anyone to defend it."

When Shilovsky arrived at his own estate the village committee came to see him, with the local postmaster at their head. He tried to instill in them the theory of the inalienability of property rights. They were unimpressed. "Give us the estate freely," they said. "We'll look after it. We don't want to use force." Shilovsky went to his younger brother's estate. While he was there he was told that his pedigreed dairy cattle had been confiscated for slaughter. "It shouldn't only be peasants who have to give cattle for the army's needs," the men said. "Let the landlords suffer as well."

He fled to the nearest railway station. On the way, he came across his herd of cattle, grazing on their way to the slaughterhouse under the supervision of two German prisoners from his estate. The station looked normal. The restaurant had clean tablecloths and waiters but the "strolling players" of the revolution were present among the crowds. A fierce-looking sailor was locked in inflammatory debate with a well-turned-out sergeant major, who interjected "No, no, that's impossible" from time to time with a sort of earnest melancholy.

Shilovsky caught the next train to Moscow, realizing that "I must give up the estate for lost and must live on what wages I could get."

The revolution of ideas, the English traveler Maurice Baring had noted in 1908, was a purely urban affair where one set of city intellectuals fought another. "Above this struggle the aristocracy floats as a nebulous mist," he wrote from the provinces. "And beneath it the peasantry have been roused from their slumber by the noise of the fight." The army had quietened the *muzhiks* then with the aid of "Stolypin neckties," as hangings were known, after then–prime minister Peter Stolypin. The Provisional Government looked to the central land committee to control them now that they were aroused again.

Established on April 21, the land committee was a miniature of revolutionary goodwill that was too perfect to survive. Russians thought that democracy was an ideal state that could be reached immediately. But the president of the American Federation of Labor, Samuel Gompers, warned in a message that "Freedom is achieved in meeting the problems of life and work. It cannot be established by a revolution only. It is a product of evolution." Gompers' advice passed unheeded.

Peasant hopes of plunder went beyond land to embrace livestock, carts, barns, mills, and greenhouses. The committee could not slake this lust; it was empowered only to make proposals to the constantly delayed Constituent Assembly. Its balance, morally magnificent to revolutionary theorists, in practice made it impotent. The committee had more than seventy members. Besides farming experts, these included twenty-seven chosen by the government, fifteen from various Soviets, and men from eleven political parties. The committee's brief covered every type of land, from desert to black earth, and people, from Kalmucks of Mongolian descent on the Caspian to the Finnic Samoyeds of the northern Urals. It reflected every opinion, from Bolsheviks to Nationalists, from Red to deepest Blue.

It was simple to break up the big estates in theory, dangerous in practice. If they were seized by the local peasants, *Izvestiya* warned, "villages close to the rich estates would get more than they should and others would get nothing." The result would be village fighting village. In northern Russia, a village might be fifty miles from the nearest estate. What use, the Soviet newspaper asked, were fields at such a distance?

In any event, it was one of the great myths of the revolution that vast tracts of arable land were on offer in European Russia. Peter Stolypin, who administered the country in the aftermath of the 1905 revolution until his assassination in 1911, had transferred land to the peasants with the same gusto with which he hanged them. Eighty million acres passed from landowners to individual *muzhiks* under his reforms. By 1917, self-employed peasants owned outright two-thirds of all land in private ownership in European Russia, and leased most of the remainder.

The land committee's chairman, Alexander Posnikov, warned its members that the *pomeshchik* landlord estates were now on a small scale and heavily mortgaged. Posnikov calculated that at most these lands would add only three to five acres per peasant household in European Russia, an amount whose importance would soon disappear. The surviving small estates were often badly run down. Owners, realizing that the wind was blowing against them, were selling off their livestock for what it would fetch. In Ryazan, there were idle fields and "emaciated livestock in the yards that must be lifted by their tails."

Eighty percent of the land in Russia was mortgaged, in most cases to the limit. "The majority of estates, in addition to the first mortgage, are burdened also by a second and third mortgage as well as by promissory notes," Posnikov said. He pointed out that those who would suffer most would not be the gentry, but "the small people for the most part, who put their savings in mortgages."

Russia had prodigious reserves of unused land, thousand-mile-thick belts of flat grassy steppe and larch and spruce forest that ran north before exhausting themselves in the mossy tundra, the preserve of reindeer and the snowy owl. Scores of millions of acres in Kazakhstan and western Siberia were primevally empty. Great tracts of land in the Don country and the plains west of the Urals remained virgin. Unused land, beyond walking or cart range, filled the gaps between villages even in the Ukraine. Posnikov reminded his committee of Tacitus, the Roman historian who had claimed that most of Germany was worthless for agriculture. Had not the modern Germans proved Tacitus wrong?

But the committee, and the peasants, were not interested in Roman historians or in a mood to go pioneering. The reverse was happening. Recent settlers to Siberia, convinced that every family would qualify for hundred of acres of land back in European Russia, overloaded the railways and river steamers as they returned west. The agriculture ministry sent out urgent circulars to stress that land resources in European Russia were so small that "even the *present* toiling population" would have to get allotments elsewhere — "in other words, they will have to *migrate*." Ministry advice was ignored.

The land committee degenerated into an argumentative mass, incapable "even to grasp the general idea of land reform," full of legal illiterates who succumbed in full to the revolutionary vice of "talking too much and incoherently." A justice ministry official who complained to Posnikov in midsummer of the slovenliness of the committee was surprised to find that the chairman was even more emphatic in his condemnation.

"And do you suppose that anything can be achieved here?" Posnikov said. "What we should do is throw out this crowd. If they could do anything, it is only you and I and those like us — people who are truly intelligent and cultured, people with economic and legal backgrounds and general higher education." The chairman of potentially the most important committee in the committee-besotted capital was open in his contempt for its members.

*   *   *

There was no consistency between ministries. The supply minister, the vigorous Alexei Peshekhonov, wanted any village that took land or crops to be liable for damages and criminal charges. Viktor Chernov at the agriculture ministry, drifting with events, was committed to land handouts; the promise to distribute land to the peasants was the main reason Chernov's Social Revolutionaries dominated rural Russia. Chernov issued no instructions to protect property in general — his ministry mentioned only "valuable cultures." The clear inference to the peasants was that, if they should be wary of taking over orchards and vineyards, anything else was fair game.

Local officials openly incited seizures. A peasant congress in Kovno in June was whipped up by leftists, including the district commissar, Belai. Belai urged the peasants to "Take all you need: fields, meadows, forests, lakes, pastures." One of Belai's subordinates, Montvil, complained to Petrograd that he was barely able to prevent seizures before the congress. After it, Montvil was powerless, the peasants taking over land "as if it were their property."

The peasants rented out a landowner's clover to graze horses without the owner's consent. When Montvil objected, the *muzhiks* shouted at him, "We elected you, and if you won't go with us, we'll throw you out." For his pains he received a telegram ordering him personally to take the "strictest measures to prevent seizures, damages to, and destruction of meadows and fields," signed by the selfsame Belai who had incited the seizures a few days before. Montvil complained to Petrograd that he was confused.

Commissars were often reluctant to admit that things were getting out of hand. Samara was in the worst of six categories for agrarian violence, a distinction it shared with Kazan, Mogilev, and Pskov. A report to Kerensky from the Samara commissar claimed, in a glorious phrase, that "conflicts were settled by telegraphic decrees by members of the executive committee." Revolutionary Russia had a touching and wholly unjustified belief in the power of the telegram.

Church land was targeted in most provinces. Faith had turned rapidly to cynicism. A peasant in Tula was astonished to be told that the English Bible was identical to the Russian one — he had convinced himself that the latter had been invented "to deceive us." In the Ukraine, priests were beaten and thrown out of their churches. In Romanovo-Borisoglebsky, deacons and psalm-singers formed armed bands to protect themselves. Rich plunder, silver, gold, and fine cloth, was to be had from churches and monasteries. Gangs broke in, beating — and sometimes, as near Konstantin Paustovsky's home village, killing — the monks and priests. Petrograd instructed militiamen to "watch incessantly, especially at night, the goings-on near monasteries and churches." Villagers were asked to organize the best possible protection for their parish priests and churches. But the militiamen were a phantom army, and local men were often the first to beat their priest and rob their church.

The grain monopoly introduced by the Provisional Government in March increased the tension between the villages and towns. All grain surplus to family needs was supposed to be surrendered to the state. In yet another layer of bureaucracy, supply committees were set up at provincial and district levels. Maximum prices were doubled to discourage peasants from hoarding.

In practice, there was no incentive for the peasants to sell. Alexei Peshekhonov, the supply minister, told the Soviet on June 6 that the "basic difficulty is this — the town lacks the products that could be given to the village in exchange for grain." Peasants hoarded grain "under the roof, under the floor, in the stove; they bury it in the ground." In the Vologda countryside, the schools inspector Alexis Babine noted that the peasants were refusing to part with any food at government prices. The inhabitants of the local town were kept alive only through a millionairess known for her charities, who had bought a large store of flour.

The fixed prices by midsummer were often less than the cost of production. Compulsory seizures by the army were attempted, and thwarted. Troops sent into villages round Nizhny Novgorod to search for hoards were met by mobs of men, women, and children more than a thousand strong. The soldiers would not fire on them.

Supply officials were beaten in Kazan, the villagers refusing to part with grain for cities inhabited by the bourgeois and "workers who work for eight hours and then sit and smoke cigars." The fixed price crumbled. The president of the Astrakhan supply committee said that, given the choice of being beaten by the starving population or being imprisoned for illegally increasing the fixed price, he would unhesitatingly choose jail.

To the crowds of deserters, committeemen, agitators, and refugees on the railways were added the *meshochniki*, the "sack peddlers" who bought wheat from the villages and sold it on the black market in the towns. Village millers did deals with local merchants to keep stocks off the markets until the price rose. Land speculation matched that in grain. Landowners went through fictional sales to get a nominal change of ownership to prevent seizures, or remortgaged estates to make them further encumbered. Foreigners — French, British, and Swedes — were active in the mortgage market. Kerensky and Chernov banned the transfer of title deeds without agriculture ministry approval on July 12, but the bureaucracy could not cope. Fake transfers continued and the agents of Swedish and British syndicates redoubled their efforts to buy up estates on the cheap.

Alexei Peshekhonov admitted the game was up in food supply on July 18. He detailed the ways in which the current harvest was being sabotaged. Peasants were smashing or impounding farm machines. They removed prisoners of war from working on estates and forced owners to pay their laborers above the government rate, and in grain and not money. "The peasants are forcibly seizing grains and fodder, hay, livestock, and equipment," Peshekhonov went on. "They are hindering the collection of grains and grasses, threshing, preparing of the fields for winter sowing, planting of crops." The supply and land committees who were supposed to be enforcing order "themselves adopt resolutions that spur the population on to commit illegal acts." To this mournful litany, with its promise of a hungry winter, the supply minister added a weary "Etc."

Despite orders to protect it, soldiers stationed on the Sheremetev family estate near Mtsensk joined peasants in looting it. Wagons were loaded with carpets, china, saddles, and milk pails from the dairy. The cellars were ransacked for wine and brandy. Drunken soldiers built a bonfire of furniture and books in front of the estate house and set fire to it. The more sober made off with cattle, sheep, and horses, dragging them with strips of brocaded cloth torn from the curtains. The damage was estimated at 7.5 million rubles and would have been worse if the alcohol tanks at the local distillery had not been fired before the mob could reach them. Near Kostroma, troops accepted packets of tobacco from peasants who had lynched merchants and stolen their stock.

Petrograd noted 1,189 "legal violations" in the countryside in June and July. Local records suggested the true number was up to eight times higher, and this concerned only complaints that were registered. Many were not, because the landowner had fled, or the local authority, if it existed, refused to log them. Alexander Posnikov, the central land committee chairman, attacked the Provisional Government for "dangerous vagueness . . . obvious vacillation and indecision."

The cities suffered. Moscow needed 2,100 wagon-loads of grain a month. In March it had got 868. In May, the grain monopoly enjoyed a brief success with no shortfall. In June, no more than 1,000 wagon-loads were shipped. By July, supplies had slipped back below the March level. In Petrograd, ambassador David Francis wrote to the American consul in Harbin appealing for "fifty pounds of breakfast bacon" to be sent to him from China.

The Bolsheviks were making little headway in the countryside. In the "sweet-scented wilderness" of rural Russia, Alexander Blok wrote, were "twisted, unhappy, and browbeaten people with ideas from before the Flood, people who have forgotten even themselves." There was some poetic licence in that — the traveler Maurice Baring had been struck by the number of *muzhiks* who quoted *Paradise Lost* to him — but the Marxist view of "reactionary" peasants was justified. They were interested in the extension of private property to themselves, not in its suppression.

Seventy percent of peasant petitions to Petrograd, some written on birch-bark, demanded that the land should be given to those who worked it. Social Revolutionary policy mirrored this. The Bolsheviks copied the SRs by calling for land handouts, but they carried little conviction and Viktor Chernov's SR party continued to dominate the villages. As to solidarity between town and country, a scant 9 percent of workers wanted land given to the peasants. No comradely love was lost between them.

Bolshevik agitators were treated with the contempt reserved for city folk. They were mocked as *belorucha*, "white hands," untouched by rural toil. "Your nails are very long," one young militant was greeted in a village. "You're not the Anti-Christ, are you?" With that, he was attacked to see "if he didn't have a tail or whether he was covered in hair."

The Shakovskys, as they moved round their estates, found the peasants to be motivated by self-interest rather than revolutionary dogma. After they had been driven from Epiphan by the deserter Chikin, the family moved to a third estate at Matovo. Here they found life had "changed not a bit, and for a while we could forget all about the revolution." They had an arsenal of guns. A cousin returned from the Romanian front with Nagan infantry rifles and hand grenades to add to the existing hunting rifles and dueling pistols. They learned that Chikin had vindictively dug up the family vaults in Epiphan and scattered the remains over the fields. But they had little need for their weapons in Matovo. When agitators were sent from Tula, and even from Moscow, the peasants considered them "foreigners." They paid the *belorucha* little attention beyond threatening to drown two of them in the duck pond.

Trouble, when it came, was the result of violent cross-hatreds between the peasants themselves. A rumor went round that a rival village was about to seize the tree nursery on the estate. The Matovo peasants became "frantic" and hacked at the young trees. Prince Shakovsky suggested that the trees must be allowed to grow — they were the only wood in the district — but "the future did not interest them." Every family came out on its cart, determined to get a bigger haul than its neighbors in a frenzy of felling in which several were maimed with axes. The wounded were brought to the big house for treatment.

The new class of peasants who had bought their own land under the

Stolypin reforms, the *otrubniki,* were deeply envied by their poorer brethren. Impoverished and landless peasants, the *bednota* on whom the Bolsheviks concentrated their slender rural resources, made little distinction between estates and *otrubniki* farmsteads. Many peasant proprietors sided openly with the landlords, attending a congress of landowners in Saratov — an aristocratic affair chaired by a count — to complain with fellow feeling of seizures. The *otrubniki* had slaved to keep up bank payments on their farmsteads, and "now those less provident and hard-working threaten us." The outline of civil war was breaking surface in the villages.

On August 4, the Provisional Government declared that fixed grain prices "will under no circumstances be raised." Talking tough, it said that prices would in fact be lowered if delivery dates were not met. By the end of the month, it had admitted failure and telegraphed immediate authority for the doubling of prices.

Its authority — any authority — was collapsing in the Russian heartland. Of the 624 districts making up the core of Old Russia, 482 witnessed violent attacks on landlords in August. In Bessarabia, an agitator urged each member of his audience to "personally choke to death one landlord." Gentry fleeing their estates in Saratov banded together and reached the supposed sanctuary of a railway station, where they were kicked and stabbed to death in the waiting room.

Prince Boris Vyazemsky also failed to survive a trip through a country station. The family estate at Lotarevo was one of the finest in the fertile Tambov black earth province, with a stud farm and hospital. The first signs of trouble came at the burial of his brother, Dmitri — an officer in one of the punitive units that had hanged and flogged their way through the Tambov region when the Red Cock had last crowed in 1906 — who had been killed in Alexander Guchkov's car at the beginning of March. The *muzhiks* stood outside the church during the funeral service, keeping their hats on and muttering.

They demanded higher wages, backing their claims with mass descents on the estate courtyard, armed with sticks and clubs. A detachment of troops was sent to protect the estate. The peasants resented the presence of soldiers. One morning in August, an ensign and soldier rushed into the big house shouting "Run for your lives!" A mass of peasants was on the move to Lotarevo. Boris refused to flee in a waiting carriage.

The prince was engulfed in the mob. Among the peasants was a city Bolshevik, a small man in a pince-nez who goaded them by telling that they were powerless in front of the prince because they were still serfs in their hearts. A village elder said that, though they respected Vyazemsky, they wanted to finish with him and take his land. The elder turned to the agitator: "As for you, the time will come when we will hang your brothers." Boris and his wife were taken to the school that he had recently built at his own expense in the village.

By evening, the peasants had broken into the estate cellars and were drunk. They accused the prince of sending young peasants to their death as chairman of the local mobilization committee. A verdict was reached. Boris was to be sent to the front. He was taken away to the station at Gryazi by a military escort at dawn. From here he was to take a train 250 miles northwest to Moscow for transfer to the front.

A train packed with deserters was standing on the track. The stationmaster tried to hide the prince in his office, but word got out to the deserters. They burst through the door, put out Vyazemsky's eyes, ran him through with bayonets, and finished him off with iron railway ties. Then they cut off his head.

The violence was worst in north and central Russia, though it had no consistency; as Paleologue noted before his departure, "each province is a center of separatism and each town a nucleus of anarchy." The Crimea was largely untouched through midsummer. It filled with refugees from the north — Grand Duke Nicholas, Felix Yusupov and his wife Princess Irina, her mother, the Grand Duchess Xenia, and her grandmother, the dowager empress. Serge Obolensky joined them, for what he mockingly called the "Kerensky revolutionaries" were convinced that his Petrograd house was joined by a secret passage to the burnt-out Okhrana headquarters, and it was frequently searched.

Obolensky spent the summer on his wife's Mordvinov estate, overlooking Yalta. He revelled in tranquillity, the "wild cherry and crab apple trees in bloom, lilacs everywhere, the weather calm and sunny . . ." He had his portrait painted by Saveli Sorine. The great portraitist was a revolutionary sympathizer, but he worked for free because he thought Obolensky was "a specific type of Imperial Guards Russian officer, and that type would soon be extinct."

In this southern idyll amid the revolution, the great problem for the refugees was not lynching but getting possessions out of their homes in the north. Art, as Felix Yusupov had discovered with his rolled-up Rembrandts, was easily portable, but there was a glut on the market as aristocrats rushed to sell and only the Americans were buying. Count de Robien snobbishly hoped that an exquisite bust of Marie Antoinette would not be snapped up by "a Transatlantic pork butcher."

The peace did not last. A band of soldiers and sailors arrived on the Yusupov estate at Aï-Todor in July. In the revolts after 1905, the peasants had hewed up and trampled everything that the owners carried out of their burning houses. But they rarely stole. Now daily thefts were reported from the great house, of silver, money, jewels, and furniture.

Princess Irina went to the Winter Palace during a visit to Petrograd to complain to Kerensky. The premier had moved to the palace on July 24, installing himself in the tsar's suite and receiving her in the study of her grandfather, Alexander III. Irina sat in her ancestor's chair, obliging Kerensky to use the visitor's seat. He promised to have the men disciplined. The thefts continued.

By August, Alexei Peshekhonov was exhausted by squabbles with Viktor Chernov at agriculture and had come to the end of the road as supply minister. To save the country, Peshekhonov said, the workers had to suffer wage cuts, the rich had to pay more taxes and part with much of their property, and the peasants had to sell their grain at moderate prices. To force this through, the government had to be "resolute and adamant." It was not. Russia was collapsing through weak government and the "triumph of greed over voluntary sacrifice."

"If we continue on this course, catastrophe is inevitable," Peshekhonov said. "Sooner or later, we shall undoubtedly have to resort to a 'strong and stable government' " — the euphemism for dictatorship. He resigned.

XVIII
"Heart of Lion, Brain of Sheep"

POWER WAS "HANGING IN THE AIR," Sukhanov said. Zinaïda Gippius thought that Kerensky had absorbed a "sort of revulsion from power, from its indispensable exterior, necessarily coercive methods. He can't, he stops, he becomes afraid . . ." Trappings took the place of authority. In place of the dictatorship urged by Peshekhonov, Russia seemed to have acquired a "show tsar." Kerensky's move to the imperial suite on the third floor of the Winter Palace, where official photographs showed him sitting at the huge mahogany desk of the tsars, was mocked as *meshchanstvo*, the affectation of a petty bourgeois.

Kerensky slept with Lilya in Alexander III's bed — though rumor had now replaced her as his mistress with the light comedy actress Timé — and traveled in one of the tsar's trains. Ambassador Francis thought that the choice of bed "is not too good politically, to say the least. . . . In Russia now it is a presumption to prophesy in the forenoon what will occur in the afternoon." The Red Flag was raised and lowered on the palace to mark Kerensky's movements, and he flew the pennant of navy minister on his open-topped limousine.

This deference was not mirrored in the streets through which he was driven by smartly turned-out aides. The sidewalks were filthy and thronged with deserters, windows dull and unwashed. The stations were carpeted with spit and sunflower shells, and drunken officers staggered along the Nevsky.

A diplomatic courier at the British Embassy, Bertie Stopford, was collecting millions of rubles' worth of jewels and money to take out of the country for Russian friends. An Oxford pal of Felix Yusupov, Stopford slipped into the abandoned Petrograd palace of the Grand Duchess Maria, got her valuables from a secret safe in her bedroom, and transferred them to a suitcase he took to London as diplomatic baggage. The rich had s. get their children out of Russia. Ten-year-old André Khilkoff-Choube. grandson of the builder of the Trans-Siberian and a playmate of the tsa ich, left for Finland with his English governess. The tsar's dentist, Ser Kostritsky, took the same route, leaving the imperial dental records behind him in his consulting rooms.

Serge Rachmaninov found that everyone was advising him to leave Russia and was trying to contact Mikhail Tereshchenko, the foreign minister, to get a passport. The composer, son of a ruined army officer who had run through five estates, had invested almost his entire earnings in his own estate at Ivanovka, in the troubled Tambov province southeast of Moscow. "Yet I am ready to write this off," he wrote to a friend. Ivanovka was in chaos. "Can you possibly catch Tereshchenko at a free moment to consult him?" Rachmaninov asked. "Can I count on getting a passport for all our family to go at least to Norway, Denmark, Sweden? It makes no difference where! Anywhere! Please talk with him and answer me quickly." There was no reply.

Maria Bochkaryova was wounded with her Women's Death Battalion. Kerensky ordered her a luxurious private room, kissing her and presenting her with a bouquet of flowers while apologizing for the troubles his offensive had caused her. The rumor mills made her another of his mistresses.

The premier shunned large meetings and treated his cabinet with near-contempt. He was becoming Bonapartist in style — the hand clenched across the chest remained leather-gloved, though it had now healed, and his simple tunics gave way to tailored uniforms — but not, Zinaïda Gippius thought, in substance. "It is a fact," she wrote, "that Kerensky is afraid. . . . Of what? Of whom?"

Not, it seemed, of the Bolsheviks. They were still underground. Lenin had moved out of his hayloft to a remote area of marshes and fields near the Finnish border, reached easily only by boat, where he lived with Zinoviev in a thatched hut. They masqueraded as grasscutters. It was a pleasant interlude. "A cool night marked with stars, the smell of hay," Zinoviev wrote. "Smoke from a small fire where venison simmers in a small pot. We go to bed in the little shack. We cover ourselves with an old blanket. . . ." The two Bolsheviks slept "closely, pressed against each other."

But the Bolsheviks were reviving. A party congress had been held in Petrograd at the end of July. Supposedly "secret," it was attended by 270 delegates who witnessed Trotsky's Interdistrict group finally throw its lot in with the party. Informers passed on details to Kerensky, but he refused to have the delegates arrested.

*　　*　　*

, retained the defense portfolio as well as the premiership. His new , at the war ministry was Boris Savinkov. Savinkov had been a famous al Revolutionary terrorist in his twenties but had now, at thirty-eight, ung violently against extremists, in particular against the Bolsheviks. The wellborn son of a military lawyer, Savinkov had joined the Social Revolutionary combat organization while a Saint Petersburg law student. He planned two high-profile and meticulous assassinations in 1904 and 1906, of the interior minister and Grand Duke Serge, the governor-general of Moscow.

He was betrayed to the Okhrana after living underground with a British passport for two years in some style — he was arrested in the dining room of a luxury hotel — and sentenced to death. The lieutenant in charge of the guard at Sebastopol Prison, where he was awaiting execution, was a revolutionary sympathizer. The lieutenant marched Savinkov out of prison as if under escort, and the two men made a dangerous voyage for four days in an open boat to political asylum in Romania.

Savinkov moved on to Paris, where he wrote two best-selling novels on espionage and terrorism, *The Pale Horse* and *What Never Happened*. At the outbreak of the war he enlisted in the French army before returning to Russia with the revolution. Brave and reckless, he served as a commissar at the front before Kerensky, a fellow mason, appointed him to the war ministry. Somerset Maugham met him and was intrigued that the archterrorist should now have the "prosperous look of a lawyer" in a stand-up collar, a quiet tie with a pin in it, and a frock coat. The British writer liked Savinkov for the endearing way he told him that "Assassination is a business like any other, one gets accustomed to it."

A loner, Savinkov's fixed gaze "shone under his barely open Mongol eyelids, with permanently sealed lips, as if meant to conceal all his secret thoughts." Joseph Noulens, the new French ambassador, found his fierce and handsome profile to be Western by contrast, so that he "combined all the energy of one race and all the cunning and mystery of the other." Winston Churchill, who met Savinkov briefly, reckoned him "one of the most interesting men alive" and a "Russian Bonaparte." Bruce Lockhart, who knew him better, thought him dangerous, a schemer, who "could sit up all night drinking brandy and discussing what he was going to do the next day." When the morrow came, because he had mingled so much with spies and *agents-provocateurs,* he would become confused and "hardly know whether he was deceiving himself or those whom he meant to deceive."

Savinkov was addicted to conspiracy, and to morphine.

The "secret" Bolshevik congress in Petrograd struck Savinkov as a heaven-sent opportunity to net the middle-level party leaders. He asked

Yekaterina Breshko-Breshkovskaya, the "Babushka" of the revolution who had been carried through Moscow in triumph in March, to persuade Kerensky to authorize immediate arrests. Breshkovskaya bowed her gray head and implored Kerensky to act: "I beg thee, Alexander Fyodorovich, suppress the congress, suppress the Bolsheviks. I beg thee to do this, or they will bring ruin on our country and the revolution." Kerensky sprang to his feet and said he would telephone instructions to Nikolai Avksentiev, the interior minister. Avksentiev was not in his office. Kerensky put the phone down and did not ring back.

Savinkov railed at the cowardice of this "narcissistic women's premier." He told Somerset Maugham that Kerensky's "morbid verbosity" was such that he had started making speeches to his chauffeur as he was being driven, adding that if the premier had had any political imagination, he "wouldn't have installed himself with his woman in the Winter Palace." The interior and war ministries had a broad brief to arrest and deport any individual who was harming the war effort. Savinkov used this authority to draw up a list of fifty right-wing and fifty leftist extremists whom he wanted expelled. Kerensky whittled the socialist list down by a half and allowed Nikolai Avksentiev to strike out all the remainder, with the exception of Trotsky and Alexandra Kollontai.

The right wing list stayed intact. Kerensky gave no explanation, but it was clear that he felt he could not risk alienating the left if he was to achieve his destiny as leader of the Russian democracy. The right was different. It was urging Kerensky to restore order, to extend the death penalty to the rear, to militarize the railways, to limit Soviet interference. He resented the pressure with fierce self-pity.

"Briefly, they [the right] think a dictatorship may be necessary," Kerensky complained. "That might not be so bad if only it could be accomplished, but . . . the thing is absolutely impossible. Where are the forces through which we could execute such a plan? Nowhere. They accuse me of inefficiency, they think I am ambitious for power. Fools! If only I could resign, get away from all this and retire to some quiet village, I'd be the happiest man in the world.

"But to whom could I resign my office? Where is the man?" Kerensky knew well that there was such a man, his new commander in chief, General Kornilov, and he feared him.

Lavr Kornilov was a wiry Cossack of forty-seven, thin-featured and tanned, ambitious with the blunt confidence of the self-important fighting man. He had something of the exotic as well as the mustachioed martinet about him. He swept round with high-hatted Turkoman bodyguards in red cloaks, with scimitars in their hands and Caucasian daggers at their belts. They called him Ulu Boyar, the "Great Boyar," as if he was a throwback to caftaned barons. But the Tartar cast to his eyes and his long service on the Asian frontiers were not matched by mental guile. Boris Savinkov thought Kornilov to be "politically illiterate." The general despised politicians for their deviousness and lack of patriotism. His colleague, General Alexeev, reckoned Kornilov to have the "heart of a lion and the brain of a sheep."

His courage was not questioned. Two years before, he had escaped after being seriously wounded and taken prisoner on the Austrian front. He impressed the Allied ambassadors, who saw him as a way of keeping Russia in the war. "If his constitution is iron, his will is steel," said David Francis, crediting Kornilov with speaking seventeen languages and having walked for six hundred miles on his escape through Austrian lines.

Kerensky had found Kornilov a problem as soon as he named him commander in chief to replace Alexei Brusilov. Kornilov took a fortnight to accept and made his own conditions: no civilian was to interfere with his operational orders and command appointments, all disciplinary measures, including the death penalty, were to apply to troops in the rear, and, in clear insubordination to his political master, he would "owe responsibility only to my conscience and the nation." The premier's irritation increased when these conditions were leaked to the press.

Mutual suspicion between the two deepened after Kornilov attended a cabinet meeting in Petrograd on August 3. The general was outlining his operational plans for the fronts when first Kerensky and then Savinkov whispered urgently that he should be careful not to disclose too much. Kornilov was still in shock when he got back to the Stavka in Mogilev. He took the warnings to mean that at least one minister — he thought Viktor Chernov — was passing on information to colleagues in the Soviet. From there, the Bolsheviks could transmit it to the Germans. What sort of government was it, Kornilov asked General Alexander Lukomsky, his chief of staff, where ministers were suspected of treason?

Shortly after, Kornilov ordered General Alexander Krymov, the commander of the Third Cavalry Corps, to move his troops from the Romanian front to Velikie Luki. The corps had two Cossack divisions as well as the Savage Division — rough tribesmen from the Caucasus, Moslems who would have few scruples at shooting Russians. Lukomsky was puzzled. Velikie Luki was two hundred miles north of Mogilev, roughly equidistant from Moscow and Petrograd, and too far from the front for the men to be used against the Germans.

Kornilov said that he wanted a reserve to deal with the possibility of a fresh Bolshevik coup in either city. If that happened, he intended to wipe out the Leninists "root and branch," whether the government approved or not. "The main thing," he told Lukomsky, "is that Russia has no authority and such an authority must be created."

On August 10 the general was back in Petrograd, arriving at the Winter Palace with two cars crammed with Moslem bodyguards; he had been warned that the government might dismiss him or the Bolsheviks assassinate him. The Moslems took up positions with machine guns outside Kerensky's office. Kornilov warned the premier that the Germans were about to make a push for Riga, threatening the capital. He upped his demands in a two-hour shouting match, insisting that defense industries as well as the railways should be militarized, and that the death penalty should be applied to all Russians who "worked for foreign powers," his longhand for Bolsheviks.

Kerensky said that this could only lead to "new and more terrible riots" and a massacre of officers. "I foresee that," Kornilov replied. "But at least those who are left alive will have their soldiers in hand." Kerensky argued that placing factories under martial law was unenforceable and lunatic. The workers would not stand for it and the garrison would not compel them. Did the commander in chief not understand that?

As to the death penalty, a great state conference was opening in Moscow four days later. Kerensky had called it as a "last attempt to save Russia," to broaden the crumbling base of his regime and stamp some unity on the state. It was essential for him to remain on good terms with the Soviet, which would have nothing to do with firing squads at the front, let alone in the rear. The Soviet had recently voted 850 to 4 in support of a Bolshevik motion rejecting execution as a device to "enslave the soldier masses to the commanding staff."

Kerensky vacillated. When Boris Savinkov pressed the issue again the next morning, Kerensky turned on his deputy, shrieking, "You are a Lenin but of the other side! You're a terrorist! Well, come and kill me. . . ." Back in Mogilev, Lavr Kornilov railed against the "molluscs" who made up the Provisional Government.

Moscow filled with delegates. Nikolai Sukhanov made the mistake of taking his boots off when he slept on the train from Yaroslavl. They were stolen and the senior representative of the Soviet executive committee arrived in his stockinged feet — a sign of the times. He spent two hours on the stationmaster's telephone tracking down a friend to bring him a spare pair. The friend had to walk to the station.

The Bolsheviks were boycotting the conference and had called for a general strike. The majority of Moscow workers, about four hundred thousand, supported the strike against the orders of the Soviet. Electricity workers walked out and the trams stopped running. Half the *drozhky* drivers stayed at home. Waiters deserted the restaurants, floor service ceased in hotels. Elevators were caught between floors by power blackouts, and the streets were dark at night because the gasworks were shut down.

Kerensky held a ministerial meeting in the Kremlin before being driven past jeering Bolsheviks to the Bolshoi, where he was protected by a thick column of military cadets. They were, Sukhanov said, his "only reliable force." A group of young girls, attracted by his lady-killer reputation, blew Kerensky kisses in the foyer. Kornilov was mobbed by well-dressed matrons with flowers when he arrived from Mogilev. "Come, *vozhd*, great leader, and save Russia!" they cried. Carried shoulder-high by officers, Kornilov paused at the Chapel of the Iberian Mother of God, where the reigning tsar had traditionally prayed on entering Moscow. The general loathed cities — they were "full of politicians" — and he ostentatiously slept on his command train rather than move to a hotel.

The white-and-gold auditorium of the Bolshoi, the stage still set for the opera *Queen of Spades*, was a brilliant spectacle. Two thousand five hundred people crammed into it, a mass of journalists jostling each other for places on the press benches. The *burzhui* parties sat on the right in frock coats and collars. On the left were the "Soviet delegates of the unshaven chin and the working shirt, with a fair sprinkling of common soldiers." In the middle, "as if crushed between two millstones," were professional men. Delegates from the minority nationalities and officers' associations sat in boxes and on the balcony. Diplomats and Allied officers were in the former imperial box.

Kerensky stumbled into the sharp divisions in the audience with his opening address. As the body of the hall applauded his promise to repress the "impossible and ruinous" demands of the separatist Finns and Ukrainians, the nationalists in the boxes glared angrily at the stage. Kerensky threatened mutineers with "blood and iron," and the socialists hissed "Bismarck!" When he thanked the Allies and said the war would be seen through to victory, the right-hand side of the hall rose for a standing ovation of the Allied ambassadors. The left sat.

He satisfied no one on capital punishment. He pointed out that he had abolished it as justice minister, only to be forced to partially reintroduce it by those who "would pervert our army." The right roared its approval. Embarrassed, Kerensky turned on them. "Who dares applaud when it is a question of death? Don't you know that at that moment a part of our human heart was killed?"

It was an unsteady performance — Madden Summers, the U.S. consul in Moscow, reported that the speech "fell rather flat." Kerensky was followed by the spokesmen of innumerable groups, the day blurring into a monotony that sent many to sleep. Kornilov woke them on the second day. Those on the right of the theater leapt to their feet when he entered, chanting "Stand up, stand up!" at those on the left. The army was becoming a rabble, the general said, which stole property and terrorized the countryside. It was a greater danger to the people of the western provinces than "any German army could ever be." Angry cries came from the Soviet seats: "Your officers are responsible!"

"Darting sharp piercing glances from his small black eyes with a vicious glint," Kornilov ignored them. Not only was an offensive impossible, he went on, but it was "even doubtful whether the army can be demobilized in an orderly manner." He put the number of deserters at two million. There was a sharp intake of breath. The audience was being told, by a general in full-dress uniform with sword and red-striped *lampa* trousers, that it was impossible for Russia to continue in the war unless discipline was restored. The hall "rocked with applause," Pavel Miliukov wrote approvingly, the Cadet leader warming to Kornilov. "All leaped to their feet except . . . the soldiers."

Kerensky, bitter at his commander in chief's success, wound up the conference in a "broken voice which fell from a hysterical shriek to a tragic whisper." The words tumbled as easily as ever. "Let my heart turn to stone . . . let all the flowers of my dreams for man wither and die," he said. "They have been scorned and stamped on today from this rostrum. I will stamp on them myself. . . . I will cast away the keys to this heart that loves the people and I will think only of the state." But he was heard out largely in silence.

At this moment, Zinaïda Gippius recorded, she "fell out of love" with Kerensky. "He is like a railway car that has left the rails," she wrote. "He sways, vacillates, painfully and without any glamor." The poetess had admired Kerensky for his spiritual qualities. Sensing that the premier had now descended into mere emotionalism, she transferred her loyalty to the stronger figure of the combat general. Kerensky had not won the left, and Kornilov had taken the right.

When Kerensky returned to Petrograd, French intelligence was warning that the Bolsheviks were plotting another coup. Boris Savinkov passed him the tip. Neither believed it, but Kerensky saw in it a useful way to clip Kornilov's wings by getting reliable units under his own control. News of the "plot" was leaked to the press on August 19. The same day, the steamer *Rus* with the imperial family aboard docked in Tobolsk, a town of sprawling wooden buildings twelve hundred miles east of Moscow and two hundred miles north of the Trans-Siberian rail line. It was, as Kerensky intended, a safe backwater. The governor's house was too dilapidated for the royal prisoners to move straight into, so they lived aboard the *Rus* while workmen repaired it. On August 10, the Russian army abandoned Riga to the Germans, the left claiming, in the poisonous cycle of lie and counterlie, that its fall was part of a plot by officers to deliver Red Peter to the Germans. "What's the odds?" people said on the trams. "We'll all die of hunger anyway."

On August 22 Savinkov arrived in Mogilev for talks with Kornilov. He told the general that a Bolshevik rising was imminent, and would coincide with a German push from Riga on the capital. Therefore, Savinkov said, Kerensky wanted the Third Cavalry Corps switched under his own personal command and moved closer to Petrograd for "merciless" action against the Bolsheviks. Since it would be embarrassing to have the capital liberated by Caucasian Moslems, the Savage Division should stay put. Savinkov said that the premier wanted General Krymov to be replaced as corps commander, lest his fierce and reactionary reputation play into Bolshevik hands. In addition, Petrograd and its suburbs were to be transferred from Kornilov's command to that of the Provisional Government, and placed under martial law.

It was apparent that Kerensky was using the alleged coup to strengthen his own military position, and Kornilov was reluctant to lose control of the Petrograd garrison. He was happy enough to move the corps nearer the capital, but he kept it under Alexander Krymov and did not separate the Savage Division from it. He had no difficulty, however, in believing that the Bolsheviks were ready to strike.

It was a dangerous game, for none of the principals — a now isolated and peevish premier, the vain and unwily commander in chief, and Savinkov, devious, spreading soft poison between the others, the onetime plotter of assassination and author of melodramatic novels — trusted each other. They were, however, sane. The fourth man who entered this twilight zone was soon found to be in need of psychiatric help.

Vladimir Lvov had a well-set-up look, with strong oval features above a heavy body. His many advantages — wealth, land, ambition, and connections — combined with instability and "incredible frivolity" to transform him into what Ambassador Francis called a "meddlesome rattle-brain." As a young man, Lvov had attended a Moscow seminary and flirted with becoming a monk before drifting into politics. High self-regard and family influence won him the position of procurator of the Holy Synod after the revolution. He made his cabinet colleagues laugh with his rambling and monkish speeches, but his vindictiveness had spread chaos in the upper reaches of the Church. He had dismissed a score of the metropolitans and archbishops on the Synod, calling them "idiots and scoundrels," by the time Kerensky had fired him from the cabinet the month before.

For all his surface plausibility and charm, Lvov was a spinner of wild intrigue and a grudge-harborer who blamed Kerensky for destroying his career. While in Moscow for the state conference, he claimed to have been approached by a patriotic group with links to big industrialists which planned to make Kornilov dictator and himself interior minister.

Lvov thought it his duty to report this to Kerensky, or so he said. He visited Kerensky in the Winter Palace on August 22. He claimed that the premier was impressed enough by his warning of a plot to agree that he, Lvov, should negotiate secretly on Kerensky's behalf to broaden his cabinet. Kerensky claimed later that nothing of the sort was discussed, but his judgment of character, never strong, was undermined by his extreme state of tension and swings of mood. Lvov returned to Moscow to assure the patriots that he was empowered to discuss the formation of a new cabinet. He then travelled to the Stavka.

Lvov arrived in Mogilev on August 24, as Savinkov was leaving after planting the false intelligence of the Bolshevik coup. Lvov saw Kornilov late that night and again the following morning, Friday, August 25. He identified himself as an envoy of the premier on an important mission. Kerensky, Lvov told the commander in chief, realized that strong government was essential and that it could be established in one of three ways. Kerensky himself could become dictator; a Directory of four strongmen, including Kornilov and Kerensky, could be formed; or Kornilov could become dictator.

Lvov seemed to be power-broking on an astonishing scale. Which option, he continued suavely, did Kornilov prefer? The general had no doubts — he would not refuse the supreme power if it was offered to him. Would it then be desirable, Lvov continued, for Kerensky and Savinkov to be members of Kornilov's new government? Kornilov agreed, adding that, with a Bolshevik rising imminent in the capital, it would be safer for the two politicians to come to Mogilev at once. The general would guarantee their safety while the new cabinet was formed.

At no stage did Kornilov ask to see Lvov's credentials, or use the Hughes wire to get confirmation from Petrograd of Kerensky's remarkable offer. Lvov was on the train back to Petrograd before General Lukomsky, an acuter man than his commander, raised doubts.

"All this is very, very strange," Lukomsky told Kornilov. "The very fact of Kerensky charging a third person with this mission seems highly suspicious. I am afraid he is hatching some plot against you." Lvov, he said, was a "blunderer" who was "quite capable of making a mess of things." Kornilov, dictatorship seemingly within his grasp, was airily dismissive. "Lvov is an irreproachably honest man and a gentleman," he said. "I have no reason to distrust him."

Petrograd was expectant. Thunderstorms broke out in the heat, "shimmering explosions, sometimes yellow, sometimes pale, sometimes covering a great stretch of sky." People on the streets told Alexander Blok that the rumbles were German artillery, or tsarist troops. Forest fires broke out on the horizon, bringing a heavy smell of moldering turf and billows of yellowish brown smoke. Beneath it, Blok thought, were the flames of "enmity, barbarity, Tartar raids, anger, humiliation, oppression, revenge . . ."

Lvov was back in the Winter Palace on Saturday afternoon, August 26. The same day that the tsar and his family came ashore from the steamer and moved into the governor's house in distant Tobolsk, Lvov neatly reversed roles. In Mogilev, he had been the premier's envoy to the commander in chief; he now appeared as Kornilov's broker, telling Kerensky that Kornilov had demanded dictatorial powers. Kerensky at first burst out laughing, but became alarmed when Lvov wrote out a list of the general's "demands." Martial law was to be declared in Petrograd; all ministers, "not excluding the premier," were to resign; "all military and civil authority" was to be placed in the hands of the commander in chief.

As soon as Lvov began to write, Kerensky said, "my last doubts began to disappear." The right-wing coup he had long awaited was imminent, he thought, and would be led by Kornilov. "The double game was manifest. . . . I saw everything with extraordinary clarity." He did not check with Mogilev to see whether the three demands, which Lvov had just concocted in front of his nose, were genuine. Kerensky trusted the bald-headed go-between as implicitly as Kornilov had, and with less reason — he had dismissed Lvov from his cabinet for his eccentricity a few weeks before. But it was convenient for Kerensky to believe Lvov; what he was saying gave the premier an excuse to rid himself of his too-popular commander in chief. When Lvov mentioned that Kornilov wanted Kerensky to go to Mogilev for "protection," the premier took it as proof that the general planned to arrest him.

Remembering the premature leaks in the Lenin affair, Kerensky now wanted proof in writing. He arranged to meet Lvov at 8:00 P.M. in the war minister's apartment, just across the square from the palace, so that they could have a recorded conversation with Kornilov on the Hughes wire.

Lvov failed to turn up. Frustrated, Kerensky initiated the conversation with Mogilev at 8:30 P.M., impersonating the absentee: "How do you do, General. V. N. Lvov and Kerensky are on the line." Using Lvov's name,

Kerensky asked: "I, Vladimir Nikolaevich, am enquiring about this definite decision which has to be taken, of which you asked me to inform Alexander Fyodorovich [Kerensky] strictly in private."

"Yes," replied Kornilov. "I confirm that I asked you to transmit my urgent request to Alexander Fyodorovich to come to Mogilev."

"I, Alexander Fyodorovich, take your reply to confirm the words reported to me by Vladimir Nikolaevich," Kerensky wired in his own name. "It is impossible for me to do that and leave here today, but I hope to leave tomorrow. Will Savinkov be needed?"

"I urgently request that [Savinkov] come along with you," said Kornilov. "I would beg you most sincerely not to postpone your departure beyond tomorrow."

"Are we to come only if there are demonstrations, rumors of which are going around, or in any case?"

"In any case," Kornilov replied.

"Goodbye," Kerensky closed the conversation. "We shall meet soon."

In truth, the conversation clarified nothing. Kerensky did not ask Kornilov to confirm whether the demands written down by Lvov were genuine. He asked only one direct question — whether he should go to Mogilev, and took the general's insistence that he should as evidence that Kornilov was planning his arrest. Lvov did not arrive until the conversation was over.

Kornilov suspected nothing, and there was jubilation at his end of the wire. Kerensky, it seemed, would soon be coming to Mogilev to cede supreme power to the general along the lines discussed with Lvov. Kornilov sat down with Alexander Lukomsky to discuss a new cabinet. "I want to have it ready for Kerensky and Savinkov when they arrive," he told his aide.

As he did so, the existing cabinet was meeting in emergency session. Kerensky outlined the military "plot." He threw Lvov's fictitious list of the "general-dictator's" demands on the table, and produced the transcript of his conversation with Kornilov. Boris Savinkov found it baffling, a classic case of cross-purposes. He urged Kerensky to get back in touch with Mogilev to clear up misunderstandings before grave damage was done.

Kerensky, after Kornilov's blood, refused to contact the Stavka. "I will not give them the Revolution," he said. At 2:00 A.M., Kornilov cabled Savinkov to advise the deputy war minister that the Third Cavalry Corps, as requested by Kerensky, would be assembling near Petrograd the following evening. Kerensky now insisted that the ministers place their portfolios at his disposal to allow him the "plenitude of power" necessary to deal with the "counterrevolution." They did so, thus giving him the right to dismiss Kornilov on his own authority. Faced by dictatorship, Kerensky made himself dictator.

The cabinet meeting broke up at 4:00 A.M. Kerensky, technically at least, now embodied the government. He wrote out a cable dismissing Kornilov and ordering him to report to Petrograd. He then retired to the Alexander III suite in high spirits. He asked Lvov to come to his study and repeat Kornilov's proposals again. When Lvov had finished, a lawyer appeared from behind a curtain — the witness Kerensky needed to have Lvov arrested for treason. Bewildered, Lvov was taken to an adjoining room where he was kept awake by Kerensky screeching operatic arias through the wall. He was later put under house arrest and treated by a prison psychiatrist.

The cable sacking Kornilov arrived in Mogilev at 7:00 A.M. on Sunday, August 27. At first it was thought to be a forgery. It lacked a serial number, and was signed only "Kerensky," without a title and lacking cabinet counter-signatures. Later in the morning, the Stavka concluded that, although the telegram was genuine, the Bolshevik rising must have started in the capital and that Kerensky had been forced to send it by the Leninists. Kornilov thus refused to resign, instead ordering General Krymov to hasten the advance of his corps on Petrograd.

There was still a chance to undo the damage. During the afternoon, Savinkov got in direct touch with Kornilov. He learned for the first time of the offer Lvov had made to the general, supposedly on Kerensky's behalf. Kornilov insisted that he had remained loyal to the government. He said that the troop movements were directed against the Bolsheviks, and pointed out that Kerensky had ordered them himself.

Savinkov rushed to the premier's office to be told he was too late. Kerensky's statement condemning Kornilov for treason had already been sent to the evening papers, and would be appearing on the streets in a few minutes. Kerensky, in "near-hysterical mood," broadcast a radiotelegram where he repeated the fictitious Lvov demands and referred to Kornilov as a traitor.

A Russian general could be called stupid without too much offense, but to call one a traitor was unforgivable. Kornilov countered with his own broadcast. He described the premier's account as an "out-and-out lie." He accused the government of colluding under Bolshevik pressure with the German General Staff to destroy the country.

Kerensky had finally provoked a counterrevolution, or so he and the country believed. Everyone was conscious of the moment. The revolution was six months old on August 27; Nikolai Sukhanov found it a "rather wretched jubilee." A breath of autumn was in the air, the magnificent summer of 1917 almost over. Sukhanov dropped into the Cirque Moderne, where Anatoly Lunacharsky was giving a Sunday lecture on Greek art to a large working-class audience. They had lunch together at the Vienna restaurant, before wandering the quays talking about aesthetics.

They were taking tea as it got dark. The phone rang. It was someone from the Soviet warning Sukhanov that an executive committee meeting was starting. Why, on a holiday? "What, don't you know?" the caller said. "Kornilov is moving on Petrograd with his troops. He's got an army corps." Sukhanov felt instant "excitement, exaltation, and joy of liberation."

In July, Sukhanov wrote, the Bolsheviks "had been in a hurry to pluck unripe fruit and got poisoned." Now it was Kornilov who was behaving like Lenin. "The coup of the generals and financiers," Sukhanov was sure, "shifted the center of gravity of the whole situation to the opposite side — a feat which the Bolsheviks could not accomplish a millionth part of." Even Irakli Tsereteli, implacably hostile to the Bolsheviks, recognized the way in which the party was being let off the hook. Downcast and dejected, Tsereteli hailed a passing Bolshevik, "Well! Now you have a holiday in your Bolshevik alley. You'll be taking the bit between your teeth again."

No one bothered to examine the credentials of the "counterrevolution" any more than they had queried those of Vladimir Lvov. They took them on trust. Had they checked, they would have found it a most curious affair. Kornilov did not lead the attack. He remained in Mogilev, protected by his bodyguards, complaining of severe ague and a loss of energy. He could not face the long drive to Petrograd over bad roads. He could have taken a train, but his supposedly bloodthirsty officers were "even afraid of the streets of Mogilev. I wanted to walk to the station. They did not let me."

He was said to have an elaborate plot, with the backing of big industrialists. In fact, what little planning had taken place was intended to deal with the supposed Bolshevik rising. Kornilov had met the magnate Alexei Putilov on a train after the Moscow conference, telling the industrialist that he was sending a corps to Petrograd, in agreement with Kerensky, to get rid of the Bolsheviks. In order to make a clean sweep and prevent them scattering, he wanted to have an advance force of officers and cadets in place. If necessary, his men would stage "Bolshevik" riots to justify intervention.

"Money is needed to put them up and feed them," Kornilov said. "Can you give it?"

He was speaking to the right man. Putilov was a member of the Society for the Economic Rehabilitation of Russia, a group of industrialists that had collected four million rubles for antisocialist work. "We raised the money," said Putilov. "But we didn't know what to do with it." He thought some of it could be made available to Kornilov.

Two colonels had duly arrived in Petrograd on Saturday, August 26, to see Putilov, asking for two million rubles to pay for food and lodging for

Kornilov's "secret army" of cadets and officers. They had a letter from Kornilov with them, but this asked for only 800,00 rubles. They explained the discrepancy by claiming that the need for the two million had been seen too late to rewrite the letter.

"Excuse me," said Putilov. "The general knows perfectly well there is no need to stand on ceremony. . . . He could have crossed out the figure and put in a new one in his own handwriting." The colonels then changed their story; they had increased the amount because of the high cost of living in Petrograd. Some of the officers had put themselves up at the Astoria. "Do something, for pity's sake!" they said. "We need the money urgently, at once." They said the action was set for the following night, Sunday, August 27.

Putilov scribbled them two checks for 400,00 rubles apiece, one drawn on his own account, the other on that of the society, and said he would raise the balance overnight and give it to them at 5:00 P.M. on Sunday at the offices of the Russian-Asiatic Bank. The colonels did not show up. Putilov tracked them down to a private room in the Villa Rodé, Rasputin's old night haunt. They were not pleased to see him. "How did you find us?" one asked, half-drunk. On being told it was his cook, he shouted, "What a fool! I have been hiding out here for three days and she tattled."

The room was filled with forty of Kornilov's officers, sitting at a banquet amid countless bottles. Although Kornilov thought he had some two thousand organized supporters in the city, and Putilov had written his checks on that basis, this was almost the sum total of Kornilov's "secret army." Putilov saw where his money was going. "Noise, shouting half-drunk speeches. . . . They would keep quiet for a while, drink, and begin over again." They told where the units were stationed, how they would deal with the Bolsheviks, how riots would be provoked. "You have gone out of your minds!" Putilov pleaded. "Here the waiters are spies, the walls are like cardboard. . . . In five minutes, the Bolsheviks will know everything!"

At 10:00 P.M. someone burst in with the news from the evening papers that Kerensky had declared Kornilov a traitor. The colonels were confused and frightened at first, but they soon calmed down and ordered more champagne. Putilov resolved not to hand over the 1.2 million rubles — "Their legs won't carry them. The money will be lost anyway." As he rose from the table, someone ran after him shouting, "But the checks? The checks?"

Such were the counterrevolutionaries whom Kornilov was supposed to have planted in Petrograd by the thousand. They squandered their funds on dinner parties and whores or embezzled them; one of Putilov's colonels disappeared, apparently to Finland, with the "last remnants of the treasury," about 150,000 rubles.

The Soviet, however, was thoroughly alarmed. It established a Committee for Struggle against Counterrevolution, which helped arm bands of workers, distributed propaganda and food, and sent out agitators to intercept Kornilov's forces. Lenin had mocked reports of tension between Kerensky and Kornilov as mere devices to frighten the Bolsheviks into supporting the moderate socialists. As the committees multiplied — there were soon 240 of them scattered through Russia, though Kornilov had at most fifteen thousand troops — the Bolsheviks cautiously backtracked. Party members were allowed to cooperate with the committees, on an informal basis.

If there had been no counterrevolution within the city, the news from outside seemed grim. Early on Monday, August 28, reports reached the Winter Palace that Kornilov's Third Cavalry Corps had entered Luga, less than ninety miles from the city, without resistance. Special newspaper editions spread panic throughout the day. Battles supposedly raged as it was reported that echelons had broken through to within a half-mile of Gatchina on the outskirts.

A pall of silence fell over the palace, Kerensky marching up and down or collapsing from fatigue on the sofas. He was "bowed with chagrin and disappointment. He looked like nothing but a deserted child, helpless and homeless. Yesterday a ruler, today a forsaken idol." The counterrevolution, which he had invented, seemed set to destroy him. He issued a public appeal, accusing Kornilov of treacherously withdrawing regiments from the front to crush the revolution: "He says that he stands for freedom, and sends against Petrograd the Savage Division."

This was a lie — Kerensky had himself ordered the Third Cavalry Corps to move — but it helped create such confusion in the army that the military remained neutral. No officer moved against the government, but none was willing to replace Kornilov as commander in chief. Kerensky at first appointed General Alexander Lukomsky, a strange move since Lukomsky was the personal friend and close aide of the "arch-traitor" he was to replace. Lukomsky rejected the appointment flatly.

All the individual front commanders cabled the Winter Palace to protest the dismissal of Kornilov, but they did not join him. Neither did right-wing politicians. With "two would-be Napoleons, one in Petrograd and the other in Mogilev and both surrounded with unsavory characters," the situation was too chaotic for sides to be taken.

The "army" marching on Petrograd under General Krymov's command was equally puzzled. Since Kornilov had not plotted to overthrow the government, he had seen no reason to provide it with a special communications network. His orders were to deal with "mercenary Bolsheviks, who lord it over Petrograd." But there was no rising in the capital, and government communiques reached Krymov's troops accusing Kornilov of treason. The officers were soon as confused as their men.

After the fiasco in the Villa Rodé, Alexei Putilov had thought it best to get out of Petrograd to a friend's estate. Driving through Luga on Monday morning, he found that the soldiers and officers were holding meetings — "Not a single platoon was ready for combat." Further along the Novgorod highway he came across disciplined units. "Ah," he thought as he drove past. "If they were to fire but a single shot everyone would scatter like rabbits." But the locals were telling the men that there were no riots in Petrograd and that they were being used against the legitimate government.

The Caucasians of the Savage Division had entrained at Dno early on Monday morning. They looked brutal enough. Glossy black mustaches and "astounded prawn-like eyes" shone amid their fur caps, felt cloaks, galloons, and daggers. They smelt of horses. But they were not much of a spearhead to throw at a city. They were under strength: only 1,350 men in all, and six hundred rifles short. A telegram advising them where to collect their missing weapons went astray.

During the morning, a bomb had been thrown at the Caucasians' trains, apparently by a provocateur wishing to make their riot-control mission more realistic. At 4:00 P.M., they were stopped twenty-seven miles from the capital. The line was cut and blocked by overturned timber wagons. A small reconnaissance detachment left the trains and was met by a delegation of Moslems sent out by the Soviet. A congress of Moslem nationalities was meeting by chance in Petrograd, and its delegates volunteered to help turn the Savage men against Kornilov.

The delegates did their work well. The divisional trains stayed where they were. The Caucasians stuck a red flag on the divisional staff carriage with the Bolshevik slogan "Land and freedom." A lieutenant colonel politely asked them to take down the flag, explaining that this was "merely to avoid confusing it with a railway signal." His men arrested him.

The Cossack divisions in Alexander Krymov's corps were no more immune than the Caucasians. They milled round Luga for much of the day, prey to agitators and railwaymen who blocked the lines on to Petrograd with freight cars. "Almost everywhere we saw the same picture," complained the Cossack general Peter Krasnov. "On the tracks or in the cars, or in the saddles of their black and bay horses . . . dragoons would be sitting or standing, and in the midst of them some lively personality in a soldier's long coat."

To Trotsky, still in prison in Petrograd, such agitators were the "secret

Vladimir Lenin, close-shaven and wearing a wig in the disguise he used to flee Petrograd after the failure of the July Days.

Communist trinity: Lenin harangues a crowd from beneath a statue of Marx and Engels.

Nadezhda Krupskaya, Lenin's wife, known as "the Fish" for her bulging eyes.

Nikolai Krylenko, the "most repulsive man in all Russia," appointed commander in chief of the Russian army by the Bolsheviks at thirty-two.

Right: The "Leaders of the Proletarian Revolution" — the Bolshevik coup in October 1917. (*From top, clockwise*): Vladimir Lenin, Anatoly Lunacharsky, Yakov Sverdlov, Lev Kamenev, Gregory Zinoviev. Leon Trotsky in center.

25 октября
1917
7 ноября
1918
Вожди пролетарской революции
Ленин.
Луначарский.
Л. Троцкий.
Каменев.
Свердлов

Maria Bochkaryova, who founded the Women's Death Battalions and was falsely rumored to be Kerensky's mistress.

Below: Crop-haired members of a Women's Death Battalion being blessed before going to the front in the "Kerensky offensive" in June.

Vladimir Antonov-Ovseenko, the long-haired Bolshevik military commissar who conquered the Winter Palace but forgot to protect his own headquarters.

Felix Dzerzhinsky, founder of the Cheka secret police and Bolshevik Terror, a fanatic whose eyelids "seemed paralysed."

Leon Trotsky after his return to Petrograd from New York.

Anti-Bolshevik military cadets during the bitter fighting for the Kremlin. The young Boris Pasternak described the shellfire in the battle as "the screams of wheeling swifts and swallows."

Wreckage in the Winter Palace after Kerensky's flight and the taking of the palace by Bolsheviks in the early hours of October 26.

Nikolai Sukhanov, the great
chronicler of the revolution,
who was sickened by its
outcome and died in the
Gulag.

Harvard-educated John Reed
allowed his Bolshevik sympathies to shine in his classic
*Ten Days That Shook the
World*. The United States
Ambassador had him tailed
as a "suspicious character."

Maurice Paleologue, French
Ambassador in Petrograd,
an "incorrigible snob" but
an acute diarist.

A detachment of pro-Lenin troops outside Bolshevik headquarters in the Smolny during Red October. Bolshevik planners originally forgot to defend the building.

weapon of the revolution." Their propaganda demoralized the Cossacks so effectively that Krymov was obliged to move his men out of the town and quarter them in nearby farms and villages.

By Monday evening, all the rail lines into Petrograd from the south and west had been cut. The suburban garrisons were on full alert. Factory workers queued up to join the Red Guards, drilling in marksmanship and weapons handling. Unarmed groups were formed for trench digging and laying barbed wire. The Putilov workers, taking a different line to that of their employer, kept shifts working through Monday night to turn out guns for new "proletarian artillery divisions." Telegraph clerks intercepted cables to and from Mogilev. Though the Bolsheviks remained in a minority, Sukhanov noted, it was clear that they were leading the resistance. The evening papers predicted a "final convulsion" the next day.

In fact, Krymov was on the verge of throwing in the towel. An industrialist, P. N. Finisov, anxious to find out what was happening to the anti-Bolshevik movement he thought he was funding, caught up with the general at 5:00 A.M. on Tuesday morning. Krymov's headquarters were in a cowshed twelve miles from Luga. Krymov complained that his indoctrinated Cossacks were refusing to advance on Petrograd without a Bolshevik rising there.

His orders had been to advance swiftly on Petrograd and "unexpectedly" occupy it. Surprise had gone — the entire countryside seemed better informed of what was going on than he was. Krymov's corps was scattered in railway sidings and in villages. Regimental commanders did not know where their squadrons and companies were. The shortage of food and forage was irritating the men, who were beginning to arrest their officers.

On his way back to Petrograd, Finisov passed a car with a colonel carrying an order from Kerensky for Krymov to halt his advance and report to him immediately. Finisov's car was running out of petrol, and the colonel siphoned him some from his own.

The country believed that momentous events were unfolding. On a Volga steamer, the passengers in the first-class saloon were in the best of spirits. A general on board followed the movements of the Savage Division on a map. A rich civilian told the British correspondent Philips Price that he hoped Kornilov would declare a "mild dictatorship for a year." He added that the army could use a few British troops as stiffening while it hunted down the Bolsheviks in the cities and the Social Revolutionaries in the villages.

In third class, a grim young fisherman warned, "If gentlemen like Kornilov don't look out, they'll all find their way to the gallows."

The rich in Petrograd were alarmed at the Bolshevik renaissance that Kornilov was sparking. Groups of armed workers were on the streets. Kerensky had allowed forty thousand weapons to be handed out. Leaders of the Bolshevik military organization played the major role in forming scratch workers' battalions. Members of the chauffeurs' union took over their employers' cars and ferried volunteers out to the expected battle in the southern suburbs. The few respectable people who were about wore a "furtive, anxious expression." The Cadet paper *Rech* warned that if Kornilov lost, the Bolsheviks, whom the majority in the Soviet has once again ceased to consider traitors," would "use all their energy to force the Soviet to embark on the realization of the Bolshevik program."

Revolutionary committees took control in the Baltic naval bases, seizing telegraphs and telephones and insisting that no orders were valid without their signatures. Sailors from the cruiser *Aurora*, Bolsheviks and anarchists, arrived in Petrograd at Kerensky's behest to defend the Winter Palace. They visited shipmates who had been arrested after the July Days in the Kresty Prison, where Trotsky was also held. "Isn't it time to arrest the government?" they asked the prisoners. But the lesson of July had been learned. The risk of a coup was too great. "No, not yet," the sailors were told. "Use Kerensky as a gun-rest to shoot Kornilov. Afterward we will settle with Kerensky."

Lenin had moved on to Finland as his haymaking disguise wore thin. A hunter on a shooting expedition had taken shelter from the rain in the thatched hut; Lenin hoped that the man had not noticed the manuscript of *State and Revolution,* which he was working on, pushed hastily under some hay. Lenin was photographed in a wig and makeup for a false identity card as "Konstantin Ivanov," a worker. No more competent a plotter than Kornilov, he was almost arrested after he got lost on his way to the country station from which he was smuggled over the border disguised as a locomotive fireman, riding on the footplate.

He was now in Helsinki, living in the comfortable fifth-floor apartment of Kustaa Rovio, the head of the city police and a Bolshevik. Despite this high-level protection, Lenin was too frightened of arrest to leave the apartment, where he lived on a diet of eggs and tea. He was, however, exhilarated by the Kornilov events. "We shall not overthrow Kerensky right now," he said. "We shall approach the task of struggling against him in a *different way.* We shall point out to the people his *weakness and vacillation.*"

The Kornilov affair ended in a whimper. Krymov's troops confronted the Petrograd units near Luga in mutual incomprehension. "The Kornilovites were especially amazed," Zinaïda Gippius noted in her diary. "They had gone to defend the Provisional Government and met an "enemy" who had also gone to defend the Provisional Government. . . . So they stood and pondered. They couldn't understand a thing."

The "counterrevolution" collapsed as the two sides fraternized. Krymov ordered the Cossacks and Caucasians to halt their advance. On Wednesday, August 30, the general agreed to appear at the Winter Palace after Kerensky had given him a guarantee of personal safety. August 30 was Saint Alexander's Day, and telegrams of congratulations on his name day poured in for Kerensky from across the country, a last echo of his popularity.

Krymov arrived in Petrograd in the early hours of Thursday, August 31. He saw Kerensky in the Alexander III study at 10:00 A.M. Shouts and loud voices were heard through the double doors. Krymov came out, saying that he was under arrest, went to a friend's apartment, asked for paper and pen to write a letter to his wife, and then shot himself through the chest with his service revolver.

Murder as well as suicide was in the air. In Helsinki's harbor four officers in the battleship *Petropavlovsk* had refused to sign a resolution condemning Kornilov. The crew shot them on Saturday evening. Louise Bryant, a young correspondent with the *Philadelphia Public Ledger,* disembarked at Vyborg the same day. She had had a good crossing from the United States, the returning Russian exiles in steerage teaching her revolutionary songs. When she landed, she found troops and sailors roaming the streets.

A group of officers had gone to the station to get out of the city. A pale young soldier went up to them on the platform, shouting, "The officers! The bright, pretty officers!" The men stamped the officers' faces with their heavy boots and dragged them away through the mud. "They threw them in the canal," Bryant wrote. "They have just finished it now. They have killed fifty and I heard them screaming."

The Germans were at Riga, and the Russians were busying themselves killing their officers. No general would replace Kornilov. Kerensky was obliged to reverse his own orders and leave him temporarily in command, issuing instructions that Kornilov's orders should be obeyed. It was, as Kornilov pointed out, an episode "unique in world history. The commander in chief accused of treason, has been ordered to continue commanding his armies because there is no one else to appoint."

It was only on Friday, September 1, that the long-suffering Mikhail Alexeev reluctantly agreed to again take up the reins as commander in chief, the post from which Kerensky had so ignominiously sacked him in June. Alexeev placed Kornilov under house arrest in a hotel before having him transferred to the Bykhov Fortress. No charges were ever brought against him, and he retained his red-cloaked bodyguards. Alexeev warned Kerensky that the officers would not stomach a trial. He leaked a copy of the Hughes wire conversation between Kornilov and Kerensky to a Moscow paper. Its last line — where Kerensky signed off with his "Goodbye, we shall meet soon" — caused a sensation. The Bolsheviks claimed that this showed clear collusion between the premier and Kornilov. Kerensky was sufficiently embarrassed to order the Bolshevik daily Rabochy Put and Maxim Gorky's Novaya Zhizn to be closed down. Gorky now split from Kerensky.

Within a week, Alexeev had resigned, explaining to a reporter from Rech, "I can state with horror that we have no army. . . . It cannot continue like this." He said that Kornilov and those arrested with him "are not adventurers; these are people who sincerely love their country." Boris Savinkov, who "understood the revolutionary temperament better than almost anyone," Bruce Lockhart thought, and "knew how to play on it for his own ends," quit the war ministry. The officer corps held Kerensky responsible for the Krymov suicide. The soldiers were angry at his failure to prosecute Kornilov, and at his continuation of the war.

Kerensky was isolated politically. The Bolsheviks, their revival sealed by the sharp leftward reaction against Kornilov, won a vote in the Soviet on the night of September 1–2, calling for a government of workers and soldiers. It amounted to a vote of no confidence in Kerensky. He formally announced a republic on September 3, an empty gesture and one that was declared illegal by the country's supreme court, the Governing Senate. A psychiatrist, Dr. Nikolai Kishkin, was appointed welfare minister, and the wags suggested he take the premier as a patient. Two days later, a stronger Bolshevik motion condemning the government was passed by the Moscow Soviet.

The Social Revolutionaries and Mensheviks were being rolled back by the Bolsheviks. In new municipal elections in Moscow, the turnout was half that of June. People were tired of talk and speeches; Blok said wearily, "I shall never join any party, I shall never make a choice, I have nothing to be proud of, I understand nothing." But half of those who did vote now supported the Bolsheviks, an increase of more than two-thirds in three months. The Cadets made modest gains as the moderate socialists were savaged by polarization, the Social Revolutionaries and Mensheviks losing 52 percent of their support. The Mensheviks began to split, the Internationalist wing of the party drifting toward the Bolsheviks.

The swing to the left obliged Kerensky to amnesty the Bolsheviks. On September 3, Trotsky was released from the Kresty on three thousand rubles bail. Within a week, he was elected chairman of the Petrograd Soviet, the Bolsheviks applauding "like a storm, ecstatically, furiously."

"Kerensky is now completely in the hands of the maximalists and the

Bolsheviks," Zinaïda Gippius wrote. "The ball is over. They haven't raised their heads yet. They sit. Tomorrow, of course, they'll get on their feet." That was what Lenin thought — the Kornilov affair "can lead *us* to power." The Bolsheviks should not speak of it in public, Lenin wrote from Finland, but in private they should realize that "even tomorrow events may put power into our hands. And then we shall not relinquish it."

XIX
"The Crisis Is Ripe"

REPRIEVED BY THE KORNILOV AFFAIR, the Bolsheviks worked "stubbornly and without letup." Sukhanov found them "at the factory benches and in the barracks every blessed day. For the masses, they had become *their own people,* because they were always there." People were swept over the heads of other parties into the "devastating fury" of Bolshevism. Party tactics were simple. "They were lavish with promises and sweet through simple fairy tales," the diarist wrote. Lenin was honing his fairy tale in Finland in the apartment of the Helsinki police chief. He continued writing his work the *State and Revolution,* cramming it with additions, brackets, and his familiar underlinings, a social engineer sketching out his blueprint for the world with manic energy.

State and Revolution took as read that the state at all times and in all places represented the interests of the exploiting class. It repeated, as absolute truth — and with added emphases — Marx's statement, "I declare the next attempt of the French Revolution: not to transfer the bureaucratic-military machine from one pair of hands to another, as was done until now, but to *smash* it. . . . *All revolutions have perfected this machine instead of smashing it.*" Lenin reminded himself of what was involved in "smashing" by reading Jules Michelet's beatification of the Terror during the French Revolution.

Lenin said that bureaucracy would disappear under socialism: "*All* will govern in turn and quickly become accustomed to no one governing." But it would not vanish overnight. "In the *transition* from capitalism," he wrote, "repression is *still* necessary." That was a matter of no consequence, for it would no longer be tsarist repression. A Bolshevik noose was a sweeter thing. "It is already repression of the minority of exploiters by the majority of the exploited," he explained. "A special apparatus, a special machine of repression, the 'State' is *still* necessary."

Russian society and the Russian state was thus condemned to smashing and repression. Lenin urged "boundless audacity in destroying the old state machine entirely . . . for the purpose of *overthrowing the bourgeoisie, destroying bourgeois* parliamentarianism." Revolution was terror and destruction. He was obsessed with its violence, mocking at moderate socialists who thought that revolution behaved in "the calm and precise manner of a German express pulling into a station. A sedate conductor opens the carriage door and announces: 'Social Revolution station! *Alle aussteigen!* All change!' " True revolution could only exist in a "furious storm of passion." The work justified Maurice Paleologue's cruel sketch of its author — "Utopian dreamer and prophet, metaphysician, blind to any idea of the impossible and the absurd, a stranger to all feelings of justice or mercy, violent, Machiavellian, crazy with vanity."

State and Revolution was intended as a testament for future generations, not for immediate publication. This was as well. Lenin was acutely sensitive to criticism, so irritated by attacks on him immediately after the July Days that he briefly gave up reading newspapers.

Some of these attacks were scurrilous. Puritanism was in fashion in revolutionary circles — when Louise Bryant crossed the border from Finland, her cosmetics were confiscated and thrown into a box filled up with "travelers' rouge sticks, French powder, brilliantine, hair dye and perfume" — and the right-wing press took great glee in accusing the Bolshevik leader of high living. *Zhivoe Slovo,* the newspaper which had first exposed the German connection, ran a story claiming that Lenin, far from being a man of Spartan personal habits, had disguised himself as "Comrade Chaplinsky" on nightly revels in Petrograd. He was said to have dined in private rooms with a Swedish actress and swilled champagne at 110 rubles a bottle. "Chaplinsky," the paper added for good measure, undertipped the waiters and called them "lackeys."

He was open to more realistic gibes on two fronts, as a dreamer and a terrorist. Lenin was commonly attacked as a "Utopian," a "scribbler," as the right-wing *Iskri* put it, who "thinks that just by writing on a piece of paper the earth will change." His socialist rivals mocked his insistence that Russia could enter a proletarian revolution without first passing through the bourgeois stage. Their objections were as much practical as theoretical. How could the small and backward Russian proletariat run a country in which the actual majority were illiterate, acquisitive, and non-Bolshevik peasants? The claim that the State would eventually wither away was similar "gibberish."

And the naked evocation of the guillotine in *State and Revolution* reinforced the charge of terrorism, that Lenin and the Bolsheviks were driving

Russia to civil war. "They turn the bourgeois and the proletariat into ene-mies," warned *Iskri,* "and repeat and repeat it." Russia had in six months become in principle the least repressive state in the world. In the United States, the Senate rejected President Wilson's suffrage bill and four women were imprisoned for picketing the White House. In Russia, women were so emancipated that they could volunteer for combat units. In Britain, men and women were being hanged for crimes. In Russia, the death penalty for civilians had been abolished together with all restrictions based on race, sex, and creed. Yet it was the Russian state that Lenin wished to *smash.*

Opponents were not alone in finding Lenin's thoughts to be, as Alexan-der Bogdanov, a cofounder of the party, put it, the "ravings of a lunatic." The central committee found his outpourings in September so bewildering that, as in March, they had some of them burnt. The desire to cut down the rich and successful, however, struck a chord of widening jealousy. Fedor Chaliapin wrote to his daughter on September 7 after a sellout concert that netted 14,500 rubles that people would go short of food to hear him sing. "Needless to say," Chaliapin told his daughter, "the newspapers turned on the poison, and I was called a thief and a marauder, and anything else that happened to creep into their little minds."

At the beginning of September, Lenin wrote to the Bolshevik central com-mittee to say that a situation was developing "with catastrophic speed" where the workers would be compelled "to wage a determined battle with the counterrevolutionary bourgeoisie to gain power." By midmonth he was confident that Kornilov had turned the tide decisively in the Bolshevik favor. He insisted that the central committee begin immediate preparations for an armed rising in letters written from Finland on September 12 and 14. Lenin's letters were near-hysterical with panic that they would be — as they were — ignored. Krupskaya went to see him twice in Finland and found him ob-sessed with the details of his coup and the plots that might abort it. "Ilyich was terribly worried, sitting up there in Finland," she said, "that the most favorable moment for the uprising would be lost." But his letters made it clear that Lenin's hesitations had gone. He was now utterly committed to a coup, at whatever risk. His certainty alarmed almost every colleague — even Trotsky, who had a similar streak of all-or-nothing — but in the end it was compelling.

"The Bolsheviks can and must take power into their hands," he wrote. "Why . . . right *now*? Because the impending surrender of Petrograd will make our chances one hundred times worse. . . . Kerensky is preparing to surrender Petrograd. The international situation *just now,* on the eve of a separate peace between the English and the Germans, is *in our favor. . . .*

Assume power at once in Moscow and in Petrograd (it does not matter where it begins; perhaps even Moscow may begin); we will win *absolutely* and *unquestionably*."

This produced gasps when the central committee members read it. There was a plan to move the government from Petrograd to Moscow, but it had been drawn up by tsarist officials the year before as a contingency in the event of a German advance along the Baltic coast. There was no evidence that Kerensky intended to surrender the city. As to the "separate peace" in the West, the British and Germans were locked in the murderous combat of Passchendaele as Lenin wrote.

Lenin continued with rambling tactical orders. "Move the loyal regiments to the most important points; surround the Alexandrinsky Theater; arrest the general staff and the government; move against the cadets. . . . Use such detachments as will die. . . . We must mobilize the armed workers, call them to a last desperate battle . . . place *our* staff at the central telephone exchange, connect it by wire with all the factories, the regiments, the points of armed fighting."

The central committee, which knew well the actual conditions in the capital, feared a repeat of the July shambles. They were not impressed that, as Bukharin recalled, Lenin had "threatened us with all sorts of punishments. We all gasped. At first we were all at sea. Afterwards, having talked it over, we made a decision . . . to burn it." Trotsky was not opposed to a coup in principle, but thought that Lenin's timing was impetuous, and that the party should first strengthen its position in the Soviets. Lev Kamenev and Gregory Zinoviev wrote off the coup as suicidal adventurism. The putsch could not succeed without Lenin's "loyal regiments" and there were none. The two moderates believed in a period of peaceful compromise with the Mensheviks and Social Revolutionaries. Kamenev moved a resolution to ignore Lenin's proposals, to call on all Bolsheviks to "follow central committee instructions alone" and to state that any kind of street demonstration, let alone an armed one, was impermissible.

No further serious discussion of armed rising was to take place until October 10. Lenin was in a fury of frustration with the senior party figures, screaming Danton's words at them from his safe haven across the Gulf of Finland: "De l'audace, de l'audace, encore de l'audace!" Danton, Lenin instructed them, was the "greatest master of revolutionary policy yet known." But was he not also the master terrorist, the man who had defended the revolutionary tribunals in France in 1973: "Let us be terrible, so that the people do not have to be"?

Lenin sought a more sympathetic hearing from a young Finnish Bolshevik, Ivar Smilga. "Give *all your attention* to the *military* preparation of the troops in Finland," Lenin wrote to Smilga on September 27. "Create a *secret* committee of absolutely *trustworthy* military men, collect (and *personally* verify) the most precise data on the composition of troops near and in Petrograd. . . . Why should we tolerate three more weeks of war and Kerensky's Kornilovite preparations?" Smilga was asked to organize troops and sailors within Finland to overthrow the "Kerensky scum." Rejected by the upper reaches of his party, Lenin was conspiring with a junior to command phantom fleets and armies — as, in childhood, he had played soldiers in Simbirsk.

Another broadside crashed into the central committee on September 29. Lenin said that its desire to delay a rising "must be *overcome,* or the Bolsheviks will cover themselves with eternal *shame* and *destroy themselves* as a party." Any postponement was *"utter idiocy* or *sheer treachery."* He wanted immediate uprisings in Petrograd, Moscow, and the Baltic Fleet, saying that success was 99 percent certain. Complaining that his articles were being edited or suppressed, he took this as a "subtle hint that I should keep my mouth shut. . . . I am compelled to *tender my resignation from the central committee,* which I hereby do." The threat to resign was a piece of Kerensky-style emotion, and no more was heard of it.

There were, however, two parts of Lenin's analysis that were wholly clear-sighted. He wanted the "briefest and sharpest" formula to back the Bolshevik takeover: "Peace to the people, land to the peasants, confiscation of scandalous profits." These simple slogans were indeed what the masses wanted to hear. The Bolsheviks had stuck since April to the same formula, which now gleamed in the confusion "like a beacon above the fog." And he was right to insist, "The government cannot do anything to save itself." Kerensky was careering deeper and deeper into crisis throughout September: he could provide neither land nor peace. Danton's "audacity" alone might topple him, and Lenin knew it.

Lenin's political audacity, however, far outstripped his personal courage, and Kerensky was aided by his antagonist's continued absence in Finland. Trotsky's release from prison showed that Lenin had little to fear physically from returning to Petrograd. But the master remained on the other side of the border from his disciples, and his epistles carried less weight than his presence could.

Damp winds blew off the Gulf of Finland into the capital. There were no warm clothes in the shops, just window after window full of flowers, corsets, dog collars, and false hair. These wares told their own story: the corsets were expensive and wasp-waisted, and the fashionable women who wore them had largely fled the capital. False hair no longer sold — except to

Bolsheviks needing disguise — because the women who remained cut their hair short in deference to their emancipation. Hothouses and gardeners still grew flowers, though their customers had departed. As to dog collars, Louise Bryant observed that few people dolled up their dogs "when there's a revolutionary tribunal round the corner."

The *svetzars* stood outside the restaurants on the Nevsky in peacock feathers with scarlet sashes and round, Chinese-looking caps, waiting to help the mighty down from their carriages. The customers had gone, but the doormen remained, "their feathers ragged and forlorn." Inside the restaurants, each table had a curt notice: "Just because a man must make his living by being a waiter, do not insult him by offering him a tip." Diners who took the advice found themselves spat at when they left.

Queues started at 4:00 A.M. for bread, sugar, and tobacco. The shops often ran out before all but the earliest queuers had been served. Alexei Peshekhonov's resignation as supply minister passed almost unnoticed. Many people were trying to live on a quarter of a pound of bread every two days. When ladies went to take tea with each other, they carried a silver sugar box and a half-loaf of bread in their muffs. Alexander Blok's mother brought him food from her estate and bunches of shaggy pink asters. The cafés were full but served only weak tea and sandwiches. Red flags flew everywhere, even on the statue of Catherine the Great in front of the Alexandrinsky Theater.

Viktor Chernov, the Social Revolutionary leader, sniped at Kerensky, his fellow party member, in a series of articles in the SR paper *Delo Naroda*. Chernov insinuated that Kerensky had plotted with Kornilov to bring in a dictatorship. Kerensky, worried that "the rumors are causing disintegration among the populace," issued vague orders to "arrest five or six people" to counter the charge that he was being "intentionally soft."

Those who feared being linked to Kornilov hid themselves away. The yellow ticket system for registering prostitutes had been abolished as undemocratic, but they found little custom among nervous officers. In London, the *Financial Times* was assuring its readers that Kerensky was "in complete control" and that investors should remember the "almost unlimited opportunities for profitable trade" with Russia that would open up after the war. Russians were less optimistic. The stock exchange had passed from fever to chill and the velvet-upholstered carriages of speculators were missing from the streets outside the bourse. Russian "Fives," the government 5 percent stock, fell from 72 to 66.5 on news of Kornilov's arrest, and the ruble slid from 222 to 282 to £10.

Almost a billion rubles of new notes were printed in September, inflation guaranteeing that they represented "no material value from which people might profit." The treasury printing works could no longer cope with guillotining the flood of notes. They were issued in sheets, the bank customers cutting off individual notes themselves. Wages at the Baltic Works had doubled in paper terms since January, but had fallen in purchase power by two-thirds. At the labor exchanges, the real wages of casual laborers had fallen by more than half. The number of strikers went above the million mark in September, up from 175,000 in June.

Factory owners wanted to abandon the struggle against fuel shortages and absenteeism. "The sole dream of the industrialist has become to give up business and close his enterprise," the employers' newspaper *Torgovo-Promyshlennaya Gazeta* complained. If closures and lockouts were still rare, it was only because of the "threat of mob law and sequestration."

In the countryside, Sukhanov reported with near glee, anarchy was "really getting underway." On September 8, Kerensky threatened all perpetrators of violence, and officials who failed to prosecute them, with three years in jail. But the Red Cock was lusty now. A landowner near Kozlovka who fired on peasants attacking his farm was pitchforked to death. Other estates were torched until the "skies east of Kozlovka were black in the day, and red at night." The army was sent in on September 14; the soldiers joined in the looting. Within a few days more than a hundred manors had burned. Most were wooden, comfortable and rambling homes, with colonnaded fronts and intricate fretwork round the windows and roofline. They burned easily and satisfyingly from the rafters to the earthen cellars, the paint exploding and setting the surrounding fields on fire. Kerensky had to order troops to protect Leo Tolstoy's estate at Yasanaya Polyana from the *muzhiks* the great writer had idolized.

Raiders carried revolvers and hand grenades as well as scythes and pitchforks. Railway passengers could see the steppe illuminated by fire at night. Alongside the track, "cows, horses, or sheep roamed the fields with ripped stomachs, mooing or bellowing from pain." In Ryazan, peasants seized the big rafts of timber being sent down the Oka River to Moscow. Wood-burning cities like Moscow, Tambov, and Orel dreaded the coming winter. Bakeries were already running out of fuel by mid-September.

Lynch law replaced justice. *Iskri* told its horrified bourgeois readers how an innocent was burned alive in the little village of Domansk in Kherson province. Cattle had begun to disappear and suspicion fell on a forty-three-year-old peasant, Philip Ostrometsky. The villagers led him out to a field where some deserters had set up camp. "Here," they said. "You can judge him." Two deserters beat Ostrometsky with staves and then set light to him. His body was left in the field all day. Only at night could his wife and children retrieve it. "Now the villagers say it wasn't him," the magazine correspondent reported. "It was his judges who stole the cattle."

The disorders were spreading "like the dreaded ringworm," or the typhus that Turkish POWs had unleashed on the villages along the Trans-Siberian line. "Even a small child could see the reason," *Novaya Zhizn* commented. "Ancient land shortage, the complete vagueness of existing land relations, and criminal inactivity by the government."

Old Russia was breaking up. Nationalist movements were accelerating in the Ukraine, Finland, the Baltic States, and White Russia, and among Cossacks, Moslems, and Siberians. The Kuban declared itself an independent Cossack state, and armed Cossacks chased the Soviets out of Rostov-on-Don and Ekaterinburg. In Kiev, the Rada, the national parliament, reported that the "organization of Ukrainian military units proceeds unflinchingly" as an "organic necessity" of an independent nation. The Rada wanted immediate peace talks with the Germans and enlarged the boundaries of the Ukraine until they included all the best farmland of South Russia as far east as the Urals.

In Helsinki, the governor-general dissolved the Sejm, the Finnish parliament, and had the doors of its building sealed to prevent illegal meetings. Sejm members broke the seals on September 15 and sat for two hours passing resolutions to make the country an independent republic. *Iskri* complained that the Finns "have become completely anti-Russian." The Finns refused to loan money to the Provisional Government and called for the withdrawal of Russian troops. Petrograd had to raise a $15 million loan from the United States to pay for its troops in Finland.

Latvian nationalists declared that legislative and executive powers were "in the hands of the Latvian people and her parliament." The Lithuanian Sejm resolved that the country should become an independent and permanently neutralized state. The Germans held talks with Lithuanian exiles in Switzerland, and proposed an independent Duchy of Lithuania with the German emperor as duke, for "Lithuanians are wholly Catholic and already inclined to the West."

Siberians declared themselves a "distinct cultural type" in which the Russian element was mixed with Turko-Mongolian stock. They demanded their own constituent assembly and an end to exploitation by western Russians. The Buryats, who retorted that they were not part of any Russian mixture, met in Irkutsk to proclaim their autonomy and to declare that the brewing of *tarasun*, their heady native drink, was again legal whatever Petrograd might say.

Old racial hatreds were stirring. Workers in Petrograd wanted the Chinese in the city, originally brought in as railway builders, to be sent back to Asia. Jews felt that the "bloodstained specter of the Middle Ages" was hovering over their heads again. Anarchy was grasping at "its favorite means of duping the masses, at the poisoned weapons of an anti-Semitic campaign." Plunder and murder raged in Bessarabia, the militia unable to cope with it. "The pogrom movement is mounting," the *Russkiya Vedomosti* correspondent reported. "Talk is heard of shifting all the blame onto the Jews." A Zionist congress declared that Jews could only hope for a normal cultural and economic life "upon recreating an autonomous national center in the historic motherland, Palestine."

Moslems meeting in Kazan resolved to organize a Moslem army and demanded a cultural and national self-determination. Crimean Tartars wanted the "return of all plundered land." Bashkirs in the heavily Russian-settled Urals, "from time immemorial the cradle of the Bashkir people," said that their land "must free itself from the wardship of other people." Moslem women held their first feminist meeting at Fiodossia in the Crimea — "after centuries they are seen in daylight and without veils," a newspaper commented — in order to complain against the "brutal exploitation and polygamy" of their husbands.

Russians turned on the Moslem majority in Turkestan, where Kerensky had spent his teenage years. Soldiers from Siberian regiments ran amok on September 10 in Tashkent, attacking Moslem passengers on trains and looting their baggage. Bolsheviks formed a committee to take power. Troops beat up the general commanding the city, looted the Moslem quarter, and sacked government offices. A squadron of armored cars was needed to put down the rising.

The only centralizing force left to Kerensky was the army, and it was dying, seized with rumors of "Yeremeev Night," when officers would be murdered in emulation of the Saint Bartholomew's Night massacre of French Protestants three and a half centuries before. The gory tale, with its peculiar Russian translation, had "somehow — God only knows how — penetrated the dark masses." Two officers were discovered disguised as soldiers on a train from Baku to Moscow. A pair of hairbrushes seen in their kit was enough to condemn them as *burzhui*. They were thrown out of the train as it crossed a deep and rocky gorge, the bodies "falling like dolls that a child has thrown away in a fit of anger."

The Germans were handing out tobacco and wine to the Russians opposite them. When an artillery commander in the 196th Regiment opened fire on the trenches to stop fraternization, the men threw fragmentation grenades into his command bunker. The British sent a film mission to "coax" the men into fighting by showing them footage of the war on the western front. "Not unnaturally," Bruce Lockhart noted, "these savage scenes served merely to increase the number of deserters."

Trains were so overcrowded with deserters that Alexis Babine, transferred from Vologda to the schools department in Samara, thought himself lucky to arrive because the car axles caught fire several times due to the weight. Stations resembled "open hives of gray-brown bees" and "stank like a vast latrine."

After the Kornilov affair, Kerensky handed the war ministry over to Alexander Verkhovsky, a thirty-four-year-old colonel. Verkhovsky thought that the only way to keep the army in being was for Kerensky to announce that he would immediately seek peace, and wanted to slash its numbers by half in the interim. He complained that Kerensky's position was so vague that "I fear lest I be betrayed." The Don Cossack division refused Verkhovsky's orders to go to Finland for police and political duties, objecting to being used as "gendarmes." Troops in Saratov moved out of their barracks and seized civilian apartments. Bolshevik agitators had only to "catch the favoring wind and fill their sails."

Sergei Pushkarev, an idealistic Menshevik, watched the process in an infantry regiment at Mariupol on the Sea of Azov. When he had volunteered to join up in August, the recruiting clerk had looked at him with astonishment. "You want to join the army, do you? What on earth for?" Pushkarev said he felt it was his patriotic duty to defend Russia. "Well, you can try," said the clerk.

Officers rarely appeared in the regiment. Each morning, the sergeants said, "Well, boys, who's going to drill today?" In Pushkarev's platoon of seventy men, only fifteen consented to training, and this consisted mostly of "talking and smoking." The troops were on duty only from 8:00 A.M. to midday. They spent their afternoons lying on the sand or swimming in the warm shallows of the sea, and their evenings arguing in the town.

The main Bolshevik agitator, a tall, lanky sergeant, won every debate. "Kerensky forces you to continue this bloody, criminal war," he would say. "Do you need it?" "No, we don't!" came the reply. "Do you need German or Turkish territory?" "No, we don't!" "Do you want to shed your blood for English and American capitalists?" "No, we don't!" Pushkarev would take the floor to argue that the Bolsheviks were making promises that they could not keep. Each time, he was shouted down: "None of this rubbish! Look, he wears eyeglasses. He's obviously a *burzhui* himself." He got himself transferred to the training company, which still had discipline.

In September, the company was sent to restore order in Bakhmut in the

Donets Basin, where the Twenty-fifth Infantry Regiment had broken into the local vodka warehouse and was looting the city. Pushkarev's company marched to the main square in strict military formation, to the visible astonishment of the local population, both sober and drunk. A disheveled soldier was holding himself upright with a lamp post. "Comrades, what regiment are you from?" he asked. "The Twenty-fourth Infantry," they replied. "Very well, comrades," he said. "Now we will drink vodka together."

Pushkarev said to him sharply, "We didn't come to drink vodka with you. We came to restore order in your city." The soldier half sobered up and said witheringly, "That's very strange! That means the Twenty-fifth will drink vodka and the Twenty-fourth will pray to God." He looked piously to heaven and Pushkarev's comrades wheezed with laughter.

The vodka warehouse was a large brick building. The entrance was guarded by armed sentries from the Twenty-fourth and a company of cadets. All night, soldiers from the Twenty-fifth came to the gates and whispered, "Comrades, comrades, give me a little bottle. Just one little *merzavchick,* one little 'scoundrel.' " When Pushkarev threatened to fire, the soldiers outside got angry: "You damned sons of bitches! We'll shoot the lot of you."

A cadet was shot in the head and died instantly. Pushkarev found it a "most unpleasant feeling . . . to be in danger of being killed in defense of vodka." When the training regiment was withdrawn a fortnight later, it, too, was being Bolshevized.

Kerensky's position was now worse than Lenin shrewdly suspected. When the premier went to Mogilev on September 26, his reception was so icy that he admitted to having a nervous collapse for two days. In the whirlpool of loathings in the army, the commissar on the northern front warned the premier, Kerensky himself had become one of the most hated men.

The swelling Bolshevik resurgence in September, Sukhanov thought, had little to do with love of Bolshevism and much to do with this "hatred for 'Kerenskyism,' fatigue, rage, and a thirst for peace, bread, and land," which bred a listlessness easy to exploit.

Only the Bolsheviks, Alexander Blok found, preserved a "precious storminess, a nontiredness." It was a quality he felt was "close to Rasputin's sensuality." He had no illusions about their methods, but thought that they would pass. "It is only to begin with that there is blood, violence, and bestiality," he said. "But then — clover, the pink clover": the socialist millennium.

A visceral anti-Bolshevik, like the landowner Pyotr Shilovsky, felt that the government was abdicating to Lenin in "deliberate suicide." A "quixotic sense of honor" alone kept Russia in the war. Shilovsky, too, was looking for "strength and vigor" and he admitted that the Bolsheviks had it. How else were the lower classes, who had been "good-natured or indifferent" to their betters, transformed into an "embodiment of ferocious, boundless hatred"?

Respectable men kept their distance from the government. Sofia Koulomzina thought her father typical of "what we would call 'decent people' — an epithet that was very strong and meant a great deal." A landowner and a moderate, when Kerensky had tried to persuade him to join the government he refused, not believing that Kerensky had it in him to achieve "anything that was politically constructive or sound." Her father made speeches and wrote his memoirs, but never rid himself of a "scepticism, an unwillingness to fight for an issue if he wasn't absolutely certain that his viewpoint would prevail." He suffered from passivity, a constant emotional withdrawal. She found these traits characteristic of the decent element in Russian public life. "The fact is," Koulomzina admitted, "my father wasn't a fighter."

Another decent man, the writer Maxim Gorky, was repulsed by public life. He could not stomach the Bolsheviks, but he had broken with Kerensky as well. Gorky threw them all on the compost heap — politics had become the "nettle of poisonous enmity, evil suspicions, shameless lies, slander, morbid ambitions." Thinkers were abandoning a public that had held them in a particular respect.

Apathy bit deep at a humbler level. *Delo Naroda* warned of the "popular weariness with conferences, voting and resolutions. . . . Meetings formerly thronged by thousands are now attended only by hundreds. In villages, insignificantly small numbers turn out to vote. The circulation of socialist papers drops; the circulation of yellow papers increases."

The Bolsheviks were the beneficiaries of this disillusionment. They cast their eyes on the Soviet, and liked what they saw. As many as eight hundred Soviets had mushroomed in the provinces after the February revolution, but their prestige sagged through the summer with their failure to cope with local crises. Many had dissolved, and moderates abandoned the survivors. *Izvestiya,* the Soviet official newspaper, complained that only half the delegates to the Petrograd Soviet were bothering to attend. Those who failed to turn up were "precisely the representatives of the majority parties," the moderate socialists on whom Kerensky depended.

Trotsky sensed a vacuum. On September 19, the Bolsheviks gained a majority in the workers' section of the Moscow Soviet. They repeated the success in Petrograd on September 25. The Bolsheviks at once incorporated the section into their party organization and, *Izvestiya* complained, "leaning on it, engaged in a partisan struggle to seize all the Soviets nationwide." The Bolsheviks had no respect for the Soviets as such, even if they were eventually to rename the country for them. The Soviets had grown up as "temporary barracks to shelter all democracy," as *Izvestiya* put it. The Bolsheviks had no desire to shelter democracy or other people. But if the Soviets could be Bolshevized, through apathy, they would become a great strategic prize — for the democratic-sounding slogan "All Power to the Soviets" would, in reality, mean "All Power to the Bolsheviks."

A democratic conference that dragged on for five days amid the red plush of the Alexandrinsky Theater toward the end of the month had a *fin de régime* air to it. The conference was arranged by Kerensky as a face-saving and temporary alternative to the delayed Constituent Assembly. Delegates came from throughout Russia, guaranteeing the moderates a majority. Most were provincials whom Somerset Maugham described as "backward and loutish people with ignorant faces and a vacuous look, the narrowness, the obstinacy of peasants." Their leaders were sick and tired. Kerensky was suffering from another bout of kidney trouble. Nikolai Chkheidze had the brilliant eyes, the "sunken cheeks and paper-pale forehead" of tuberculosis. Irakli Tsereteli's lungs seemed finally broken by his seven years' hard labor in Siberia. Julius Martov was husky with an infected throat.

Sessions dragged on until 4:00 A.M., delegates often giving a "long, sustained speech of an hour's duration." Maugham was bored, for "they make no attempt to enliven with story or jest." Fifty races were said to be represented, their delegates sometimes speaking in a language no one else understood. The daughter of the aristo-anarchist Prince Peter Kropotkin looked on in disdain, peering through the only pair of lorgnettes in the theater.

Maugham found Kerensky to be "green with fright." There was a gangway over the orchestra pit that led from the stage, and Kerensky walked down it every now and then as though he sought to appeal to each man personally.

"I cannot speak to the conference of the Democracy, whose will I carried out and with which I created the Revolution," Kerensky began, "until I feel that there is no one here who could slander me personally." The Bolsheviks booed his immodesty. When he spoke of the army, a voice mocked him from the stalls, "And what of the death penalty, Marat?" He retorted, "When just a single death sentence is signed by me, the Supreme Commander, then I will permit you to curse me."

It seemed weakness, not strength, for what was the point of death sentences if the Supreme Commander would not sign them? Boris Savinkov had told Maugham how Kerensky had handed him a telegram saying, "Will you see about this?" It was a plea for clemency from a woman whose son had been sentenced to be shot for desertion. Only Kerensky could make such a decision, but he handed the cable to Savinkov "to rid himself of a responsibility he dreaded." Maugham thought it doubly telling that Kerensky never asked Savinkov what he had done — though neither apparently did Maugham himself, for he did not record it.

Olga Kerensky was attending the conference, "dressed always in black, pale and wistful." When the Bolshevik barracking of her estranged husband over the death penalty became too great, she snapped *"Da volna!"* — "that's enough!" Kerensky ignored her.

The conference, intended to underpin the principle of coalition government, achieved nothing. Trotsky, "vehement, serpent-like," played cleverly with resolutions. A coalition was acceptable — provided that it did not include the Cadets, which was the basis of the coalition. Irakli Tsereteli lost his normal self-control in frustration: "The next time I deal with Bolsheviks, I will insist on having a notary and two secretaries!"

The Bolsheviks walked out, while delegates "ran into the hallways, screaming, pleading, weeping." Only when he again threatened to resign was Kerensky able to persuade the rump of the conference to accept a coalition with the Cadets. The crisis, Lenin realized with glee, was ripening.

XX

The Muddlers

ON SEPTEMBER 25, Kerensky appointed a new cabinet. It was the seventh major ministerial reshuffle since March, the fourth cabinet, and the third coalition. Trotsky noted that each cabinet "moved further away from mass opinion and lasted less long than its predecessor. The new cabinet was hardly born when it began to die, and sat waiting for the undertaker." Though elections showed a swing to the left in the country, a third of the ministers were bourgeois. The chairmen of the Moscow war industries committee and stock exchange were given posts. It was clear that a further and more sweeping transition was coming — but "to what? To a German occupation? To a Bolshevik New World? To the last democratic hope, the Constituent Assembly?"

The new government received its first humiliation the day after it was formed. Kerensky saw the British, French, and Italian ambassadors in the Winter Palace. Sir George Buchanan was the senior member. Kerensky could tell from Buchanan's "faint almost girlish blush" and the moist glimmer in his eye that the Englishman was upset. Buchanan told the premier that the Allies would withdraw the military aid piling up in the Arctic ports and at Vladivostok unless he adopted rigorous measures to maintain internal order.

This was breathtaking condescension; it suggested that the Allies no longer realized what was possible in Russia, and threw Kerensky into a "mental storm." The war was crucifying his government. Could the Allies not recognize this? He summoned Somerset Maugham to the palace to ask the British agent to take a secret oral message to Lloyd George in London. Kerensky wanted Buchanan replaced by someone more sympathetic, and he pleaded with the British prime minister to enter negotiations with the Germans. The message had a desperate ring. Even a peace the Germans would refuse would do — anything that he could tell his soldiers "is being done for peace."

Otherwise, he told Maugham, when the snows arrived, "I will not be able to keep the army in the trenches. I don't see how we can go on. Of course, I don't say that to the people. I always say that we shall continue whatever happens, but unless I have something to tell my army, it's impossible." His large, sallow face reminded Maugham of a theatrical producer who, though he could "excite in others the desire to do things for him," was himself so afraid of doing the wrong thing that he would rather do nothing. Kerensky would hardly let Maugham go, talking on "as though he was too tired to stop."

Maugham had already warned London that Kerensky "is losing popularity and it is doubtful if he can last." The Germans were paying out millions to support the Bolsheviks, but London was balking at the $50,000 a year that Maugham was proposing for a program of pro-Menshevik espionage and propaganda to keep Russia in the war. The British sent a destroyer to Norway to pick up Maugham and take him to London. Before it had set to sea, King George V invited a rebellious and monarchist Russian general, Gurko, to have tea at Buckingham Palace. Kerensky was so irritated by this show of Allied contempt that he threatened to send a telegram of sympathy to Sinn Fein separatist rebels in Dublin.

The German navy won control of the Gulf of Riga at the beginning of October. Kerensky criticized the Baltic Fleet as disorganized and unreliable. "Kerensky-Bonaparte, traitor to the revolution," the sailors cabled back, "we send you our curses." Revel, the last stronghold between the Germans and Petrograd, was evacuated by the Russians on October 3. The Germans were within 250 miles of Petrograd with no reliable units facing them.

In the capital, the somber news arrived amid "dark trees waving skeleton arms in the wind . . . seagulls wheeling and flashing white wings against a dull, grey sky." People talked of a bombardment from the sea, or calculated how long it would take German ground troops to reach the city, three weeks or four. Everyone who could leave was going. The women and children in the British colony left to make their way home through Finland and Norway.

It was asked daily whether the government was going to evacuate the city. Every morning, a different decision was published in the papers, only to be contradicted in the evening. Mikhail Rodzianko, the old Duma chairman, was in favor. "I say, to hell with Petrograd," he bellowed. "People fear our central institutions in Petrograd will be destroyed. Let me say that I am glad if they are because they have brought Russia nothing but grief." The

British embassy was told in secret that it was likely to be moved to Moscow, where a Yusupov mansion would be placed at its disposal.

Barges and trucks were filled with the treasures from the Hermitage and sacks full of papers from the ministries. At the Winter Palace, Kerensky's few remaining petitioners had to squeeze past crated paintings and antiques. A barge at the quay in front of the palace was so overloaded with files from the foreign ministry that it sank. "*Nichevo,*" said watching soldiers as it went under. "It doesn't matter." Plans to "offload" key defense plants by moving them deeper into Russia away from the Germans were attacked by the Bolsheviks as a counterrevolutionary plot. Putilov workers had already demanded that the first to be offloaded should be "idlers, drones, men and women in monasteries, those who live off their incomes, those who do not work or serve."

The rumor mills that had so wounded the empress nine months before now ground at Kerensky's reputation. He used the imperial Rolls-Royce, the imperial box at the theater, the imperial bed to service his supposed string of mistresses. One of his aides was also a womanizer, and when the aide's girlfriends rang him at the Winter Palace Kerensky amused himself by answering and flirting violently with them. Kerensky became a Napoleon who "can speechify but cannot act" to the left-wing press. The right attacked him for his conceit in having, tsarlike, two aides standing rigidly to attention as he spoke.

Kerensky was tormented too by "friendly" ambassadors, rural atrocity, continual leaks by the commission investigating the Kornilov affair that suggested his complicity in it. The Bolsheviks could be held responsible for nothing. They could adapt their policy to the moment, and, where they had no policy, they had slogans. Giving land to the peasants was the main plank of the Social Revolutionaries. The Bolsheviks happily admitted to stealing this SR policy.

In the cities, the Bolsheviks spoke vaguely of "workers' control." The workers would have the factories, as the peasants would have the land. There was no economic program. Instead, the Bolshevik M. A. Larin complained in the party newspaper *Rabochy Put,* there was a vacuum. Larin had been asked to fill it as an emergency measure and did so with a Utopian brew: the national debt would be canceled, workers replace managers, and laborers earn the same as skilled men.

Every day hundreds of thousands of hungry, tired, and angry people listened to Bolshevik propaganda. It was the simplest message, carried by men who set off from Petrograd, wrapped in heavy overcoats with a shabby suitcase containing a little food and many pamphlets. "The rich have lots of everything, the poor have nothing," Sukhanov paraphrased the campaign.

"Everything will belong to the poor. . . . This is the message of your own working-class party, followed by millions — the sole party fighting against the rich and their government for land, peace, and bread."

It did not matter that it was lies — that Lenin had railed against giving land to the peasantry for fifteen years as pandering to their *burzhui* instincts, that civil war, not peace, would accompany the desire to smash existing society — for it "flooded the whole of Russia in endless waves." "After all," said the young writer Boris Pasternak, "what everybody needed were not empires, but bread, salt, and paraffin."

Pasternak thought that only a maniac could have wanted to continue the war. The only question in the air was what the next day held in store — that something was amiss was obvious to the meanest child. So the last days of September "slyly passed on the doubts and unanswered questions to a dull, foggy October."

With Lenin invisible, Trotsky was the main party figure. The mutual insults the two had exchanged during their long feud were not forgotten. Trotsky, recognizing the killing instinct in Lenin, had compared him with Robespierre to the extent that a "vulgar farce resembles historic tragedy," condemning his style as "hideous, dissolute, and demagogical." He referred to Lenin's Swiss exile as his "Zurich bird-cage." Lenin, for his part, described Trotsky as a "hollow bell," a "phrase-monger," and "Balalaykon," a slovenly and complacent chatterer.

"Trotsky, as always," Lenin had written sarcastically in 1915, "is, in principle, opposed to the Socialist Chauvinists [the defensists], but in practice he is always in agreement with them." Lenin coined the word "Trotskyist" to describe an individualist and opportunist, the reverse of the good party man. The two appeared temperamental opposites. Lenin could be mistaken for a drab-suited grocer; Trotsky dressed with panache, his collar always clean and his nails carefully manicured. Lenin was sardonic; Trotsky could belly-laugh.

Trotsky drank wine, read French novels, loved New York, was sensitive to praise, and wrote with wit and wide learning. He was courageous — a former war correspondent and a Siberian escapee — and Bruce Lockhart thought he would "willingly die fighting if there was a big enough audience to see him do it." He liked to refer to himself in the third person — "Trotsky" — but he had little pomposity. His mind was "wonderfully quick" and he had an intuitive grasp of political — and military — tactics.

Lenin, wrote Bruce Lockhart, who was to know both men well, was "impersonal and almost inhuman," his vanity "proof against all flattery." He drank little, ate badly, and was indifferent to an audience — the Russians were to see less of Lenin than they had of Nicholas II. He was brave in thought, almost recklessly so, but not in personal deed. He demanded obedience, while the key to Trotsky's spirited life — two marriages, adulation in the 1905 revolution at twenty-six, sled rides to freedom, the New World — had been his refusal to obey.

Against all odds, the two had grown closer after their return from exile. They discovered traits in common. They shared an instinct to go for the political jugular and a relish for risk. Both put the end above any qualm over means, though this tendency was more developed in Lenin. The catalyst of their rapprochement was Trotsky's newly found willingness to be led; he admired Lenin's sense of certainty and control and his ability, in a world full of talk, to "come to an essential conclusion." Trotsky thought of Lenin as "indestructible" — "it seemed as if Lenin would never wear out," he wrote later. A rare intimacy developed between them. Trotsky was to describe Lenin as "always active, alert, even-tempered, and gay." Many Bolsheviks wrote of Lenin with awe; Trotsky, almost alone, displayed affection.

Lenin recognized the younger man's brilliance and drive. Energy, physical and mental, was a rich gift in unstable times. Kerensky, though he was flagging now, had stamped himself on the revolution with an eighteen-hour day. Trotsky was capable of a similar work rate and, like Kerensky, his talents were broad. He spoke, wrote, organized, and analyzed. The telephone was invaluable — Trotsky and Kerensky both used it compulsively. But mass radio did not exist. It was not enough, as Julius Martov did, to make an eloquent speech in the Soviet and leave it at that. A speech had to be repeated elsewhere, and gutted for pamphlets and the press, before it had impact. Trotsky had tenacity as well as flair.

Lenin had offered Trotsky senior party membership back in May. Trotsky had turned him down. "Don't you know why?" Lenin said at the time. "Ambition, ambition, ambition." Trotsky remained a political freelance well into the summer. He was in the Kresty Prison when he was finally elected to the central committee, and did not attend his first meeting until two days after his release.

A jealous pique against the newcomer remained among the original Bolsheviks. Trotsky tried to offset this by his accessibility — he, and his pretty little wife, who hardly spoke anything but French, were always available for interview by the foreign press. He had a warmth and humor that non-Bolsheviks found attractive. Raymond Robins, the head of the American Red Cross mission in Russia, thought Trotsky a "four kind son of a bitch, but the greatest Jew since Jesus."

Like Lenin, Trotsky was by temperament a single-party man, instinctively opposed to power-sharing. He supported the projected coup for the same reason that Zinoviev and Kamenev opposed it: it would ruin conciliation and democratic cooperation on the left. But his misgivings were restricted to its timing. He had led the walkout from the democratic conference, and he was now preparing to do the same at its successor. The conference had appointed from among its members a Council of the Republic, or preparliament, to represent the nation until the constituent assembly met. Members of all parties were due to attend it on October 7. The Bolsheviks, in a minority, could expect nothing from it.

Lenin had opposed even the brief Bolshevik presence at the "idiotic babbling" of the democratic conference. He regarded parliaments as "despicable talking shops" and thought parliamentarianism was no more than an "example of what is rotten to teach the masses." He was outraged when the party, again ignoring him, voted to participate in the preparliament. "It is an *incorrect* tactic," Lenin fumed from Vyborg, having moved there to be closer to Petrograd while still safely in Finland. "There is no doubt that at the 'top' of our party there are numerous vacillations which may become *ruinous*." A walkout was agreed only after Trotsky's intervention.

Kerensky opened the preparliament in the Maryinsky Palace at 5:00 P.M. on October 7. The ushers and stenographers had been borrowed hastily from the Duma. Chill rains fouled the streets outside with mud and slush, which lay untouched by municipal clearance gangs. Trams were running only intermittently. Kerensky opened the proceedings with unusual humility. He asked delegates to "tell us the truth, but only the truth." The Bolsheviks at whom this was aimed were late into the hall, having just finished a bitter row over the timing of the walkout.

Trotsky, the "very incarnation" of the bourgeois caricature of a revolutionary, his "huge forehead surmounted by great masses of black, waving hair," lips "heavy and protruding," a man who struck Bruce Lockhart as "all temperament, an individual artist," caused a sensation. For most of the frock-coated *burzhui*, the "famous leader of the bandits and hooligans" was a novelty. Trotsky had become the public face of Bolshevism — Lenin absent, Zinoviev and Kamenev unhappy at the impending walkout, Bukharin too "clerkly and nervous," Stalin too young and coarse — and its perceived persona flashed in his liquid eyes and "cruel, cascading mouth."

Trotsky accused the government and the bourgeoisie of using the "bony hand of hunger" to strangle the revolution and of preparing to surrender the capital as part of a government conspiracy. This drew fury from the right, shouts about Germans and sealed trains, and a cry of "Bastard!" Unabashed, Trotsky said that the Bolsheviks had nothing in common with the preparliament or with Kerensky's "government of national treachery."

With that, the sixty Bolsheviks walked out to cries of, "Go catch your German trains." The majority were pleased to see this "particular breed of wild beast" leave the society of mankind. They gazed after them with disdain, waving their hands — "Good riddance!"

Nikolai Sukhanov was, almost alone, utterly depressed. He felt that there was "only one place for the Bolsheviks to go — to the barricade. If they cast away the electoral ballot, they must take up the rifle." They were now taking up arms against the entire old world. By the strength of their own small party alone, surrounded by millions of casual and unreliable fellow travelers, they were attempting to create an unheard-of proletarian state and a new society. "And they wanted to do this in our ruined, half-wild, petty bourgeois, economically shattered country."

Sukhanov cursed them for putting an "end to the united front of the democracy forever." The civil war that would surely follow could have been avoided, he thought. The new coalition government could "no more have lasted than any other product of Kerenskyism," and the Bolsheviks had it in their grasp to become a major factor in the preparliament. The non-Bolshevik left was splitting into Mensheviks and Menshevik Internationalists, Social Revolutionaries and Left Social Revolutionaries, the desire of the extremist wings for immediate peace and land share-outs little different from the Leninists. With this support, Sukhanov reckoned the Bolsheviks might have produced a majority and a legitimate government.

But — "all these abstract calculations would only have been significant if the Bolsheviks hadn't been Bolsheviks."

Lenin could comfort himself, in his own calculations of support, that the people were already smashing the state on his behalf. In a village near Baku a mob marched to the square, led by half a dozen ragged soldiers. Each had something red on him — an armlet, a handkerchief round the head. One of them carried a flag, a woman's red petticoat tied to a stick. An old man in the middle of the mob wore a general's uniform and was bleeding from a little cut just below the eye. Three ladies with him had loose hair and disordered clothes.

The old man raised his hand for silence. A hush fell on the mob, automatic, because a general's uniform remained a symbol of authority. The general said that he had served his tsar and country with devotion — "This my single fault. I love Russia, I love my people, I demand that you let me go!"

"*Demand!*" said the man with the flag, a red-headed peasant called Mikhail Vereshchenko, a deserter from the Galician front. "The swine demands! This is what I do, comrades, to a demanding swine." He spat in the general's face. An old crone in the crowd did likewise. She was wearing a looted evening dress in yellow silk, which she had pulled over her own clothes so that the gown had burst down one side and her gray rags showed through.

One of the general's ladies fell to her knees and begged for mercy. The red-haired man dropped his flag, took a rifle and knocked her over the head with the butt. Blood ran out of her ears. The general moved on the man. Vereshchenko ran him through the belly with his bayonet. There was a screech from the crowd. The mob turned on the two surviving ladies and trampled their bodies "like a manure heap." Two or three bayonets swayed above their heads, a "bright crimson against the sunlit walls behind."

Probably, the Cossack onlooker Maria Yurlova thought, the general had ordered thousands of men to as miserable a death. "Whichever way I looked at it," she said, "it seemed that nobody was in the right, that a murder like this condemned both the killer and the killed. And that was the final disillusion."

On the railway line into Baku, towns and villages "crouched along the track like animals." In the city, soldiers and workers were milling in the main square. A soldier claimed that the empress, being German, had sold Russian soldiers to the Germans at ten kopeks a head. Who else was responsible for the slaughter of the troops? "Speculators, Jews, and officers!" went up the cry. The stores had been looted. There were no officers around to murder.

"Those yelling soldiers," Yurlova wrote, "and the speakers throwing their arms in the sky, and a sense that no order existed . . ." The civil war implicit in the Bolshevik walkout would, those concerned knew well, extend the disorder throughout Russia.

Trotsky's tactics for the Bolshevik rising were opaque. Deception was essential. It would be wrong to organize a coup under the "bare slogan of the seizure of power by a party." The country was not in the mood for single-party power. An uprising carried out under the slogan of defending the rights of a fresh All-Russian Congress of Soviets was, he realized, something quite different. It would be "covered by the authority of the Soviet" and gain a spurious "Soviet legitimacy." Thus, "while moving forward all along the line," Trotsky later explained, "we maintained an appearance of defensiveness."

He could not do this with a properly convened Soviet Congress. The Bolsheviks would be in a minority and the majority would not accept a Bolshevik coup. Timing was crucial. Lenin was worried that the Constituent Assembly would forestall him. Elections were due to begin on November

12, with the opening session fixed for November 28. Once the people made their will known through a democratic election, the Bolsheviks could no longer claim to act on their behalf.

The Bolsheviks had no chance of outright victory in a national election. Party strength was concentrated in the big industrial and garrison town — Petrograd, Moscow, the Urals, and the northern armies and Baltic Fleet — and even here was far from a majority. The Social Revolutionaries dominated the provinces and the other armies. The coup had to take place before the election.

But how to get a Bolshevik-packed All-Russian Congress of Soviets? The Social Revolutionaries and Mensheviks were opposed to holding any Congress, fearing that it would interfere with the Constituent Assembly and give the Bolsheviks a platform for mischief-making. Trotsky was able to use his position in the Bolshevik-dominated Petrograd Soviet to have a Congress convoked for October 20. Since this was a national affair, however, the party would lack a majority. He thus strove to invite delegates only from those local Soviets, mainly in central and north Russia, where there was Bolshevik control.

This was achieved through holding a Northern Congress of Soviets, an artificial invention that, as the Soviet executive committee pointed out, had no official standing whatever. Nevertheless, this Bolshevik front invited delegates to the All-Russian Congress on blatant party lines.

It was, as Trotsky said, a well-calculated blow. The radios aboard Bolshevik-crewed battleships were used to coordinate the plan to select only Bolshevik delegates. Bolshevik agitators had a skillful campaign based on the letter "K" to whip up feeling in the chosen areas — "Do not preserve the K which leads the world to slaughter. That includes the first murderer, Kolka, Kerensky, Kornilov, the Kadets, the Kossacks, all one letter K." "Kolka" was the slang expression for Nicholas II, so well-respected in exile in old-fashioned Tobolsk, in fact, that the townsfolk were bowing and crossing themselves when they passed by his quarters in the governor's mansion. "Kadet" was the Russian rendition of the Cadet party. Trotsky was delighted with the "K" propaganda — he noted that there was "no coughing, or hawking or nose-blowing," the first signs of boredom, among audiences exposed to it.

Selection for the Congress was a farce. One Bolshevik Soviet with fifteen hundred members was asked to send five delegates, more than the whole Social Revolutionary–dominated city of Kiev. Alexander Genevsky, the member of the party's military organization who was involved in planning for the coup, was delighted. "For the first time," he said, "the Bolsheviks dominated a congress without serious opposition." *Izvestiya*, the official

Soviet newspaper, complained that the Bolsheviks were not only convening a wholly illegal pseudo-congress, but were also flouting every accepted rule for its composition.

The Soviet executive committee, still more concerned with Kornilovite reaction than Bolshevik coup, caved in. It recognized the congress, insisting only that the opening should be delayed to October 25 to allow provincial delegates time to get to Petrograd on the collapsing rail network. Trotsky had won a prize of great value, a handpicked congress, stuffed with Bolsheviks and their allies and certain to legitimize Bolshevik action.

On October 9, the panic following the fall of Revel threw up another opportunity for Trotsky. A Menshevik moved a resolution in the morning calling on the Petrograd Soviet to form a revolutionary defense committee to prepare the defense of the city against the Germans. Caught unawares, the Bolsheviks voted against it since they already had their own Bolshevik military organization, the Voenka.

In the afternoon, the Bolsheviks realized their mistake. The one problem he had not resolved, Trotsky admitted, was reconciling an armed Bolshevik force with a Soviet containing anti-Bolshevik parties. He seized on this as the way out. Provided the Voenka became its main element, there was every advantage in supporting a Soviet defense committee. It would combine Soviet respectability with Bolshevik control. It would give the Bolshevik coup military legitimacy, just as the packed Soviet Congress due to open on October 25 was designed to give it a political fig leaf. Trotsky described it as "defense-camouflage." When the Menshevik resolution came up again at the Soviet that evening, the Bolsheviks reversed their position: they would support the new defense committee, provided that the committee had full charge of the city's protection both against the Germans and what they claimed was a "fully prepared assault of the military and civil Kornilovites." The Mensheviks, well aware that by "Kornilovites" the Bolsheviks meant the Provisional Government, opposed the amendment. The defense of the city, they argued, was the responsibility of the government and the army alone.

The Mensheviks failed, however, and the amendment was passed. Renamed the Military Revolutionary Committee, or Milrevkom, the new body was empowered with the "allocation of combat and auxiliary forces . . . the elaboration of a working plan for the defense of the capital . . . protection against pogroms and desertions . . . maintenance of revolutionary discipline." With this "dry" revolution, Trotsky was later to say, nine-tenths of the rising was secured. It was a skillful piece of political engineering. Using the real threat of the Germans, and the nonexistent one of the "sheep-brained" general snugly locked up in comfortable quarters in the Bykhov

Fortress, the Bolsheviks contrived to obtain the widest possible brief for a Soviet-backed military force under their own control.

No decision to mount a coup had yet been taken. That could only be achieved by Lenin's physical presence in Petrograd. As the burning, suppression, and editing of his work had shown since March, the party had no slavish regard for Lenin as a strategist. The idolatry would come later. There was admiration for his tactical skills, in particular the simplicity and power of his slogans — by now the cry of "Peace, Land, and Bread" was resounding through Russia over and over like the beat of the surf. Against that, he had spent not much more than three months in Russia over the past ten years. His grasp of the country's realities remained suspect. The melodramatic predictions he was making at the beginning of October — that Germany, Italy, France, and Britain were on the verge of social collapse and that world revolution was imminent — suggested that his global perception was equally shaky.

Lenin was more difficult to resist in person than on paper. For then, as Trotsky wrote, the party was exposed in full measure to "this Leninist anxiety, this pressure, this criticism, this tense and revolutionary distrust." Without it, the party might not have "straightened its front at the decisive moment, because the resistance at the top was very strong." At its critical moment, the party was subject not to the inevitable force of history, but to the power of an obsessive personality. Trotsky himself was swamped, Bruce Lockhart finding him "as incapable of standing against Lenin as a flea would be against an elephant."

It is not known when or how Lenin slipped back to Petrograd on the five-hour journey from Vyborg, although rumor had it that he again crossed the frontier disguised as a locomotive fireman. It may have been as early as October 3. Although he was not to be on public display for another fortnight, it is certain that he was back by October 10. He stayed in the genteel fifth-floor apartment of a Bolshevik agronomist, Margarita Fofanova, in a comfortable new residential block on the corner of Bolshoi Sampsonievsky Prospekt on the city outskirts close to the Finland railway line. Fofanova was thirty-four and separated from her husband; she had sent her two children to their grandparents in the country on party orders. The Kshesinskaya palace was still out-of-bounds to Bolsheviks.

At 10:00 P.M. on October 10, Lenin crossed the city for the first Central Committee meeting he had attended in three months. It was held in Sukhanov's snug flat in an art deco building at the Karpovka, a comfortable block with parquet flooring, intricate stone and ironwork, and a *burzhui* clientele of lawyers and doctors. Sukhanov, a Menshevik deeply opposed to a coup, knew nothing of it. The great diarist's wife, Galina, was a Bolshevik and had suggested that her husband should sleep near his office that night.

Twelve Bolsheviks took part in the meeting, in wigs and makeup, glued-on mustaches, and false beards. That evening, Kerensky was preoccupied with plans for a visit to Mogilev. The chance for an immense haul of those plotting to overthrow him — the already famous: Trotsky, Zinoviev, Kamenev, Kollontai, Lenin; and those who would only later stir the human conscience: the secret policeman Felix Dzerzhinsky, the tsar-killer Yakov Sverdlov, the mass liquidator Joseph Stalin — passed unnoticed.

Lenin wore a wig of gray hair that sat deep on his domed brow. It had been ordered from a Helsinki wigmaker who had worked for the Maryinsky Theater and whose normal clientele were aristocrats. He had been puzzled at Lenin's insistence on a gray model, for most of his customers wanted to look younger. Lenin wore glasses and had shaved his beard. Alexandra Kollontai thought he looked "every inch the Lutheran minister." Gregory Zinoviev, his shock of hair a trademark, had shaved his head and wore a beard.

Yakov Sverdlov, a party fixer and organizer whose fierce black eyes under his pince-nez reminded Bruce Lockhart of a "Spanish inquisitor," opened proceedings with a rambling denunciation of a "new Kornilov-type plot" that was supposed to be going on in Minsk. Lenin spoke for an hour by candlelight — the power was off. He said that the time would never be riper for a rising. He claimed that a mutiny in the German navy — a small affair, in fact, which had already been put down — was simply an extreme manifestation of the growth throughout Europe of the "world-wide Socialist revolution." Internally, there was a "shift of the people's confidence toward our party." To wait for the Constituent Assembly would be suicidal, for the voting "will obviously not be on our side."

The dangers were clear to Kamenev and Zinoviev. The rising might alienate the "huge third camp" of the small bourgeoisie, shopkeepers, minor officials, and substantial peasants. "Comrade Lenin's proposal means to stake on a single card the fate of our party and the future of the Russian and the world revolution," said Kamenev. "We have no right to stake the future on an armed uprising."

Toward 3:00 A.M. Lenin took a child's squared exercise book and wrote a resolution in pencil in it: "Recognizing . . . that an armed rising is inevitable and that its time has come, the Central Committee suggests that all party organizations be guided by this." No timing was agreed on, Trotsky continuing to insist that the rising should appear to be linked to the Soviet Congress and must await its convocation. A vote was taken. Kamenev and Zinoviev continued to dissent, but the resolution was passed. The exhausted conspirators broke off for a breakfast of black bread, cheese, and carrot tea — queueing for ordinary tea took five hours — before setting off into the sleet-sluiced streets to pass the word — "It's time to move from words to deeds."

Party agitators were not the only ones privy to the conspiracy. Most of Petrograd knew that the Bolsheviks were planning something. "Literally every edition of the bourgeois papers shrieked about the Bolshevik preparations for an attack," admitted Alexander Genevsky. "Even an approximate date was marked — October 25." Nadezhda Alliluyeva, the sixteen-year-old schoolgirl daughter of the family Joseph Stalin was staying with, who was growing fond of the lodger, wrote to a girlfriend, "There are rumors going around that the Bolsheviks are going to do something but there's probably nothing to it."

No one was fooled when the Bolsheviks put forward an obscure teenage Left Social Revolutionary medical orderly, Pavel Lazimir, rather than one of their own, to become chairman of the Milrevkom on October 16. "The Bolsheviks won't answer the straight question of whether they are preparing a coup," a Menshevik complained. "The projected Milrevkom is nothing but a revolutionary staff for the seizure of power."

"In whose name does he ask this question?" taunted Trotsky. "In the name of Kerensky, of counterintelligence, the secret police, or some other body?" He won some laughter, but the Menshevik point was made. The real power in the Milrevkom lay with Bolshevik figures familiar from the July Days, Trotsky and the Voenka leaders Nikolai Podvoisky and Vladimir Nevsky.

The cabinet met on October 16. It issued a brief statement that the "most resolute measures would be taken and were being taken" against a Bolshevik rising. Kerensky flirted with drafting Cossacks and bicycle troops into the capital. There was no deep alarm. A coup was unlikely now that it had lost any element of surprise. The Bolsheviks had bungled in July — "Can they really be such bunglers still that they advertise their position?" Kerensky was assured by the Petrograd chief of staff that, though the Bolsheviks were planning a protest demonstration, it would be peaceful. Sukhanov was surprised that Kerensky did not move now, but found the "inflated puppets" in the Winter Palace felt confident.

It looked as though Kerensky was right.

A Bolshevik Central Committee meeting was held the same evening. The Voenka men responsible for getting units in place and plans ready wanted more time. Podvoisky insisted on a ten-day delay, citing reports from the grass roots. Vasilevsky Island was not militant, Narva not ready for action;

in Kronstadt, "morale has fallen and the local garrison there is no good for anything in a militant sense. . . . No one is ready to rush into the streets." Comrade after comrade continued the litany. V. V. Shmidt of the trade union section said that demonstrations could not be expected, because of the fear of dismissals. As the economy fell deeper into chaos, thousands were being laid off from plants. Alexander Shlyapnikov added, "A Bolshevik rising is not popular, rumors of it even produce panic."

The minutes showed Lenin's reaction to this tale of woe: "He sees no pessimism in what is being said here. He shows that the bourgeoisie do not have large forces on their side." To Kamenev and Zinoviev, this was absurd. "We have no machinery for an uprising," Lev Kamenev said. "Our enemies have much stronger machinery and it has probably got stronger this week." Zinoviev moved a resolution that only "reconnaissance" and not action should be allowed. Though Zinoviev lost, six supported him, with fifteen against.

Lenin did not get back to the Fofanova apartment until 4:00 A.M., exhausted by the strains of the conspiracy, the late hours, the trip across the city through slushy and darkened streets. His wig fell off and dropped in the mud. He arrived carrying it, too dirty to wear, in his hand. Margarita Fofanova agreed to give it a good going-over with soap and water.

Lenin was worried about his disguise. He lived in a small room in the apartment and put the wig on when he went into other rooms for fear of unexpected visitors. He never got the hang of wearing the wig. "He kept trying to straighten it," Fofanova wrote, "and he was always asking people if he had got it on properly." He refused to go out onto the little wrought-iron balcony, except to check the state of the drainpipe for use as an emergency exit. He had to rely on Fofanova to bring him the newspapers, his only real source of news, which he worked through, underlining articles in blue pencils. He suffered headaches.

On October 17, Maxim Gorky's *Novaya Zhizn,* which had a big working-class circulation, carried an editorial confirming — for those who still needed confirmation — that the Bolsheviks were preparing a "criminal" insurrection. It said that leading party figures were anonymously circulating leaflets against the rising.

Lenin furiously dashed off a letter to the Bolshevik paper *Rabochy Put* saying that there must be agitation "*in favor* of a rising. Let our anonymous individuals come right out into the light of day and let them bear the *punishment* they deserve for their *shameful vacillation.*" The letter came out on October 18, its prompt publication making it clear that Lenin was back in Petrograd, something that his wig and makeup were studiously designed to avoid.

The "anonymous vacillators" came out into the open in *Novaya Zhizn* the same morning; Kamenev and Zinoviev declared in a joint article that they were opposed to the party taking any armed move in the immediate future. They stressed that a large group of their colleagues shared their belief that insurrection would be "inadmissible and fatal to both the proletariat and the revolution. . . . To risk the fate of the party, the proletariat, and the revolution and rise up in the next few days — would be to commit an act of despair."

Gorky attacked the Bolsheviks in the same issue. He said that Petrograd, as in July, could expect to see trucks packed with people holding rifles "in hands trembling with fear" who would shoot "at the windows of stores, at people, at anything. . . . People will kill each other, unable to suppress their own animal stupidity." Gorky called on the Central Committee to refute the rumors that it was controlled by "crazed fanatics."

Cooped up in his room in the Fofanova apartments, Lenin feared that Trotsky would turn against the coup. His suspicions were unfounded. Sukhanov watched Trotsky working a crowd of three thousand. Leather coat flying, eyes intense behind the pince-nez, Trotsky painted in the misery of the trenches. "Soviet power" would end it. There was suffering and hunger — the Bolsheviks would send "a soldier, a sailor, and a working girl" into every village, and they would come back "with the stores of the rich." "The Soviet government will give everything the country has to the poor and to the soldiers at the front," Trotsky went on. "You, *burzhui,* you own two coats? Give one to the soldier freezing in the trenches. You have warm boots? Stay at home. Your boots are needed by a worker."

The crowd "verged on ecstasy" and Sukhanov thought they would burst into a religious hymn at any moment. Trotsky was talking of defense, not of the aggressive coup he planned, and who could resist? As one, there was a mass of "uplifted hands and burning eyes."

Sukhanov watched with an "unusually *heavy* heart." Trotsky knew what he was doing well enough — the "essential thing was the *mood.*" But the Bolshevik ideas were no more than the "most fantastic notions." The smashing of the credit system, the seizure of banks, parity of wages, the "crazy notion" that factory workers could administer a state — Sukhanov thought that "all these 'ideas' were, first, so disproportionately few in comparison with the immensity of the tasks, and second, so unknown to anyone in the Bolshevik party, that you might say that they were completely irrelevant."

Lenin fretted over the party's military incompetence. Late on October 19, he summoned the chieftains of the military organization — Vladimir Nevsky, Vladimir Antonov-Ovseenko, and Nikolai Podvoisky — to a meeting in an apartment a few blocks away from the Fofanova hideaway. He sat

Podvoisky on a sofa and peppered him with questions about Red Guard commanders. Podvoisky described one as a wonderful fellow. "Is he a good shot?" asked Lenin. "Can he fire a big gun? Can he drive a vehicle if necessary?"

Podvoisky said he did not know that sort of detail. "How are you going to direct a rising if you don't know what sort of men your commanders are?" said Lenin. "It's not enough that they are good agitators.... An uprising is not a meeting to listen to speeches." Podvoisky was tired. After a long day spent trying to organize the coup, he had traveled out from the Smolny to meet a man in a wig who now demanded that all Red Guard commanders without training in street fighting should be replaced immediately. The Red Guards had no proper command structure, and their training was at best a few hours of drilling in a factory yard.

Against that, on paper Kerensky could call on scores of thousands of experienced professionals. But the premier's moral force was spent. Everything was breaking up "like ice on a river in spring," the art critic Mikhail Babenchskov thought. Babenchskov saw Kerensky as a man who had stopped at the bank. Beyond him a Bolshevik strode on, though the ice was splitting under his feet, ignoring the dangers, "his eyes fixed on some point far ahead, avidly breathing in the cold wind off the sea."

Zinaïda Gippius telephoned Blok to ask him to write for the anti-Bolshevik paper *Chas — The Hour*. He refused. "You don't want to be with us," she said. "I suppose you're not with the Bolsheviks by any chance, are you?"

"Yes," said Blok. "If you put it that way, I am more with the Bolsheviks."

Brandy and morphine, Kerensky's secretary said, had become "the only way he can keep up." His kidney was troubling him — his doctor had ordered him to drink only milk — and he was suffering from stomach cramps. "He really is hysterical," the secretary told Louise Bryant. "He weeps here, and he is so dreadfully alone. I mean, he cannot depend on anybody." Olga and his two boys were never seen in the Winter Palace and there was no domesticity to offset his growing exhaustion. The secretary thought he could not take much more of it, and that "we're going to wake up one day without a Provisional Government."

Kerensky was in a black depression when Bryant spoke to him in mid-October, in Nicholas II's beautiful little private library with its bound set of Jack London novels and stories in English. She noted that he seemed less cultured than Trotsky or Lenin, speaking only Russian and a few words of French.

As a man, Louise Bryant preferred Kerensky to Lenin. She said that any reporter interviewing both would favor Kerensky "because he *liked* him best." The premier had "personality plus — one cannot but be charmed by his wit and friendliness. . . . Lenin is sheer intellect — he is absorbed, cold and unattractive." She thought that Lenin was politically the more dogged and thorough, with "all the qualities of a 'chief' including the absolute moral indifference which is so essential to such a part." And, despite his intellect, Lenin's propaganda appeals were marvels of simplicity, where Kerensky resorted to theatrics.

Kerensky told her that the people had lost the will to resist. He was pinning his last hopes on the Constituent Assembly. "It must be the deciding factor, one way or the other," he said. Bryant was not sure he would last that long, the news from the country was so bad.

Blok had dreamed in August of "yellowish brown billows of smoke . . . menacing the villages, bushes and grass flaming in wide strips, and God sends no rain and the crops have burned and what there is still will burn." Now, in the welling October madness, his own country estate at Shakmatovo fell victim. The family factotum, Nikolai Lapin, wrote to Blok's mother, stubbornly, in the old style, addressing her as "Your Excellency Gracious Lady." The mob had swept up the gravel drive to the house, with its big colonnaded porch, and "executed devastation. Such outrage and hooliganism there is no describing." Blok's writing table was broken open with an axe and the drawers rooted through. The library door was smashed in.

"They played on the piano, smoked, spat, tried on the *barin's* caps, took the binoculars, the dagger, knives, money, medals and what more I don't know," Lapin reported. "I felt sick and went away." He managed to sell a thoroughbred horse, all that was left, for 230 rubles. He warned Blok's mother that he had been told to inform on her if she came. "There are people who are sorry for you," he concluded. "And people who hate you."

The weather had been hot through most of the summer, with delayed frosts and excellent winter crop shoots throughout European Russia. There were no natural, only human, reasons for the incipient starvation. "There is no scarcity of food in Russia," said David Francis, "but very imperfect and inadequate transport." The breadline outside a bakery near the U.S. embassy stretched for two blocks. *Iskri* had photographs of food trains looted by soldiers along the Volga near Kamyshin. The ruins of the Mariankova model estate smoldered in front of the camera. The estate laboratories had experimented with high-yield sugar beet. All its best seeds had been destroyed.

Russkiya Vedomosti apologized to its readers that it had room to print only a fraction of the mutinies and pogroms that flooded daily into its newsroom. Kharkov, Tambov, and Ostrog "merge into one dark picture of murders, pillages, arsons, and debauch." Mobs ferreted for axes and crowbars to break into liquor cellars. Landowners and shopkeepers suspected of speculation were beaten to death with clubs, and the same fate "awaits Jews, just because they are Jews." Members of land committees were kicked senseless by the mobs that had elected them. In Rostov, the town hall was dynamited. Gangs of deserters made road travel dangerous in Pskov.

Autumn with the *muzhiks,* Trotsky noted with satisfaction, was the time for politics. "The fields are mowed, illusions are scattered, patience is exhausted. Time to finish things up!" The politics were not Bolshevik and agitators continued to be beaten, but the hostility did not inconvenience the party. The conspiracy was restricted to the capital. The fury in the provinces assisted by underscoring Kerensky's impotence.

In Tobolsk, sullen guards refused to allow the imperial family to drink a case of wine that had been sent from Petrograd with Kerensky's permission. The bottles were thrown into the river unopened. The Tobolsk commissar, ignoring Kerensky's orders to treat the tsar with humanity and politeness, insisted that Nicholas be photographed for his files full face and profile, "as your police photographed us."

On October 20, Kerensky made a final attempt to bring the army to heel. Any unit that repeatedly flouted orders was to be designated a penal unit, a status that could be applied to entire divisions. Its troops were to be fed prisoners' rations. No leave or promotions would be granted and pay would be at prerevolutionary rates — the ruble had lost three-quarters of its value since March.

Kerensky was undermined by his war minister the same evening. Alexander Verkhovsky declared that the government must sue for peace at once, to "take the ground from under Bolshevik feet. . . . We cannot fight." It was the first time a minister had stated the obvious so baldly. Mikhail Tereshchenko gave up fathoming a government that talked of penal units and peace on the same day. "C'est un maison de fous," he said — a madhouse.

Kerensky, furious, dismissed Verkhovsky the next day. He did not wish to alarm the public, however. A story was concocted that Verkhovsky was being sent on a fortnight's rest cure and that his replacement, General A. A. Manikovsky, was deputizing for him. Dr. Nikolai Kishkin, the psychiatrist and welfare minister, had his own chilly vision of a lunatic who sacked the war minister on the eve of a coup.

"Passivity and indecision are the symptoms of our government's mental illness," Dr. Kishkin said. "Our premier should be blamed for the whole distressing situation."

*   *   *

The target area for the coup was equally passive. The rich were having a last dance in Petrograd. Louise Bryant found it odd to go to Holy Russia and find it so apparently unholy. The shrines along the streets loomed black, unlit and forgotten. Eight months before, nobody had passed a church without crossing himself: now only the odd passerby made the gesture, absentmindedly, like an old courtier bowing to a dead king. The final scraps of the old banquet of tsarism were being devoured, and everything could be had for big money. Cab drivers were charging five rubles for the ten-minute ride from the French embassy to the Hotel de l'Europe, twenty times the prewar rate. Soldiers hired themselves out by the hour to wait in queues, and sold off their chocolate rations at eleven rubles the pound.

Donon's restaurant on the Moika was packed at lunchtime and Rasputin's favorite, The Bear, served stylish Georgian dinners. Electricity was cut off at midnight, for economy of coal and fear of raids by Zeppelin airships. Devotional candles were stolen from churches, and gambling clubs were "champagne sparkles by candlelight" into the early hours, with twenty-thousand-ruble stakes. Officers still clicked their spurs accurately and wore their gold-trimmed crimson *bashliki* and Caucasian swords in brothels and hotel lobbies. Prostitutes in jewels and expensive furs walked up and down, and crowded the cafés.

Felix Yusupov was back from the Crimea to liberate more paintings and jewels. He found social life agreeable once more and gave supper parties in the palace on the Moika. He spent one evening at Tsarskoe Selo, where the daughters of Grand Duke Paul Alexandrovich performed a play written in French by their brother. The daughters of noblemen and rich *maradiors*, ghouls or speculators, arrived to study at the conservatory or to trawl for husbands.

The *maradiors* were having a vintage month. The American journalist John Reed, newly married to Louise Bryant, knew three brothers who had never known such profits. One gambled in foodstuffs, with coffee bought in Vladivostok for two rubles a pound selling in Petrograd for thirteen. Another sold gold from the Lena mines to mysterious parties in Finland. The third owned a chocolate factory. The stock exchange had a flurry of activity, with Russian "Fives" putting on 2 rubles, to 71.5, and the *Economist* noting a smart recovery in Baku oil stocks.

Life was back to normal after the alarms of Kornilov. Sukhanov, touring barracks and factories, found 'no desire for fresh adventures.' A girl of good family burst into tears when a tram conductress called her "comrade," thinking such liberties were past. A group of monarchists were confident enough to break up a performance of the burlesque *Sins of the Tsars* at the Troitsky comedy theater, threatening to lynch the cast for "insulting the

Emperor." *Iskri* ran a sympathetic story about the governor's house in Tobolsk where the emperor was held, saying that his four daughters had to share two bedrooms. "There is no garden either," the magazine noted, "so they cannot go out for walks."

In the Petrograd salons, Mikhail Rodzianko was raising funds for a secret plan to create a force of White Guards. The units were to be disguised as depots for winter training. Colonel Georgy Polkovnikov, commanding the Petrograd military district, gave daily press conferences. The message was always the same: "All necessary measures have been taken for the suppression of any uprising." Ambassador Francis, not convinced, chartered a small steamer to stand by to evacuate Americans from the capital if necessary.

Lenin remained in the Fofanova coop, fearing to emerge, spewing out his bile on the "*blacklegs*" Kamenev and Zinoviev for "*betraying* to Kerensky the decision to conceal from the enemy preparations for the insurrection and the date appointed for it." The conspirators were bickering among themselves over the shattering of surprise, the master element in a coup. If any trouble came, the mine owner Mikhail Auerbach was reassured by a deputy minister, it would pass like the next storm in a series — "sleep well."

Only Trotsky maintained a high profile among the conspirators. He rushed from factory to barracks, seeming "to be speaking at all points simultaneously." His message — he was accusing the government of "outrageous counterrevolution" in allowing the the near-bankrupt tram system to charge soldiers five kopeks a ride — appeared more hysterical than menacing.

The others were unknowns. Sukhanov saw deference paid to a "short fellow with a modest look, pince-nez, a black goatee, and flashing Jewish eyes," and had to ask who it was. It was Yakov Sverdlov, who in a few days would be titular head of Russia.

The preparliament sat day after day in the Maryinsky Palace, a "hostile, divided house," unable to carry out a single measure. Mensheviks and Menshevik Internationalists, Social Revolutionaries and Left Social Revolutionaries squabbled among themselves and with the Cadets in the seats opposite. The fragmented left bickered with Cadets, who had attracted all the "dark forces" of reaction, so that a party that was "once honest and liberal has become hated and despised," while all the time "people left their old parties and joined the absent Bolsheviks."

XXI

"We Had the Revolution Last Night"

IT WAS AN ENDURING MYTH that Lenin had created a party with a unique and disciplined core of professional revolutionaries. Lenin himself believed it. In his centrally heated hideout, he saw the rising as a carefully planned operation, in which loyal regiments and insurgent detachments of workers, connected by telephone to all the points of armed fighting, would strike at predetermined targets to a strict timetable. Lenin had read his Clausewitz, and he was convinced that the "*technical* preparation" of insurrection was all-important, and that it had been mastered.

In the event, timekeeping was so vague that no one — rebel or loyalist — was able to say at what hour or on what day the rising began. The mayor of Petrograd was obliged at one stage to send a delegation to ask the participants if it was already underway. They were unable to give a categorical reply. The Bolsheviks had so little military experience that Alexander Genevsky — a temporary lieutenant who had been gassed after a few months at the front and declared unfit for active service — was asked to become a "general." He was instructed to keep in touch with Podvoisky by ringing a Smolny telephone number, 148-11, but found it engaged when it was not out of order. Failure to master the telephone system reduced the rebels to sending runners through the streets. The key force of sailors arrived a day late. Lenin himself was in hiding for much of the coup, and an embarrassment when he came out of it.

The rising was a lash-up, tied together with string, kept in the air by the skill of Trotsky and his craftiness in flying it under false colors. It survived largely because the enemy was initially reluctant to take it as a serious threat and because the bulk of onlookers — workers, soldiers, officers, *burzhui*, politicians — gave a collective shrug and declared themselves neutral.

Neutrality was the key, for it enabled a small number of players to struggle for a prize — control of the capital — quite beyond their natural strength. Trotsky claimed that the overwhelming mass of the garrison was "standing openly on the side of the workers." Both soldiers and workers were in fact standing on the sidelines. Sukhanov thought that at best a tenth of the garrison was actively pro-Bolshevik and "very likely many fewer."

That was generous. Trotsky's mass turned out to be rather less than 5 percent of the quarter of a million men garrisoned in and around the city. Worker support was less still. It was not a spontaneous and popular rising, like the great wave of February, but a coup whose success rested on the yet greater indifference accorded to Kerensky. The nominal supreme commander of nine million men was reduced to some bicyclists, women volunteers, a few Cossacks, half-trained officer cadets, and forty war invalids commanded by an officer with artificial legs.

Most onlookers, remembering the July rout, believed that a Bolshevik coup would lead to a countercoup from the right. Some right-wingers relished the prospect of a Bolshevik coup. Stepan Liazonov, an industrialist known as the "Russian Rockefeller," told John Reed that the Bolsheviks would not last a day. "The government can declare a state of siege," Liazonov said, "and the military commander can deal with these gentlemen without legal formalities." David Francis, the U.S. ambassador, thought sadly that this opportunity might be lost. "Beginning to think the Bolsheviks will make no demonstrations," he cabled Washington. "If so, shall regret as believe sentiment turning against them and time opportune for giving them a wholesome lesson."

Francis's disappointment was premature. On Saturday, October 21, garrison delegates gave Trotsky a rapturous ovation and promised allegiance to the Milrevkom. They did so on the spurious grounds that the Milrevkom was an authority properly constituted by the Soviet for defense against counterrevolution. About two hundred Milrevkom commissars, nearly all Bolsheviks and many, like Trotsky, on parole for their part in the July Days, were sent out to the regiments. They told the men that no orders were valid unless signed by the Milrevkom.

It was mutiny to deny the government command of the garrison in its own capital, but Kerensky was reluctant to treat it as such. On Saturday night, Milrevkom delegates were sent to Colonel Polkovnikov to insist that three commissars should countersign all staff orders. It was a stupid and potentially dangerous move; the conspirators were showing their hand before their forces were in place. Polkolnikov could have had the delegates arrested on the spot. Instead, he politely refused to accept their demand, and took no further action beyond providing them with a car for their return journey — the last trams of the night had stopped running — and calling a staff meeting.

The staff reassured itself that nothing serious was afoot — after a brief exchange of opinions no definite decisions were taken," *Rech* reported the next day. Kerensky turned down an offer to organize an anti-Bolshevik force from the fifteen thousand officers in the city. Many of them spent the following days getting drunk in disgust.

Ten cadets turned up unexpectedly late that night at the British embassy to protect it against possible disorders. The diplomats were more concerned than Kerensky. "I only hope they do come out," the premier told Buchanan, "and then I will put them down." The headquarters of government forces, the military staff in the Mikhailovsky Palace, remained unguarded. Nobody entering it was as much as asked for identification. Milrevkom commissars had installed themselves in the Cartridge Factory plant, and fresh ammunition would only be issued now on their orders.

Trouble was expected on Sunday, October 22. Cossack units planning a religious procession canceled it to reduce the tension in the city. The rest of the day passed without incident. Vladimir Antonov-Ovseenko, a thirty-three-year-old journalist and former officer from a military family, was finalizing Bolshevik strategy. He had been an army captain before being sentenced to death for inciting mutiny in 1905 and fleeing to Paris. He had returned in May. He looked more like a poet than a military man, his face delicate, his hair long and bushy, and usually he wore a bow tie. Instead of concentrating his nebulous forces on a few key targets, Antonov drew up a list that included almost every landmark in the city — the Winter, Tauride, and Maryinsky palaces, every railway station, banks, telephone exchanges, warehouses, and municipal electricity and water works.

He forgot, however, to include the defense of his own headquarters. The Smolny was the new seat of the Soviet, and home to the Bolsheviks after the loss of the Kshesinskaya palace. Long gray blocks under a blue-and-gold cupola, this former boarding school for the daughters of the nobility was sited at the beginning of the long westward bend of the Neva. The doors off its cavernous dark corridors still bore the names of vanished teachers of French, mathematics, biology, and drama. The Soviet Congress was scheduled to meet in its brilliant white-and-gold ballroom, and the Milrevkom was centered in a shabby room on the top floor.

No unit had been earmarked for its defense. Neither had Antonov calculated how long it would take for the sailors of the Baltic Fleet to arrive from Helsinki and Kronstadt. They were likely to be his main strike force, in view of the indifference of the soldiers barracked in the capital.

Kerensky threatened energetic measures if the Milrevkom did not renounce its claim to command the garrison. He took none on Sunday although, acknowledging for the first time that all was not well, he abandoned the Alexander III suite in the Winter Palace that night and slept in the General Staff building across the square. Government defense forces in the center of the city consisted of a little under seven hundred teenage cadets from military schools, forty bicycle troops and thirty-seven officers, and some volunteer invalids. Kerensky was confident that "we have more strength than we need."

It was as well for his peace of mind that he was not relying on the forces in the trenches. As he slept, a cable came in from the commissar of the western front; the entire command structure, it said, was crushed by the elemental scale of violence and Bolshevization. The mood "is panic. There is nothing left but to give up. Disintegration has reached its limit." On the northern front, "gaunt and bootless men sickened in the mud of desperate trenches."

Kerensky awoke on Monday, October 23, to headlines about the Verkhovsky affair. The rabidly patriotic *Obshcheye Delo* was claiming that "General Von der Verkhovsky" was proposing a secret separate peace with Germany. "Citizens, save Russia!" it cried. "To your feet! Russia is being betrayed!" To leaf through the newspapers that morning was to guarantee confusion. On the far right, the war minister — although now on his "rest cure" — was accused of selling the nation to the kaiser. In the center, a Bolshevik coup was predicted as a racing certainty. The Bolshevik press wrote luridly of a Kornilovite counterrevolution.

Evidence of the Bolshevik coup, however, abounded at the Smolny. The girls' school had a disheveled but nonetheless military air. "Everything was dirty and untidy and smelt of cheap tobacco, boots, and damp greatcoats," Sukhanov observed. "Armed groups of soldiers, sailors, and workers scurried about. Gray wolves lived in the Smolny now, and they were going on with their work."

Mikhail Tereshchenko lunched at the British embassy. The young foreign minister dismissed with a laugh the idea that the coup had begun. He was, the ambassador's daughter Meriel Buchanan said, "perfectly confident that they would be able to deal with the rising if it happened." After the liqueurs, he strode out unconcerned into the sour twilight. At 7:00 P.M., Trotsky was claiming gaily in the Soviet session at the Smolny that "an insurrection is going on."

Kerensky was in session with his ministers and the General Staff officers deep into Monday night. A proposal to arrest the members of the Milrevkom was postponed. The latest justice minister, Pavel Malyantovich, had been Trotsky's defense counsel at his trial in 1905 and still had a sympathy for his former client. Kerensky felt it necessary to get the backing of the preparliament before so provocative a step was taken. He did, for the first time, approve of troops being brought into the capital. Orders were given for another company of cadets, a rifle regiment, the First Women's Battalion, and a battery of horse-drawn artillery to move to the Winter Palace.

There was still no question of forming attack groups. Measures were defensive. It was agreed that all owners should be called on to place their automobiles at the disposal of the General Staff, to prevent the rebels seizing them. No revolvers were to be sold without permits. The Milrevkom commissars were to be removed. But no *burzhui* was willing to hand over his car, and the staff was to become a net loser of automobiles. Rifles were being distributed to workers. The commissars stayed put.

Three active steps were taken. The Bolshevik papers were to be suppressed — together with a couple of far-right publications for balance — the telephone lines to the Smolny disconnected, and the Neva bridges raised. Soldiers of the pro-Bolshevik Pavlovsky Regiment were on duty in the General Staff building and passed these details on to the conspirators. The government knew what the rebels were doing, and the rebels knew what the government was doing.

Late that night in the still-undefended Smolny, the American journalist John Reed met a Bolshevik with a revolver. "The game is on," the man said dramatically. "Whether we move or not the other side knows it must finish us or be finished." The Oregon-born, Harvard-educated son of a judge, Reed was at thirty reporting for the leading socialist journal in the United States, *The Masses*. He had been a member of the Harvard swimming team and the editorial board of the *Lampoon* before joining the staff of *The Masses* in 1913. The following year he was arrested in Paterson, New Jersey, for inciting a strike among silk mill workers. As a war correspondent he had won a major reputation reporting on the Mexican revolution. Tall, handsome and light-hearted, Reed had married the intense and pretty Louise Bryant a few days after the Rasputin murder. The newlyweds had shipped out of New York for Russia in July, Reed escaping a charge of sedition for an antiwar article — "knit a straitjacket for your soldier boy" — in *The Masses*. His sympathies were with the Bolsheviks, and he was excited that the standoff was crumbling.

In the predawn dark of Tuesday, October 24, a detachment of cadets broke into the print shop of the Bolshevik newspapers *Rabochy Put* and *Soldat,* smashed the printing plates, and sealed the doors with sealing wax. Trotsky was jubilant. "Although an insurrection can only win on the offensive," he wrote, "it develops better the more it looks like self-defense." A piece of official sealing wax on Bolshevik doors might not amount to much as a military measure, but "what a superb signal for battle!" The Milrevkom called on the garrison to defend the Soviet against the "counterrevolutionary conspirators."

Kerensky watched loyal troops take possession of the Neva bridges from a window on the top floor of the Winter Palace. At midday, he went to the Maryinsky Palace to get a vote of confidence from the preparliament. White, excited, his eyes red with sleeplessness, he said that he thought it best "first to give the people every opportunity of rectifying their conscious or unconscious error." "But that's just what's bad," came the frustrated shout from the right. "All days of grace are now past," Kerensky answered, "with special attention for Bronstein-Trotsky." The Milrevkom was to be arrested.

As he spoke, Kerensky was handed a telegram from the Milrevkom to the garrison, ordering it to "make ready for battle." It suited him as well as sealing wax had Trotsky. With a lawyer's glee, Kerensky said with slow drama, "Those who dare to lift their hand against the state are liable to immediate, decisive, and permanent liquidation." The Mensheviks laughed at his theatricality.

"The Provisional Government is constantly being reproached with . . ." he went on. "Silliness!" cried the stooped Julius Martov, to more laughter. " . . . with weakness and extraordinary patience," Kerensky continued. "No one has the right to say that for the whole time I've been at its head, it has resorted to any measures of pressure whatever until the state was threatened with immediate danger and destruction." With its pride in decency and its indecision, it was a fitting valedictory for his government. Finally, the applause came. Kerensky left before a vote was taken, certain of support.

On his way out he saw Sukhanov, who had often taunted him. With a "resolute gesture, but a glum look, he stretched out his hand," the diarist wrote. "I never saw him again."

The Milrevkom remained disconnected from the telephone system. Its couriers ran through the streets or caught trams with orders. It had, however, a wireless station of sorts. The crew of the cruiser *Aurora*, moored in the Neva, had disobeyed government orders to leave the river. Trotsky ordered its radio room to instruct any listeners to its broadcasts to "sit continually, accumulating all possible information on the plans of the conspirators." The city was uncertain who was conspiring against whom. A company of pro-Bolshevik Litovsky guardsmen told the militiamen outside the *Rabochy Put* plant that the orders to close it were illegal. The militiamen duly removed the seals and the print run was resumed with new plates.

Military cadets and the girls from the First Women's Battalion were in charge of the government's bridge-lifting operation. The Liteiny Bridge remained down after its squad of cadets was disarmed by Bolsheviks. Alexander Genevsky, commanding a mixed Bolshevik squad of Grenadiers and chemical engineers, removed part of the machinery to immobilize it. There was no fighting — "neither side felt like a serious brawl," Sukhanov thought. The Nikolaevsky Bridge was raised in the morning. In the afternoon, the Milrevkom ordered the crew of the *Aurora* to lower it. The captain refused, but after he allowed himself to be symbolically arrested the cruiser was brought up to the bridge and it was lowered. The women at the Troitsky Bridge were baffled by the lifting machinery and failed to raise it.

The chaos at the bridges, traditional trouble points, unnerved the city. At around 2:00 P.M. government offices and shops began closing. On the Nevsky, hooligans looted passersby, tearing clothes, shoes, boots, and jewelry from them. Government pickets got into furious arguments with motorists who refused to hand over their cars. No lamps had been lit in the dusk. A mass of people rushed to get across the Troitsky Bridge before it closed, cab-drivers whipping up their tired horses to a frenzied gallop, motors hooting desperately, tram bells clanging. Gray on the gray Neva, thin blocks of ice scraped the hull of the *Aurora* and half-frozen flakes of snow drifted out of leaden skies from the sea.

A delegation from the city hall arrived at the Smolny to ask on behalf of the mayor whether a rising was taking place. Trotsky told them that it was, although not a shot had been fired and they were unconvinced. Trotsky found it a sweet moment. A few weeks ago the Bolsheviks had been no more than a "trademark, without printing press, without treasury, without departments." Now the mayor was asking the Milrevkom, for whom arrest warrants were now out, what was to be the fate of the capital and the nation.

In a casual way, the Milrevkom began to take the initiative. Two unarmed commissars were sent at 5:00 P.M. to take over the central telephone exchange. The office was being guarded at Colonel Polkolnikov's orders by a detachment from the Kexholm Regiment, which was sympathetic to the Bolsheviks. After an argument, the switchboard operators agreed that the commissars could stay. The lines to the Smolny were restored and the exchange was noted as being under Milrevkom control. Since the commissars had no technical knowledge, and the operators refused to cut government lines themselves, it was a prize of dubious worth.

A coded telegram was sent to Lenin's young devotee Ivar Smilga in Helsinki: "Send regulations." This was the signal to dispatch fifteen hundred sailors from the Baltic Fleet, the main Bolshevik strike force. It was not received until midnight, and it took a further two hours to round up the sleepy seamen. Cadets from the Pavlovsky Academy refused to obey government orders to move out of their barracks for fear of the Grenadiers stationed nearby. For their part, the Grenadiers ignored appeals from the Milrevkom for fear of the cadets.

The preparliament resumed at 6:00 P.M. in the Maryinsky Palace. It was in a mood to cry plague on both houses. Fedor Dan spoke for the Social Revolutionary–Menshevik bloc. Dan was anti-Bolshevik enough — he was responsible for the vigorous anti-coup line in *Izvestiya* — but he was married to Julius Martov's sister, and had caught his brother-in-law's famous indecision. "The bulk of the working class will not embark on the criminal adventure the Bolsheviks are urging on it," Dan said. "But while we wish to struggle against Bolshevism in the most decisive way, we do not wish to be an instrument in the hands of the counterrevolution."

Martov, limping on one leg, exchanged bitter repartee with a right-wing delegate who jeered him as a minister in the future Bolshevik government. Martov retorted, "I am short-sighted and cannot see whether that was a former minister of Kornilov's cabinet. . . . In no circumstances shall we collaborate with Kornilovites." Martov's formula, negative to both Bolsheviks and Kerensky, was to appoint a committee of public safety to supervise the impartial restoration of order. At moments demanding decision, Sukhanov observed, Martov reverted to his "Hamletism and ultrarefined analytical web-spinning." Though the moderate socialists were at risk to Lenin, Martov's neutral resolution was passed by 122 votes to 102, only the Cadets voting to back Kerensky.

It was a grievous blow for the premier. The maintenance of order was to be entrusted not to the government but to an as-yet-nonexistent committee. In Martov's personal spite against Kerensky, and in his fear of the phantom armies of reaction, Trotsky realized that the Menshevik leader was also dooming the preparliament. The moderates were "working out the formula for their own funeral," Trotsky sneered. All the good men of preparliament were neutral. The preparliament's session ended at 8:00 P.M. The military cadets and women still guarding the bridges, having waited in vain for promised evening relief units, went back to their barracks.

The Provisional Government assembled in the Malachite Hall of the Winter Palace at 9:00 P.M. The Bolsheviks in the telephone exchange had attempted to cut off the palace lines, but two were still working. Kerensky read Martov's speech carefully and said with shock, "Why, in a concealed form there's actually *no* confidence!" He considered resigning.

Lenin was pacing the floor in Margarita Fofanova's apartment. Party leader and coup instigator, he had been isolated from both for three days.

Every other Bolshevik was circulating freely, except for Lev Zinoviev, and he had the excuse that he had predicted failure. Remote, unaware of Trotsky's maneuvering, Lenin worried that the rising had been aborted, that the Central Committee had betrayed him. At 6:00 P.M. he had scribbled a note: "Now everything hangs by a hair. . . . It would be disaster to wait . . . the government is tottering. We must at all costs, this very evening, this very night, arrest the ministers." The Milrevkom had no forces available to take the ministers. Only in the past few hours had it scraped together some troops and four machine guns to defend its Smolny headquarters. Lenin gave the note to Fofanova with orders to take it to Krupskaya.

Shortly after 10:00 P.M., a Finnish comrade who acted as Lenin's bodyguard arrived with half-accurate news that the Neva bridges had been raised. Lenin at length decided that his place was in the Smolny. The two men caught a tram, empty like the streets, and got off near the Finland Station. The Finn had exaggerated. The Liteiny Bridge was still down and they crossed it without incident. Legend had it that the two were stopped by a government patrol who let them go as a pair of harmless drunks. But the morning papers, which were finalizing their editions at 10:00 P.M., were reporting that Petrograd was perfectly quiet and that "nowhere, not even at a single point, had anything serious happened."

Lenin fretted about his disguise. He was in his wig and a large pair of spectacles, but had forgotten his makeup in his excitement. He wrapped a handkerchief round his face as if he had a toothache. When he arrived at the Smolny shortly before midnight, the sentries refused to let him in. His Soviet pass was white and out of date. New passes were red. The Finn bellowed that a member of the Soviet was being denied admission, and Lenin slipped into the building.

He contacted Trotsky, who was amused at the disheveled gray-haired figure, finding he looked "quite odd." Dan, back from the Winter Palace, where he had been persuading Kerensky not to quit, had no difficulty in spotting Lenin. He nudged a colleague with his elbow and they winked at each other. "They have recognized us, the scoundrels," Lenin said forlornly.

The delegates for the Soviet Congress had started assembling in the Smolny. Everywhere, Sukhanov found "the greatcoats and gray features of the provinces. The mood was gray. Faces were tired, dull, even gloomy. There was no enthusiasm." Dan was urging them to condemn a coup. "We've been listening for eight months!" they yelled at him. "We've heard all that! It's too late!" Trotsky tried to whip them up: "Our enemies will capitulate immediately and you will take the place that is rightfully yours, the place of master in the Russian land." The response was leaden.

At midnight, Kerensky began searching urgently for reinforcements. He wired General Krasnov on the northern front to bring his cavalry corps to Petrograd. He left the Winter Palace at 2:00 A.M. to go to the General Staff building and telephone the First, Fourth, and Fourteenth Don Cossack regiments "in the name of freedom, honor, and glory of the fatherland" to come to the aid of the government. The men got up a mass and decided they had no intention of making a living target of themselves.

At 2:00 A.M. in the Smolny, in reply to Lenin's insistent questioning, Trotsky pulled out his watch and said, "It's begun." Lenin, so Trotsky said, made the sign of the cross.

As the city remained "sunk in a deep sleep," small groups of Bolshevik troops moved out of their barracks in the early hours of Wednesday, October 25. They showed no enthusiasm or spirit and were visibly relieved at the lack of resistance. They took the Neva bridges, the main telegraph office, post offices, the railway stations, the Central Bank, and the power stations. It was unnecessary for them to attack a target — at best, an onlooker noted, they surrounded them.

No shots were fired. Pickets of cadets, outnumbered, retired and the stronger squad took their place. The mathematics were simple. Kerensky had at most two thousand loyalists. The Milrevkom could call on about six thousand troops and sailors and a small number of Red Guards. Almost all the troops were from the Pavlovsky and Kexholm regiments. The whole operation resembled the changing of the guard, but without its precision.

No early attempt was made to seize Kerensky and the Winter Palace, although the capture of both was supposedly a priority and Kerensky was all but unguarded. He catnapped in the palace, waking to find his telephone had been cut off. When he looked out of the windows, he saw that the palace bridge was controlled by Bolsheviks. Pavel Malyantovich, the justice minister, went looking for him at 9:00 A.M. Nobody stopped Malyantovich or asked for his papers. He wandered into Kerensky's empty office, where he could have "taken any papers I wanted, or planted a bomb."

He came across a general reading a newspaper and asked him where the prime minister was. "No idea, my dear sir, ask the duty officer," the general said. He then looked up over his spectacles, saw that Malyantovich was still wearing his hat, and snapped, "The hat, you know, should be taken off." A cadet gestured to a door, with no sentry outside it, and Malyantovich let himself in. Kerensky was in the room, his face "sleepless, pale, and aged." He was putting on a coat of English cut and had a curious but stylish sportsman's cap.

Alexander Konovalov, a Moscow millionaire and the deputy premier, said that Kerensky was going off to Luga to rally a bicycle battalion. Were there not enough loyal troops among the quarter of a million in the capital? "I know nothing," said Konovalov. "It's bad." Malyantovich thought it was bad indeed if, to defend the Russian state, it was "necessary to go to Luga to meet . . . a battalion of cyclists."

Thirty cars were drawn up outside the palace. None was in running order. The distributors had been removed during the night, apparently by Bolsheviks. An ensign, Boris Knirsha, had been sent out to see if he could requisition one that worked. The British embassy turned him down. So did Vladimir Nabokov, the cabinet secretary, who was having his morning bath. The Americans were more generous.

An embassy official, Sheldon Whitehouse, was buttonholed by a Russian officer — presumably Knirsha — who "said he wanted my car to go to the front." Whitehouse was not happy. "This car is my personal property," he said, pointing at the Winter Palace, "and you have thirty or more automobiles waiting." Whitehouse was told they were all out of commission. He relented, although he tried and failed to remove the American flag flying from the car, a Renault complete with chauffeur. Whitehouse was assured that he would have the car back as soon as Kerensky returned from the front with enough troops to put down the coup — "within five days."

Ensign Knirsha was also able to scrounge an open-topped Pierce-Arrow tourer. Its tank was almost empty and Knirsha was loaned eight gallons of gasoline by the Anglo-Russian Hospital.

Kerensky told Alexander Konovalov that he was leaving him in charge of the capital. He bade farewell to the palace garrison — "As supreme head of the Provisional Government and the army, I know nothing for certain" — and went down to the Pierce-Arrow. It followed the Renault, whose American driver did not know where they were going. The chauffeur circled the palace square several times, before accelerating under the arch of the General Staff building and speeding down the Morskaya past the Maryinsky Palace. The driver became lost on the Voznesensky and stopped for instructions. The Pierce-Arrow cut in front and led the way out of the city to the Pulkovo highway.

The route took the two cars through the Bolshevik cordons that were supposedly sealing the city center. Kerensky, sitting in the open back of the tourer, was recognized by scores of pedestrians and rose to acknowledge them with salutes. On the outskirts, Kerensky said, a patrol of Red Guards "came rushing toward our machine from all sides, but we had already passed them." He drove on without incident to lunch at Gatchina. Behind him, government ministers were able to make their way to the Winter Palace without difficulty, while in the Smolny Lenin prepared to announce their overthrow.

Lenin's proclamation was published at 10:00 A.M. It stated that the Provisional Government had been deposed and that authority had passed into the hands of the Petrograd Soviet and the Milrevkom, in whose joint names it was signed. The Milrevkom had no license, from the Petrograd Soviet or any other entity but the Bolshevik Central Committee, to replace the government. The Soviet Congress, which was designed to legitimize the coup, had not yet officially opened. Its delegates milled round the Smolny in confusion.

The city ignored Lenin's claim. Trams were running, the banks were open, and factories were working. Sir George Buchanan took a morning stroll from the British embassy along the Neva embankment to Palace Square and noticed nothing out of the ordinary except for the guards on the bridges. Ministers continued to arrive at the Winter Palace by cab. Troops in the intermittent cordons were bored, smoking and standing easy. "Incredible!" muttered the commander of a group on the Moika. "The order was to march. But why — no one knows. Against one's own people, after all. All rather strange." Sukhanov found the atmosphere quite frivolous and un-warlike. The soldiers looked as if they would scatter at the first blank shot — "but there was no one to do any shooting."

Motor torpedo boats and armed trawlers had sailed up the river but the bulk of the Bolshevik sailors from the Baltic Fleet had yet to arrive. Pavel Dybenko, the "laughing Bolshevik," good-natured sailor-president of the fleet's central committee, a bearlike man of twenty-eight with broad shoulders and beard and sharp eyes, had spent a sleepless night trying to organize the sailors. Captain Rengarten, chief intelligence officer aboard the flagship, was kept awake by the rumble of feet. Eventually, fifteen hundred had been packed off by train but they played little more part in the coup than the officers. When the latter were asked to move units with artillery to the capital, Rengarten found that nobody showed the least desire to defend Kerensky and the government. Admiral Rasvozov, the fleet commander, was opposed to supporting either side for fear of starting a civil war.

At noon, a few detachments and an armored car arrived in leisurely fashion at the Maryinsky Palace. The preparliament was ordered to disperse. A hasty vote was taken and its members agreed to go home. As they trooped down the stairs, the troops examined their papers carefully. The Cadets expected to be taken off to the Peter and Paul Fortress, but they were only looking for government ministers. They found one, the assistant labor minister, but he protested that he was a Menshevik and a good socialist and they let him go.

When Sukhanov arrived at the palace, the men had searched the building and found no one of note. "By the way, did I happen to know where the government was?" they asked him. "They had to arrest the ministers but they just didn't know where they were."

The opening of the Soviet Congress was postponed to allow time for the ministers to be rounded up. Lenin, still heavily disguised with wig, bandaged face, and spectacles, was bombarding Nikolai Podvoisky in the Milrevkom office with lists of targets to be taken. Podvoisky was a publisher by trade, a neat figure in starched collar and cuffs, a fitness fanatic and amateur gymnast, and his slow and overdetailed approach to military affairs so frustrated Lenin that at one stage Lenin threatened to have him shot. Podvoisky had originally promised to take the Winter Palace in the morning. This slipped to 3:00 P.M.

At 2:35 P.M., Trotsky felt compelled to hold an extraordinary session of the Petrograd Soviet to prevent the Congress delegates drifting away from the Smolny. He claimed that the government had "ceased to exist" — though it continued to meet in the Winter Palace — as the result of a movement of "such enormous masses" that it had no parallel in history, which was passing almost unnoticed in the streets as he spoke. The only sign of revolt that most passersby saw was the odd armored car, siren blaring, still bearing the names of the first tsars but with Bolshevik initials splashed in red paint on their gray bodies.

An "unknown, bald, clean-shaven man" rose to his feet in the Smolny. Only when he began to speak, in a throaty, rasping voice with a familiar stress on the end of the sentences, was it clear who he was — "Eh — Lenin!" The wig had gone, and so, Philips Price thought, had his self-confidence. He found Lenin's delivery weak, apparently with excitement and slight indecision. The *Manchester Guardian* man felt Lenin was still doubtful about the outcome of the coup. "The old state apparatus will be uprooted and a new machinery created," Lenin started. "To end the war . . . it is clear that capitalism itself must be conquered. In this task we shall be helped by the world workers' movement which has already begun to develop in Italy, Germany, and England. . . . Enough of playing games with the capitalists. We shall win the confidence of the peasants with one decree, to abolish *pomeshchik* land ownership. We will institute workers' control over production. We shall create a proletarian socialist state. Long live the socialist world revolution!"

Complaining — in German — that the sudden transition from the underground to power had made him "dizzy," Lenin disappeared again. By contrast, Gregory Zinoviev's worries no longer creased his enormous forehead. "Well, Comrade Sukhanov," Zinoviev said, with his slight lisp and low, effeminate voice. "You didn't expect the victory to be so quick and easy?" But what Lenin had outlined struck Sukhanov as a potential death sentence, if not by civil war, then by starvation.

A few Bolsheviks realized this. "It's insane! Insane!" said the trade union vice president, David Ryazanov, biting his beard. "The European working class won't move!"

Sukhanov was so unimpressed by it all that he went home to eat supper by the stub of a candle. He thought that the Bolshevik regime would be ephemeral — "and a majority of them themselves were convinced of the same thing." Normally he would not have dreamt of leaving the Smolny cauldron. Now food came into his mind easily. "It was a question," he said, "and not for me alone, of the blunting of perceptions. People were used to every sort of happening. Nothing had any effect."

The continuing siege of the Winter Palace was so sloppy that John Reed and Louise Bryant were able to stroll into the building during the afternoon. Palace servants in their tsarist blue uniforms took their coats, and cadets with the familiar red shoulder straps and rosettes of the military schools were glad to show them round. Louise Bryant found the poor, uncomfortable, unhappy boys, reared in genteel isolation and now "without a court, without a tsar, without all the tradition they believed in."

The boys came from academies where, by tradition, cadets never held an intellectual conversation and could talk only of wine, women, and horses. Chemistry and engineering were considered beneath them and books on these subjects were touched only with gloved hands. Baffled by the revolution, the cadets all said they were keeping one bullet for themselves. Bryant hoped they would not have to use it. Packing cases and mattresses littered the floors, along with cigarette butts and empty wine bottles; many of the defenders were drunk. The journalists were taken to the Gold Room. The cadets, mainly teenagers who sprinkled their chatter with French phrases to prove they were cultured, said proudly that it was one of the finest rooms in all Europe.

Keepsakes were exchanged — a silver Caucasian dagger, a ring inscribed "God, tsar and Lady." A photographer arrived to take pictures of the Women's Battalion. The girls, most from poor homes in the provinces, were not happy. With their close-cropped heads and simple, coarse sunburned features, they could have been taken for boys had they not been so small. They looked like dwarfs in comparison to the guardsmen besieging them outside the palace. The girl soldiers had hoped to be honored. Instead, one said, "we were insulted on the streets. At night, men knocked at our barracks and cried out with blasphemies." They had been told they were going to take part in a ceremonial parade and were uneasy about shooting down fellow

Russians. The Bolshevik troops outside were equally worried about them — "people will say we shot Russian women," one muttered.

A captain greeted the journalists in thick but fluent French, unaware that Reed and Bryant were committed to the other side, Reed to the extent — or so the U.S. embassy claimed — of keeping colleagues from the Associated Press out of Smolny meetings on the grounds that they were capitalists. The captain smelled of alcohol. "I am very anxious to get away from Russia," he said. "I have made up my mind to join the American army." He gave them his address and asked them to put in a word for him with the American consul.

The ministers felt themselves in a void of total indifference. They thought Colonel Polkovnikov was too unenergetic and sacked him as Petrograd commander, entrusting their defence to Dr. Nikolai Kishkin, the psychiatrist and welfare minister. Then they had some sausage and cheese sandwiches. "Doomed people, lonely, abandoned by all, we walked around in the huge mousetrap," Pavel Malyantovich noted in his diary. The *Aurora* had been moored across the cold waters of the Neva and its guns were clearly seen from the palace windows. It was lying close to Pyotr Shilovsky's townhouse, to which he had retreated after abandoning his estate. Handsome sailors were calmly moving about on deck, and Shilovsky noticed that "our female servants, not excluding the English nursery-governess, lost no opportunity of getting to know our new neighbors." He learned from the servants that the cruiser had come to get rid of Kerensky; "whether he was removed or not did not seem a matter of concern to anyone."

A fresh detachment of engineering cadets arrived during the afternoon under a lieutenant, Alexander Sineguba. He found the small detail of Cossacks in the palace to be tired and irritable at having to defend "women and Yids." The commissary was thick with tobacco smoke and reeked of wine and vodka. Many rooms were being used as hospital wards for soldiers wounded at the front, and doctors and nurses scurried about the corridors.

Two cyclists arrived with an ultimatum from the Milrevkom, threatening to open fire if the palace did not surrender by 7:10 P.M. The ministers asked Admiral Verderevsky what would happen if the cruiser shelled the palace. "It will be turned into a heap of ruins," he said, adding that its turrets were higher than the bridges and that it had a clear field of fire. The ministers still had hopes that Kerensky would shortly appear with reinforcements. They had discovered some working telephone lines, and were heartened to get through to Moscow and find that no trouble had been reported. They declined to give themselves up.

The General Staff building was also under an ultimatum. After failing to get any instructions from the ministers, it was surrendered at 7:40 P.M. to a small group of Pavlovsky guardsmen who were waiting outside the doors. "What military order could we have issued? None," said Malyantovich. "The Bolsheviks walked in and sat down and those who had sat there got up and walked out and that is how the army headquarters was taken."

Kerensky arrived in Pskov as darkness fell. He asked General Krasnov to send his Third Cavalry Corps to the city, the same unit that Kornilov had used two months before. A young officer refused to shake the premier's hand — "I am a Kornilovite!" Krasnov was also unimpressed. "Pale, unhealthy, with an ill-looking skin and swollen red eyes," he described his supplicant. "A face with traces of heavy, sleepless nights. Clean-shaven like an actor. His head too large for his trunk. Military jacket, breeches — looks like a civilian who has got himself up for a Sunday ride." Krasnov said he would do what he could.

In London, Somerset Maugham passed on Kerensky's three-week-old secret appeal — "unless I have something to tell my army, it's impossible" — to Lloyd George. Although Maugham had promised Kerensky that he would deliver it verbally, he wrote the plea out on a piece of paper because of his stammer. The British prime minister looked at it and said simply, "I can't do that."

Posters announcing the fall of the government were being distributed by trucks and stuck up on billboards in Petrograd. Louise Bryant was allowed on a truck by sailors who threw posters off the tailgate, after she had removed her yellow hatband for fear of nonexistent snipers. Olga Kerensky was arrested for ripping a poster down in a show of loyalty to her husband, but was soon released. Zinaïda Gippius went for a stroll, and thought the weather showed the difference between the February Revolution and what was happening now, between "the beaming heavens of spring and today's dirty, dark gray, slimy clouds."

The coup did not interfere with the evening life of the city. Trams and cabs were operating normally, making an occasional detour to avoid a cordon. Elegant figures settled into their seats at the Alexandrinsky Theater to watch *The Death of Ivan the Terrible,* while opera buffs listened to Chaliapin singing in *Boris Godunov* at the Maryinsky. Cinemas, nightclubs, and bars were full. The Restaurant de Paris was turning away diners without reservations. The ministers in the Winter Palace had already had an early supper of soup, fish, and artichokes. After the meal they ordered the palace lights to be put out. In the resulting confusion, among both besieged and besiegers, four cadets from the Constantine Academy were slightly wounded, probably by their own side. The Constantine cadets left the palace without informing the ministers, who were now being served tea in crystal glasses with silver holders bearing Nicholas II's monogram. Fifteen hundred miles to the east in Tobolsk, their former owner had been asleep for five hours.

Vladimir Antonov-Ovseenko had ordered the *Aurora* to open fire on the palace when a red light was shone from the Peter and Paul Fortress. The cruiser was fresh out of the dockyard for repairs, however, and had only blank ammunition. The fortress garrison could not find a red lamp. At 9:40 P.M., a purplish flare was seen from the fortress and the *Aurora* turrets opened up with blanks. The remaining cadets replied with machine gun fire until they realized that, for all the smoke and noise, no shells were falling on them. Pyotr Shilovsky, a few yards from the cruiser, did not hear the salvoes — "I must have slept through them."

The ministers used one of the open telephone lines to dictate an appeal "To All, All, All" to respond to the Bolshevik's "insane attempt" at taking power. It was read out in the Duma. Pitirim Sorokin, the young SR journalist and philosophy teacher who had been so impressed by Kerensky's protection of tsarist prisoners in February, had been lying sick in bed all day until the artillery fire sent him hurrying to the Duma. Alexander Konovalov, the millionaire deputy premier, got through to the Duma on the telephone and his despairing shouts were relayed to the delegates — "The massacre has begun! . . . Hurry!" A two-hundred-strong delegation set out, singing the "Marseillaise," to go to the Winter Palace and "die with the government."

They were blocked on the Nevsky by a patrol of sailors in three automobiles, loaded down with machine guns and grenades. "Let us pass!" the Duma men said. "Let us sacrifice ourselves!" The sailors were unimpressed. "Go home and take poison," one said. "But don't expect to die here." A delegate asked what would happen if they pushed forward. "We may give you a good spanking," a sailor replied. "But we won't kill any of you — not by a damn sight!" The would-be martyrs turned around and returned to the Duma to form a committee — this one "To Save the Fatherland and the Revolution."

The cadet guard at the palace, expecting the Duma delegation, let a large group of Bolsheviks into the building. When they discovered the men were armed, some flamboyantly with several pistols, they arrested them. "What a guard," sighed Malyantovich. "They mistake armed men for members of the Duma! Strange!" Two hand grenades thrown by sailors exploded. Some cadets were grazed and Dr. Kishkin treated them. The sailors were arrested. The ministers were told, to their relief, that the Women's Battalion was leaving. Malyantovich found this the "first cheerful news of the entire day." The women were disarmed, told to "go home and put on female attire," and disbanded. A month later Louise Bryant came across a dozen of them, living in a little house in a deserted garden, working as nurses. The Cossacks had already gone, loading their ponies with equipment and clattering off with a promise of safe conduct from the Pavlovsky men in the palace square.

Beyond the darkened square, the besiegers could see trams, lighted shop windows, and the blinking electric signs outside movie houses. Rich old men in fur coats shook their fists at soldiers whose cordons inconvenienced them, and the soldiers argued back feebly with embarrassed grins. Reed had a ticket to the Maryinsky Theater, but he found it "too exciting out of doors."

At about 11:00 P.M., the six-inch guns of the Peter and Paul Fortress opened fire at the Winter Palace with two live rounds. The explosions startled Vladimir Nabokov, the eighteen-year-old son of the cabinet secretary, recovering from an appendix operation, who was writing a poem in the family house on the Morskaya. One shell missed the 1,500-room target by several hundred yards. The other hit the Alexander III suite but did little damage. A few minutes later, the three-inch guns joined in with thirty-five rounds. Most fell in the river. Only one hit was recorded, which chipped a cornice.

The Soviet Congress at last opened, the Smolny stifling and filthy, rifles, bayonets, and fur caps scattered everywhere, to the sound of the cannonade. The Bolsheviks had packed it well, so that they and their Left Social Revolutionary allies had two-thirds of the delegates. Its makeup was sharply different from that of the Petrograd Soviet. The Moscow workers now present, Nikolai Sukhanov thought, resembled their Petrograd comrades "as much as a hen does a peacock," but even they were sophisticates compared to the gray mass of delegates. They were crude and ignorant men who had crept out of "trenches and obscure holes and corners." Their devotion was made up of "spite and despair," their socialism was "hunger and the unendurable longing for rest."

Trotsky called it the most democratic of all parliaments in the history of the world, but it had been boycotted by the main peasant organizations and by the army committees. Most delegates were from the north and central provinces. The fertile southeast, Siberia, the Cossack territories, and the Ukraine were hardly represented. The majority were young — the old type of peasant in long beards, the middle-aged intellectuals, and mature soldiers were missing. One in ten came from tiny — and pro-Bolshevik — Latvia.

Julius Martov, bent with galloping tuberculosis, his hand trembling on his hip, demanded a peaceful solution; his speech was received with limp applause in which a few Bolsheviks joined, unnerved by their party's aggression. Other Mensheviks, and Social Revolutionaries, called for a government recognized by all in place of a "military conspiracy organized behind the back of the Congress." The leader of the Jewish Bund, one of the oldest socialist movements in Russia, declared solidarity with them. Delegates from the front said that the army was being stabbed in the back.

The moderates were met with jeers — "Go over to Kornilov! Lackeys of the bourgeoisie!" They prepared to walk out. In doing so, Sukhanov rued, "we completely untied the Bolsheviks' hands . . . yielding to them the whole arena of the revolution."

With the exit of the "pure in heart," no influence remained to push the Congress toward a united front and the defusing of civil war. Sukhanov was later to think that this failure to remain was his "greatest and most indelible crime." The field was left open to the Bolsheviks, with only a few Left Social Revolutionary youngsters to check them. But Sukhanov and the other conciliationists thought it unlikely the Bolsheviks would last out the week.

In a rolling speech of triumph, Trotsky told the departing moderates, Sukhanov among them, that they were miserable bankrupts. "A rising of the masses of the people needs no justification. . . . Our insurrection was victorious. And now we are told: renounce your victory, make concessions, compromise. No, here no compromise is possible." He told them to go "where you ought to be — in the dustbin of history!" The sound of gunfire outside exhilarated Trotsky. "It bothers nobody," he said. "On the contrary! It helps speed the work along."

Late-night trams still crossed the Troitsky Bridge. The war ministry reported to Mogilev that, apart from a stretch from the Moika to the palace, all the other streets were open. The crowds "are amazingly indifferent to what is going on." Rebel troops were gradually closing in on the palace. "In the beginning the insurrectionists showed no determination, only later, when they saw there was no resistance."

Malyantovich fell asleep in the Malachite Hall of the palace, where the columns, fireplaces, and tables were worked from the green and coppery stone. When he awoke he was told that another section of cadets had left. The telephone kept ringing with sympathetic calls from well-wishers urging the ministers to hold out until morning. Mikhail Tereshchenko was less resigned than the others. The young sugar magnate looked "so well groomed and so angry."

More Bolsheviks were found wandering in palace corridors, and were disarmed without resistance. "How many of them are there in the palace?" a minister asked. "Who is actually holding the palace — us or them?" Nobody knew. At 2:00 A.M., a friend rang Malyantovich to ask how he was. "Not bad, in cheerful spirits," he replied. He lay back on a divan to get some sleep, but shortly a noise flared up and began to rise and draw nearer.

The ministers grabbed their overcoats. The noise grew and swept the hall like a "wave of poisoned air." A cadet rushed in, drew himself up to attention and saluted, excited but determined. "What are the orders of the government?" he asked. "To fight to the last man?" Wearily, the ministers shouted, "It's not necessary! It's useless. No bloodshed!"

A little man, a wide-brimmed artist's hat pushed back on his long red hair, with a high starched collar and a flowing tie in place of his usual bow, flew into the room like a chip tossed up by a wave. An armed mob behind him "filled up the room like water." He shouted in a shrill and jarring voice, "I inform you, all you members of the Provisional Government, that you are arrested. I am Antonov-Ovseenko, a representative of the Milrevkom."

Antonov was furious to have missed Kerensky.

The ministers were lined up in a column and marched along the Millionaya and over the Troitsky Bridge to the Peter and Paul Fortress. There were shouts, "Run them through! . . . Chuck them in the river!" But no attempt was made to lynch them. The day's casualties were no more than a couple of dozen, most caught accidentally in random cross fire.

Lev Kamenev, in a worn and shiny jacket, a "quick-moving little man with a wide vivacious face" in Reed's description, announced the fall of the Winter Palace "smiling slyly" in the Smolny ballroom at 3:00 A.M. There was particular applause when Kamenev read out Tereshchenko's name in the list of arrested ministers, but no general enthusiasm. It was late and the Congress was "getting fed up with all this." A Left Social Revolutionary said that it was inadmissible to arrest socialist ministers. Trotsky snapped that he had no time for such trifles. It was the very first day, Sukhanov thought, and "this new ruler was showing his teeth over 'trifles.' An omen for the future."

Occasional bursts of gunfire echoed round the streets. The ballerina Tamara Karsavina had gone on to supper with friends on the Millionnaya after her performance at the Maryinsky. They sat playing cards — a game called "Cheating" — until it was quiet. Much of the city had seen no fighting at all between Kerenskyites and Bolsheviks. "The man in the street," said Pyotr Shilovsky, "did not even grasp very clearly what the difference was between them."

A Bolshevik lieutenant searched Antonov's men as they left the Winter Palace. "Comrades, this is the people's palace," he said. "Do not steal from the people." He laid out his confiscations on a table. It was a meager haul — the broken handle of a Chinese sword, a wax candle, a coat hanger, a blanket.

The Soviet Congress was adjourned at 6:00 A.M. until the following evening. Cold mist stole over the streets and the watch fires by the bridges, the shadow of a "terrible dawn gray-rising over Russia." The delegates shuffled out past the armored cars and machine guns guarding the doors of the new cradle of socialist revolution. Tamara Karsavina was going to bed in her apartment. She looked out of the window and saw a solitary figure in soldier's uniform creeping from a barracks gate toward the Champs de Mars. A shot rang out. "The figure fell on the snow. I drew the curtain."

Delo Naroda assured its readers that nothing untoward had happened the previous day. Some barricades had gone up, "but this should not be taken too seriously. They are no more than piles of wood." Paul Anderson, a young American who was working with the YMCA, was not so sure. He hurried off to the Astoria Hotel to ask John Reed what had happened. "Well," said Reed. "We had the Revolution last night."

XXII
The Brotherhood Grave

NEWSPAPERS, though they had gone to press well before the palace fell and had no definitive stories on the coup, became news themselves on Thursday morning, October 26. *Pravda,* now resurrected, crowed with triumph at the striking down of the "bourgeois gang." The rest of the press slashed at the Bolsheviks. "The promise of immediate peace — is a lie!" the Social Revolutionaries raged. "The promise of bread — a hoax! The promise of land — a fairy tale!" At Lenin's orders, bands of sailors went to news kiosks and distribution depots to seize copies of non-Bolshevik papers and burn them in the streets.

No such auto-da-fé had taken place under the tsars. Kiosk owners, egged on by their customers, kicked and scratched to recover the bundles. An occasional worker or soldier cheered the sailors, on the grounds that the *burzhui* "used to beat us and we, having seized a club, are going to smash them." The great body of neutrals in the city was infuriated and alarmed by the flaming heaps of newsprint. Zinaïda Gippius wrote in her diary that the city was now "headed by a handful of swindlers." "So this was the start of the new regime!" thought Sukhanov. "The trampling into the mud of democratic principles."

A mass explosion of anger was only prevented, Sukhanov said, because "absolutely no one believed the Bolshevik regime could last." Philips Price, the *Manchester Guardian* correspondent, met a banker at the telegraph office who gave the Bolsheviks a few days. The staff showed him piles of telegrams from soldiers' committees at the front, all of which promised help in "expelling the traitors and usurpers."

Philips Price wanted to "laugh at the absurdity of it all." It was as if a bunch of private soldiers and workers had set themselves up in London, refusing to have any truck with Whitehall, with Buckingham Palace ringed by troops while the king escaped through a side door dressed as a washer-woman. He thought it inconceivable that the Bolsheviks could master the technical apparatus of the administration. He thought Russia was doomed to become a second Carthage, a hewer of wood and drawer of water for the financial magnates who would soon reappear.

Several Bolsheviks agreed with him. Philips Price filed a story to Manchester claiming that party moderates, shocked at the way Lenin and Trotsky were intent on "turning themselves into cheap editions of Robespierre," hoped for a coalition government to exert a "sobering influence."

Sobriety was in short supply. As Pitirim Sorokin went to work on *Delo Naroda*, he found the aspect of things was horrible. A swarm of soldiers and workers was plundering the cellars of the Winter Palace. "Broken bottles littered the square," he wrote. "Cries, shrieks, groans, obscenities filled the clear morning air." He worked off his venom on the Bolsheviks in an article that afternoon, describing them as murderers, ravishers, brigands, and robbers. A band of Red Guards broke into the offices in the evening to arrest the editors, but they had gone home. It was time for non-Bolsheviks to change into disguise. Sorokin stopped shaving, as many bearded men took to the razor.

The Committee for Salvation was sitting in the municipal Duma. G. I. Schreider, the majestic, white-haired mayor of Petrograd, told a packed meeting that no "government by bayonet" was legitimate. A few Bolsheviks in the hall were hissed and booed, walking out to cries of "German traitors!" To violent applause, the powerful railwaymen's union announced that it was joining the Committee for Salvation. The union was taking the rail network into its own hands and would not allow access to any "usurpers."

A delegate of the postmen's union said that no mail would be delivered to the Bolsheviks in the Smolny. A telephonist confirmed that all phone lines to the Smolny had been cut off. News came in that Kornilov had escaped from his golden cage at Bykhov. Kerensky was said to be marching back at the head of an army of Cossacks.

It was well after 9:00 P.M. when the second session of the Soviet Congress opened at the Smolny. Lenin had spent much of the day drafting decrees on peace and land, while his colleagues argued over what to call the new government. A cabinet with ministers sounded too bourgeois. Trotsky thought that a Council of People's Commissars — Sovet Narodnik Komissarov — had the right ring to it. It paid lip service to the Soviet and it had the sort of punchy abbreviation the Bolsheviks did so well, Sovnarkom.

Seven out of the fifteen commissars — Sukhanov thought that the very word smacked of policemen — had served prison terms for terrorism and had spent long periods in the underground. Their aliases were given in parentheses beside their real names — Ulyanov (Lenin) as chairman, Bronstein (Trotsky) at foreign affairs, Dzhugashvili (Stalin) at nationality affairs. Trotsky was the only Jew on the list. The Bolsheviks were well aware that many workers and soldiers mistrusted them as a "Yid party." Lev Kamenev and Gregory Zinoviev, born Rosenfeld and Radomyslsky, were given important but lower-profile jobs, respectively on the central executive committee and as editor of the Bolshevized *Izvestiya*. Not a single ministry acknowledged its new commissar.

Some commissars admitted that they were totally unqualified. David Ryazanov at commerce, though not reconciled to the coup, told all who would listen that he had no idea of business. The new commissar of finance — Viacheslav Menzhinsky, whom Lenin had appointed because he had once worked as a clerk in a French bank — sat alone in the café on the top floor of the Smolny, stubble-chinned and dressed in a rancid goatskin cloak, nervously trying to work out sums on the back of an envelope. The State Bank had already refused to make any funds available to him. A red-haired young man called S. S. Pestovsky came to see Menzhinsky, looking for a job, and mentioned that he had studied finance, among other things, at London University. Menzhinsky, relieved, got up and said emphatically, "In that case we shall make you the director of the State Bank." He went off and returned with a piece of paper to that effect signed by Lenin.

An announcement that the death penalty had been abolished started the session off to cheers. Lenin had not yet arrived in the hall. Trotsky recorded that Lenin was utterly indignant when he was told of the abolition, exploding, "How can you make a revolution without executions? Do you expect to dispose of your enemies by disarming yourself? What other means of repression are there?" He added sarcastically, "Prisons?" The significance of this — while not one tsarist official had been executed by the Provisional Government — made as little impression as the obvious untruth of Lev Kamenev's speech to the congress. As newspapers burned outside and lines of fresh prisoners shuffled off to the Peter and Paul Fortress, Kamenev claimed that the free press had been restored and political prisoners released.

Lenin entered, shabby and unshaven, his pipelike trousers too short for him, in a soft white collar and a black tie with little white flowers on it. Given the floor, he said, to an overwhelming human roar, that "we shall offer peace to the peoples of all the belligerent countries." There would be no annexations, no indemnities, and all would have the right to self-determination. The secret treaties would be published. He was willing to negotiate in writing, by telegraph, or at a conference. Lenin had no doubt, he said, with his "great mouth seeming to smile," that German and British workers would help achieve a just peace.

Soldiers sobbed like children, Reed recorded, and an immense sound soared into the quiet sky. Delegates flung their caps in the air and sang the slow and melancholy "Death March" in memory of the martyrs at the front. A young worker, his face shining, shouted, "The war is ended! The war is ended!"

No such thing had happened, as Sukhanov observed. The bloodiest conflict in history could not be solved by the simple stratagem of posting a letter or sending a cable. The German position at the front was so strong that it was impossible to expect any but the most humiliating peace terms. Why else had Kerensky been forced to continue the war? As to the secret treaties, Lenin could not publish them. The foreign ministry did not recognize the Sovnarkom and refused to hand them over.

Next came land. "All private ownership of land," Lenin began, "is abolished immediately without compensation." All the estates of landlords, the church, the crown, and the monasteries were to be seized and transferred to district Soviets until the Constituent Assembly met. Any damage to confiscated property was a serious crime, to be punished by revolutionary tribunals. Hired labor was forbidden. The sweetener was in the tail: "The lands of peasants and of Cossacks serving in the army shall not be confiscated."

The decree was badly written, and Lenin stumbled and became confused while reading it. It was not his own work, but was taken from the Social Revolutionaries; he had written down much of it verbatim earlier in the day from a two-month old copy of the SR land program. He claimed that this did not worry him — "Isn't it all the same whoever composed it?" But the concessions to the peasants and Cossacks ran counter to his own beliefs, in which *all* land would be confiscated, and were included as a temporary measure to prevent peasant hostility. Trotsky looked on "calm and venomous, conscious of his power." The land decree was put to the vote at 2:00 A.M. and passed with a single hand against.

At 2:30 A.M. Kamenev read out the final decree on the Constitution of Power. It established the Sovnarkom as a "temporary" government which would serve only until the Constituent Assembly met in November. The "People's Commissars" were to be "controlled" by the congress and its central committee. But the congress was due to be dissolved in a few hours. Its central committee, elected shortly after the final decree was read out, had seventy Bolsheviks out of a hundred members. The provisional status of the Sovnarkom was necessary because the Bolsheviks doubted that even a packed Congress would submit to single-party rule. To the original fiction of a Soviet-inspired coup, they now added another, that they would submit to the will of the Constituent Assembly.

Not all were convinced. Menshevik Internationalists and Left Social Revolutionaries explained that their refusal to enter the Sovnarkom was a protest against tyranny and the suppression of their newspapers. A railwayman, hard-faced and stocky with a look of implacable hostility, said that his union recognized neither the Congress nor the Sovnarkom. Not a single train would be available for the Bolsheviks.

At 7:00 A.M. on Friday, October 27, the Congress finally dissolved. The streetcar drivers' union was more sympathetic than the railway men, and trams had been kept waiting at the Smolny to take the delegates back into the city. Paul Anderson, the American YMCA volunteer, breakfasted with the family he was staying with, rich manufacturers with a townhouse that ran to a ballroom. They asked where he had been. "At the Soviet," he said. "Oh, the Soviet!" they laughed. "It will be gone in a fortnight."

The Duma was crowded throughout Friday as delegations — of Mensheviks, Social Revolutionaries, employers, trade unions, and merchants — came to pledge their support to the Committee for Salvation. On the steps, Boy Scouts distributed copies of banned newspapers, while a worker with a revolver and a red band on his arm tried in vain to confiscate them.

Red Guards made many arrests, and the sight of columns of prisoners shuffling off to the Smolny irritated and repelled passersby. The Smolny had become, Sukhanov said, "not only the General Staff but also the supreme police institution, the supreme tribunal and the jail." Count Tolstoy, a sleek fat Bohemian and a literary man like his famous namesake, was crossing the Troitsky Bridge when two Red Guards took him to the Peter and Paul Fortress for no better reason, it seemed, than that he was wearing a frock coat and a fur cloak. Shops and banks shut and ministries locked their doors as almost everywhere it was decided not to recognize Bolshevik authority.

An officer told John Reed that the Bronneviki, the armored car crews, were coming out against the Sovnarkom. "Do you want to see the turn of the tide? Come on!" Reed trotted after him to the Mikhailovsky riding school where the lumbering gray machines were based. They were highly effective in breaking up demonstrations — "whoever controlled the Bronneviki controlled the city." A lithe man in a leather coat with lieutenant's shoulder straps was urging the men to support the Provisional Government.

He appeared to have won them over when Nikolai Krylenko arrived in the gloomy building, summoned urgently from the Smolny. Krylenko had been named a commissar for war, jointly with Vladimir Antonov-Ovseenko and Pavel Dybenko, the day before. He was the former tsarist ensign whom Kerensky had out-argued at the front before the offensive, short-legged with an unnaturally large forehead and squinting eyes. Louise Bryant thought him a "violent little person," a *burzhui*-hater whose favorite phrase was: "Those who do not work shall not eat." At first he was barracked — "Shut up! Down with the traitor!" Krylenko got into his stride, warning them that Kornilov was coming back, that cadets and the Death Battalions — "who are *never* neutral" — would shoot them down in the streets. "The government is in your hands," Krylenko said. "You are the masters. Great Russia belongs to you. Will you give it back?" A vote was taken. Only fifty men stood with the lieutenant in the dim light.

Reed was delighted. The U.S. embassy was keeping a wary eye on him. He had lost his pocketbook shortly after he arrived in Petrograd and it had been handed in at the U.S. consulate. Ambassador Francis had gone through it carefully, finding the addresses of several Russo-American extremists who had returned from New York, and a letter from Reed to a woman in Croton-on-Hudson. In the letter, the young journalist said that "I do not think my benefactors are going to lose much on this trip of mine." Francis wondered who the "benefactors" were. One of Francis's agents reported that Reed had told him that he was a socialist, that workers should run factories themselves, that Russian workers were far advanced politically from Americans, and that, if the Bolsheviks got to power, the "first thing they will do is throw out all the foreign embassies."

It was not what Francis expected of a Harvard man, and he had Reed tailed as a suspicious character.

If Reed was happy that the Sovnarkom was about holding its own in Petrograd, the news from elsewhere was mixed. In Moscow, Boris Pasternak was walking home on Thursday night when he heard a "scattered knocking in the distance, like someone hammering nails into a plank." These were the first shots as the local Milrevkom took the Kremlin, with the help of the pro-Bolshevik commander of a guard regiment. A Committee for Salvation was rapidly being formed by the city's energetic mayor, V. V. Rudnev, and on Friday evening cadets were preparing to launch a successful attack across Red Square on the walled complex of palaces and churches.

An appeal was published in the local paper in Saratov, a big provincial town on the Volga six hundred miles southeast of Moscow. It called on citizens to resist the expected Bolshevik takeover. "Owing to the unpopularity of Kerensky and to the physical and moral flabbiness of our Christian citizens," the schools inspector Alexis Babine wrote in his diary, "only about 150 people came forward."

Kerensky was only twenty-five miles out from Petrograd, comfortably quartered in the old imperial palace at Gatchina. He had arrived in excellent spirits, protected by a Don Cossack cavalry regiment, leading it in with a Napoleonic air, his hand thrust between the folds of his jacket. He seemed more at risk from an extreme right-wing officer in the palace — who threatened to kill him with a hand grenade and was arrested for his pains — than from the Bolsheviks. Ensign Knirsha was busily sending "To All, All, All" telegrams assuring provincial governors that the news of a coup was a lie. Kerensky was relaxed enough to play a game of billiards, and to telephone friends to say he would be back in the capital in the morning. He spoke with Olga, his infidelity perhaps shaken by events, and she went to bed "reassured and joyful."

In the British embassy, Sir George Buchanan met with his French counterpart Joseph Noulens to plan for the stationing of Anglo-French troops in the city after Kerensky's return. David Francis advised the two hundred American railroad experts assembling in Seattle that they should sail for Vladivostok as planned on November 6, since he had "no confidence in the survival of the Soviet government." The men duly embarked on their mission to breathe life back into the Trans-Siberian.

The stock exchange, after an initial panic, recovered its nerve. Share prices were back to their Monday levels. The ruble slid further, but foreign investors took little account of Bolshevik activity. "So far as the coup d'état is concerned," the *Economist* reported in London, "the only effect is to leave Russian government bonds slightly lower than they were before."

Beneath the surface conviction that Lenin had played and lost, however, Philips Price noted a shift in mood. "There was a different feeling in the air," he wrote. "It seemed as if there was, for the first time in many months, a political force in the country that knew what it wanted." Poorer students, small shopkeepers, "high collared" proletarians — the urban element halfway between have and have-not that the Russians called *meshchanin* — were interested in two things alone. They wanted to see if the Bolsheviks could bring food to the towns and make an end to the war. They had been bitterly hostile to the Leninists all summer. "Now, they were saying: 'Give these people a chance.'"

On Saturday, October 28, Peter Krasnov's Cossacks were skirmishing toward Tsarskoe Selo, and cadets and Cossacks took the Moscow Kremlin. Boris Pasternak watched them advancing toward Red Square from the windows of his father's Moscow apartment. He saw a Cossack shot, and crawl back for cover among half-bare lilac bushes, leaving a fine dark trail behind him. Rounds came through the apartment windows and lodged in the ceilings. The Pasternaks took shelter at the back of their apartment, until this was made dangerous by shrapnel from White artillery firing from Arbat Street. Boris and his artist father took refuge in a ground floor flat.

Young Pasternak poked his head out from time to time to listen to the firing. The twenty-seven-year-old poet had not believed in "whizzing bullets" as a literary description and he was curious to improve on it firsthand. Listening carefully, he found that bullets "squealed," and that the shells were "swooping down . . . with a clatter like crows or pigeons, and crying with a special cutting shriek that sets the air on edge, the scream of wheeling swifts and swallows."

Over Petrograd, two aircraft flew low down the Nevsky dropping leaflets that instructed the garrison to lay down their arms and assemble on the Champs de Mars to await Kerensky. The telephones to the Smolny remained cut off. Telegraphists and postmen refused to distribute Sovnarkom decrees. The big government wireless station at Tsarskoe Selo fell to the Cossacks. "Each day it becomes clearer that the Bolsheviks cannot govern," *Novaya Zhizn* commented. "They issue decrees like hotcakes and cannot carry them into life." Anyway, it said, the directives "read more like newspaper editorials than legislation."

The Petrograd garrison considered it had done enough work. As far as Kerensky's forces were concerned — "well, they were still somewhere near Gatchina, let the local garrisons fight them, they were closer." Nikolai Podvoisky went to the barracks of the Volhynian Regiment to hasten it on its way to attack the Cossacks. The men told him unceremoniously that they would not budge. Podvoisky rushed back to the Smolny to tell Lenin that he had failed to get a single unit to move out.

Lenin went into a terrible rage, and his face became unrecognizable. He shouted at Podvoisky, "You will answer for it if the regiments do not leave the city instantly. Do you hear me, at this very moment!"

Antonov-Ovseenko and Dybenko set off for Tsarskoe Selo in a car commandeered from a *burzhui*, Antonov wiry and bespectacled in a shabby raglan coat, Dybenko massive and bearded, toying compulsively with a blue steel revolver. The chauffeur refused to let them take two military bicycles with them, for fear it would spoil his paintwork.

As the two war commissars sped down the Suvorov Prospekt, they realized they had no food. They thought they might be gone for some days. They had no money and borrowed some from a Russo-American correspondent, Alexander Gomberg, who was traveling with them. Provisions safely aboard, they turned onto the Nevsky and blew a tire. They had no spare. Antonov stood in the road and waved down a car driven by a soldier.

He explained that he was the military commissar. The driver told him that he did not care if he was the devil himself — "You can't have this car."

A battered car flying an Italian flag drove up. Antonov stopped it. The owner, a Russian, was in the back, hoping that the foreign pennant would save it from requisitioning. He was dislodged and the car taken. Ten miles out, the commissars stopped in a village. Here they discovered that, apart from some desultory trench-digging, no defense line had been established. Depressed, they returned to the Smolny.

By the less complicated means of taking an evening commuter train, John Reed arrived in Tsarskoe Selo without effort and in half an hour. The only sign of military activity was a freight train drawn up in a siding, with troops warming themselves at bonfires by the track. Reed had an excellent dinner at the station, where he met a French officer who confirmed that Kerensky was still in Gatchina but that all was quiet. "Ah, these Russians," the Frenchman said. "They are original! What a civil war. Everything but the fighting!"

The barber shops were all crowded and there were Saturday night queues outside the town bathhouse. Reed was sure that Bolshevik troops and Cossacks were mingling happily inside. He went to the Catherine Palace. A colonel asked him how he had got there without being killed. Kerensky's Cossacks were only a mile away and sporadic fighting was going on round the town.

Reed asked the colonel if he was for Kerensky.

"Well, not exactly *for* Kerensky," the colonel hesitated. "You might say that none of the *soldiers* are for Kerensky; but some of them just don't want to fight at all. The *officers* have almost all gone over to Kerensky's forces, or simply gone away. We are — ahem — in a most difficult position, as you see." The colonel, weary not with hardship but by being "so long, three years, away from my mother," gave Reed an escort back to the station. Shortly after he left, Krasnov's troops moved into the town. They were not the army corps that haunted Lenin, who was desperately ordering the fleet to send a battleship and two destroyers up the Neva to act as floating artillery. Krasnov had twelve hundred Cossacks, an infantry company, one tank, and a small armored train.

On the short ride back to Petrograd across the damp and featureless plain, Reed saw knots of soldiers standing by bonfires, and armored cars at crossroads, the drivers hanging out of the turrets shouting at each other.

The darkened city was tense. The Committee for Salvation was in an emergency session, delegates rushing from barracks to barracks to whip up the men with unfounded stories of Bolshevik atrocities. The most persistent was the gang-rape of the Women's Battalion, in fact safely disbanded. Reed was told that the cadets would move at midnight. A soldier, with a small boy to hold his pot of paste, was sticking up notices signed by Podvoisky as president of the Milrevkom, declaring a state of siege in the city and suburbs.

In Saratov, the expected Bolshevik move had started at nightfall. Rifle volleys and cannon fire marked an attack by Red Guards and rebel troops on the city hall, defended by a few hundred cadets, officers and citizens. Three were killed and eighteen wounded as it fell. Alexis Babine sat up late, hoping that a rumor that Cossacks were coming was true, securely locking his gate against armed and other rabble. The cannonade continued in Moscow. "No one spoke any longer," said Boris Pasternak, "whispered questions getting an indifferent, muttered reply."

Early on Sunday, October 29, officer cadets, anticipating Kerensky's imminent arrival, moved through the city. When it came down to it, the only people prepared to risk their lives for the Provisional Government were teenagers of good families from military academies. They did not do so out of respect for Kerensky — none mentioned him as a source of inspiration — but from a traditional loyalty to authority. In four years' time, the Kronstadt sailors arraigned against them were to turn on the Bolsheviks. It was to military cadets that the Bolsheviks looked to cross the ice to the naval base to destroy their ex-employees. For now, the cadets seized the central telephone exchange.

When Antonov arrived on an inspection tour, he was taken prisoner. A party of sailors settled down behind barricades of wood and tin sheets to besiege it. At 7:00 A.M., a patrol surrounded the Vladimir Academy and gave the cadets twenty minutes to surrender. They refused and two armored cars cruised around the building raking it with their machine guns. The cadets telephoned a Cossack regiment for aid, but the cavalrymen refused to budge.

The cadets had acquired some armored cars now — Ambassador Francis credited them with breaking into a garage during the night, chloroforming the guards, and driving off with eight vehicles. Louise Bryant watched one stall on the square in front of Saint Isaac's. Some sailors opened up on it and it replied with a burst of machine gun fire which killed seven onlookers. The sailors charged it as the panic-stricken driver failed to get the motor running. Yelling, the sailors thrust their bayonets through the observations slits again and again. Fighting broke out in the lobby of the Astoria Hotel, in the telegraph office, and between armored cars.

Artillery was brought up to the Vladimir Academy and the walls were slowly reduced to rubble. At 2:30 P.M., the cadets hoisted a white flag. Soldiers and sailors raced into the building. Five cadets were beaten and stabbed to death. As the surviving two hundred were herded off to the Peter and Paul Fortress a mob set on them, killing eight more.

The dreamy standoff of the past week was over, and both sides were in a mood for atrocity. "Now blood has been spilled there is only one way — pitiless struggle," Trotsky said in the almost-deserted Smolny. "It would be childish to think we can win by any other means." An American banker saw a general killed on the Neva embankment, his blood seeping onto the pavement. Young girls dipped their toes in it as they passed, laughing.

After an eight-hour siege, the defenders of the telephone exchange panicked when an armored car drove off the Nevsky and opened fire with its machine gun. The American correspondent Albert Rhys Williams was in the building. Cadets tore off their belts and caps. One pleaded with Williams for the loan of his overcoat — "anything to disguise their rank." A captain put on a cook's apron he found in the canteen, and plunged his arms into a sack of flour and, "already white with terror, becomes the whitest White Guard in all Russia."

At the cadets' urging, Williams found Antonov in the room where he was being held prisoner. A deal was struck, Antonov's life for those of the cadets. The cadets were led out of the building as the pretty telephonists huddled around their switchboards. Some of the cadets were kicked to death or thrown into the river as they were marched off to the Peter and Paul Fortress. Those who tried to flee across the rooftops were tracked down and hurled into the streets.

Watchers in the British embassy saw artillery being brought up to the engineering school, where groups of cadets had fled for sanctuary, at about 5:30 P.M. A white flag fluttered from a window. With dusk, the fighting flickered away with some two hundred dead and wounded. Embassy staff gave the cadet guards on the door civilian clothes so that they could slip out unnoticed.

Although the line of prisoners showed a victory in the capital, the Bolshevik central committee was not confident. Meeting without Trotsky and Lenin, it voted to accept the railwaymen's demand to broaden the Sovnarkom by including other socialists. While Trotsky exulted in the Smolny — "we've won the power, now we must keep it!" — his colleagues were in the rail union headquarters negotiating an end to one-party rule. As the talks dragged on, there were frequent demands that Lenin and Trotsky should be excluded from any new government.

The impetus of Kerensky's advance, however, was slipping away during Sunday. Kerensky spent most of the day in his room, according to Count Zubov, the director of the Gatchina Museum, "lying on the couch and swallowing tranquilizers." Their distant home fastnesses on the Don were beginning to have a hypnotic attraction for his Cossack strike forces. "What have we to do with Russia, Kerensky, and the Bolsheviks?" they muttered. "Let us go to the Don, the Bolsheviks will not get there!"

General Krasnov advanced to Pulkovo. Here an astronomical observatory was located on the sandy heights that interrupt the plain, gray as a windless sea, that stretched to the southern edge of the city seven miles away. His troops could plainly see spires and factory chimneys pluming their smoke into the inky sky. If Lenin thought that several army corps were marching against him, Krasnov for his part estimated that he was opposed by fifty thousand Bolshevik troops and workers. In fact, all that faced him were some hastily dug scrape trenches and a few machine guns. Krasnov stopped.

In Moscow, the Milrevkom considered its position "critical." It had lost control of the railway stations and telegraph offices as well as the Kremlin. It was, however, able to use a lull while it negotiated with the local Committee for Salvation to bring in fresh forces from the suburbs and nearby towns.

On Monday, October 30, the Milrevkom decreed that all those guilty of fighting for the Provisional Government would face military revolutionary courts. In the talks at the rail union, Fedor Dan and Julius Martov were accusing the Bolsheviks of "Red Terror." It was the first use of the term, justified, they thought, by the rapidly filling prisons. Posters were being pasted in the streets, headlined "To the Pillory," urging the people to destroy the Mensheviks and Social Revolutionaries. The Committee for Salvation was outlawed.

Committee members went into hiding. Reed was taken to see two of them in an apartment block off the Nevsky. Reed's contact knocked at the door in a special manner and a woman let him into the flat. A man in uniform emerged from behind the window curtains, and another dressed as a worker came out from a closet. They said they were both Social Revolutionaries and would be shot if the Bolsheviks caught them.

At noon, Lenin arrived at the Smolny to oversee preparations for what was expected to be a desperate battle at Pulkovo. He ordered Putilov workers to mount armor plate on railway engines and wagons and drive them out to the front with artillery pieces aboard. He fussed over the disposition of Red Guard units and the destroyers whose guns were meant to protect the approaches to the Moscow railway line. There was traffic chaos in the city, its streets still bustling, as the Neva bridges were raised to allow the destroyers and their "scallywag crews of indescribably dirty workmen and sailors" to pass upriver. Podvoisky, nominally commanding the Milrevkom forces, complained that there were now two headquarters. "One was in Lenin's offices and one in mine," he said. "This dualism got on my nerves." Podvoiski threatened to resign. Lenin flew into a rage. "I'll hand you over to the party court; we'll shoot you!" Lenin shouted. "I order you to continue with your work and I'll continue with mine."

A stream of trucks, haycarts, and marching men passed through the Moscow Gate and out along the Moscow highway toward Pulkovo. Krasnov's troops, without promised reinforcements and confused by the Bolshevik agitators who had been haranguing them during their two days of lethargy, finally advanced in a skirmish line along a river. Now only six hundred strong, they were outnumbered by ten or more to one.

They had little difficulty in scattering the motley army and Red Guard units. Dybenko's sailors held. The ground was marshy and cut by rivulets and the Cossacks had no stomach for fighting dismounted, falling back when they realized that they could not break the three thousand sailors, who kept up a steady fire. By midnight the only serious contact in Kerensky's counterthrust had been broken off.

In Saratov, the government alcohol stores were looted. Most of the liquor spilled from the vats into the streets, but some soldiers succeeded in getting drunk. No Cossack counterattack had developed.

Six hundred miles away in Moscow the Milrevkom ended its truce and went on the offensive. Fierce street fighting continued throughout Tuesday, October 31. On the main streets, the great banks and mercantile houses were wrecked by shellfire and casualties were heavy. "Whenever we didn't know just where the cadets were, we bombarded their pocketbooks," a Bolshevik explained. Madden Summers, the U.S. consul-general, was married to a Russian girl whose aunt owned the big Dom Gagarin building where the Bolsheviks were headquartered. It was wrecked, Summers reported sadly, as the "morgues filled up with cadets and Bolsheviks." He added that "large numbers of students aged from ten to sixteen" had been murdered in mistake for military cadets. Fires raged in the Metropole Hotel — though none of the Americans staying there was hurt, the consul-general reported that several lost their luggage. The thick red walls of the Kremlin were pocked with shrapnel as the Bolsheviks slowly squeezed at the pockets held by the Committee for Salvation.

In Saratov, it was being said as a fact that Kerensky was back in Petrograd and that Lenin and Trotsky had been hanged. In truth, Kerensky had failed.

Pavel Dybenko met with General Krasnov in Gatchina late on Tuesday night. Early in the morning of Wednesday, November 1, the two came to an agreement. The Cossacks would have safe conduct to the Don, retaining their horses and their arms. In return, Kerensky would be handed over to

Dybenko. The premier awoke to unfamiliar faces in the palace. Sailors were infiltrating the grounds and Kerensky was warned that the Cossacks planned to betray him. The exits were heavily guarded and Kerensky spoke of suicide — unnecessarily; the Leninists were as incompetent in arranging his arrest as he had been with Lenin's.

A young Social Revolutionary soldier brought Kerensky a sailor's uniform, which he put on along with a pair of aviator's goggles. The flying sailor was led through a crowd of fraternizing Cossacks and sailors to the main gate where a car was waiting for him, and driven off at high speed toward Luga.

Outcast and fugitive, Kerensky disappeared but was not forgotten. Everyone, Meriel Buchanan found, had an "odd belief that he would still achieve something and even those who hated him shared this." He was said to be hiding in Finland, to have been seen in a third-class railway carriage, to have been murdered by a mob, to have been elected a member of a remote town council in Siberia, to be living in Petrograd disguised beyond recognition. The Bolsheviks, enraged at their second failure to seize him, searched for him. Seven months later, a Serbian soldier sporting a fine mustache passed through Bolshevik security checks and got on a train bound for the Arctic port of Murmansk. His British visa, signed by Bruce Lockhart, was in order though his Serbian papers were false. The "soldier" — who had been a peasant, country gentleman, and Swedish doctor in beard and blue-tinted spectacles in other recent incarnations — boarded a boat for Scotland.

The British press baron Lord Beaverbrook asked Kerensky, in exile, what would have happened if he had made a separate peace with Germany. "Of course, we'd be in Moscow now," Kerensky replied. "Then why didn't you do it?" "We were too naive," Kerensky said. Naïveté, Bruce Lockhart thought, was Kerensky's proper epitaph.

On Thursday morning, November 2, Louise Bryant failed to get to Tsarskoe Selo after her interpreter, convinced that Kerensky's Cossacks were still a threat, swallowed the Smolny passes issued to her. The only interview she achieved was with a peasant who presented her with an apple and a dirty sandwich and told her, "America is a great nation! I know about America. Sewing machines come from America."

The interpreter's fears were groundless. In Moscow, the Committee for Salvation was ordering its men to lay down their arms. It then dissolved itself, assuming that the Constitutional Assembly would soon take power. Though civil war was beginning on the peripheries, organized resistance to the Bolsheviks ceased in the two main cities. Prayers for the Provisional Government were dropped from church services for the first time since the revolution, though few in Moscow thought the Bolsheviks would survive. "The animals!" the manager of the National Hotel, its windows shattered by shell blasts, told John Reed. "But wait! Their time will come. In just a few days now their ridiculous government will fall, and then we shall make them suffer!" The hotel dining room was closed, and Reed ate at a vegetarian restaurant called "I Eat Nobody."

The five hundred who had been killed on the Bolshevik side were buried in two massive pits, fifteen feet deep and fifty yards long, in Red Square in front of the Kremlin wall. The churches were dark and silent and no sacrament or prayers were said over the crude and crimson-daubed coffins. Wreaths hung in the leafless branches of the linden trees like strange, multicolored fruit. A Latvian military band played the funeral hymn. The clock above the great Spassky Gate in the Kremlin had been damaged by shellfire. It played two tsarist tunes at noon and midnight, and the Bolsheviks had the mechanism changed so that it sounded the "Internationale" and the revolutionary funeral song, "You Fell in Sacrifice." All those with bad consciences, "monarchists, counterrevolutionaries, speculators," hid behind drawn blinds, afraid of a reign of terror. Only the proletariat attended, the coffins being lowered from noon until after dark.

It was called the "Brotherhood Grave" but there was no room in it for dead cadets, who were thrown into holes in the ground. The Social Revolutionaries and Mensheviks had proposed a joint funeral. "Imagine!" a Bolshevik said. "It is impossible to teach them anything! They compromise from sheer habit." Fellow socialists were comrades no more.

XXIII
Grazhdanskaya Voyna

MANY IN PETROGRAD WERE INDIFFERENT to Kerensky's overthrow. Maxim Gorky made a careful study of a gardener in the Alexander Park. In March, the man had cleared a fresh snowfall, oblivious to the shots, klaxons, and red flags around him. During the July Days, he remonstrated with a curious crowd following the progress of rebel troops. "What are you up to, walking there?" the gardener shouted. "Isn't there enough path, that you have to trample the grass?" Now, stolid as ever, he was lopping branches and deadheading roses by the side of the path — "stubborn as a mole, and apparently as blind as one too."

In the provinces, the shrewdest made little sense of events. Those who presumed that the Sovnarkom had some connection with the Soviet were confused when Soviet loyalists condemned it as a single-party dictatorship. The Bolsheviks themselves floundered. In Saratov, the party impatiently waited for clarification promised by the central committee in Petrograd — "Alas! None came."

The Petrograd press had given some inkling of central events to a country spread across six time zones. The Bolsheviks had suppressed it. The Fifteenth Grenadier Regiment in Tiflis, the key element in the local Soviet, complained on November 9 that it had ceased trying to divine where its loyalties should lie. In the space of a day, it had received telegrams from the war and interior ministries, the Milrevkom, a Committee for Salvation, and a front committee, all giving contradictory instructions. The regiment appealed to its divisional committee. "They answered us that just as you cannot make anything out of it, neither can we."

During November the Milrvekom sent 106 commissars and more than 600 agitators to the provinces in an effort to explain "Soviet" power and to consolidate it. They had physical backup from some two hundred heavily armed units, manned largely by sailors from the Baltic Fleet. Results were mixed. Within weeks, led by the Finns, Finland, Lithuania, Latvia, the Ukraine, and Estonia — those parts of the Western borderlands that were not yet fully overrun by the Germans — were to declare themselves independent.

The revolution, by lifting the suppression that had bound the Russian empire together, reactivated the fault-lines below the surface. The pressures building were religious, ethnic, linguistic, cultural, commercial. The peoples on the western edge felt that the pull to the backward and Orthodox Russian East robbed them of a more prosperous and enlightened destiny in the West. Germany was the contiguous Great Power. Only Finnish volunteers fought in any numbers for the Germans. But the power and development of German industry made the economic comparison between Russia and Germany irresistible.

The comparison showed in bitter political jokes. One had an American visiting Germany and being amazed that his train was on time despite the strain on the railroad system. "Why do you find that odd?" his German host snapped back. "Don't you know there's a war on?" The American moved on to Russia, where he was equally astonished to find that his train was a day late. "So?" said his Russian companion. "Don't you know there's a war on?"

Finland had been part of the Swedish kingdom for six hundred years until it was ceded to Russia in 1809. Finns were consciously Scandinavians, not Russians, and the majority were Lutheran Protestants with a prejudice against the incense and chants of Russian Orthodoxy. The Baltic States had close cultural and commercial ties with Scandinavia — Estonian was linguistically close to Finnish — and had westward-looking Catholic and Protestant communities. The western Ukraine also had substantial numbers of Catholics; Ukrainians thought of themselves as occupying the eastern borderlands of Central Europe, not the western periphery of Russia.

Similar centrifugal forces were at work within the Russian heartlands, and to the east and south. The country was studded with Soviets, at the province, city, suburb, town, village, army, and regimental level. The coup's main catchphrase, "All Power to the Soviet," was often taken at face value to justify local autonomy. Bolsheviks in the industrial towns generally, but by no means always, followed the example of the twin capitals and threw out their socialist rivals.

In Smolensk, a Cossack regiment fought Bolsheviks, while a Cossack division in Saratov declared itself neutral. Kursk ignored the Bolsheviks for four months and the villages in the black earth provinces for longer. In the

Caucasus, only Baku went Bolshevik, while nationalists prepared takeovers in the rest of Azerbaijan and in Georgia and Armenia.

Tashkent was the sole Bolshevik center in Central Asia, and after capturing its fortress from a company of cadets the Bolsheviks were obliged to retake it from Cossacks later in the month. Kazakhstan declared autonomy. Bolshevik progress in Siberia was slow. In November, Krasnoyarsk was the one Red spot on a White vastness, held by elements of the Fifteenth Siberian Regiment and Bolshevized Hungarian prisoners of war. Social Revolutionaries controlled Tomsk and there was fighting in Omsk.

By mid-November, however, the Bolsheviks controlled most of the central and northern cities of Old Russia. They did so on what most thought to be an academic basis. It was assumed that the Constituent Assembly would — as Lenin and Trotsky had promised — be running the country within a few weeks, with the legitimacy of an election behind it; this expectation allowed the fifty Bolsheviks in Orsha to disperse its Committee for Salvation, many times more numerous, without a shot being fired. Their opponents, the Bolsheviks bragged, were "pitiful, for they did not realize that they could have 'combed us out' in a moment with a couple of machine guns, since we were holding on only by psychological effect."

The army shared the belief that the coup would be reversed by the Constituent Assembly and the pressure of protest strikes in major cities and on the railroads. Officers received "To All, All, All" messages from the Sovnarkom but nobody took them seriously. Army headquarters were no long interested in initiatives. The Kornilov affair had shattered the attractions of a military takeover. Viktor Manakin, commanding a shock battalion in Mogilev, found himself "defending the Stavka, but the Stavka did not want itself to be defended."

Anton Dukhonin, the commander in chief, felt that politicians should be left to bicker among themselves. He did not feel himself obliged to carry out the political instructions of exotic and distant Sovnarkom commissars. On November 8 he was ordered by telephone to propose an immediate cease-fire to the Germans — at the front, German trenches were topped with huge cartoons showing President Wilson pushing Russians into battle, while shielding American troops with his arm. Dukhonin at first stalled, but eventually said he would only carry out the orders of a government supported by the army and the country. Lenin dismissed him for refusing to obey orders and for bringing "incredible misery to the toilers of all countries." Dukhonin was, however, instructed to continue his duties until he was replaced as commander in chief by Ensign Nikolai Krylenko. A full general was to be replaced in command of the world's largest army by a former schoolteacher of thirty-two, a narrow-eyed semihysteric with the lowest commissioned rank.

It took Krylenko ten days to leave Petrograd for Mogilev in an armored train, with a bodyguard of fifty sailors from the *Aurora* and a squad of Red Guards. Ominously, Krylenko had already branded Dukhonin an enemy of the people. All those who supported him were to be arrested "regardless of their status, their political position, or their past." This clearly applied to a group of strongly anti-Bolshevik generals, including Lavr Kornilov, who were in Mogilev. As Krylenko's train neared Mogilev, Kornilov urged Anton Dukhonin to move south to the Don territories, where Mikhail Alexeev was mustering an anti-Bolshevik Volunteer Army.

Dukhonin refused, and the other generals left Mogilev to make their way the thousand miles to the Don, disguised as an engineer ensign, a private soldier, and civilians. At 1:00 A.M. on November 20, with Krylenko expected by the hour, Colonel Manakin made a final attempt to get Dukhonin out of Mogilev, offering to take him "wherever you can start the formation of a new army free of Bolsheviks"; Manakin's battalion was about to pull out of town with its own train. "I cannot answer you," the general said, covering his face in his hands. "It's so horrible to be a lump of flesh." Earlier in the evening, Dukhonin and his chief of staff had changed into civilian clothes, ready to flee, but "we looked at each other and became ashamed."

Krylenko's train steamed into Mogilev at 6:00 A.M. Dukhonin was summoned to the station, that sad place from which Nicholas II had set out for the last time as tsar, to hand over his command to the tubby ensign. A crowd of soldiers and sailors roared when Dukhonin arrived at the station. When he was taken on board Krylenko's train, they jeered and drummed on the side of the carriage with their rifle butts. Dukhonin appeared at the carriage step, as though to talk to the mob.

He was shot before he could open his mouth, his body pitchforked with bayonets across the platform and dumped on the track. It was several hours before anyone dared remove it. Krylenko — an "epileptic degenerate," according to the British diplomat Bruce Lockhart, the "most repulsive type I came across in all my dealings with the Bolsheviks" — was a few yards away. Krylenko found it "not possible" to identify the assassins.

The murder of a commander in chief in full view of his successor was an immediate and decisive shock for officers and for those of similar class who were equally threatened. They followed Lavr Kornilov and the Cossacks, drifting south to the valleys of the Don and Kuban, to the intact estates of the Crimea and Caucasus, to pit a consciously White cause against the Reds. Non-Bolsheviks by the million were to fight for the Reds — staff officers,

Cossacks, Kerensky's war minister Alexander Verkhovksy. Czech prisoners of war and the former terrorist Boris Savinkov, as well as Americans, Canadians, Japanese, French, and Britons fought with the Whites. Republicans wore white epaulettes, as parliamentarians served under the five-pointed Red Star. But, in so far as simple color-coding survived the shading loyalties and cross-hatreds of civil war, White already meant right, and Red, left.

Within a few hours of Dukhonin's death, Russian and German armistice delegations were meeting. Krylenko ordered firing to cease on all fronts and for fraternization to begin. "A power which had for three years absorbed millions of the best soldiers and thousands of guns of the Central Powers," the British prime minister Lloyd George wrote, "had finally withdrawn from the fighting line." By the end of November German strength in the West had risen from 150 to 160 divisions, while other units awaited transport from the East.

Formal negotiations opened in tents, railway cars, and the ruined red-brick fortress at Brest-Litovsk, a town on the banks of the Bug which the Russians had fired when they abandoned it in 1916. As the delegates met, the army dissolved, the men "voting with their feet," as Lenin put it. The men helped themselves first to the contents of their regimental depots — food, uniforms, blankets, machine guns which they sold for a few hundred rubles apiece — and looted the garrison towns. At Vinnitsa, the men of a heavy bomber squadron sold off the officers' cutlery and china, typewriters, and furniture. The seasoned timber kept for airframe repairs went for firewood. The soldiers burst into a riverbank liquor store, piercing the storage tanks with such eagerness that vodka flowed into the stream. They ran down the bank with teakettles to take their fill of this precious if dirty mix of water and spirits. Then they went home.

The terms the Germans were to impose on Lenin explained why Kerensky had felt compelled to keep fighting. Russia was to lose sixty-two million of her population, a million and a quarter square miles of arable land, and a third of her industry. White Russia was almost all occupied; the Ukrainian breadbasket became a German protectorate in all but name; the Baltic states were sliced off; and the independence of Finland was confirmed. Parts of the Caucasus were ceded to Turkey. German defeat a year later was partially to undo the humiliation, but this redemption was made possible only by the success of capitalist British, French, and American soldiers on the western front.

There was no peace on the home front. *Grazhdanskaya Voyna* — civil war, an affair not of coups but of troops with distinctive and long-term loyalties fighting in campaigns — arrived swiftly. On the afternoon of Dukhonin's murder, Viktor Manakin was faced with a similar prospect of lonely death on a crowded station platform. The train carrying his battalion was halted outside Zhlobin, ninety miles down the track from Mogilev. The yards were packed with other trains carrying deserters home — "the peculiar method for demobilizing the army at this time."

Manakin walked to the stationmaster's office to check on the delay. Railway stations were dangerous places, for news reached them swiftly along the telegraph. The men knew of Dukhonin's murder. Manakin, though he had spoken with him not many hours before, did not. The room filled with soldiers, eyeing his colonel's epaulettes. A mob waited for him outside the door. His revolver was torn away. He broke free and walked a few steps until he was surrounded. The men discussed whether to kill him on the spot or to wait. Those at the front kept their eyes lowered, "as if to say, 'We have nothing to do with this!' " At the back, they were shouting, "Kill him!"

Manakin was hit on the head by something thrown from behind. The men in front of him were still reluctant to strike him in the face. They began to push him around in the circle from one edge to another. "I was clearly aware that if I should fall, they would trample me to death," Manakin said. "A fallen enemy is no longer frightening." He felt his strength going. Shots rang out. His troopers, running from their train, were firing in the air. Courteously, the circle evaporated. They had had their fling at lynching and, now that order was reestablished, they willingly demurred.

On November 24, Trotsky ordered Krylenko to get ready to "wipe off the face of the earth the counterrevolution of the Cossack generals and the Cadet bourgeoisie." Two days later, the first units of Alexeev's Volunteer Army paraded at Novocherkassk on the Don. Anti-Bolshevik politicians — including Pavel Miliukov, Mikhail Rodzianko, and Boris Savinkov — were beginning to arrive from the north to give a political edge to the cause. On December 2, the Volunteers took nearby Rostov in street fighting, their first major engagement.

Recruitment was informal. Serge Obolensky, commanding a small group of volunteers, came across a friend in a Yalta street dressed in felt hat, dark suit, waterproof coat, high buttoned boots, gloves, and a fine cane. He urged him to join the White cause, and the man did so at once, "cane and all." The Reds enlisted sailors from the Black Sea fleet and convicts freed from Yalta prisons. Obolensky fought off an attack mounted through the gardens of the Massandra Palace on a hill overlooking Yalta. The Reds withdrew, leaving the bodies of their comrades hanging on the wires that supported the rose bushes.

The Whites moved into the city, both sides finding it difficult to identify one another in their old tsarist-designed uniforms and civilian clothes. Two men with rifles challenged Obolensky in a street: "Who are you?" "We're Whites," said Obolensky. At that, the two opened fire and ran. "We shot back," said Obolensky. "They missed and I think we missed." Obolensky jumped over a wall for cover, and landed on a plum Gypsy guitar player who had played at his parties in Petrograd.

Vladimir Antonov-Ovseenko struggled to put a Red force together in Kharkov to slice between the Don country and the Ukraine. In the nascent Red Army, where the Russian Flying Club was commandeered to form an aviation unit and electricians from the Petrograd tram depot were drafted as technical troops, officer ranks were abolished and commanders elected in an attempt to create a "free army of armed citizens." Large units of sailors from the Baltic Fleet, sometimes two thousand strong, were sent to track down the Whites.

Manakin ran into them as his train steamed south for the Don to join the emerging White armies. In Kursk province, Bolshevik sailors in black coats rushed onto the track. They renounced ambush so as to "give battle on even terms. This was a peculiar kind of chivalry characteristic of sailors." Manakin's men opened fire, and several sailors fell. After a while, a delegation of sailors came forward. "What are you fighting for?" they asked. "For our people and for the future of our country," said Manakin. "We are too," said the sailors. "Why should we keep on fighting?" Manakin said, "You stop first." The sailors semaphored each other and the train was allowed to steam on.

Despite such quixotic honor, Manakin realized that "We were beginning the Civil War." Atrocity was its companion.

The Reds retook Yalta and threw fifty White prisoners off the jetty that stretched out into the bay, visible from the terraced slopes of the town. Stones were attached to their feet, and on sunny days the corpses could be seen beneath the sea, waving their hands with the currents. A White officer found a prisoner wearing Obolensky's looted overcoat — it had the English maker's label, "Davis, London," sewn into it — and shot him. *Burzhui* learned to soak their hands in alcohol to crack the skin and to rub dirt into them. Bolsheviks at checkpoints might shoot a man if his hands were soft.

" 'Perfect love driveth out fear,' " Alexander Blok quoted John 4:18 in his diary. "Do not fear the destruction of fortresses, palaces, pictures, books. . . . Fortresses are in our hearts." His optimism was not shared by his friends and he found himself losing them. The distant armed clashes of civil war in the south were reflected elsewhere by a less formal type of class warfare, in which the possessions of bourgeois and noble "plunderers" were in turn plundered by the poor under the slogan "*Grabi nagrablennoe*,"

"Loot the loot." This was a matter of indifference to Lenin; it helped to uproot Russian society.

Blok's Petrograd apartment house in Offitserskaya Street closed tight at dusk after the coup, guarded by a rota of armed residents. There were shots under the windows in the evenings as thieves raided nearby wine cellars. Patrols of Red Guards shot at people who did not take their fancy. David Francis passed a large crowd in the street on his way to the U.S. embassy. His chauffeur, curious, went back to see what was happening and reported to the ambassador in his study. A branch post office had been robbed of twenty-eight thousand rubles and a nineteen-year-old girl teller shot dead. Francis was by now "so accustomed to such outrages that I remarked only that I was sorry . . . and continued to dictate to the stenographer."

Spoil from pillaged apartments was sold at the Alexandrinsky Rinok, the booming thieves' market. Old Bokhara rugs, amber, silver chains, Bristol glass, Chinese porcelain, furs, and cameos stacked the stalls. Somerset Maugham bought two magnificent bead purses.

Pickpockets swarmed in the streets, Meriel Buchanan complained, and firing broke out most nights — "nobody quite knows why." Red Guards swept by the embassy in a car with its lights out, a "machine gun rattling away out of the back window, for no particular object." An old general walking past, his long beard and fur cap silver in the moonlight, was spat at by soldiers.

Felix Yusupov came across worse. He saw a group of sailors kicking a general and beating him with their rifle butts as he dragged himself along the ground, whimpering. "To my horror," Yusupov said, "I saw blood streaming from the two gaping holes in his swollen face where his eyes had once been." Soldiers dossed on the marble floors of the Moika Palace. Yusupov fled to Kiev, but found more shooting, between Bolsheviks and Ukrainian nationalists. Only when he got to the Crimea, and was met at the station by his big Delaunay-Belleville car flying a pennant with his coat of arms on the door, did he feel temporarily safe. In a few days, a band of sailors arrived in the courtyard of the Aï-Todor house with banners reading "Death to the *burzhui.*" Felix noted that one was wearing a diamond bracelet, another a looted brooch. When they discovered that he was Rasputin's murderer, they congratulated him and insisted that he sing to them on his guitar, before shaking hands with him again and again and riding off.

In Moscow, anarchists moved into the finest houses. Broken bottles littered the floors, "magnificent ceilings were perforated with bullet holes . . . wine stains and human excrement blotched the Aubusson carpets. Priceless pictures had been slashed to strips." The Poets Café, in a converted laundry, set out to shock the respectable. It was painted "cannibal orange." The

Futurist poet Vladimir Mayakovsky, blasphemous and suicidal, read his verses each night and scratched a line on the wall — "I like watching children die." When an anarchist fired his revolver into the café ceiling, Mayakovsky quieted the customers by telling them that the past was being destroyed: "Today to the last buttons of our coats life is being made anew!"

The rich drank away their fears in cellar cabarets, like the Podpolye, where the star, a young singer called Vertinsky, his face powdered white, had encore after encore for his lament for dead officers:

> *I do not know why*
> *or for what purpose*
> *Who sent them to death*
> *With relentless, untrembling hand.*
> *Only it was all so useless*
> *So pitiless.*

The song, Bruce Lockhart thought, reflected the mood of an anti-Bolshevik audience whose soul and morale were lost. It was the song of "a class which had already abandoned all hope," a class which "would go to almost any length to avoid death by fighting."

Town militias were replaced by Red Guards, untrained and including ex-convicts and robbers who particularly favored the roads leading from the railway stations. At provincial meetings, "you hear threats against Mensheviks and Social Revolutionaries, who are called 'bloodsuckers,' 'fat bourgeois,' and so on. It is hard to understand what these newborn Bolsheviks really want. All one hears are wild outcries calling for murder, plunder, etc."

A local doctor was shot in the stomach by robbers in Saratov who followed him home after he had cashed a check for three thousand rubles for the town's Deaf and Dumb Asylum. When the militia arrived at the house, the cook thought they were robbers — they looked like highwaymen — and ran to the attic for safety. The militiamen in turn mistook the cook for a bandit, and shot him dead. Housebreakers were cornered by a crowd of women in a building opposite the lodgings of Alexis Babine, the schools inspector. The women became "perfectly frantic," and got hold of heavy sticks of wood and "pounded the captives on their heads, even after they, dead, had been placed on a sleigh."

Soldiers were selling off machine guns in the town market in Saratov, and "one could buy any number of muskets and ammunition." Troopers in a cavalry squadron sold off revolvers at 250 rubles apiece, and their horses for 80 rubles.

At Grozny railroad station in the South, a soldier flicked cigarette ash into an officer's plate of soup. The officer ordered another plate. When it was brought, the soldier spat in it and stood staring at the officer. The officer, so Alexis Babine was told by a friend, "threw himself back in his chair, stared in return, pulled a revolver out of his side pocket and shot the offender." Then the officer shot himself.

In Tula, it was reported in mid-November that the villages were having a "big drunk." Expeditions armed with rifles, revolvers, and clubs set out to "procure the 'national wealth' as vodka is called. Sometimes they meet rival expeditions and a pitched battle takes place. . . . Venereal disease is spreading fast."

Grain was turned into vodka. "Practically every village has fifteen to twenty distilleries," the report continued. An epidemic of gambling was taking place: flush with cash they could not spend on consumer goods, the peasants were "all playing *vingt et un*."

XXIV
The First Chekist

IT HAD STARTED SNOWING in Petrograd on November 5 and continued day after day. Winds swept huge drifts in which automobiles stalled. Driving down the Nevsky in a sled, a surer method of progress, was like going on a mountain switchback. Boys used the slopes of the Neva bridges as toboggan rides, icing the roadways and careening unchecked into pedestrians. Trams broke down and nobody bothered to mend them. People went up into their attics with axes to pillage the rafters for firewood, and roofs collapsed under the weight of snow. Rations were cut to a half pound of bread a day and one egg a week. Protest strikes gathered strength.

Having weathered Kerensky's counterthrust, Lenin had to fight his own party once more to preserve its domination. The railway union continued to be bitterly hostile to the coup and to one-party rule. The railwaymen were the cream of Russian labor; literate and politically sophisticated enough to grasp the danger of a purely Bolshevik government, they were refusing Sovnarkom orders to drive troop trains.

Lenin was enraged when he learned of the compromise that Lev Kamenev had discussed with the union as the price of its cooperation. Lenin was to be replaced as chairman of Sovnarkom by the Social Revolutionary leader Viktor Chernov. The Social Revolutionaries were the largest party in the country and the union insisted that this be recognized. Under the Kamenev scheme, the Bolsheviks would be offered minor ministries in administration weighted in favor of Social Revolutionaries and Mensheviks. This was nonsense, Lenin said, and "must be stopped at once." "Diplomatic camouflage for military action" was one thing — Lenin had no objections to tricking the union into providing transport. But serious negotiation was heresy.

The Bolshevik central committee continued to doubt Lenin's judgment. It voted ten to four in favor of maintaining discussions with the other socialist parties. Trotsky's intervention was crucial. Lenin set the strategy — one-party rule — but it was Trotsky who carried out the tactical maneuvers to achieve it. Admirers liked to say that Lenin was a "finely tuned and powerful engine," with Trotsky as his "drive shaft." Automobiles were still a novelty, the one luxury the Bolsheviks did not deny themselves — Lenin had started the revolution with a Renault and, like Trotsky, would end the civil war with a Rolls-Royce — and automotive comparisons were often made.

There was nothing mechanical, however, in the relations between the two men. Their qualities blended — even Lenin's rare sense of malice was matched by Trotsky, whom Bruce Lockhart described as "an incarnation of belligerent hate." Trotsky was able to accept a Lenin diktat and sculpt it to a subtler shape.

He did so now. Trotsky assured the committee that the "whole petty bourgeois scum," railway union included, would come over to the Bolsheviks once "it learns that our authority is strong." The petty bourgeois were, serf-like, looking for a "force to which to submit." Why not hedge for time? Negotiations could continue with the sympathetic Left Social Revolutionaries, to give the veneer of coalition, while they were broken off with the powerful mainstream parties.

In a fresh vote, a majority of the central committee now voted to condemn opposition parties. Lev Kamenev and Gregory Zinoviev again led a revolt. *Izvestiya* ran a letter from them on November 4. The central committee, the two men wrote, "insists on a purely Bolshevik government no matter what the consequences and how many victims the workers and soldiers will have to sacrifice. . . . We cannot assume responsibility for this fatal policy, pursued in opposition to the will of the vast part of the proletariat and the troops." They resigned from the central committee. Lenin called them "deserters and blacklegs." Four out of the eleven new people's commissars also quit.

The resignations did not greatly concern Lenin, for the principle of rejecting genuine power-sharing was safely established. He casually suggested that Yakov Sverdlov should replace Kamenev: "I would like you to become the chairman of the central executive committee, what do you say?" On November 8, Sverdlov was elected by the Bolshevik-packed committee. Eight months after the abdication of Nicholas, the thirty-two-year-old son of an engraver, twice exiled and three times imprisoned, a frail man with a startling bass voice and hooded black eyes "like a modern Spanish inquisitor," became the titular head of the Russian state.

The manifest illegalities of Sovnarkom decrees produced furious protest. The press decree was seen as a suppression of freedom of expression on a scale never indulged by tsarist censors. Even Bolsheviks were embarrassed. Anatoly Lunacharsky, conscience-stricken, felt he could no longer continue as People's Commissar for Enlightenment. "What next?" Lunacharsky wrote. "This is more than I can stand. I am helpless to halt this terror." His resignation was refused. The Milrevkom in Moscow unilaterally abolished the press decree on November 21. The Left Social Revolutionary P. P. Proshian, a natural ally in other respects, thought it a "clear and determined expression of a system of political terror and incitement to civil war."

A more furious onslaught came from Maxim Gorky, who turned "dark and black and grim" at the mention of Lenin and Trotsky, his voice like a dog bark. Gorky wrote that the two "have already become poisoned with the filthy venom of power," destroying the rights of the individual for which the democracy had struggled. Lenin was a "cold-blooded trickster who spares neither the honor nor the life of the proletariat. . . . He does not know the popular masses, he has not lived with them." Gorky compared Lenin to a chemist in a laboratory — except that, where a chemist employed dead matter to gain results valuable for life, Lenin was working on the living flesh of Russia.

Gorky was "especially suspicious, especially distrustful" of a flaw in the Russian soul. Not long ago a slave, as soon as he got his hands on power the Russian became the most unbridled despot.

Those who resigned, Lenin guessed correctly, would soon return. They had nowhere else to go. He was indifferent to Gorky's accusations, counterattacking immediately, spraying insults and violent slurs. *Pravda* accused Gorky of betrayal and becoming an enemy of the people. Such campaigns of vilification were, as countless Russians were to discover, immensely wearing on the nerves. "I can't sleep," Gorky soon complained. "My mood is so heavy that it is simply a catastrophe."

To mounting criticism that Sovnarkom decrees had no basis in law, Lenin replied that the government could not be bound by mere formalities; its legitimacy rested not on the vote but on the untested "confidence of the broad masses." Critics were "petty bourgeois scum" trading in "parliamentary obstructionism." The flavor of Sovnarkom sessions reminded one observer of the sitting of an underground revolutionary committee. The commissars sat in greatcoats and the "forbidding leather jackets" that were their trademark. The talk was crude and rough, for most were ex-convicts, inured to violence and contemptuous of the law, having spent much of their lives on the wrong side of it.

The truth was simple. "From the moment the Provisional Government was declared deposed," Trotsky was to reminisce, "Lenin acted in matters large and small as the government." Once a decree had been signed by Lenin and published in the official *Gazeta,* it became law. Many important decisions were issued as secret circulars. Within a few days of the coup, Russia was reverting to an autocracy more secretive and extreme than that overthrown with such joy in February.

Not all of those who sensed that dictatorship was the real pattern beneath the Soviet camouflage were content to wait until the Constituent Assembly was convened.

Companies of Red Guards stood by fires at street corners, stopping passersby to ask questions. "These men," Meriel Buchanan complained, "unkempt, unwashed, unshaved, totally ignorant, had become the real rulers of Petrograd." British subjects were more or less prisoners in Russia, kept as hostages and forbidden to leave while Russian pacifists remained interned in England. German and Austrian prisoners swaggered around, confident that their side had won. Government buildings were silent and empty. More shops joined the strike day by day, while soldiers, seeing how easy it was, broke the shutters and looted them.

From early November on, almost the whole of the civil service, and managers and staff in many private companies, refused to work in a spontaneous gesture of outrage at the illegality of the Bolshevik regime. When the commissars descended from the Smolny to take possession of their ministries, they found, along with mountains of paper and folders, only couriers, cleaning people, and doormen. All the officials, down to the typists, had either left or sat silently at their desks.

Staff locked themselves in their rooms when Trotsky paid his first visit to the ministry of foreign affairs on Alexander Square. Workmen had to be brought to force the locks. When Trotsky told them that he was the new commissar, six hundred officials greeted him with ironic laughter and went home. He searched for the secret treaties to discover that the former assistant foreign minister, Neratov, had disappeared with them.

At public welfare, Alexandra Kollontai burst into tears before arresting the strikers to force them to hand over the keys to her office and the safe. When the safe was opened, she found that the former minister, Countess Panina, had taken all the funds off with her. The countess refused to hand them back unless ordered to do so by the Constituent Assembly. The two women loathed one another, Panina noting cattily that Kollontai "dresses very well, which is exceedingly unusual among women interested in revolutionary ideas." At the Commissariat of Enlightenment, teachers and education officials walked out. Lunacharsky said that he could persuade empty-headed clerks to return, but "all the intellectual workers stubbornly insist on their opinion that we have usurped power."

Mass layoffs accompanied the collapse in business orders and the attempts at worker control. "If you establish control, then I will close the factory," the director of the big Triangle rubberworks warned his staff. "I cannot work under control." He was as good as his word. White-collar workers and skilled engineers walked out of the Putilov works.

The work force, far from welcoming the coup as Bolshevik propaganda insisted, was surly and uncooperative. When the Putilov foundries managed to get sixty wagonloads of coal through a "pusher," the works committee called for volunteers from the twelve thousand men laid off on two-thirds pay to unload them. Only two turned up. The jobless turned to traditional scapegoats. "The people have come to understand the dirty deeds of the Yids," the self-styled Party of the Unemployed threatened. "Jews have settled on all the committees. We suggest they leave Petrograd within the next three days."

"In the orgy of a newly acquired freedom," the chairman of Spies Petroleum complained, "there is no limit to the demands of uneducated labor intoxicated with the academic theories of political agitators." The directors of North Caucasian Oilfields announced on November 12 that they were capping a new well, for it "has become ruinous to produce until this spasm of madness had subsided." The big producers had drawn up a protest against the requisitioning of oil — "but to whom are we to deliver it?" British shareholders in the Irtysh Corporation were told that a two-hundred-foot-thick seam of gold ore freshly discovered in Siberia would remain unexploited until a stable government returned.

Foreign shareholders were, nevertheless, urged not to dump Russian stocks. "The position has been usurped by a group of people who are in no sense representative of those whom they claim to lead," the chairman of the Russian Corporation, A. W. Tait, told his annual general meeting in London. "They cannot hold the reins of government for any time."

Private banks, pharmacies, schoolteachers, and the management of public utilities struck. The State Bank and the State Treasury, though the former continued to pay out more than half a billion rubles a week to the army and other institutions, refused to hand over a kopek to the Sovnarkom. On November 7, Viacheslav Menzhinsky, the bank clerk turned finance commissar, entered the State Bank by the Catherine Canal with an escort of armed sailors and fruitlessly demanded ten million rubles. "Without money, we are helpless," he complained. "The wages of the railroad men, the telegraph workers, must be paid. All the bank clerks in Russia have been bribed to stop work. . . . But Lenin has issued an order to dynamite the vaults."

Menzhinsky was back on November 11 with an ultimatum in place of dynamite: if funds were not forthcoming within twenty minutes, the staff would lose their jobs and pension rights. Those of military age would be drafted. The bank would not budge. Staff voted to continue to deny the Bolsheviks any funds. The *Financial Times* in London finally abandoned its optimism that day, with the sarcastic headline "Russian Millennium — Lenin Abolishes Capital and Land Ownership." It noted that Russia was desperately short of finance — "but what group of banks will advance money to a government the avowed purpose of which is to bring about a complete social upheaval?"

Lenin had the bank director brought to the Smolny and kept under guard. This had no effect and on November 17 he sent two Bolsheviks off to the bank with orders not to come back without the money. They rounded up bank officials and forced them to open the vaults at gunpoint. Five million rubles were taken in sacks back to the Smolny and tossed on Lenin's desk. As in prewar days, the Bolsheviks were back in the bank-robbing business.

Fearful of assassination, Lenin worked, ate and slept in the Smolny, access to his office guarded by Latvians. Running a government was a new and often puzzling task. Party members were frightened of Lenin, or could not get past his security, so that they left him well alone, while every little difficulty was brought to Trotsky. The foreign commissar lived in one room at the top of the Smolny building, partitioned off like a poor artist's studio. At one end were two little cots, where Trotsky slept with his wife, and a cheap little dresser. At the other end was a desk, where he worked without a stenographer. There were no pictures, no comfort anywhere. Trotsky was overstressed, and flew into rages.

Strikebreaking was a further priority. An Extraordinary Communication pasted on city walls accused "criminals" in "government institutions, banks, railroads, post, and telegraph" of counterrevolution: "THE MILREVKOM GIVES THESE CRIMINALS A LAST WARNING. In the event of the least resistance on their part the harshness of the measures against them will correspond to the seriousness of their crime." Bank workers countered with their own leaflets: "We cannot take part in plundering the people's property. . . . Save the people's property from robbery!"

Red Guards and soldiers were used to gain entry into public offices from mid-November on. Striking senior staff were dismissed and imprisoned, and office juniors were tempted to return to work with giddy promotions after signing pledges of subordination to the Sovnarkom. But most ministries were working only fitfully by Christmas, and some not at all.

* * *

The same coercion was used in food supplies. Bands of sailors and Red Guards roamed the capital, routing into warehouses, freight yards, and barges. Heavily armed expeditions of Kronstadt sailors were sent to the South and to Siberia with roving commissions to capture cities held by the Whites and to get food. A notice would be pinned up on a fence — the usual way in which the Bolshevik rulers announced their will since local newspapers were suppressed — saying that all the houses in a town would be searched for provisions. Armed squads then went to work, concentrating on *burzhui* properties.

The painter Marc Chagall dreaded the Bolshevik orders pinned on fences that greeted citizens when they awoke. "The factories were stopping," Chagall wrote. "The horizons opened. Space and emptiness. No more bread. The black lettering on the morning posters made me feel sick at heart." Chagall went without food for days, sitting watching "a bridge, the beggars and the poor wretches weighed down with bundles." Lenin, Chagall thought, had turned Russia, "upside down the way I turn my pictures."

Passenger trains on the Trans-Siberian were held in sidings to allow freight trains loaded with bolts of cloth and metal bars to steam eastbound for Siberia. The goods were to be bartered with peasants for grain and potatoes. Private stocks of fuel were confiscated.

"Speculators" picked up in the Astoria were marched off to the Kresty. "Jimmy," who had learned to mix his famous cocktails at the Waldorf-Astoria in New York, closed his bar in the Hotel de l'Europe. Advertisements were made a monopoly of Bolshevik newspapers, and private printing plants and paper supplies became Soviet property. Non-Bolshevik papers that were still appearing suspended publication in protest, or disobeyed the law and were closed. Neratov, the former assistant foreign minister who had refused to hand over the secret treaties to Trotsky, was frightened enough to return them to the ministry. Trotsky caused an international scandal by publishing the treaties in *Pravda*.

The "rich classes and their sympathizers" were threatened with starvation if they did not stop "inciting strikes and . . . interrupting communications." They would, the Milrevkom warned, be "deprived of the right of receiving food." Lest they survive on their existing supplies, "all reserves which they possess will be confiscated." The assets of Russo-Asiatic Consolidated, one of the greatest mining enterprises in the world, with interests in copper, coal, gold, and riverboats, were seized on grounds of the company's economic "sabotage."

As the ruble collapsed to 385 to £10, the rush to transfer assets abroad accelerated. The price of jewelry in Paris slumped further with the oversupply of fine pieces from Russia, and the specialist art market in icons was swamped. Anatoly Lunacharsky forbade the export of any work of art more than twenty-five years old, but smugglers had no difficulty in bribing officials on the Finnish frontier. A School of Proletarian Drama was set up to banish the *burzhui* "theater of frivolity." The Commissar of Enlightenment reorganized the Imperial Porcelain Factory in Petrograd to serve the new state by producing plates with portraits of Lenin and Marx and quotations from Saint Thomas More — "Everywhere I see the conspiracy of the rich seeking their own ends in the name of the general good." The famous Gardner factory in Moscow replaced its china figures of officers and tsars with Red Guards, sailors, and women sewing Red banners. At the Fabergé works in Petrograd, which had crafted an exquisite Easter egg for the tsar each year since 1884, management was taken over by a workers' committee.

Serge Rachmaninov took advantage of a proposed concert tour in Sweden to abandon his 120,000 ruble investment in his Ivanovka estate. The composer took with him a single small suitcase with the first act of his *Monna Vanna* and the score of Nikolai Rimsky-Korsakov's *Golden Cockerel*. No one saw him off on the train from Petrograd, though Fedor Chaliapin sent him a farewell note attached to a can of caviar and some homemade white bread for the journey. The customs official at the border, searching for jewelry and gold, thought that Rachmaninov's musical manuscripts were child's exercise books and let them through.

In Tobolsk, Nicholas was shocked by the coup. He regarded Lenin and Trotsky as German agents, and the children's tutor for the first time heard the tsar regret his abdication. Kerensky, and with him his orders for humane treatment of the royal family, had gone. The guards had become surlier. They ordered Nicholas to remove his colonel's epaulettes — epaulettes were a symbol of "counterrevolution" and during the civil war White officers were to have them nailed into their shoulders when they were captured by Reds. Nicholas wore his secretly in his room, covering them with a cloak when he went out. Fuel was kept short and Alexandra was suffering badly from chilblains. The family busied itself by putting on a performance of Chekhov's *The Bear*, young Alexis eagerly dressing up in a beard while his father played the title role.

Kerensky was hiding sixty miles southeast of Petrograd in an isolated cabin belonging to the uncle of one of the Social Revolutionary soldiers who had smuggled him out of the palace at Gatchina. He wrote an appeal to the Russian people. "Come to your senses!" he said. "Don't you see that your simplicity has been abused, and that the Bolsheviks have shamelessly deceived you? . . . This is me speaking to you, Kerensky." He justified his record — "only now, with the violence and horror of Leninist coercion, is it clear even to the blind that when I was in power, there was real freedom and democracy."

The appeal reached Petrograd. Viktor Chernov dismissed it as the "cry of an exhausted and wounded soul."

Voting for the Constituent Assembly began in Petrograd on November 12, a day marked by the trashing of the offices of the Cadet newspaper *Rech* by Bolshevik heavies. Moscow voted on November 19. The election continued to the end of the month elsewhere, carried out on the terms set by the Provisional Government, in all territories except those occupied by the Germans, with all men and women of twenty and over entitled to vote. The elections were free — few incidents were reported and seventeen parties put up candidates in Petrograd alone — and the turnout was high. Seven out of ten went to the polls in the twin capitals, with 100 percent levels claimed in some country districts. The results doomed the assembly.

Socialists won more than two-thirds of the total, but the Social Revolutionaries outstripped the Bolsheviks by 40 to 24 percent. The Mensheviks, ruined by Julius Martov's indecision, scraped 2.6 percent and the Left Social Revolutionaries 1 percent. On the right, the Cadets polled 4.7 percent. Ominously, nationalist parties — Ukrainian, Georgian, Azerbaijani, Armenian, Kazakh — won almost 14 percent of the total all-Russian vote, with outright majorities in many of their own regions.

Analysis was gloomy for the Bolsheviks, the results like a bone in the throat. A good performance in the big cities relied heavily on support from the garrisons, now rapidly disbanding. The Cadets ran a good second in Petrograd and Moscow, and beat the Bolsheviks in eleven provincial capitals. Well organized and financed, they remained a powerful threat. The countryside remained overwhelmingly loyal to the Social Revolutionaries, despite the Bolshevik theft of their policies. In the 707-seat assembly, the Bolsheviks would muster only 175 delegates against 410 Social Revolutionaries.

On November 20, without waiting for the complete results, the Sovnarkom decided to postpone the opening of the assembly indefinitely. It ordered enquiries into electoral "abuses." On the night of November 21, enraged members of the Petrograd Soviet, the trade unions, and all socialist parties but the Bolsheviks and Left Social Revolutionaries formed a Union for the Defense of the Constituent Assembly.

The following day, Lenin issued a decree dissolving existing courts, including the Senate, the highest appeal court. Only minor local courts were to remain. The former law student abolished the legal profession itself, the office of the procurator, the attorney general, and most of the magistrature. In their place came Revolutionary Tribunals, empowered to try counterrevolutionary and economic "crimes" and to impose penalties at the "dictates of revolutionary conscience." In effect, Lenin was smashing the rule of law in Russia, replacing judges with amateurs without professional qualifications other than the ability to read and write, and the possession of a "revolutionary conscience." Lenin had criticized the Paris Communards of 1871 for their failure to destroy the French legal system; his own contempt for due process of law was again on view on November 23, when he ordered the arrest of the Constituent Assembly's electoral commission for its refusal to hand over its files to the Sovnarkom for verification.

The Defense Union declared that it would open the assembly on November 28, in defiance of Lenin's orders. Large crowds on a day of rare blue skies accompanied deputies elected to the assembly to the Tauride, carrying banners: "Long live the Constituent Assembly, the Master of Russia!" The palace was blocked off by pro-Bolshevik Latvian riflemen. Pitirim Sorokin, elected a Social Revolutionary deputy, climbed the wrought-iron gates and opened them. The Tauride commandant, the "exceedingly repulsive" Moisei Uritsky, was forced to let the deputies enter after Sorokin had slyly congratulated the troops for their "welcome" to the "highest authority in Russia."

In the afternoon, Lenin issued a "Decree concerning the arrest of the leaders of the Civil War against the Revolution." This did not, of course, refer to the Bolsheviks' own assault on the Provisional Government. It was used by Lenin to declare the Cadets to be enemies of the people. During the night, armed Bolshevik squads arrested every leading Cadet they could track down. Several of those seized had been elected to the assembly. Their parliamentary immunity was ignored. The Cadet party itself was outlawed, and denied membership in the Constituent Assembly.

The decree, the lawyer and Left Social Revolutionary Isaac Steinberg said, was "almost an invitation to terror issued by the most authoritative institution in the country." Lenin had no time for such niceties. "It is senseless even to discuss the question of legality," he said. "The Cadet party constitutes the general staff of the civil war." Alexander Blok realized what was afoot — it was the "gray-purple, the silver stars and amethyst of the blizzard." He surrendered to its force: "I love the Cadets in my blood . . . but I would be *ashamed* to support them."

The following day, after the remaining delegates had passed a resolution calling on the nation to defend the Constituent Assembly, the Latvians forced them to leave and sealed the palace.

Having attacked the *burzhui*, Lenin now turned on the peasants. The Congress of Peasants' Deputies, representing the great bulk of the population, had backed the Committee for Salvation against the coup. It met in Petrograd at the end of November. Bolshevik attempts to rig its membership by packing it with garrison troops failed and it retained a Social Revolutionary majority. The Bolsheviks responded by shouting down speakers, yelling, booing, and invading the rostrum. Lenin appeared at the session on December 2. "You will bring Russia to the point where Nicholas will be replaced by Lenin," a Social Revolutionary shouted, pointing at him. "We need no autocratic authority." Lenin responded with a sarcastic attack on the Constituent Assembly. After he had left, the delegates passed Chernov's resolution acknowledging the legitimacy of the Constituent Assembly and condemning Bolshevik measures against the Cadets.

The congress was chaired by Maria Spiridonova, the Left Social Revolutionary, the tiny figure who had murdered the Tambov police official on a station platform as a nineteen-year-old in 1906. With her big gray eyes and soft brown hair worn in a coronet braid, she was said to have the greatest political following of any woman in the world, for the peasants adored her. But Bruce Lockhart thought her "more hysterical than practical," and the Bolsheviks found her easy to mold. She obligingly ruled that the resolution was not binding.

On December 4, Bolsheviks and Left Social Revolutionaries again reduced the congress to a shambles, putting up such a racket of taunts and screams that no speaker could be heard. The Social Revolutionaries walked out, singing the Marseillaise, to resume the congress in the Agricultural Museum on the Fontanka. On December 6, the Bolshevik and Left Social Revolutionary rump declared their own sessions to be the only legitimate congress.

As a minority, the Bolsheviks were well attuned to the strategic use of terror. "There is nothing immoral in the proletariat finishing off the dying class," Trotsky had declared on December 2. "This is its right. You are indignant . . . at the petty terror which we direct against our class opponents. But be put on notice that in one month at most this terror will assume more frightful forms, on the model of the great revolutionaries of France. Our enemies will face not prison but the guillotine."

The proletariat, in the strict sense of the industrial working class, accounted for fewer than five people in a hundred. The new commissar for foreign affairs was proposing as "nothing immoral" a pogrom so grotesque — "finishing off" an entire class — that his statement was ignored. Both Trotsky and Lenin were still considered exotics, "washed up unexpectedly from abroad." Their thought was a mystery to Russia at large.

It was only dimly appreciated inside the party that the systematic use of terror was natural policy to Lenin. In July, Prince Lvov had willingly handed over the premiership to Kerensky because he felt that Kerensky could bring himself "to fire at the people." In the event, Kerensky had no stomach for such work. Firing at the people slipped easily into Lenin's vision of a world composed only of friend and foe. Lenin was at pains to conceal his encouragement of terror. Within a few months, it was proposed at a meeting to kill foresters who were short on a wood quota — "when a dozen or two have been shot, the rest will tackle the job in earnest." Lenin remarked carefully, with his "sly smile," that "the shooting of foresters, though adopted, should be omitted from the official minutes."

Lenin believed in the physical elimination of foes — real, imagined, or potential — on an intellectual basis. Leninist terror had little to do with the heat of the moment. Nine years before, commenting in an essay, "Lessons of the Commune," Lenin had isolated as its major failure the "excessive generosity" of the Paris working class — "it should have *exterminated its enemies*" instead of feebly attempting to exert moral influence on them. Terror was a form of pesticide to be used on people whom Lenin dehumanized as "harmful insects . . . scoundrel fleas . . . bedbugs."

He now had opponents to imprison, funds to find, and strikers to return to work. He detailed controls to be imposed on the moneyed classes. All those with an income of more than five hundred rubles a month, those with capital in excess of a thousand rubles, or those owning shares or property, were required to sign a declaration stating their address and income. Failure was punishable by a fine of five thousand rubles and a year's imprisonment. The same sanctions applied to those guilty of "sabotage or evasion of work in banks, government or public offices, joint-stock companies, railways, etc."

A system of registration needed a repressive agency to enforce it. Lenin approved the creation of a *Chrezvychainaia kommissia po borbe s kontr-revoliutsiei i sabotazhem* — "Extraordinary Commission for Struggle against Counterrevolution and Sabotage." It gained its working name from the Russian initials for Extraordinary Commission — "Ch K," pronounced "Cheka." Its brief was to "investigate and liquidate" all attempts at sabotage and counterrevolution and to hand over those responsible to revolutionary tribunals.

Such a commission needed a man of rare qualities to run it. "Where are we going to find our Fouquier-Tinville?" Lenin asked.

It was a precise question — Lenin had refreshed his knowledge of the

French Revolution during his stay in Finland three months before. Fouquier had been the chief prosecutor of the French revolutionary tribunals. He was quiet, bureaucratic, and vindictive, attaining a grisly record in personally dispatching a daily average of twenty-six victims to the guillotine over the course of a month. Fouquier obliged Chrétien-Guillaume Malesherbes, the noble liberal who had defended Louis XVI at his trial, to watch as his daughter and granddaughter were guillotined before him, and had Malesherbes's seventy-six-year-old sister executed for good measure.

Fouquier worked with catchall accusations — "spreading false news," "depraving morals." No witnesses or defense counsels were permitted to interfere with the flow of guilty verdicts in his courts. When he himself fell, and awaited his own appointment with the "national razor," fellow prisoners banged the walls of their cell in protest at being confined with a "monster."

Fouquier had a favorite phrase. When he felt a trial had lasted a few minutes too long, he would inform the jury that it had "heard enough to be illuminated."

Such was the man Lenin wished to recreate. Lenin found his technician of terror in Felix Dzerzhinsky. The son of minor Polish nobility, now forty years old, Dzerzhinsky had been arrested for revolutionary activity at twenty and had spent nearly eleven years in tsarist jails and at hard labor, including a year in solitary confinement. Above a slender and haggard figure, his black hair was long and waving as a poet's, his face abnormally thin and angled, the lips and receding chin concealed by a jutting mustache and a "satanic pointed beard." Dzerzhinsky was exceptionally hard-working and meticulous, his manners correct and his speech quiet. Bruce Lockhart found him "grim and formidable . . . without a ray of humor in his character." His deep-set blue eyes "never twinkled . . . his eyelids seemed paralyzed."

Dzerzhinsky had a favorite expression of his own: "We don't want justice, we want to settle accounts."

On December 7, the Sovnarkom agreed to the establishment of the Cheka and to Dzerzhinsky's appointment as chairman. The same day, the man the Chekists most wanted to capture slipped further from their grasp. Fearing betrayal, Alexander Kerensky left the cabin where he had been hiding and set out in a sled along the frozen Malaya Vishera River. His destination was a small, filthy hut in the wilds near Novgorod. On December 8, Lenin sent "arch-important" orders for "not less than 100 *absolutely reliable* Party members" to be sent to the Cheka. That night, and uninterruptedly thereafter, squads of Chekists set out in trucks to search, interrogate, and arrest.

Cheka powers were broad. In December, Lenin drafted a *dekret* nationalizing banks. In it, he outlined a universal labor obligation intended to enliven class hatred and to humiliate the rich. "The first step: consumer-labor, budget-labor booklets for the rich, control over them," Lenin wrote. "Their duty: to work as ordered, else — 'enemies of the people.' " The Cheka's role in this was noted by an addition and a parenthetical phrase in the margin: "Dispatch to the front, compulsory labor, confiscation, arrests (execution by shooting)." It was confirmed the following month that the "parasitic elements of the population" — a phrase so vague that the Cheka's embrace could be and was extended to any group on a simple sadistic whim — were to be "destroyed."

The Bolsheviks were reluctant to acknowledge their new creature — the announcement of its formation was restricted to two sentences in *Pravda*. The link with the Okhrana was reinforced by the siting of the Cheka head-quarters in former tsarist police offices on Gorokhovaya Street in Petrograd. The *intelligentsiya*, the thinkers and artists who traditionally struggled with the national conscience, were revolted. The Bolsheviks made great play of inviting the literary and artistic intelligentsia to meet at the Smolny for discussions.

Alexander Blok, walking about "young and merry and wide awake with shining eyes," attended. Few others came, he admitted — Vladimir Mayakovsky, a couple of actors and theatrical producers. Blok mocked the rest — they "run around and squeal 'Oh! Oh! We're burning!' " — but his own welcome for the Bolsheviks was a reversal of intelligence. He hoped that the "brain of the country" might be "ripped out quickly, cruelly, and authoritatively." Conceding that he was welcoming a throwback to Tartar cruelty, he warned the West that "If you destroy our revolution . . . we shall open wide the gates to the East. Your skins will go for Chinese tambourines."

Blok's fellow Russians were less eager. Dzerzhinsky had to staff the Cheka largely from minorities — Poles like himself, Armenians, Jews, and Latvians. "*Soft, too soft is the Russian,*" Lenin had complained. "He is incapable of applying the harsh measures of revolutionary terror."

Lenin took steps to protect the harshness. On the night of December 9, the Left Social Revolutionaries were persuaded to enter the Sovnarkom as junior partners. Some concessions were made to obtain this coalition fig leaf. The Social Revolutionaries were able to insist on a slight easing of censorship, and on the convocation of the Constituent Assembly for January 5. The twenty-nine-year-old Left Social Revolutionary lawyer, Isaac Steinberg, became justice commissar. The Bolsheviks refused point-blank to abolish the Cheka.

Steinberg despised Dzerzhinsky as a "gleaming fanatic" driven by an "unquenchable hatred for his class enemies." It was, Steinberg said, "my lot to fight against Dzerzhinsky from the very start on this question of priority: law and justice versus security of the regime." On December 15, Steinberg ordered all Cheka prisoners to be released. Dzerzhinsky ignored him and, secure in Lenin's approval, arrested members of the Defense Union four days later.

Russia, Alexander Blok thought, "has infected man with health. . . . Cosmos is born out of chaos." It was not a view that would survive. Shortly before he died, in 1921, his poems suppressed, Blok wrote, "She's gulped me down at last, that filthy, grunting, mother-of-mine Russia, like a sow her piglet." The year 1917 in Russia, the *annus mirabilis* of plurality and tolerance, had become the birthing pit of the one-party state, the leader, and the execution cellar.

Epilogue

IT WAS NOT UNTIL LATE DECEMBER, Louise Bryant said, that the "rich people were beginning to fear that the Soviet government might stick." The official brutality of the Cheka was matched by the people. Shortly after Christmas, Maxim Gorky saw a crowd standing on a bridge at the Fontanka. "They're drowning thieves," someone explained. "Hey, he's howling!" said another as the crowd strained to catch the death shouts. "It looks," Gorky wrote, "as if these people brought up on torture have now been given the right to torture one another freely."

The Constituent Assembly, the "real master" of Russia so eagerly awaited since March, opened in the Tauride on January 5, 1918. A demonstration was organized by the Defense Union to march to the palace with banners calling for "All Power to the Constituent Assembly." Bolshevik troops under Nikolai Podvoisky opened fire on fifty thousand marchers on the Liteiny, scattering them and tearing their banners to pieces. "Their dress was neat and poor," Edgar Sisson, President Wilson's special representative in Russia, noted of the demonstrators. "The ornate were not here." All were unarmed. There were around fifty casualties.

Lenin entered the Tauride, cautiously, through the back door, at 1:00 P.M., "excited and pale like a corpse." He was protected by bodyguards — a member of the party central committee on his way to the palace in a sled had been ambushed in an alley by thieves who made off with his fur coat. The palace square was filled with troops and Red Guards. Latvians and Kronstadt sailors, armed with rifles, grenades, and revolvers, were inside the building. "It's going to be a regular Wild West show," said the socialist mayor of Stockholm, present as an observer. "Everyone's carrying a gun."

Only half of the delegates elected in November were present, but the Bolsheviks were well outnumbered. Lenin did not let the session begin until he was told at 4:00 P.M. that Podvoisky had broken up the pro-Assembly crowds in the streets. Lenin had mislaid his Browning revolver and was irritated at having to go into the hall without it. When a delegate started speaking in Ukrainian, the Bolsheviks howled that they did not want to hear any language except Russian. It was a warning to minority aspirations.

Viktor Chernov was elected chairman of the Constituent Assembly. The vote was taken slowly and carefully, by putting balls into glass jars. The Bolsheviks yawned at this display of democracy. A Bolshevik motion was put by Yakov Sverdlov requiring the Assembly to renounce its authority to legislate, the purpose for which it had been elected. Sverdlov also demanded that the Assembly ratify all Sovnarkom decrees. All banks, and factories, mines, railways, and means of production and transportation, were to belong to the Soviet Republic. General compulsory labor was to be introduced to "destroy the class of parasites."

The great Constituent Assembly, for which more than thirty-six million people had voted in November, was asked to rubber-stamp Lenin's diktats and to dissolve itself. Lenin sprawled on a staircase, his head nodding, his hand over his eyes, pretending to be asleep. His attitude reminded Sisson of a "goat-getting stunt." "Boring!" Lenin said of the proceedings. The Bolsheviks, taking their cue from Lenin and lolling in their seats, were defeated by 237 votes to 136. The Bolshevik delegates walked out, declaring the Assembly to be counterrevolutionary.

The great names of the Russian democracy rose to speak, Chernov himself, Matvei Skobelev, Irakli Tsereteli, his attack on the Bolsheviks "cracking like whip lashes and cutting as deep" as he described their policy as no more than "conquest from without and civil war from within." A sailor, sitting in Sisson's box, cursed Tsereteli in a monotone and raised his rifle at him. Another sailor amused himself by sighting at Chernov along his gun barrel, grinning the while.

Lenin stayed on until 10:00 P.M., delighted by the sailors taking their imaginary potshots at the parliamentarians below. He did not address the Assembly, lest he appear to legitimize it. Instead, Lenin chatted with John Reed and Albert Rhys Williams about the difficulties of learning Russian, advising the American correspondents to start by learning the nouns and to leave the grammar until last. The Bolsheviks met in another part of the building, and passed a resolution dissolving the Constituent Assembly.

Sisson took himself off to try to find some food at 1:00 A.M. The Tauride canteen had nothing but tea. At 2:30 A.M., Pavel Dybenko ordered the sailors in the hall to end the session. A little later, the anarchist commander of the guard, the sailor Anatoly Zheleezniakov, a veteran of the Villa Durnovo, tapped Viktor Chernov on the back and told him to close the session because the guard was tired. "We are also tired," Chernov replied. "But exhaustion cannot interrupt our work which all Russia is watching." The sailors started turning off the lights, one by one.

At about 4:00 A.M. on January 6, the Assembly broke up. When delegates returned to the Tauride at 5:00 P.M. to resume the session, the entrance was blocked by troops. The only session of a Russian parliament, elected freely and with universal suffrage, had lasted a little over twelve hours. On January 8, the Bolsheviks opened their own pseudo-Assembly, the Third Congress of Soviets, in which they and their Left Social Revolutionary allies had 94 percent of the seats in place of the 25 percent of the vote the two parties had mustered in November.

The dictatorship that followed was, as Peter Struve had observed of Lenin, marked by the quality of its hatred. During the civil war that now spilled through the country, the malice first consumed or forced into exile those opponents on which it could lay hands. It did so, not simply by the individual, but by the class. The terror broadened in a ripple effect, to engulf the better-off peasants who had been far from the original center, and eventually to swamp, with rare exceptions, the Bolshevik leadership of 1917 itself.

Under a variety of acronyms, Chekists were the functionaries of terror. Their first known victim was "Prince Eboli," a Petrograd robber and blackmailer shot for masquerading as a Chekist in February of 1918. He was followed by countless others, for Felix Dzerzhinsky developed his agency swiftly and well. When Lenin moved the government to Moscow in March 1918, Dzerzhinsky sought a headquarters. He found it in the offices of the Iakor Insurance Company at 11 Bolshaia Lubyanka in the city center. The Lubyanka had many rooms and entrances and a wealth of rambling and soundproof cellars.

Administratively, Dzerzhinsky had created a formidable instrument by the time of his death by heart attack in 1926, at the age of forty-nine. Chekists and their descendants — the OGPU (1922–34), NKVD (1934–43), NKGB (1934–6), MGB (1946–53), MVD (1953) and KGB (from 1953–) — minted concepts and words. They introduced the "isolator" and the "Gulag," and added the "swan dive," "bridling," and the "conveyor" to the lexicography of torture. In reward, the square outside the Lubyanka was named for Dzerzhinsky, and his statue remained until August 1991 on a plinth of honor at its center, overlooked by the largest toy store in the Soviet Union. Dzerzhinsky, as Isaac Steinberg remarked, was "always affectionate to children."

The novelty in Bolshevik philosophy lay in a little phrase of Dzerzhinsky's; the Cheka's task, he said, was to "stifle crime at its inception." A victim need not act before he was "liquidated," the pretty word that re-placed "executed without trial." The accused need not, indeed, have thought of acting. His existence was sufficient grounds for its termination. Members of the imperial family were among the first to suffer from this innovation. The Bolsheviks murdered every Romanov they could find. Lenin did not want to give the Whites a "live banner to rally round."

On the night of June 12, 1918, a Cheka squad seized Grand Duke Mikhail and his English secretary in their hotel in Perm. They were mur-dered in nearby woods, and the body of the Romanov who had been tsar for a few hours fifteen months before was burned in a smelting furnace.

At 2:30 A.M. in the morning of July 17, in the Urals city of Ekaterinburg, to which they had been transferred from Tobolsk, Nicholas and Alexandra were asked to escort their family into the basement of the house where they were being held. Their crippled son and four daughters, the family doctor and three servants, and Anastasia's pet King Charles spaniel, went down-stairs with them. A truck was parked outside the house. Its engine was running and served to muffle the shots as a Cheka execution squad shot and bayonetted the humans and the pet to death. The process took twenty minutes. Charles I of England and Louis XVI of France had been brought to trial before execution; the Romanovs were killed as in a gangster massacre.

The bodies were dumped in a mine shaft. Feeling it not deep enough to hide their handiwork, the Cheka men were removing them to another shaft when their truck became mired in mud. The bodies were doused in sulphu-ric acid and dumped in a shallow grave. When mortality reached out for Lenin, after a series of strokes in 1924, his body was embalmed and placed in a granite art nouveau mausoleum on Red Square more ostentatious than that of any tsar.

On the same day that Nicholas and Alexandra died, other Romanovs were seized by the Cheka ninety miles away at Alapayevsk. The Grand Duchess Elizabeth, Grand Duke Serge Mikhailovich, and the three sons of Grand Duke Constantine were beaten and thrown, still alive, into a mine shaft where they died of exhaustion and starvation. A peasant heard hymns being sung from the shaft. When the bodies were found by Whites, the injured head of one of the boys was seen to have been carefully bandaged with a handkerchief. In January of 1919 four more Grand Dukes, including Nikolai Mikhailovich, the liberal historian, were executed in the Peter and Paul Fortress. Maxim Gorky pleaded for Nikolai Mikhailovich. "The rev-olution does not need historians," Lenin replied.

The Dowager Empress Maria, who had last seen her son Nicholas on the railway station at Mogilev, survived the civil war. Together with her daugh-ters the Grand Duchesses Xenia and Olga, and Felix Yusupov, she was evacuated to the West aboard a British battleship. The dowager empress returned to her native Denmark. Xenia settled in Britain. Olga, the tsar's younger sister, died above a barbershop in a poor section of Toronto, Canada, in 1960.

The tsar's first cousin, the turncoat Grand Duke Cyril whom Maurice Paleologue had observed marching to join the revolution, escaped to France. He declared himself "Tsar of all the Russias" and held court in a village in Brittany. He died at the American Hospital in Paris in 1938. Grand Duke Nicholas, the giant commander in chief whom Alexandra had despised, died at Antibes in the south of France in 1919.

Anna Vyrubova, Alexandra's confidante, was fortunate not to have accompanied the imperial family to Siberia. She escaped from Petrograd to Finland, where she died in 1964 at eighty.

Rasputin's assassins had mixed fortunes. Felix Yusupov, his supply of Rembrandts gone, had his coffers replenished by a $375,000 settlement in a defamation action against the Hollywood producers of a movie called *Rasputin the Mad Monk,* and died in France in 1967. Grand Duke Dmitri was saved from the Bolsheviks by his exile to Persia. In 1926, Dmitri married an American heiress in Biarritz. During the 1930s he was a champagne salesman in Palm Beach, Florida. Dmitri died at fifty in Davos, Switzerland, in 1941. Vladimir Purishkevich died of typhus while fighting for the Whites in southern Russia during the civil war.

The monk Iliodor, who had incited spurned women to kill Rasputin, went to New York. He became a Baptist and worked for a time as a janitor in the Metropolitan Life Insurance Building on Madison Square. Iliodor died in New York in 1952. Rasputin's daughter Maria became a lion tamer, touring the United States before settling in Los Angeles. The Yar restaurant, where Rasputin reveled in Moscow, is now the restaurant of the Hotel Sovetskaya.

Among the military men, Lavr Kornilov was killed during the civil war by a Red shell at Ekaterinodar in April of 1918. The Reds dug up his body, kicked it around the streets, and burned it in the municipal slaughterhouse. Long-suffering Mikhail Alexeev died of pneumonia in October 1918 while leading White armies. Nikolai Ruzsky, the northern front commander, was captured by Reds and executed by a squad of Bolshevik sailors at Pyatigorsk in May 1918.

Peter Krasnov, the Cossack general, fled Russia after the civil war, wrote novels in France and, in 1944, raised a Cossack force to fight with the Germans in Italy. Krasnov was handed over to the Russians by the British in 1945. *Pravda* reported in January 1947 that he had been executed. Admiral Alexander Kolchak, the former Black Sea Fleet commander, was seized by the Reds in Irkutsk as his White force retreated east through Siberia in January 1920. Fearing a White counterattack, the Reds took Kolchak from prison in the predawn gloom of February 7 and shot him by the headlights of a lorry on the banks of the Angara River.

Colonel A. P. Kutepov, who led the tsarist counterforce in Petrograd on February 27, 1917, was evacuated with White troops from the Crimea in 1920. He headed a White officers' emigré organization in Paris, where he was kidnapped in January of 1930. It was presumed that Stalinist agents were responsible. He was not seen again.

Among the White survivors were Colonel Viktor Manakin, the shock battalion commander, who escaped to Yugoslavia, and General Anton Denikin, who died peacefully in Ann Arbor, Michigan, in 1947.

Bolshevik military men fared badly. The three joint commissars of war were murdered by their own side. Pavel Dybenko, the bearded sailor who routed Krasnov, was arrested in January of 1938 and accused of spying for the Germans and the United States. He had been army commander in Samarkand when a party of Americans visited the town, though he had not met them. Despite his marriage to the Bolshevik heroine Alexandra Kollontai, Dybenko was shot six months later. She, remarkably, survived stints as a Soviet ambassador in Scandinavia to die peacefully at eighty in 1952.

Vladimir Antonov-Ovseenko, the conqueror of the Winter Palace, was serving as political commissar in Republican Spain during the civil war in 1938 when he was recalled to Moscow. Bravely refusing to sign a confession, he was sentenced to ten years for espionage but was in fact shot. When he was taken from his cell in the Butyrka Prison in Moscow, he gave his shoes, overcoat, and jacket to other prisoners. "I beg anyone who gets to freedom," he said, "to tell the people that Antonov-Ovseenko was a Bolshevik and remained a Bolshevik until his last day." He was then led away.

Nikolai Krylenko, the "epileptic degenerate" who had replaced General Dukhonin as commander in chief, became a notably venomous and sadistic prosecutor after the civil war, an expert in the extraction of forced confessions. By the 1930s, Krylenko wished to "liquidate" even the "neutrality of chess. . . . We must organize shock brigades of chess players and begin immediately a Five Year Plan for chess." Appointed People's Commissar for Justice, comment enough in itself on "Soviet legality," Krylenko was arrested in January 1938. Just as French prisoners had with Fouquier-Tinville, Krylenko's fellow inmates objected to being incarcerated with someone so "notorious and universally despised." He was tried, with 127 others, at the end of July 1938. His hearing lasted twenty minutes — his own forced confession was faultless. He was shot.

The "repulsive" Tauride commandant, Moisei Uritsky, was assassinated in Petrograd in August of 1918, on the same day that Lenin was shot and wounded in Moscow by the Social Revolutionary terrorist Fanny Kaplan. Fedor Raskolnikov, hero of the Baltic Fleet sailors, was a fleet commander in the civil war. He was serving as Soviet ambassador to Bulgaria when he was recalled in April of 1939. Raskolnikov defected, after writing an abusive letter to Stalin, and died in unexplained circumstances in the south of France a few months later.

Six hundred Baltic Fleet sailors were massacred by a Bolshevik force that advanced over the ice to crush a mutiny at the Kronstadt base in March 1921. The sailors had rebelled against the "nightmare rule of communist dictatorship." "Lenin said that 'Communism is Soviet power and electrification,' " they said; "but the people are convinced that the Bolshevik form of communism is commissarocracy plus firing squads."

Lieutenant A. I. Semashko, who led out the First Machine Gun Regiment in the July Days, fled from his post as First Secretary at the Soviet Embassy in independent Riga, Latvia, in 1922. Genrikh Yagoda, in whose house Petrograd Bolsheviks regrouped after the July Days, became chief architect of the purges as head of the NKVD until he followed his victims in front of a firing squad in 1936.

Vladimir Nevsky, of the Milrevkom, and agitator in the July Days, became a leading historian and director of the Lenin library. Nevsky was arrested in 1936 and executed a year later after refusing to remove books that Stalin found offensive from the library. "I'm not running a baggage room," he said. Serge Mstislavsky, who had watched the February mutiny unfold from his window in the military academy, split with the Social Revolutionaries and joined the Bolsheviks during the civil war, surviving to become a movie scriptwriter after it.

Of the writers, John Reed returned to the United States to write his classic *Ten Days That Shook the World* on the events of October. He helped to found the Communist-Labour Party, later the Communist Party of the USA. In 1919, he and his wife Louise Bryant appeared before a Senate investigating committee after they had made "incendiary" speeches. Reed was indicted on sedition charges, but fled New York on a forged passport and sailed to Finland as a stoker. Reappearing in Moscow, he became a member of the Communist International. In August of 1920 he contracted typhoid on a trip to Baku and died a few days later in Moscow. Reed, whose wife died in the United States in 1936, is buried on Red Square close to the Kremlin Wall. No such distinction was accorded to Alexander Blok, who died in August of 1921 of "venereal disease, malnutrition, and despair."

Shortly before his death, Blok acknowledged one Bolshevik quality — "their quite unique ability to stamp out custom and to liquidate the individual."

The poet Vladimir Mayakovsky, who designed propaganda posters to put in empty store windows during the civil war, committed suicide in 1930. "Love's boat has smashed against the daily grind," Mayakovsky wrote before shooting himself. Maxim Gorky had uneasy relations with the Bolsheviks. Lenin closed *Novaya Zhizn* in 1918. Gorky went abroad in 1921, first to Germany and then to Italy, before returning to Russia in 1931. He died in 1936, probably murdered by his doctors at Stalin's orders. Gorky's birthplace, Nizhny Novgorod, was renamed Gorky for him. It is not, perhaps, an honor he would have appreciated. A neighboring city is called Dzerzhinsky.

Nikolai Sukhanov probably lived a little longer. He started writing his *Notes on the Revolution,* with its fatal reference to Stalin being no more than a "gray blur," during the civil war. He wrote an epitaph for 1917 — the Bolsheviks "by virtue of their characteristic willpower and organizational ruthlessness constituted themselves the heirs of the revolutionary upsurge after it had spent itself." In the 1920s, Sukhanov went back to his old work as an agronomist. He was found guilty in the so-called "Trial of the Mensheviks" in 1931 of plotting to overthrow the Soviet state and to restore capitalism. Sukhanov arrived at the "isolator" camp at Verkhne-Uralsk where he may have survived until 1940.

The diarist and schools inspector Alexis Babine emigrated to New York in 1922 and worked at the university library at Cornell until his death in 1930. Zinaïda Gippius died in France in 1945. Maurice Paleologue wrote his diaries in France, was elected to the French Academy, and died as Paris was being liberated in August of 1944. His colleague Sir George Buchanan went on to become the British ambassador to Rome, but his later years were dimmed by the hostility of fellow countrymen who wrongly held him responsible for failing to evacuate the imperial family to safety in Britain at the start of the revolution.

The British writers and secret service agents Somerset Maugham and Bruce Lockhart died, laden with honors, respectively in 1965 and 1970. Arthur Ransome, the British foreign correspondent, became friendly with the Bolshevik leadership and married Trotsky's secretary. Ransome became a best-selling writer of children's books and died in England's Lake District in 1967. Morgan Philips Price, the *Manchester Guardian* man who did not think the Bolsheviks would last a week, became a British Labor MP and died in England in 1973.

Marc Chagall, after a brief spell as a commissar for fine arts at Vitebsky, left Russia for Paris in 1922. He died in France in 1985. Fedor Chaliapin also left for the West in 1922. Ten years later, Chaliapin declared that "The practice of Bolshevism proved even more dreadful than its theories. . . . Bolshevism has become completely saturated with that awful intolerance and bigotry, that obtuse smugness which is Russian philistinism." The great basso died in Paris in 1938. Serge Rachmaninov died in Los Angeles in 1943.

Tamara Karsavina, the prima ballerina who witnessed Red October from her bedroom window, was married to a British diplomat and died in London, aged ninety-three. In 1922, she met her fellow dancer Mathilde Kshesinskaya in Monte Carlo. Kshesinskaya had lost everything in Russia, including her suitcase of jewelry and her palace. She had, however, retained a house in Cap d'Antibes and married her Grand Duke Andrei. Karsavina found her as "cheerful as ever, without a single wrinkle." Kshesinskaya ran a ballet school in Paris for thirty years, taught Dame Margot Fonteyn, and also lived into her nineties, dancing a jubilee performance at Covent Garden in London in 1936 when she was sixty-three. The Kshesinskaya palace in Petrograd became a shrine to Lenin.

The young writer who had been so interested in the sound of gunfire in Moscow in October, Boris Pasternak, published his novel *Dr. Zhivago* in 1957. The following year he was awarded the Nobel Prize in literature; the Soviet regime forced him to decline it. Pasternak died in 1960.

Anti-Bolshevik politicians had a greater chance of dying of natural causes than their Bolshevik foes. The Cheka never did catch Alexander Kerensky. In January of 1918, posing as a Swedish doctor, he returned to Petrograd where he was hidden away in a student's flat. He moved later to Moscow. In May of 1918 a friend approached Bruce Lockhart and begged him to arrange for Kerensky to be smuggled out to Britain. Bruce Lockhart stamped a British visa in a false Serbian passport, and Kerensky joined a party of Serbian troops who were being repatriated from Murmansk aboard a ship bound for Scotland. After helping to organize anti-Bolshevik resistance movements from Paris, Berlin, and London, he narrowly escaped capture by the Germans during the fall of France in 1940. He moved to the United States, where he spent a long period working on Provisional Government documents at the Hoover Institution at Stanford, California. Despite his missing kidney Kerensky lived into his ninetieth year, dying in New York in 1970. He is buried at Putney Vale in London. His secretary, Pitirim Sorokin, became a Harvard professor, dying in 1968.

Yekaterina Breshko-Breshkovskaya, the "Babushka" who served as Kerensky's hostess at the Winter Palace, died in exile in Czechoslovakia at the age of ninety. Kerensky's ex-wife Olga and the two boys lived in desperate poverty and were briefly held by the Cheka in the Lubyanka before escaping to England. Oleg, the eldest son, became one of the world's leading bridge designers and Gleb had a successful career with English Electric.

Nikolai Chkheidze emigrated to France, where he died in 1926. Fedor Dan and Viktor Chernov also escaped to France, both moving on to die in New York shortly after the World War II. Mikhail Tereshchenko, the Provisional Government foreign minister and sugar magnate, died in England in 1958. Irakli Tsereteli escaped to Paris and died in 1959. Nikolai Avksentiev, the Social Revolutionary interior minister, died in New York in 1943.

The Octobrist Alexander Guchkov, though beaten up by the White Guards in Berlin in 1922, lived on in exile until 1936. Vladimir Nabokov, the cabinet secretary, was less fortunate. He was murdered by Whites who held the Provisional Government responsible for the Bolshevik coup, in Berlin in 1922. His son Vladimir, who had been startled by the shelling of the Winter Palace, went on to the United States to write *Lolita* and *Pnin*. Mikhail Rodzianko, the Cadet leader, died in Yugoslavia in 1924. Julius Martov, dying of tuberculosis, emigrated to Germany in 1920, where he edited a Menshevik journal before his death in 1923.

Prince Georgy Lvov died in France the following year. Pavel Miliukov, after joining Alexeev's Volunteer Army, escaped to continue his scholarship in France, where he died in 1943. Vladimir Lvov, eccentric to the last, returned from the safety of exile to Russia in 1922, working briefly for the Soviet regime before returning to France, where he was believed to have died as a street derelict. Nikolai Nekrasov, the one-time Cadet transport minister, threw his lot in with the Bolsheviks and served as an engineer on canal projects before disappearing into the Gulag.

Boris Savinkov, Kerensky's deputy in the Kornilov affair, served as a foreign representative for the Whites. Aided by Western secret services and Russian business interests, he formed an anti-Bolshevik union in Paris in 1921. In August 1924, he was arrested while trying to cross the Polish border into Russia. His death sentence was commuted to ten years' imprisonment, but it was announced in 1925 that he had "committed suicide" in the Lubyanka. Maria Bochkaryova, the leader of the Women's Battalion, also returned to Russia after the civil war and disappeared, fate unknown.

The passionate nationalist Vasily Shulgin was the longest-lived of all the major players in the Revolution. He emigrated to Yugoslavia, writing his book *Dni* and returning to Russia in 1925 on a mission provoked by Chekists. Shulgin went "clandestinely" over the Polish border. Those whom he met were subsequently arrested for anti-Soviet plotting. Shulgin returned to Yugoslavia, where he was arrested by the Red Army in 1944. He was released from a Soviet prison camp in 1956. After his remarkable odyssey, Shulgin died peacefully at Vladimir in Russia in 1976 at the age of ninety-eight.

Tsarist politicians, so carefully protected from lynch mobs by Kerensky, were vulnerable under the Bolsheviks. Boris Stürmer, the former premier, and Alexander Protopopov, the despised interior minister, were shot. Harmless old Ivan Goryemkin, another former premier, was caught by a mob in Petrograd in 1918 and strangled. Former war minister Vladimir Sukhomlinov escaped across the Gulf of Finland and died in Berlin in 1926. His voluptuous and much younger wife divorced him and returned to Russia to marry a Georgian officer her own age. They died in the Red Terror.

Most leading Bolsheviks did not enjoy longevity. Yakov Sverdlov died of influenza in 1919 at thirty-three; Nicholas's deathplace, Ekaterinburg, was renamed Sverdlovsk in his honor. Inessa Armand succumbed to cholera the following year. Joseph Stalin, emerging after Lenin's death as the "Kremlin mountaineer, the murderer with a cockroach whistler's leer," reaped the most of the remaining Old Bolsheviks in the 1930s. Stalin himself died in office in 1953. Nadezhda Alliluyeva, the schoolgirl in whose apartment Stalin was lodging during October of 1917, married him but committed suicide in 1932.

Gregory Zinoviev was shot with Lev Kamenev after a show trial in 1936. Nikolai Bukharin survived for a further two years before meeting the same fate. Alexander Shlyapnikov, undercover artist and organizer of the train that brought Lenin to the Finland Station, died in prison in 1937. Ivar Smilga, to whom Lenin had confided before the October coup, was shot the same year. Martyn Latsis, Dzerzhinsky's sadistic deputy at the Cheka and pioneer organizer of labor camps — "We are not waging war against individual persons, we are exterminating the bourgeoisie as a class" — was shot in 1938. Karl Radek, the mop-haired mimic on the sealed train, sided with Trotsky against Stalin and was expelled from the party in 1917. He recanted and switched his propaganda talents to Stalin. This did not save Radek from being tried for treason in 1937; he was shot in 1939.

Leon Trotsky, war commissar and victor in the civil war, went into exile in 1928 and was murdered in Mexico by a Stalinist agent with an ice pick in 1940. The Left Social Revolutionary Maria Spiridonova, the train platform assassin, turned against the Bolsheviks in 1918. After twenty years of further imprisonment and exile in Central Asia and Siberia, the frail ex-terrorist was shot by the NKVD in Orel Prison in September 1941 as the Germans advanced on the town.

Mikhail Kalinin and Vyacheslav Molotov were among the few to be more fortunate, or more perspicacious in cultivating Stalin. Kalinin, who had suggested freeing the prisoners in the Kresty on February 27, 1917, became titular head of the Soviet state under Stalin. The former German city of Konigsberg in East Prussia, taken by the Red Army in 1945, was renamed Kaliningrad in his honor.

Vyacheslav Molotov, the young Bolshevik press expert, rose in the party hierarchy through backing Stalin. He became commissar for foreign affairs in 1939 in time to sign the Molotov-Ribbentrop nonaggression pact in August of that year. He survived the subsequent war, during which the "Molotov cocktail" gasoline bomb was named for him. After 1945, he was known as the "Mister *Nyet*" of the Cold War. He fell under Nikita Khrushchev but, now that removal from office no longer involved execution, survived to become ambassador to Mongolia. He died at ninety-six in 1986.

Russia became the Soviet Union in 1922. Its new title was ratified in 1924, the same year that Petrograd became Leningrad. Finland escaped, not to return. The Ukraine and Georgia enjoyed only the briefest of independence during the civil war. Lithuania, Estonia, and Latvia maintained their new independence until 1940.

The Russian bourgeoisie ceased to exist as a class. By mid-1918 it was common to see well-dressed "former people" laboring and street cleaning under guard. Trainloads were sent off to the civil war fronts to dig trenches — "rich, smart lawyers, and stockbrokers from Petrograd side by side with cabbies, floor polishers, bath attendants, Tartar rag and bone merchants, escaped lunatics, shopkeepers, and monks, all lumped together with the exploiting classes."

There were 51,105 priests in Russia at the time of the Bolshevik coup. By 1940, fewer than 500 priests and 7 bishops remained. The better-off peasants, defined as *kulaks* and exploiters, suffered an "ethnic catastrophe" during the forced collectivization of farms after 1929. OGPU agents, descendants of the Chekists, like "raging beasts" rounded up Russia's best farmers and their families and drove them, "stripped of their possessions, naked, into the tundra and the taiga." Those too poor to be classified as *kulaks* were sentenced as *podkulachniks,* people aiding the *kulaks.* At least eight million peasants died as the land promised them by the revolution was taken by the state.

The Communist Party — the word "Bolshevik" was officially dropped in 1952 — survived as the ruling party in the Soviet Union until its disgrace following the unsuccessful coup in August of 1991. The Soviet Union itself ceased to be a monolith in the same month, as the centrifugal forces so evident in 1917 reasserted themselves.

The citizens of Leningrad voted in 1991 to return its name to Saint Petersburg. The cellar where the murder of Rasputin began in the Moika Palace is closed to the public. The staircase leading down to it was blocked off and the basement windows were impenetrable with grime and cheap gauze curtains for many years. At the beginning of 1992, wax figures of Rasputin and Yusupov were placed in the cellar, which has been repainted, ready to welcome tourists and their hard currency to the new Russia.

Bibliography

Books, and bias, on the events of 1917 are abundant. Although much material remains to be translated, there is a wealth of accounts by eyewitnesses and by major actors for the reader in English. Nikolai Sukhanov's brilliant and energetic *The Russian Revolution 1917* (Oxford, 1955) helped to cost the author his life under Stalin. Leon Trotsky continued to write in opposition up to the time of his own murder. His works, a blend of propaganda and vigorous writing, include *The History of the Russian Revolution* (3 vols; London, 1932–3), *My Life* (New York, 1970), *Lenin* (New York, 1962) and *The Young Lenin* (New York, 1972).

Lenin's *Collected Works* (New York, 1927–45) are voluminous. Olga Krupskaya wrote her *Memories of Lenin* (2 vols.; London, 1935) after her husband's death. Viktor Chernov, disillusioned, wrote *The Great Russian Revolution* (New Haven, Conn., 1936). Alexander Shlyapnikov's *On the Eve of 1917* (London, 1982) gives a vivid picture of life in the Bolshevik underground, matched by Boris Savinkov's *Memoirs of a Terrorist* (New York, 1931). Anatoly Lunacharsky wrote *Revolutionary Silhouettes* (New York, 1968).

Alexander Kerensky wrote widely about events and his part in them, notably in *The Catastrophe* (New York, 1927) and *The Crucifixion of Liberty* (New York, 1934), and in an ambivalent book on the Kornilov affair, *Prelude to Bolshevism — The Kornilov Rebellion* (London, 1949). He also published, with Robert Browder, a useful collection of government and other documents, and press articles and editorials, *The Russian Provisional Government* (3 vols.; Stanford, Calif., 1961).

Pavel Miliukov brought a liberal view to *The Russian Revolution* (2 vols.; Gulf Breeze, Fla., 1978 and 1984). Mikhail Rodzianko wrote *Memoires: Le Regne de Raspoutine* (Paris, 1928). The memoirs of the ill-fated cabinet secretary Vladimir Nabokov are published in *The Ordeal of a Diplomat* (London, 1921).

The Allied ambassadors also wrote accounts, David Francis in *Russia from the American Embassy* (New York, 1921), Sir George Buchanan in *My Mission to Russia* (New York, 1923), and Maurice Paleologue in *An Ambassador's Memoirs* (London, 1973 ed.). Sir George's daughter, Meriel, wrote *Petrograd, The City of Trouble* (London, 1918) and *Dissolution of an Empire* (London, 1932). Paleologue's successor Joseph Noulens wrote *Mon Ambassade en Russie Sovietique* (2 vols.; Paris, 1933).

Accounts by Western journalists include John Reed's mood-catching and partisan *Ten Days That Shook the World* (New York, 1919), Louise Bryant's lively *Six Red Months in Russia* (New York, 1918), Morgan Philips Price's *Reminiscences of the Russian Revolution* (London, 1921), and Albert Rhys Williams's *Through the Russian Revolution* (New York, 1921). Arthur Ransome's experiences are included in Hugh Brogan's *The Life of Arthur Ransome* (London, 1984). The Russian journalist Konstantin Paustovsky wrote *The Story of a Life* (New York, 1964).

Serge Mstislavsky's account of the February revolution is included in his *Five Days Which Transformed Russia* (London, 1988), first published in 1923. Ilyin Genevsky wrote another self-congratulatory memoir of military events, *From February to October 1917* (London, 1931). For a White point of view, see Anton Denikin's *The Russian Turmoil* (London, 1922), and for an Allied approach, Alfred Knox's *With the Russian Army* (2 vols.; London, 1921). Marina Yurlova's *Cossack Girl* (London, 1934) gives an unusual view of the collapse of the Imperial Army. *The War and the Russian Government* (New Haven, Conn., 1923), by Paul Gronsky and Nicholas Astrov, shows the financial strains imposed by the war.

Robert Bruce Lockhart's *Memoirs of a British Agent* (London, 1985), with its lively character sketches and account of Kerensky's escape, was written in 1932. His fellow agent, Somerset Maugham, covered his dramatic interview with Kerensky and his recollection of Savinkov in *A Writer's Notebook* (London, 1949).

Of the ballerinas, Tamara Karsavina wrote *Theatre Street* (New York, 1961) and Mathilde Kshesinskaya *Dancing in Petersburg* (New York, 1961). The artist Marc Chagall included bitter memories of Russia in *My Life* (London, 1965). Fedor Chaliapin told his *Autobiography* (London, 1968) to Maxim Gorky, whose own comments on events are collected in *Untimely Thoughts* (London, 1970). For Gorky's provincial descriptions, see *Fragments from My Diary* (London, 1986). Boris Pasternak gave his vivid account of the fighting in Moscow in *Safe Conduct* (London, 1959). For Alexander Blok's comments, see *The Life of Alexander Blok* (2 vols.; Oxford, 1980) by Avril Pyman.

Felix Yusupov covered the murder of Rasputin in *Lost Splendor* (New York, 1953). His fellow conspirator Vladimir Purishkevich wrote his account in *Comme j'ai tué Raspoutine* (Paris, 1923). Serge Obolensky wrote *One Man in His Time* (London, 1960).

Alexandra's correspondence with Nicholas is published as *Nicky-Sunny Letters* (Hattiesburg, Miss., 1970). Anna Vyrubova, Alexandra's confidante, escaped Russia to write *Memories of the Russian Court* (New York, 1923). Pierre Gilliard, tutor to the imperial children, wrote *Thirteen Years at the Russian Court* (London, 1921). Sir Bernard Pares, who was present in Petrograd, described *The Fall of the Russian Monarchy* (London, 1939). A description of Saint Petersburg and other places is given in Karl Baedeker's *Russia* (Leipzig, 1914).

Alexis Babine wrote his reminiscences in *A Russian Civil War Diary* (Durham, N.C., 1988). The memoirs of Pyotr Shilovsky, Count Alexei Bobrinskoy, Sofia Koulomzina, and Arvids Jurevics are included in *The Other Russia* (London, 1990), by Michael Glenny and Norman Stone. Other contemporary accounts are given in Dmitri Mohrenschildt's *The Russian Revolution of 1917* (London, 1971) and in *Witnesses to the Russian Revolution* (London, 1964) edited by Roger Pethybridge.

Other contemporary documentation is collected by James Bunyan and H. H.

Fisher in *The Bolshevik Revolution* (Stanford, Conn., 1934) and by Martin Mc-Cauley in *The Russian Revolution and the Soviet State* (London, 1975).

There are innumerable biographies (and hagiographies) of Lenin — with David Shub's *Lenin* (London, 1966) prominent among them — and of Trotsky, including Isaac Deutscher's trilogy, of which *The Prophet Armed* (London, 1954) covers the revolutionary period, but few of Kerensky. Richard Abraham's *Alexander Kerensky: The First Love of the Revolution* (New York, 1987) fills a gap.

Norman Stone's *The Eastern Front* (London, 1975) gives general insights into the Russian army, as Erich von Ludendorff's *Meine Kriegserinnerungen* (Berlin, 1919) does from a German standpoint. S. A. Smith's *Red Petrograd* (Cambridge, 1983) covers the working class in the capital, and Marc Ferro's *The Bolshevik Revolution* (London, 1980) is strong on the *muzhiks*. George Katkov's *Russia 1917* (London, 1967) and E. N. Burdzhalov's *Russia's Second Revolution* (Bloomington, Ind., 1987) are interesting on the February events. Documents on October have been suppressed, but light is cast by S. P. Melgunov's *The Bolshevik Seizure of Power* (Santa Barbara, Calif., 1972).

W. H. Chamberlin's *The Russian Revolution* (2 vols.; New York, 1935) and Victor Serge's *L'An 1 de la révolution russe* (Paris, 1930) are among earlier histories. There are two excellent modern accounts for the reader wishing to cover the sweep of events leading up to and beyond 1917: Harrison Salisbury's *Black Night, White Snow* (New York, 1978) and Richard Pipes's majestic *The Russian Revolution* (New York, 1990).

Edmund Wilson's *To the Finland Station* (New York, 1940) remains a classic history of Marxist thought. Arthur Koestler's *Darkness at Noon* (New York, 1941) is a superb account, in fictional form, of disillusion with communism. The events that caused such rejection are best seen in Robert Conquest's *The Great Terror: A Reassessment* (London, 1990).

Index